# The Return to Scripture
# in Judaism and Christianity

# Theological Inquiries

*Studies in Contemporary
Biblical and Theological Problems*

General Editor
Lawrence Boadt, C. S. P.

PAULIST PRESS

# The Return to Scripture in Judaism and Christianity

## *Essays in Postcritical Scriptural Interpretation*

*Edited by*
Peter Ochs

PAULIST PRESS
New York • Mahwah

## ACKNOWLEDGMENTS

The Publisher gratefully acknowledges use of the following: "Toward a Postliberal Theology," from *The Nature of Doctrine: Religion and Theology in a Postliberal Age,* by George A. Lindbeck; copyright © 1984 George A. Lindbeck; used by permission of Westminster/John Knox Press; "Zu einer neuen Verdeytschung der Schrift." *Beilage Zum Ersten Band Die Fünf Bücher Der Weisung* (Köin: Jakob Hegner, 1968 [1954], translated by Alan Swensen and edited by Steven Kepnes; Reprinted with permission of the Balkin Agency, Amherst, Mass., as an agent for the Estate of Martin Buber; "On Man's Role in Revelation," from *From Ancient Israel to Modern Israel to Modern Judaism, Intellect in Quest of Understanding: Essays in Honor of Marvin Fox,* edited by Nahum Sarna (Scholar's Press for Brown Judaica, 1990), reprinted with permission from Brown Judaic Studies, Brown University, Providence, Rhode Island; excerpts from *From Tradition to Commentary* (Chapter One) by Steven Fraade, reprinted by permission of the State University of New York Press, Albany, New York; "Extra-Biblical Exegesis," from *The Garments of Torah,* by Michael Fishbane, copyright © 1989 Indiana University Press, Bloomington, Indiana; reprinted with permission of Indiana University Press; "The Uses of Scripture in Classical, Medieval Judaism: Prooftexts in Maimonides' Code" from *The Return to Scripture in Judaism and Christianity* (Chapter Seven) is printed as an altered version of an article entitled, "Biblical Interpretation in the First Book of Maimonides' Code," in *The Judeo-Christian Tradition and The U.S. Constitution,* A Jewish Quarterly Review supplement, 1989, pp. 29–56. Excerpts adapted from *The Bible and the Narrative Tradition,* edited by Frank McConnell. Copyright © 1986 by Oxford University Press, Inc. Reprinted by permission. These excerpts have been condensed and revised as per the instructions of the late Hans Frei. Excerpts from *Peshat and Derash: Plain and Applied Meaning in Rabbinic Exegesis* by David Weiss Halivni. Copyright © 1991 by David Weiss Halivni. Reprinted by permission of Oxford University Press, Inc.

**Library of Congress Cataloging-in-Publication Data**

The Return to Scripture in Judaism and Christianity: essays in postcritical scriptural interpretation/edited by Peter Ochs.

    p.  cm.—(Theological inquiries)
    Includes bibliographical references and index.
    ISBN 0-8091-3425-X (pbk.)
    1. Bible. O.T.—Criticism, interpretation, etc., Jewish.
2. Bible—Criticism, interpretation, etc.—History—20th century.
I. Ochs, Peter, 1950–  . II. Series.
BS1186.R48  1993
220.6'01—dc20

93-24518
CIP

Published by Paulist Press
997 Macarthur Boulevard
Mahwah, NJ 07430

Printed and bound in the
United States of America

# CONTENTS

FOR MY PARENTS,
SIDNEY AND RUTH OCHS

# PREFACE

The scholars who have contributed to this volume of essays also inspired it. They are Jewish and Christian thinkers who, without melding their different religious traditions and scholarly methods, have developed complementary responses to what they believe is wrong with modern scholarship in Judaism or Christianity. The purpose of this collection is to draw attention to the similarities among these responses and to the possibility that they may contribute to a family of *postcritical* methods for interpreting the scriptural traditions.

The scholars represented in this collection employ modern methods of critical, scientific inquiry to clarify the language, the historical contexts and the didactic messages of the biblical traditions of religious and moral instruction. They do not, however, find these methods sufficient. They argue, in various ways, that the biblical traditions communicate to their practitioners some rules of action that cannot be deciphered within the terms set by the canons of critical reason that emerged in the European renaissance and enlightenment. This does not mean, however, that the biblical traditions are in this respect irrational, for among their unique rules of action are rules for interpreting the traditions themselves, including the traditions' primary texts of scriptures and of scriptural commentary. In their efforts to identify these indigenous rules of interpretation, the scholars represented here have begun to articulate rules of reason that expand and transform the modern, critical canons. In some ways, these *postcritical* rules appear *postmodern:* they emerge out of criticisms of the modern search for sources of individual self-certainty, and they emphasize the communal, dialogic and textual contexts of knowledge and the contributions made by interpreters to the meaning of what they interpret. In other ways, however, the postcritical rules appear *premodern:* they describe themselves as rules of *reasoning* that serve the theological and moral purposes of particular traditions of scriptural interpretation. The postcritical rules belong, in other words, neither to postmodernity nor to premodernity, but rather to a dialogue that is now unfolding between a contemporary family of scholars and their scriptural traditions.

Saving my comments about these scholars for Chapter 1 and for the introductions to each section of the book, I will take the time here only to acknowledge the contributions they have all made to the general development of this project, however much they may be innocent of claims I have made about them. My thanks go the Research Council of Drew University and to the Spencer Foundation for supportive grants; to the Reverend Lawrence Boadt, C.S.P., my editor at Paulist Press, for gentle guidance; to Paula Massa of Drew University for word processing; and to my wife, Vanessa L. Ochs, for editing my editings.

I lovingly dedicate this volume to my parents, whose marriage commingled the energies of reason and of faith in a paradigmatically postcritical way.

Chapter One

# AN INTRODUCTION TO POSTCRITICAL SCRIPTURAL INTERPRETATION

## PETER OCHS

### AN OVERVIEW OF THE POSTCRITICAL APPROACH

"Postcritical scriptural interpretation" refers to an emergent tendency among Jewish and Christian text scholars and theologians to give rabbinic and ecclesial traditions of interpretation both the benefit of the doubt and the benefit of doubt: the former, by assuming that there are dimensions of scriptural meaning which are disclosed only by way of the hermeneutical practices of believing communities and believing traditions of Jews or Christians; the latter, by assuming, in the spirit of post-Spinozistic criticism, that these dimensions may be clarified through the disciplined practice of philological, historical and textual/rhetorical criticism. Among Christian scholars, this tendency emerges, illustratively but not exclusively, in what Hans Frei terms the attempt to recover the scriptures' *sensus literalis* or in what George Lindbeck has called a "cultural-linguistic" approach to interpreting church doctrine. Among Jewish scholars, the tendency emerges, for example, in Moshe Greenberg's "holistic" method of interpreting scriptural texts, David Weiss Halivni's examination of the rabbinic principles of legal (*halakhic*) exegesis or also in Michael Fishbane's study of "intra-scriptural midrash."[1]

The Christian scholars whose work is represented in this volume tend to identify in the scriptural narrative a dimension of unreduced meaning that stands the tests of both critical scholarship and of faith. They tend to interpret the plain sense of the scriptural text as the text's meaning for a normative community of Christian interpreters. Unlike strictly modernist interpreters, they thereby practice what the semiotic philosopher Charles Peirce would call a three-part hermeneutic: claiming that the *text* (the first part) has its *meaning* (the second) *for a normative community* (the third), rather than identifying the meaning of the text with some historical or cognitive "sense" that is available to any educated reader. Following this approach, these postcritical Christian scholars tend to argue that questions of truth may be raised only within the context of a normative community's exegetical practices. These scholars refrain from adopting a prioristic methods of resolving competing claims among various normative communities. Instead, some tend to advocate an ethnographic method of understanding other communities in terms of the multiplicity of their practices and of their complex conceptual structures. While taking pains to avoid repeating what they consider the errors of reductionism, these scholars attempt to promote dialogue among practitioners of the various scriptural traditions. To locate a common language of discourse, they examine shared textual sources and layers of shared practice and, therefore, of shared meaning.

The postcritical Christian scholars have a special interest in the exegetical practices of rabbinic Judaism. They speak, for one, of a need to reappraise those tendencies in patristic theology which encouraged the delegitimization of Judaism and, with it, the mistreatment of Jews *and* the misrepresentation of Christianity's Jewish origins. At the same time, they speak of the "midrashic method" of the rabbis as a prototype for their own emergent methods of scriptural exegesis.

Stimulated by developments within the traditions of both rabbinic and modern academic scholarship, the Jewish scholars represented in this volume are concerned to identify specific elements of this rabbinic practice of scriptural interpretation, or of the related practices of Jewish exegetes trained in the rabbinic methods. They make non-reductionistic use of the tools of critical scholarship—historical, philological and textual—to identify the hermeneutical rules which emerge in rabbinic practice but which may possibly be adapted to or observed in other practices as well. These rules may provide the basis for dialogue among Jewish and Christian postcritical scholars, since they belong both to the ethnographic description of rabbinic Judaism and, when examined separately, to any of several contemporary projects of hermeneutical reconstruction.

The scholars represented in this volume do not necessarily describe their work as part of any larger movement, in particular, of a postcritical movement. There is as yet no generally recognized terminology for describing their several but related methods of interpreting scriptural narrative. Are these methods of narrative or ethnographic or pragmatic or performative or postcritical interpretation? I hope that this collection of representative essays will verify my own claims that these scholars share a family of methods, that it is helpful to call these "postcritical methods," and that it is helpful to isolate a paradigmatic set of rules for postcritical scriptural interpretation. Should my own claims prove unconvincing, I trust that readers will nonetheless find these essays of value in themselves, as individually powerful illustrations of recent trends in scriptural hermeneutics.

## A HISTORY OF THIS PROJECT

This collection represents an expanded, literary version of a more intimate dialogue that took place in 1987–88 after Moshe Greenberg's Yale faculty seminar on methods of biblical interpretation. Greenberg, the late Hans Frei, George Lindbeck, Steven Fraade and I met several times to explore the relations between Greenberg's "holistic" method of Bible interpretation and Frei's "realistic" method.

Greenberg has introduced his holistic method as an alternative to what, in a 1980 essay, he calls the "two opposed axioms [that] have served, historically, for the interpretation of the Bible: one theological, the other historical-analogical."[1a] He explains:

The theological [axiom] maintains that without insight gained from faith in the divine origin of Scripture, its message cannot be understood. . . . Historically, the product of

this axiom has usually been an exegesis that puts into
Scripture what ought to be believed rather than attending
to what it says.[2]

The historical-analogical axiom arises as a reaction to this.

The reaction, which reached fullest articulation in ch. vii
of Spinoza's *Theological-Political Tractate* (first printing,
1670), insisted that nothing but what Scripture itself revealed of its sense might be used in interpreting it. The
ordinary process of induction, so fruitful in arriving at an
understanding of nature, was adequate for—was indeed
the only legitimate basis of—interpreting the Bible.[3]
. . . Having voted for scientific universality, the interpretation of Scripture became linked in the 19th century to
the career of literary-historical interpretation at large. The
analogy of the latter was decisive for the former: ". . . The
character of a particular party of the OT cannot be decided
by an *a priori* argument as regards what it *must* be; it can
only be determined by an application of the canons of
evidence and probability universally employed in historical or literary investigation."[4]

Noting increasing scholarly dissatisfaction with the reductionistic
tendencies of this modern axiom—its tendency to narrow literary
options to those already available in contemporary western literature—Greenberg proposes his alternative:

. . . a holistic interpretation, "emphasizing the organic or
functional relation between parts and wholes" (Webster).
As the religious person approaches the text open to God's
call, so must the interpreter come 'all ears' to hear what the
text is saying. . . . For an axiom he [or she] has the working
hypothesis that the text as he has it has been designed to
convey a message, a meaning. For if it does have design
and meaning, they will be discovered only by effort ex-
pended to justify such an assumption.[5]

To guard, finally, against uncritical acceptance of established or *ad hoc* readings, the holistic interpreter "appropriates something of the historical-analogical [axiom], namely, the inference from the text itself of principles of its interpretation."[6] This is, through historical-philological work, to reconstitute the range of possible significations inherent in the text at the time "when it had reached its present disposition."[7]

As presented in *The Eclipse of Biblical Narrative,* Frei's critique of what he calls the tradition of "mediating interpretation"[8] provides a logical-semiotic framework applicable as well to Greenberg's critique of the historical-analogical axiom. Frei argues that, emerging in the eighteenth century with John Locke and the latitudinarians in England and the neologians in Germany, this tradition sought to mediate between the hermeneutical and theological extremes of an "orthodox dogmatism and [the naturalists'] radical skepticism about revelation"—that is, between the "rigorous affirmation and denials of the historical positivity of revelation."[9] The mediators

> tended to insist that belief in the factual occurrences reported in the Bible, especially those connected with Jesus, was indispensable. At the same time they either said or hinted broadly that the religious meaning or truth communicated through these events must be understood by reference to a content of religion and morality broader than the Bible.[10]

Frei argues that the mediators' mediation was illusory, because it retained the semiotic premises that generated the dialectic of orthodoxy and naturalism in the first place. These were the premises that the ostensive reference of scripture can be separated from its explicative sense and that its meaning is to be identified with ostensive reference. The mediators claimed that the stories of scripture point to their meanings referentially, but that this reference is ideal, appearing in the text as a token of some universally generalizable truths of experience. Dichotomizing text and referent in this way and privileging the latter, the mediators treated their preferred method of identifying reference as if it were foundational: as if, in other words, mediating theology were a privileged means of identifying the meaning of scriptures. Frei's critique thus offers a framework for Greenberg's. Modernist readers, like the mediators, locate the meaning of scripture in an ostensive referent "behind" the biblical text: in antecedent historical events, in an authorial intentionality or in a conceptual order to which these readers have privileged access.

Like Greenberg's, Frei's alternative to the modernist reading is to relocate meaning within the biblical text itself in its intratextual context. Following Erich Auerbach,[11] he seeks to recover the premodern practice of reading the biblical text as "realistic narrative." The Bible is to be read as a collection of stories that are "history-like," not because they point outside themselves to a privileged realm of real events, but because they portray lives lived in a way that reshapes the descriptive and performative languages of the community of biblical interpreters. This is history as paradigm. The question Greenberg put to his holistic method, however, may also be put to Frei's notion of realistic narrative: "How can such an approach be guarded against uncritical acceptance of things as they are, and against reading in *ad hoc* explanations or making fanciful connections?"[12] Greenberg's response is to "appropriate something of the historical-analogical [approach], namely, the inference from the text itself of principles of its interpretation."[13] The goal is to expand our attentiveness to the range of semiotic possibilities latent in the text as given: not by reading back to some antecedent ground against which the text can be measured, but by reading forward from the text in its philological-literary-historical context to the variety of environments in which it can be legitimately interpreted. Frei's method is, similarly, to look for semiotic richness within the text rather than outside it and to locate meaning in the relation between the text and its community of interpreters rather than between the text and some antecedent ground.

While similar, these two responses to modernity are not identical. In our Yale dialogue, the subtle differences between them were displayed in subtly different descriptions of what it means to return from ostensive reference back to the "plain sense" of scripture. As I recall our discussions, Frei, and to an extent Lindbeck, said that "plain sense" reading respected the integrity of the words of a scriptural text in its intratextual context *and* displayed the performative force of that text as token of an authoritative community's code of religious behavior. They argued, in sum, that the plain sense of the biblical text *is* its meaning for the authoritative community of interpreters. Greenberg, generally supported by Fraade, on the other hand, tended to distinguish plain-sense and performative (or interpretive) readings, limiting the plain-sense or *peshat* to that aspect of the text which, in the integrity of its intratextual context, rendered all reference possible.[14] In other words, Greenberg reserved the notion of plain-sense for that as yet presemantic or uninterpreted field of meanings from which all meaningful interpretations could be distinguished. In a tradition of Jewish hermeneutics, this is the way he guarded against the foundational or dogmatic attempts of traditional and modern readers to replace the text itself with *their* privileged readings of it, whether historical, legal or theological. Frei, on the other hand, applied the notion of plain-sense to that one meaningful interpretation among others that would serve as a reliable code of behavior for the community of believers. In a tradition of Christian hermeneutics, this is the way he guarded against modernist efforts to distinguish the text in its ostensively *literal* and thus objective meaning from the text in its performative and thus merely subjective meanings.

Our dialogue never blurred the potential differences between Frei's and Greenberg's approaches. At the same time, the dialogue always worked as a dialogue: each text scholar respected the concerns that moved the other. This indicated to me that all four scholars discussed their differences with respect to commonly held assumptions about what was at stake today in the study of biblical hermeneutics. Before exploring differences among individual scholars or between Jewish and Christian scholars, I was therefore moved, as a preliminary exercise, to identify the assumptions these scholars shared. My first hunch—and the one which led me to collect this volume of essays—was that they shared in some version of the approach to scriptural interpretation that I had first encountered in the rabbinic studies of Max Kadushin, z"l, my teacher at the Jewish Theological Seminary in the early 1970s.

Through a series of six books, published between 1932 and 1987,[15] Kadushin sought to describe the complex conceptual structures of rabbinic Judaism. His method was to identify the collection of rabbinic exegetes as a community of interpreters whose work provided the context in which scriptural texts had meaning for the Jewish people. He argued that this meaning was embodied in the practice of rabbinic exegesis itself and that the rules which informed this practice represented the conceptual order of rabbinic Judaism. He devoted most of his work to examining these rules by examining the system of virtues, or what he called "value-concepts," that were displayed in rabbinic literature. Kadushin believed his work challenged those who assume that conceptual order is to be understood only on what he called a philosophical model. He argued that this assumption leads to one of two errors: either imposing an extraneous conceptual scheme on rabbinic Judaism, or else denying that rabbinic Judaism displays any conceptual order. Instead, he examined religions as indigenous systems of value-concepts. The scholar's task, he said, is to observe how these concepts interrelate with one another and how they guide concrete behavior.

After the Yale seminar, I collected more examples of recent Jewish and Christian studies that might share in Kadushin's general approach, and I attempted to reduce these examples to their shared rules of inquiry.[16] As reported in this collection, I have found that Kadushin's work displayed rules of inquiry that were similar to those displayed in the works of Greenberg, Frei, Lindbeck and Fraade and of eight additional Jewish and Christian scholars. Borrowing a term from Lindbeck's book, *The Nature of Doctrine,*[17] I labeled the approach they all shared "postcritical" inquiry. The label is not itself compelling; until something better comes along, however, it serves to mark the facts that these scholars share some interests and that someone believes they share a rule of interpretation.

In his book, Lindbeck contrasts the "cultural-linguistic" approach of postcritical (or "postliberal") theology with precritical "propositionalist" and critical "experiential-expressivist" approaches. According to Lindbeck, the propositionalists are traditionalists who read church doctrines as "truth claims about objective realities" and scriptures as referential signs of those claims.[18] He says the experiential-expressivists are liberal scholars, for whom "doctrines [are] ... nondiscursive symbols of inner feelings, attitudes or existential orientations."[19] They read scriptures as nonreferential signs (for example, metaphors) that give expression to "common core experiences" that are available to all humans at all times.[20] According to the "cultural-linguistic" alternative, "meaning is constituted by the uses of a specific language." Scriptures therefore display their meaning intratextually, which means within the context of scripture as a system of symbols. These symbols are to be interpreted by the community for which they are meaningful as rules of conduct: first, the conduct of scriptural reading itself, and, then, the everyday conduct that is enjoined by this reading.

In Lindbeck's terms, then, Kadushin was a postcritical scholar. The "propositionalists" against whom he argued were the philosophers who imposed extraneous conceptual schemes on the rabbinic texts, claiming that the texts referred ostensively to the objective meanings of scripture. The "experiential-expressivists" were the philosophers (and irrationalists) who denied rabbinic Judaism displayed any conceptual order; for them, the rabbinic texts expressed either the rabbis' subjective beliefs or else the root experiences that are common to all humanity. Against these two approaches, Kadushin offered his "cultural-linguistic" alternative: for the rabbis, scripture was a system of symbols, or value-concepts, whose meanings were displayed, within the rabbinic community, in its everyday and its scholarly conduct.

I believe Kadushin's approach is refined in the postcritical Jewish *and* Christian interpretations collected in this volume. There are, indeed, differences between the Jewish and Christian participants in this collection, and these differences present a significant subject for future study. For now, however, my immediate concern is to attend only to the postcritical tendencies shared by both communities of scholars. These tendencies do not pertain to the everyday practices of either tradition, but only to either tradition's repertory of rules for self-correction. Without blurring distinctions between the communal practices of Jews and Christians, the goal of this study is to show how both can make use of comparable tools for repairing those practices today.

## THE RULES OF POSTCRITICAL SCRIPTURAL INTERPRETATION

In this long section, I take up the technical question of what general tendency of interpretation may be exhibited, in different particular ways, in the works of Jewish and Christian scriptural interpretation represented in this collection. My approach is, first, to select five representatives of the postcritical approach. Among Christian hermeneuts, these are Frei and Lindbeck, whose work is closely intertwined and whose differences represent principally a division of scholarly labor between historical and doctrinal/interpretive studies. Among Jewish hermeneuts, these are Fraade, Fishbane and Halivni, whose independent studies illustrate what I consider the moderate, radical and conservative modalities of Jewish postcritical interpretation.[21] I then retell what I consider the most critical steps in each of their arguments, largely as presented in the essays included in this volume, but with some additions from other writings of theirs. Since their arguments are complex, this retelling may serve some readers as a simpler introduction to their work. My own purpose is, of course, more tendentious, since I am not merely describing but also arguing that their arguments display a consistent pattern of postcritical interpretation. I redescribe this pattern in semiotic terms, which I borrow in part from the philosophy of Charles Sanders Peirce.

Frei's critique of mediating theology provides a point of departure for introducing the formal, semiotic model of postcritical interpretation. In Peirce's terms, Frei has introduced a distinction between the biblical text, as a *sign,* and two different ways of mapping its meaning. The way taken by the mediating theologians is to suggest that a given text simply refers to a given meaning. This is, in the language of the French semiotician de Saussure, to draw a two-part distinction between signifier (*signe*) and signified (*signifié*). In these terms, the mediators placed the signified, as ostensive referent, outside the signifier the way we would say, for example, that the exit sign in a theater indicates the way to go but is not itself that way, nor part of that way. According to Peirce, some signs (the ones he calls *indices* or *indexicals*) work this way, but verbal signs generally do not. Verbal signs do not merely point away from themselves, and they do not have merely one referent or object. Instead, he says, they are genuine representations, or *symbols*. This means that they are signs that refer to some object or referent only with respect to some mode of interpretation (or what he calls some *interpretant,* or interpreting agency or mind). Through this definition, Peirce indicates his claim that verbal signs normally have more than one possible referent and that a given mode of interpretation offers a means of distinguishing among a field of possible referents. This claim leads to a triadic semiotic model of the interpretation of verbal symbols. In this model, a symbol is a *sign* (1), that displays its *meaning* (2), with respect to some particular *interpretant* (3).[22]

In these terms, we may describe postcritical interpretation as a critique of attempts to apply an inadequate, dyadic semiotic model to the interpretation of genuine symbols, such as biblical texts.

*The first stage of postcritical scriptural interpretation is to identify mediating or modern interpreters as interpreters who reduce biblical interpretation to a dyadic semiotic by assimilating the mediating or modern interpretant of a biblical text to its meaning or referent.* This is to treat the biblical text as if it had a referent independently of any particular interpretant and as if this referent were intrinsically mediating or consistent with a modern understanding. It might be, for example, to identify the "meaning" of Exodus 14 exclusively with the historical referent of "a tidal event in the Sea of Reeds in the year 1534 BCE," or with the conceptual referent of "the power of hope to liberate those in spiritual bondage."

*The second stage of postcritical scriptural interpretation is to identify the consequences of a dyadic scriptural semiotic.* These are to introduce a series of dichotomizations that lack warrant in the biblical texts—between text and ostensive referent; between the text's reference and its performative or, in J.L. Austin's term, its perlocutionary force;[23] between the intrinsic meaning of the text and its meaning for the contemporary interpreter; and between literary and historical, "subjective" and "objective," or "scientific" and "religious" methods of biblical interpretation.

*The third stage of interpretation is to locate signs of a triadic semiotic within the biblical text itself, in particular as it is read in the primordial communities of rabbinic or of Christian interpreters.* Such a semiotic provides general rules of interpretation which, when defined in the contexts of contemporary study, restore the activities of mediation which are missing from modernist practices of interpretation. Postcritical scholars define and refine these rules in ways that address the particular instances of modernist interpretation that concern them. As a result, there is no single, postcritical model of scriptural interpretation, but, rather, a family of models, each of which may be redescribed in terms of this three-stage pattern of postcritical interpretation.

## CHRISTIAN POSTCRITICAL INTERPRETATION IN THE WORKS OF FREI AND LINDBECK

Frei's essay on "The 'Literal Reading' of Biblical Narrative in the Christian Tradition" and Lindbeck's excerpt from *The Nature of Doctrine* illustrate what I consider the three prototypical stages of postcritical scriptural interpretation.

Frei's critique of mediating theology provides the central paradigm for what is logically, but not rhetorically, the *first stage of his argument.* As described above, Frei criticizes the mediators for introducing a dichotomy between the biblical text and its ostensive referent and for privileging the latter. Extending his criticism forward, he describes contemporary phenomenological hermeneutics as the latest expression of the mediating tendency. Frei notes that, as practiced by Paul Ricoeur, David Tracy and others, phenomenological hermeneutics introduces an empirically unwarranted disjunction between texts, as "discourse," and the consciousness which interprets them, or "understanding." To mediate the two, the hermeneuts refer to the text's "power of disclosure," through which it reveals to the understanding worlds of meaning otherwise hidden within discourse. Frei argues that, as shown by the deconstructionists, this attempted mediation is introduced, by *force majeure,* into an interpretive scheme which in fact precludes genuine mediation. In the manner of a Cartesian project, the scheme has an Archimedean point: its unquestioned adoption of the category of "self-presence," of which "understanding" is the prototypical manifestation. Once self-presence is made the only agent of meaning, interpretation is reduced to the terms of a binary opposition between mere presence (as silent or undisclosed signification) and self-presence (or self-referential signification). In other words, text and reader are as isolated as windowless monads or as speakers of foreign tongues without an interpreter. The text's capacity for "disclosure" is supposed to bridge the gap, but—for Frei and the deconstructionists—this reduces to the reader's capacity to attribute his or her own form of self-presence to the text, rereading the text's signifiers as metaphors for elements in a newly constructed, self-referential system of meanings. The text lacks its own hermeneutic agency.

In the *second stage of his argument,* Frei finds a context for this dichotomous move within the types of interpretation that were available within traditional Christian readings of scripture. He calls this interpretation literal, typological and prescriptive. Beginning with the letters of Paul, Christians have traditionally read the stories of the life of Jesus literally, interpreted it as an antitype of the "Old Testament" texts as types, and adopted it as prescriptive for their communal life. While reading the Jewish scripture allegorically, patristic interpreters read the gospel story in its plain sense: " 'Jesus' . . . is the subject, the agent, and patient of these stories . . . and the descriptions of events, sayings, personal qualities, and so forth, became literal by being firmly predicated of him."[24] In modern times, however, the persistence of allegorical readings of the Jewish scriptures has become problematic. Without allegorical interpretation, there may be no way to maintain both Testaments in the canon and read both literally. It does not seem possible, however, to maintain allegorical readings and also acknowledge the autonomy of the Jewish scriptural tradition. Moreover, allegorical reading of the "Old Testament" sets a precedent for allegorical readings of the New Testament as well. Frei's thesis is that liberal readings of scripture since the reformation have tended to follow this precedent: phenomenological hermeneutics, in particular, read the gospel accounts as types of which some conceptually articulated universal principles are the antitypes. Frei concludes that deconstructive theory successfully deconstructs *this* modern theory of figuration, while then overgeneralizing its deconstruction into the unwarranted claim that *all* literal or referential readings are illusory.

Frei's most general complaint is against unwarranted generalization. For him, phenomenological hermeneuts, deconstructionists, and even the "new critics" and narrativists with whom he shares
some methodologies all err by straining to claim that their arguments are generally valid, rather than valid specifically as responses
to the particular problems which have stimulated them. He argues
that, when applied to scriptural interpretation, phenomenological
hermeneutics extends the ancient method of allegorical reading to
the gospel stories themselves: rereading the narratives of Jesus as
"carnal shadows of the true 'secondary' world of 'meanings' understood in 'disclosure.' "[25] The story of Jesus is at most a metaphor of
generalizable events in the life of consciousness, disclosed in this
case to contemporary understanding. This understanding discloses
itself to the activity of hermeneutical theorizing itself, which, in
turn, discloses itself to nothing other than the self-presence of consciousness. There is, in other words, no mediator between the text
and its signification for consciousness. On the one hand, the life of
consciousness has no referent outside its own self-presence; on the
other hand, as historical referent of the narratives or as a character
within the text, Jesus lacks personal agency of his own.

[In the denouement of his essay, Frei extends his critique of the
contemporary mediators to related, if less egregious, attempts to
reduce meaning to self-presence and to substitute the authority of
general theory for the authority of a sacred text. He argues that
David Tracy's "analogical" theology retains the phenomenological
presupposition of self-presence, even if in a more cautious expression. He notes that, as "an immanent subversion" of phenomenological hermeneutics, deconstruction tends to fall prey to the same
tendencies it effectively criticizes: extending its critique of referential readings beyond the domain of the allegorical *cum* ontological
tradition it services. He argues that "new criticism," with which he
otherwise shares many rules of interpretation, fails to acknowledge
its debt to the tradition of plain-sense reading in Christianity. The
"new critics" prescind selected features of plain-sense reading and
then generalize these features into a general theory of reading, of
which they claim Christian plain-sense reading is a limited example.
This, says Frei, is a clear case of over-generalization. He offers a
comparable critique of recent narrative theology: "it is once more

a case of putting the cart before the horse . . . if one constructs a general and inalienable human quality called 'narrative' . . . within which to interpret the Gospels and provide foundational warrant for the possibility of their existential and ontological meaningfulness."[26]]

In the *third stage of his argument,* Frei explains that the problem that stimulates his inquiry is Christianity's task "of regaining its autonomous vocation as a religion, after its defeat in its secondary vocation of providing ideological coherence, foundation and stability to Western culture."[27] His project, then, is to pull in the reins of his religious community's hermeneutical pretensions, deconstructing what he considers its onto-theological illusions and finding in their place a particular text with a foundational and redemptive story and with various traditions of reading that story plainly and performatively.

As an alternative to the mediating theologies, Frei offers a "modest" theory for describing how scripture is in fact read within the religious communities for which it is authoritative. He concludes that the letters of Paul prescribe a non-dichotomous hermeneutic according to which the Jesus narratives are to be read literally and performatively and the "Old Testament" narratives are to be read typologically. Frei does not adopt the Pauline hermeneutic directly, because, as he suggests, contemporary exegetes cannot tolerate two potential correlates of the ancient typological method: Christian supercessionist readings of Jewish scriptures and liberal supercessionist readings of the gospels. Instead, he reaffirms the Pauline hermeneutic in a way that would be appropriate for contemporary exegetes. The most conspicuous rule of this hermeneutic is *to respect the integrity of the scriptural text in its sensus literalis.* This literal sense refers to the way the Christian community both ascribes to Jesus of Nazareth the stories associated with him and adopts those stories as the community's code of behavior and belief.

Because Frei's and Lindbeck's modest theories of literal sense reading are so intertwined, I will, for economy of reporting, resume the discussion of this stage of Frei's argument after introducing the first two stages of Lindbeck's argument.

The *first stage of Lindbeck's postcritical argument* is his critique of "propositionalist" and "experiential-expressivist" approaches to religion. As reported above in different terms, Lindbeck describes the propositionalists as "cognitivists," who consider religions as systems of propositions or truth-claims about an objective reality.[28] He says the experiential-expressivists consider religions, in Bernard Lonergan's terms, as "diverse expressions or objectifications of a common core experience,"[29] which is "the dynamic state of being in love without restriction" and "without an object."[30] Lindbeck's version of Frei's critique is to argue that both these approaches are extra-textual, replacing the authority of the biblical text with the authority of certain conceptual, historical or experiential descriptions of which the text is considered a merely instrumental (or dyadic) sign.

In *the second stage of his argument,* Lindbeck examines the dichotomizing consequences of extra-textual reading. In *The Nature of Doctrine,* for example, he argues that extra-textual interpreters reduce church doctrines to either term of a rigid dichotomy. Describing doctrines as "informative propositions or truth claims about objective realities," propositionalists assume that "if a doctrine is once true, it is always true, and if it is once false, it is always false."[31] He argues that they consequently fail to provide or account for ecumenism or for the emergence of new or varied doctrines. Describing doctrines, on the other hand, as "noninformative and nondiscursive symbols of inner feelings, attitudes or existential orientations,"[32] experiential-expressivists tend to privatize Christian religious experience. Lindbeck argues that they can provide and account for doctrinal change, but not for the power of doctrines to authorize and sustain communal discourse.

Peirce's semiotic offers another way of articulating Lindbeck's critique. According to Peirce, a proposition may be defined as the application of a relative predicate (or *rhema*), which delivers all its *meaning* or content, to an existential subject (or *index*), which refers the predicate to some observable actuality/ies or moment/s of experience.[33] "This book is red," for example, may be redescribed as the application of "———the character of being red and a book" to "what I am pointing to." In these terms, Lindbeck may be said to argue that propositionalists describe doctrines as the applications of certain characters (such as, "the dead are raised") to universal indices (*"it is true in all possible worlds that . . ."*); while experiential-expressivists describe doctrines as unquantified relative predicates which are neither true nor false ("the dead are raised," make of this character what you will). In Peirce's semiotic, an alternative would be to describe doctrines as rules, or modes of interpretation. These are neither propositions nor mere predicates, but rather ways of formulating propositions, or of applying certain types of predicates to certain types of indices on certain types of occasion. In this case, there would no single way of defining a doctrine—since every pur-ported definition would display only a single application of the doc-trine—but there could be certain paradigmatic applications which served, for certain communities, as preferred or authoritative ways of exhibiting the doctrine. In this approach, however, we would have to redefine our use of the term "true."

For propositionalists, "true" indicates that a proposition cor-responds to some objective order of things; for experiential-expressivists, it is either an unhelpful designator (" 'the dead are raised' is neither true nor false"), or it indicates only that a predicate expresses an identifiable feeling or quality (" 'the dead are raised' expresses this or that to me"). The rule approach would require distinguishing among two categories of truth-terms. In some essays, Peirce used the term "expressiveness" to refer to the capacity of a predicate to display the quality it displays; "veracity" to refer to the conformity of an assertion to the speaker's belief; and "truth" to refer to capacity of an argument (or statement of a rule) to carry the force it claims to carry.[34] To take one example, "the dead are raised" has veracity if, for a speaker, "the dead are raised" expresses the quality the speaker sought to express. All three of these terms refer to what we may call types of *validity:* the correspondence between a sign and its intended use. Peirce used the term "strength," or prag-matic force, to refer to the influence of some rule or genuine symbol in the life of some community of speakers.[35] Unlike the various types of validity, then, *strength* refers to the correspondence be-tween a symbol and some change *in the world.* To illustrate, suppose there is some genuine symbol or rule of which "the dead are raised" is true, in the sense of *valid.* We would say that the rule is strong if it, in a significant way, guides or transforms the behavior of a given community of speakers. We would say that the specific locution, "the dead are raised," is valid if it succeeds in exhibiting this rule to the particular community to whom it is addressed.

In this Peircean approach, propositionalists would be those who assimilate strength to validity by identifying a rule with one of its context-specific locutions; experiential-expressivists would be those who exclude considerations of strength, identifying rules only with the expressive qualities or predicates that attach to their context-specific locutions.

I mention the Peircean approach because it anticipates in a formal, and perhaps formalistic, way Lindbeck's rule theories of doctrine and of religion. In the *third stage of his argument,* Lindbeck makes use of these theories to clarify, for theoretically minded scholars, his intratextual method of scriptural interpretation. Along with Frei, he labels his theories "modest" in order to preserve the priority of text over theory: if his interpretations are compatible with a triadic semiotic, that is only because intratextual Bible reading recommends such a semiotic to the philosophic interpreter, not because Bible readers need to arm themselves with semiotic theory in order to read the Bible.

With Frei, then, Lindbeck reads the Bible intratextually, which means within the context of scripture as a system of literary signs. These signs are interpreted by the community for which they are meaningful as rules of conduct, both the conduct of scriptural reading itself and the everyday conduct that is enjoined by this reading. In this approach, the Bible is not a sign of some external reality, but a reality itself whose meanings display the doubly dialogic relationships between a particular text and its context within the Bible as a whole, and between the Bible as a whole and the conduct of the community of interpreters. What I am calling the community of postcritical Christian interpreters emerges as the community for whom the gospel narratives recommend this hermeneutic itself. As Lindbeck has written,

> If one characterizes the literal sense as that which a community of readers takes to be the plain, primary and controlling signification of a text . . . then, as Frei has suggested . . . the narrative meaning of the stories about Jesus

was the uniquely privileged *sensus literalis* of the whole of
scripture for the groups by and for whom those stories were
composed.[36]

The narrative meaning is the meaning *of* the text *for* its community
of readers.

Lindbeck offers a rule-theory of doctrine consistent with this
understanding of narrative meaning. Christian doctrines are the
way the Christian community, as "the story-shaped Church," reads
the biblical narratives as directives for communal belief and
practice.

> Church doctrines are communally authoritative teachings
> regarding beliefs and practices that are considered essential
> to the identity and welfare of the group in question.[37]

Such doctrines have expressive meaning or validity for those who
practice them, and they display their meaning propositionally with
respect to specific contexts of practice, which are specific ways of
describing the world and how to act in it. However, the pragmatic
force of such doctrines extends beyond any specific context. Lindbeck therefore describes them as rules: patterns of imitating the character of Jesus in the gospel narratives and, thereby, of transforming
everyday beliefs and actions in the various ways that are dictated by
each context of action.

Addressing theoretically minded scholars, Lindbeck and Frei
suggest that their intratextual method of interpretation is consistent
with a semiotic or cultural-linguistic understanding of religion as

> at once . . . a determinate code in which beliefs, ritual and
> behavior patterns, ethos as well as narrative, come together
> as a common semiotic system, and also as the community
> which is that system in use.[38]

This religion is to be described through the kind of method Clifford
Geertz (after Gilbert Ryle) called "thick description":

> It is, first, description of details as parts of 'interworked
> systems of construable signs . . . within which they can be

> intelligibly . . . described.' Second, it is description from
> the actor's, participant's, or language-user's point of view,
> yet without mimicry or confusion of identity on the part of
> the interpreter.[39]

The assumption here is a semiotic and a pragmatic one: first, that a religion may be understood as a system of signs; second, that such signs display their meaning in use, which means in the way they inform behavior in the community of sign users. In Peirce's formulation, the signs in question here are genuine symbols, which may be redescribed as laws of behavior or as sets of conditional resolutions to act, manifested in the behavior of symbol users as sets of observable actions. From this perspective, to study a religion is to learn these laws of behavior, as displayed in those sets of observable actions.

In this approach, scripture functions within its community of interpreters as the paradigmatic token of that community's religion, or semiotic code. To enact that code is to act in such a way that one's actions are tokens of the genuine symbols of which scripture in its literal sense is the paradigmatic token. If the genuine symbols could be conceptually defined, then the student of this approach might be tempted to imitate what Frei called the allegorizing practice of phenomenological hermeneutics: substituting conceptual descriptions of the symbols for their scriptural tokens. The symbols are displayed, however, only in indefinite series of conditional resolutions to act. The text of scripture itself is the only enduring token of these series. For Frei and Lindbeck, the literal sense of scripture is the paradigmatic form in which the Christian community of interpreters reads the text as such an enduring token.

It is at this point that both Frei and Lindbeck advertise the importance of rabbinic studies for postcritical Christian theology. For Frei, the demise of Christian onto-theology marks the demise, as well, of Christian universalism: not the universal import of Christianity, but the subordination of scripture reading to the terms of universal theories about the meaning of human experience as such. Frei believes that, relieved of the burdens of foundationalism, Christian scriptural interpretation may be more similar to rabbinic scriptural interpretation than previously assumed.[40] In an essay entitled

"Doctrine in Christianity: A Comparison with Judaism,"[41] Lindbeck notes that both he and the Jewish philosopher David Novak share the conviction "that biblical religion has to do with chosen peoples, and that is why the social or communal role of doctrines is primary."[42] He says, "my suggestion is that Christianity has been and could again be much more like Judaism in this respect than is often supposed."[43] The rabbinic community, or *kahal,* then becomes a prototype for the community of Christian interpreter-practitioners.[44]

## FRAADE'S MODERATE JEWISH POSTCRITICAL INTERPRETATION

Steven Fraade's "The Turn to Commentary in Ancient Judaism" is a version of the introduction to his book, *From Tradition to Commentary: Torah and Its Interpretation in the Midrash Sifre to Deuteronomy.*[45] His book displays the Jewish postcritical approach in what I'll call its moderate or centrist form. He presents his book explicitly as an alternative to two dialectically opposed tendencies in modern scholarship in rabbinics, which he calls "the hermeneuticist and historicist fallacies."[46] He argues that, on the one hand, by viewing "the historicity of commentary's *representations* apart from the hermeneutical grounding of its performance," historicists allow the text only to face "out upon history and society." On the other hand, by "viewing the hermeneutics of commentary's *interpretations* apart from the sociohistorical grounding of its performance," hermeneuticists allow the text to "face in upon itself." Concerned to minimize subjectivistic readings, historicists attend strictly to the objective aspects of meaning: the syntactics of the text itself and the referential relation of the text to what they take to be its meaning for the historically specific society in which it was redacted. Concerned to reclaim dimensions of textual meaning lost in historicist readings, "hermeneuticists" focus their attention on the possibilities of interpretive activity of which they take the rabbinic texts to be symptomatic. Schleiermacher's goal remains prototypical of their effort "to understand the author better than he understood himself," or at least to privilege the scholar's empathetic understanding as the irreplaceable source of hermeneutical reconstruction. In Lindbeck's terms, then, historicists are modern propositionalists, for whom the meaning of rabbinic texts is to be found only in their objective reference; hermeneuticists are modern experiential-expressivists, for whom the meaning of rabbinic texts is to be found only in readers' subjective responses to them.

Fraade's response is that, however useful it may be "for the maintenance of our disciplinary boundaries," the modern attempt to bifurcate these two tendencies distorts the meaning of rabbinic literature. His goal is to reintegrate the two tendencies by giving voice to a third mode of inquiry which, true to his approach, he identifies only by performing it. I find the following characteristics of his performance to be the most telling.

Without disclaiming critical inquiry, he seeks to reclaim a dimension of textual meaning that is lost in the ancient texts themselves. His method is to find *within these texts* a mode of inquiry that, when reappropriated within the context of modern scholarship, would enable that scholarship to reclaim the dimension of textual meaning it had lost. His method is thus dialogic—in his terms, a "shuttling back and forth" between modern and ancient discourses in order to recover both the overlooked meaning of rabbinic literature *and* the appropriate method for disclosing it. He calls this the method of *commentary* and sets out both to *describe* rabbinic scriptural commentary *and* to *perform* his new variety of modern scholarly commentary.

Fraade notes that, like other commentaries, rabbinic commentaries "begin with an extended base-text, of which they designate successive subunits for exegetical attention, to each of which they attach a comment or chain of comments, which nevertheless remain distinct from the base-text, to which the commentary sooner or later returns ... to take up the next selected subunit in sequence."[47] Like other commentaries, rabbinic commentaries are therefore paradoxical, in that they derive their rhetorical framework from the sequence of subunits in their scriptural base-texts at the same time that they atomize and re-order those sub-units for the sake of analysis.[48]

He sets out to engage the "rabbinic turn to commentary" in its aboriginal form, both by studying rabbinic commentaries in their textual entirety and integrity and by focusing on "one of our earliest compilations of rabbinic exegesis ... against the backdrop of its only known antecedents as biblical commentary": the prophetic *pesharim* of the Dead Sea Scroll and the allegorical commentaries of Philo. Through detailed studies of selected, individual texts, he isolates the major hermeneutical traits of these antecedents that are of relevance to a study of rabbinic commentary. As a type, the *pesharim* represent "deictic" commentary, which means they refer each phrase of their biblical base-texts to specific (in this case, allegorical) referents. As a type, Philo's allegories represent "dialogical" commentary, which allows the commentator to interact with the base-text by posing questions of it and proffering answers.

Examining the *Sifre* to Deuteronomy in its textual integrity, Fraade notes how it integrates both deictic and dialogic forms of commentary, while emphasizing the latter. He considers, for example, *Sifre's* commentary on Deuteronomy 32:7:

> Remember the days of old (*olam*), consider the years (*shenot*) of each and every generation; ask your father and he will inform you, your elders and they will tell you. "Remember the days of old": [God said to them:] Take heed of what I did to the earliest generations . . . . "Consider the years of each and every generation": You can find no generation without people like those of the generation of the flood . . . but each and every individual is judged according to his deeds. "Ask your father and he will inform you": These are the prophets as it says, "When Elisha beheld it he cried out [to Elijah], 'Father, father' " (2 Kgs. 2:12). "Your elders and they will tell you": These are the elders, as it is said, "Gather for Me seventy men of the elders of Israel" (Num. 11:16).[49]

Fraade explains how the atomized element "father" is taken to refer deictically to "prophets" and "elder" to "elder." *Sifre's* overall reading is dialogic, however. In this commentary, *Sifre* interprets the scriptural passage as referring to a biblical past, from earliest times to the present. In "another interpretation" brought after this one, *Sifre* interprets the passage as referring to the future, from the sufferings of the present ("whenever God brings sufferings to you") to the ultimate future (" 'Consider the years of each and every generation':

This is the generation of the Messiah")—a time when Israel will hear directly from her "father" (now referring to "the Holy One"). The only elements common to each interpretation are the "elders," referring each time only to "elders." Fraade interprets these "elders"— standing in between the prophets of the past and the God revealed in the distant future—to mean the rabbinic sages themselves: the "inspired class" which mediates between revelation and redemption. *Sifre*'s commentary has thereby interacted dialogically with its base-text, eliciting from it a message about the role of the rabbinic sages in Israel's relation to God.

Here is a sampling of the other features of *Sifre*'s commentary to which Fraade draws our attention.

● The commentary allows for multiple interpretation of the base-text, while still respecting the integrity of the text's plain sense. No matter how many interpretations it brings, it bases these on a reading of all the words of its Deuteronomic text in their intratextual setting.

● By bringing the base-text into dialogue with all of scripture, the commentary provides a medium through which scripture can refer to and interpret itself.

● The commentary presents itself as the product of collective and cumulative, rather than of merely individual, activities of interpretation.

● It effects a dialogical relationship between scripture as a whole and the interpretive rabbinic community, through which textual meaning and communal practice are mutually transformative. Thus the words of Torah become the sages' words.[50] The goal of commentary is to stimulate continuous study and the continuously transformative activity which accompanies it. Fraade's comment about the "elder" as the rabbinic sage is a brief sampling of his analyses of ways in which the sages included themselves and their mode of inquiry into scripture's subject matter.

Fraade concludes that rabbinic commentary, so described, "requires that our own critical interpretation of its texts adopt two converging perspectives: that of their formation and that of their reception." As literary historians, modern rabbinic scholars must examine how rabbinic redactors integrated various traditions into running commentaries. As hermeneuts, they must also receive and respond to the commentary as if they were its intended students, thereby achieving some understanding of its performative method and force. Fraade is proposing, in sum, "that the critical analysis of a rabbinic scriptural commentary take itself the form of commentary, one that in its own way is dialogical, alternating between the perspectives of the text's formation and reception, as between that of the ancient student of the text and the modern critic of it."

The leading principles of his modern commentary thereby reappropriate the principles of rabbinic commentary: to respect the integrity of rabbinic and prerabbinic base-texts in their plain-sense; to bring these base-texts into dialogue with comparable texts, so that the modern commentary may serve as a medium for the ancient text's self-reference; to engage the modern reader in an activity of reinterpreting the base-texts as well as of re-evaluating modern methods of interpretation; to contribute to the collective work of transforming modern rabbinic scholarship.

In sum, Fraade's book displays the three prototypical stages of postcritical scriptural interpretation. In *the first stage of his argument,* he criticizes the bifurcation of modern rabbinic scholarship into historicist and hermeneuticist tendencies. In *the second stage,* he identifies ways in which historicist and hermeneuticist scholars distort the meaning of rabbinic texts by reducing meaning to either mere reference or mere interpretive form. In semiotic terms, this means that they either reduce interpretation to reference or reduce reference to interpretation. *In the third stage of his argument,* Fraade locates paradigms for non-reductive interpretation within what he considers primordial texts of rabbinic Judaism. Like Lindbeck's, Fraade's interpretive paradigm is doubly dialogic: displaying the dialogic relation between a particular text and its intratextual context in an entire document at the same time that it displays the dialogic relation between this document and the performative life of its community of interpreters.

The moderate form of Fraade's inquiry corresponds to his criticizing both historicist and hermeneuticist tendencies with generally equal force. In his recent book, *Peshat and Derash: Plain and Applied Meaning in Rabbinic Exegesis,*[51] Halivni is responding primarily to the excessive subjectivity of contemporary legal interpretation; he therefore places particular emphasis on the conservative, or objectively referential, aspect of his postcritical inquiry. On the other hand, in his recent book, *The Garments of Torah: Essays in Biblical Hermeneutics,*[52] Fishbane responds primarily to the excessive objectivism in both traditional and modern text interpretation; he therefore places particular emphasis on the more radically interpretive aspect of his inquiry. These two works display the limits of Jewish postcritical scriptural interpretation. Offering context-specific criticisms of either of two poles of modern/premodern interpretation, Halivni and Fishbane articulate their triadic semiotics in the dichotomizing forms of context-specific polemics.

## HALIVNI'S CONSERVATIVE JEWISH POSTCRITICAL INTERPRETATION

Halivni's "Plain Sense and Applied Meaning in Rabbinic Exegesis" is a composite of parts of four of his essays, two from earlier manuscripts of his book *Peshat and Derash: Plain and Applied Meaning in Rabbinic Exegesis.*[53] Read according to its own *peshat,* Halivni's *Peshat and Derash* offers a theological/hermeneutical recommendation about how observant rabbinical scholars may resolve conflicts they perceive between the *peshat,* or plain-sense, of the scriptural text and the *midrash halakhah,* or the scriptural readings the Talmudic rabbis have offered for the sake of making legal judgments. Briefly stated, he offers an historical-like account and justification of the rabbis' identifying their *midrash halakhah* as the correct *peshat* in those cases where the conflict would have consequences for legal decision making.[54]

At the same time, as Halivni indicates in his Preface, the performative form of his book also delivers part of its message. Divided into separate scholarly and theological parts,

> the structure of the book . . . mirrors its central theological proposition—that rabbinic exegesis and halakhah (legal norms) are integrally, but not always inextricably, linked.[55]

On the one hand, "the critical scholar . . . [has] an allegiance to the dictates of objective truth and accuracy—indeed, to peshat."[56] On the other hand, Halivni's theological method is the "systematic mining of rabbinic theological sources," drawing "inferences" that relate these sources to issues of existential concern.

As a dialogue between these objective ("scholarly") and subjective ("theological") methods, Halivni's book as a whole represents a postcritical inquiry: interpreting the rabbinic corpus (as symbol) as it bears on an issue of immediate existential concern (its interpretant). This appears to be Halivni's concern to respond, on the one hand, to Orthodox critics of his anti-authoritarian Talmudic science and, on the other hand, to Conservative critics of his persistently orthodox religious practice. In response, he suggests that all his critics share in the mistaken belief that science and practice share a common authority and that the results of each should therefore be harmonized. He believes that this leads contemporary Orthodox scholars to reduce their exegetical science to the changing standards of authority and convention that govern religious decision making (*halakhah*) and that it leads contemporary Conservative scholars to reduce their process of religious decision making to the objectifying standards of science that govern exegesis. As an alternative, he offers an historical-hermeneutical account and justification of the exegetical approach exemplified in the Rashbam's work.[57] As text scholar, exemplifying "the highest genre of *Torah Lishmah* [the study of Scripture for its own sake]," the Rashbam searched for the *peshat,* even at the expense of his own legal readings.[58] As *posek,* or adjudicator ("one of the greatest *posekim* of his time"), he relinquished his fidelity to *peshat;* responding to the needs of his community, he no longer, in Halivni's words, "had the luxury" of studying the text for its own sake.[59]

There is also a third dimension of Halivni's book: the critique of modernist reductionism implicit in his response to traditionalist reductionism. In this regard, Halivni's scholarly discussion of the evolution of rabbinic exegesis is most telling. Like Fraade, Halivni has sought to avoid the reductive tendencies of modern inquiry by reclaiming for a modern rabbinic commentary the indigenous rules of rabbinic exegesis. He has sought to examine these rules, however, as they are displayed not only in single documents, but also in what he considers the singular trajectory of rabbinic exegesis in its evolution from the Second Temple period to today. Reducing an extensive collection of rabbinic documents to their operative rules of interpretation, he has observed a tendency that links one to the other in historical sequence. He says this is a progressive tendency to respect the integrity of scriptural and rabbinic texts in their extended intratextual contexts (*peshat*) and the integrity of the halakhic process (*midrash halakhah*) in its time-bound, communal context. In a 1979 article, Halivni distinguishes what he calls his "dialectically critical method" from both the "conceptual method" of traditional Talmudic study in the *yeshivot* and the "critical method" of "academically trained Talmudic scholars."[60] He says

> The conceptual method concentrates mainly on the *logical exploration* of the statement under discussion, the critical method concentrates mainly on the *textual state* of the statement under discussion, and the dialectically critical method concentrates mainly on the *evolving* nature of the statement under discussion.[61]

While "the weakness of the conceptual method is its loose connection with the text," the weakness of the critical method is its "adhering too closely with the text, to the point that it restricts itself almost completely to meanings that lie on the surface of the text."[62] But

> There is more to a text than meets the eye. Deliberation, indeed meditation on a text, yields not only new nuances that have not been contemplated before, but may also affect the very direction and purport of the text. . . . Communication with a text means pondering over it long enough until it opens up and reveals the many and varied allusions that otherwise would have remained buried beneath the surface. . . . The critical scholar ignores these allusions . . . ; by denying validity to non-explicit meaning, he is imparting to textual learning a quality of *shallowness* that is unwarranted by its content.[63]

While sharing the "critical scholar's concern for an accurate text," the dialectically critical scholar looks for meaning "beneath the textual surface," by "seeking out [the present text's] antecedents and tracing their fluctuations and subsequent development" "through dialectical means"—that is, by generating hypotheses about how the text may have evolved and by engaging the text's argumentation on the basis of these hypotheses.[64]

Restated in terms of a postcritical semiotics, Halivni's thesis is that, in its evolutionary trajectory, rabbinic exegesis tends to draw a tripartite distinction among the *peshat* of the text (as *symbol*), time-bound interpretations of the text's references (as *meaning*), and the time-bound contexts of interpretation (as *interpretants*). Here, *peshat* (as "extended intratextual context") refers to the unburdened presentation of the symbol as locus of possible meaning. This means that referential, hermeneutical and pragmatic studies of the *peshat* are true to the extent that they *do not fail to uncover* whatever possibilities of signification are displayed by the text in its intratextual context. They are false if they misrepresent those possibilities *or limit them* by attending preferentially to certain possibilities over others.[65] The plain-sense scholar (*pashtan*) displays the semantics of the text and identifies the range of meanings that might possibly attend such a text as interpreted with respect to the range of known interpretants. The interpreter (*darshan*) explores the possibilities of meaning that are available with respect to single interpretant.[66]

Halivni argues that "contemporary critics" misconstrue this evolutionary trajectory because they have evaluated it in terms of the modern standards of "original [authorial] intent" and of "literal sense."[67] From this perspective, he says, these critics believe that rabbinic exegesis has through the years "zigzagged" back and forth between concern for *peshat* and for *derash*. Thus

> Talmudic interpretation of the Bible is generally considered by modern exegetes to be quite distinct from the peshat, out of tune with the 'natural' meaning of the biblical text it purports to explain. In contrast, medieval exegesis, especially that of Rashbam . . . and Ibn Ezra . . . is regarded as close to peshat (relatively speaking). . . . Postmedieval exegesis is again unacceptable, harking back to talmudic interpretation of the Bible.[68]

According to Halivni, however, authorial intent and literal sense are the preferred standards of only one, more recent phase in the evolution of rabbinic hermeneutics. To interpret earlier phases according to these standards is to remove them from their historical contexts and impose on them an alien intentionality. The result is to read into previous modes of exegesis a dichotomy between "natural" *peshat* and "artificial" *derash* that is not evident in those modes.[69]

Halivni's argument may be redescribed in terms of the paradigm of postcritical interpretation. *In the first stage of his argument,* Halivni criticizes interpretive tendencies either to overly harmonize *peshat* and *derash,* and thus, with the seminarians, to assimilate reference and interpretation, or to overly dichotomize the two, and thus, with the moderns, to ignore the relations between reference and interpretation. *In the second stage of his argument,* he claims that each of these errors results from a failure to respect the integrity of the scriptural or rabbinic texts as genuine symbols. *In the third stage of his argument,* he seeks to reclaim for modern rabbinic commentary the rabbinic tradition's progressive respect for the integrity of *peshat* as extensive intratextual context. Understood this way, the study of *peshat* does not compete with midrashic interpretation; instead, it prepares readers, in the integrity of their contexts of interpretation, to engage the text in the integrity of its context of symbolization.

## FISHBANE'S RADICAL POSTCRITICAL INTERPRETATION

"Extra-Biblical Exegesis: The Sense of Not Reading in Rabbinic Midrash" illustrates the theological context of Fishbane's investigation into the rules of inner-biblical and early rabbinic text interpretation. In these remarks, I will describe that context as it is more fully displayed in Fishbane's *The Garments of Torah: Essays in Biblical Hermeneutics*[70] (in which the essay also appears) and as it is served by the discoveries of his *Biblical Interpretation in Ancient Israel.*[71]

In *Garments,* Fishbane celebrates the maieutic voice of scripture: the capacity of its mystery to challenge the limits of language, to deflate ontological pretensions, and to decenter. At the same time, he identifies the dialogic partner to whom this voice is addressed and for whom it would be redemptive: what he calls, after Martin Buber, the monologic modern self, alone in its autonomy the way Roland Barthes says the interpreter is left with nothing else than his or her "will-to-power."[72] *Garments* records Fishbane's search for ways of renewing a modern culture that has lost its connection to sacrality, to community and, thus it appears, to the conditions of meaning which the biblical traditions once provided. He organizes the book into three parts, reflecting the "three typical moments whereby cultures renew themselves hermeneutically," as well as what I take to be the three elements of his own program for renewing the culture of scriptural reading. These elements are: first, to examine the range of exegetical possibilities inherent in the *peshat* of the scriptural text; second, to identify the forms of exegesis, in the Bible and in rabbinic literature, that emerged in response to epistemological dislocations in biblical and early rabbinic cultures; and, third, to identify the epistemological dislocations that stimulate modern exegetical scholarship and, then, to reintroduce the forms of biblical and rabbinic exegesis which may respond to these dislocations.

Part I of *Garments* delivers the lesson of Fishbane's *Biblical Interpretation in Ancient Israel:*[73] that scripture interprets itself and, thus, that scriptural revelation is a revealed activity of interpretation. The pragmatic force of this lesson is that scripture is a living dialogue in which the modern reader has a part. This is what Halivni calls a "non-maximalist conception of revelation," and what a postcritical semiotician may term the genuinely symbolic character of scripture, which calls the reader to hear and respond to the complaints of which it is a sign. Fishbane interprets this pragmatic message through the language of the kabbalah:

> Rabbi Simeon said: If a man looks upon the Torah as merely a book presenting narratives and everyday matters, alas for him! . . . The Torah, in all of its worlds, holds supernal truths and sublime secrets. . . . The tales related in the Torah are simply her outer garments, and woe to the man who regards that outer garb as the Torah itself, for such a man will be deprived of portion in the next world. . . .[74]

The words of the Torah are garments; the inner message lies within —in Fishbane's reading, I take this to mean the inner message for the modern, solitary self for whom the words of scripture have otherwise lost their sacrality.

The question, of course, is how that message can be heard once again. Fishbane's response begins with his scholarly study of the genres of innerbiblical exegesis. These appear in his work to be signs of the Torah's inner life, sewn into the "garments" themselves. In the language of postcritical semiotics, these genres are tokens of the semiotic law according to which the scriptural text, as symbol, displays its meaning to its various interpretants. To study them, in other words, is to study tokens of the divine semiosis. Fishbane catalogues the genres as "scribal," "legal," "*aggadic,*" and "mantological"—exemplified in a plurality of specific exegetical strategies, or logia, of which there is no over-arching logos. The lack of any single archetype means that the divine semiosis cannot be reduced ultimately to any language other than that of the biblical text as a whole, alive with all of its semiotic indeterminacies and, thus, its drive to be actualized in as yet undisclosed ways. Kadushin described the rabbinic value-concepts in just this way, as having a "drive to concretization." He claimed the value-concepts named certain rules of knowledge-and-conduct, however, such as "loving-kindness" (*gemilut hasadim*) and "God's mercy" (*middat ha-rahamim*). In Fishbane's work, the logia are strictly rules of exegetical conduct, such as scribal correction, "lemmatic legal exegesis" (legal interpretation bound to an authoritative legal text), analogical aggadic exegesis, and the recontextualization of historical narratives as oracular signs. A fruitful subject of study would be to examine the relations among exegetical rules and behavioral rules: are they independent, is one subordinated to the other, or both to a third set of rules?

In "Extra-Biblical Exegesis: The Sense of Not Reading in Rabbinic Midrash," Fishbane offers a case-study which, as I read it, shows how the rules of exegesis may be tokens of value-concepts, or, in his terms, of rabbinic theologies. The context is his identifying scribal corrections of the biblical text as occasions for the rabbis' playfully suspending the authority of the text as written and substituting for it some semantic marks of their own theological innovations. Fishbane identifies two aspects of this embedded theology: "divine empowerment through ritual praxis and divine pathos in response to human suffering."[75] To illustrate the rabbinic theology of divine empowerment, he notes how the homilist of the *Pesiqta de-Rav Kahana* rereads Job 17:9—"But the righteous one holds fast to his way, and the pure of hands will increase [his] strength (*yosiph ometz*)—to mean

> that God—who is both righteous and pure of action—gives strength (*koach*) to the righteous in order "that they may do His will." This construction concluded, the Joban passage is then further applied to both Moses and the righteous. On this last application, R. Azariah interprets the verse to mean: "Whenever the righteous do the will of the Holy One, Blessed be He, they increase strength (*mosiphin koach*) in the *dynamis*"—that is to say, they empower the divine principle of immanent power through their performance of the commandments.[76]

To illustrate the rabbinic theology of divine pathos, he notes how the homilist of *Exodus Rabbah* (XXX.24) rereads Isaiah 56:1, "for My salvation is near to come (*ki qeroba yeshu'ati lavo*)."

> [The homilist] begins with a philologist's observation: "Scripture does not say '*your* salvation' (second person plural) but '*My* salvation.' " And he adds: "May His name be blessed! For were it not [so] written [in Scripture], one could not say it." . . . [the *derashah* continues] "If you [Israel] do not have merit, I shall perform [the salvation] for My *own* sake (*bishvili*); for *kivyakhol* [as it were], as long as you are in trouble, I am with you, as it says [in Scripture]: "I am with him (Israel) in trouble (*'imo anokhi be-tzarah*) (Ps. 91:15).[77]

If biblical exegesis is indeed a form of ritual praxis, then its appearance within the Bible itself would seem to illustrate, within the biblical context, the rabbinic concept of divine empowerment through biblical exegesis! If, furthermore, human suffering provides the occasion for biblical exegesis, then this exegesis may provide the occasion for divine pathos. I take this, in fact, to be the pragmatic message of Parts I and II of Fishbane's book. And I take it to be consistent with a stronger claim that remains merely implicit in his work: while not the only stimulus to interpretation, human suffering is the archetypical stimulus. Other stimuli give rise to referential or iconic readings of the Bible, that is, efforts to identify precisely what the Bible means or how to live in its image. But only suffering gives rise to genuinely symbolic readings, by which I mean readings which engage the revealed word in a mutually transformative dialogue.

Developing this theme, Part II of *Garments* displays Fishbane's conviction that crises and dislocations in Israel's hermeneutical life mark the occasions of symbolic, or dialogic, scriptural interpretation in traditional as well as modern practice. Here, Fishbane examines the "axial ruptures in cultural system," which he believes stimulated the major hermeneutical innovations in Israel's life.[78] The first was Israel's primary break with the mythic cosmology of the ancient Near East, corresponding to the emergence of Torah as an autonomous source of meaning and law. The second was Israel's secondary movement "from a culture based on direct divine revelations to one based on their study and reinterpretation."[79] Beginning in the time of Ezra, this shift corresponded to the emergence of hermeneutics as Israel's prototypical mode of religious discourse. As Fishbane notes in *Biblical Interpretation,* "the common denominator underlying the socio-historical, textual, and mental settings of legal exegesis is *conflict,*" and "the historical exigencies that elicited the literary transformations [displayed in the *aggadah*] . . . [express] a particular type of crisis or dislocation which affected the continuity of perception of the . . . [authoritative content of scriptures]."[80] Sufferings —crises and conflicts—accompany semiotic dislocations, where conditions of interpretation that once apply no longer apply— where, therefore, God's word has for the moment lost its referentiality and the loving God has become the hidden God (*'el mistater*).[81] Yet, paradoxically, by freeing the dialogic partner to his or her solitary autonomy, God's absence stimulates this partner to imitate God's own creative activity. Searching (*l'derosh*) the scriptural sources[82] for new conditions of interpretation, the human partner renews the dialogic relationship with a God made closer through hermeneutic absence.

In Part III, Fishbane describes the hermeneutical dislocation of the modern reader, symbolized by the collapse of modern scholarship's dichotomous presuppositions—subjectivistic on the one side (in Fishbane's terms, "fideistic," or "personalistic") and objectivistic on the other ("philosophical," "objective," or "historical-philological"). At the center of these presuppositions is what Buber calls the monologic self, dislocated by its own autonomy from the capacity to listen and to hear. Paradoxically, however, this dislocation both insulates modern readers from the sacrality of scripture and offers them the occasion to rediscover the vitality of scripture as a genuine symbol. In the approach of Buber and Rosenzweig, this is to rediscover scripture as a *spoken* word: "Only responsiveness to the claims of the hour can open the heart of this monologic self and give him the one thing needful—speech."[83] In Rosenzweig's terms, this is God's speech, which, addressing us by name, says "Love Me!"[84] For Fishbane, modernity is thus redeemed by its potential receptivity to God's love, as offered by the words of scripture when they are read "from deep to deep," that is, from the the depth of one's own suffering heart to the depth of scripture's inner meaning.

Fishbane thus draws a tripartite distinction among the scriptural word as *symbol* (the subject of Part I) and the *interpretive contexts* of its referentiality or *meaning.* He divides these contexts into two sets: the contexts of scripture's historically primordial meanings (the subject of Part II) and of its present meaning (Part III), which is also the interpretive context of his own inquiry. Restated in terms of the postcritical paradigm, Fishbane has argued, *first,* that modern scholarship has errantly dichotomized subjective and objective approaches to the study of scripture; *second,* that this scholarship maintains the dislocation of the modern self from scripture as a source of speech and, thus, of God's love; *third,* that the route to relocation begins with the performative study of innerbiblical exegesis itself: scripture displays the route to its own reclamation.

## CONCLUSION:
### POSTCRITICAL INTERPRETATION AS PRAGMATIC INQUIRY

The scholars described in this essay or presented in this collection have not declared themselves representative of a postcritical tendency in Jewish and Christian scriptural interpretation. My argument is simply that it is possible and helpful to redescribe their various arguments according to a single, general paradigm. Thus far, the Jewish postcritical interpreters have not offered such a general paradigm. Frei and Lindbeck have offered a theory of intratextual reading, informed by the practices of "new criticism" and associated with Wittgenstein's theory of language and Geertz's interpretation of religions as cultural and symbol systems. They also suggest that the rabbinic practice of midrashic interpretation may offer Christian scholars a prototype of this kind of intratextual reading. I have found that Peirce's semiotic provides both the precision and flexibility needed to extend their intratextual paradigm to rabbinic as well as Christian interpretation.

Summarized in a sentence, the argument of both Jewish and Christian postcritical interpreters is that modern scholars have reduced biblical interpretation to the terms of a dyadic semiotic that lacks warrant in the biblical texts. The postcritical scholars claim that, as read in the primordial communities of rabbinic or of Christian interpreters, these texts recommend a triadic semiotic, according to which the text displays its performative meanings *with respect to* its community of biblical interpreters.

Readers may still find the concept of "triadic semiotics" too abstract. To bring it down to earth a bit, I will, in closing, restate the postcritical paradigm once more, this time in terms of Peirce's theory of pragmatism, which is a theory about how abstract inquiries like this one are connected to our everyday practices in the world. According to Peirce's theory of pragmatism,[85] our everyday reasonings about the world and about what we are supposed to do in it are informed by deep-seated rules of knowledge that we do not ordinarily have reason to question. Instead, these rules set the largely unperceived context in terms of which we question and correct our understanding of particular facts and behavioral norms. At times, however, our incapacities to correct problems in everyday understanding stimulate a deeper level questioning: what Peirce calls a "pragmatic" inquiry, designed to adjust our deep-seated rules of knowledge to changing conditions of life. Postcritical inquiry is a pragmatic inquiry of this kind, stimulated by the doubts certain text scholars have about the fundamental rules of scholarship they inherited from modern academia. More specifically, these are doubts about modern scholarship's capacity to sponsor pragmatic inquiry when it is called for and to recognize pragmatic inquiry when it is already in place. The postcritical claim is that modern scholarship tends to define rational inquiry on the model of everyday inquiry: as if reason operates only when a community's deep-seated rules of knowledge are in place and when the task of inquiry is strictly referential, that is, to identify facts and norms with respect to these rules. Modern scholarship therefore tends to reduce the pursuit of knowledge to the terms of a binary opposition between referential, rational inquiry (when the deep rules are in place) and non-referential irrational inquiry (when they are not). In the case of scriptural studies, the effect is to assume either that scriptural texts are simply referential (in which case they display their meaning by pointing ostensively to certain facts or norms) or that they are non-referential (in which case they are either silent or display their meaning only expressively or metaphorically). The postcritical complaint is that this binary opposition excludes the possibility that scriptural texts may have pragmatic reference: that is, that they may represent claims about the inadequacy of certain inherited rules of meaning and about ways of transforming those rules or adjusting them to new conditions of life. To the degree that they refer pragmatically, scriptural texts will not disclose their meanings to modern methods of study.

In terms of the theory of pragmatism, semiotics functions as an instrument for reclassifying the elements of scriptural texts as records of pragmatic inquiry. We have previously described a genuine symbol as a *sign* that refers to its *object* (or meaning) with respect to some particular *interpretant* (or system of deep-seated rules). Peirce distinguishes symbols from *indices* and *icons*. An index refers to its *object* by virtue of some direct force exerted by the object on the sign. This means that an index is indifferent to its interpretant, the way modern scholars suppose a referential text simply refers to some facts independently of any particular context of reference. An icon (image) does not refer to its object ostensively; instead, it appears to its *interpretant* to share certain characters with its object. The icon therefore displays its meaning metaphorically, through similarity, the way modern scholars suppose a non-referential text is either silent or fully subject to the interpreter's attributions. According to Peirce, the genuine symbol does its referring by virtue of some implicit law that causes the symbol to be *interpreted* as referring to its object.[86] This means that, while a symbol displays its meaning only to a particular interpretant, it is not fully subject to the interpreter's attributions. Instead, a symbol *influences* the way its interpretant attributes meaning to it. The symbol therefore engages its interpretant in a dialogue, the product of which is *meaning*. As agent of a semiotic law, the symbol engages its interpreter in some tradition of meaning. Transferring agency to the interpreter, the symbol also grants the interpreter some freedom to transform the way in which that meaning will be retransmitted. *In this way, the symbol is the fundamental agent of pragmatic inquiry.* It is itself the interpretant of a community's deep-seated rules of knowledge (its semiotic law), of which it serves as an agent. At the same time, the freedom it grants its own interpreter serves as a sign that these deep-seated rules are also subject to and, we presume, in need of change. The simultaneously conservative and reformatory activity of interpreting a symbol is what we call pragmatic inquiry. In the process of inquiry, the interpreter can use his or her freedom for nought—that is, without accepting the responsibility to hear the symbol's complaints, as it were, and to determine what changes need to be instituted in its semiotic law. Or the interpreter can use his or her freedom for the good of this law, inquiring after its needs for change.

For postcritical scholars, scriptural texts do not always function as genuine symbols and thus as signs of the need for pragmatic inquiry. When they do not—that is, when textual elements refer iconically or indexically—then modern scholarship offers useful instruments for scriptural study. To the degree that scriptural texts function as symbols, however, modern scholarship fails to serve as their agent. This is a serious failing, indeed, since it represents a failure to *hear* the text's call for help, as it were: a failure to make use of the freedom the text grants its interpreter to search after (*l'derosh*) those deep-seated problems of which it is a sign. Postcritical interpretation attempts to reform the deep-seated rules of modern scholarship in order to render that scholarship useful as an agent of this kind of search.

APPENDIX:
THE POSTCRITICAL METHOD OF PHILOSOPHIC INTERPRETATION

For the technically-minded reader, I offer here a description of the method of inquiry I employ in this project. This is a form of philosophic analysis of which cultural anthropology is a vaguer and more well known illustration. Like an ethnographer, I have attempted to become a participant-observer of an intriguing practice, in this case, the scholarly practice of "postcritical interpretation." As a philosophic ethnographer, I assumed that it would be possible and useful to identify this practice by describing what Peirce would call its *logica utens,* or embedded rules of operation. The science of description here is logic, but as a postcritical science of how a particular class of scholars might best articulate its rules of reasoning, rather than as a modern, foundational science of how scholars in general ought to reason. I assume that the purpose of any logical science, with all its technicalities, is to locate a means of classifying and evaluating practices and, thereby, correcting them if necessary. A postcritical logic would be distinctive only in the specificity of its pragmatic context. This means that the purpose of logical description is not to hold a mirror to the practices, but rather to make a useful claim about how they may be evaluated—useful, that is, *for* responding to some problem, and useful *to* some particular community of practitioners. In the case of this project, the identity of the community remains in question. Unless this proves to be an atypical case, a postcritical logic may therefore display its performative dimension in the way it helps nurture the community for which its claims are meaningful.

In this project, the first stage of logical description has been to reduce a given scholar's practice to a few identifiable rules. The second stage has been to compare this practice with other ones for which related rules could be constructed. These rules are not related by strict similarity, but in the way they appear to contribute to the resolution of similar problems. The third stage has been to attempt to collect a family of such practices by constructing a general paradigm of inquiry that each practice could be said to illustrate in its response to these problems. This is the paradigm of what I have called the three stages of postcritical scriptural interpretation: criticizing attempts to reduce biblical interpretation to a dyadic semiotic, tracing the consequences of such attempts, and offering in their stead various models of triadic biblical interpretation.[87] In constructing this paradigm, I am not attempting to understand the work of a number of scholars better than they understand it themselves, but rather to offer a new claim about what would happen if their various works were juxtaposed. To offer comments about what would happen is to move from logical description to a non-foundational metaphysics, which amounts to what may be called a speculative anthropology. This is to envision what the behavioral consequences would be if a given logical construction were adopted as a rule of actual practice.

I will conclude by envisioning three of these consequences. The first consequence of collecting the various forms of postcritical scholarship under some general paradigm would be to provide a dialogic model of rationality. To have abandoned the foundational pursuit of universal norms of reasoning is not to have abandoned the pursuit of regional norms. The paradigm of postcritical scriptural interpretation delimits a regional universe of practice within which rules of reasoning and criteria for truth and falsity could be articulated. To be sure, these rules and criteria would not be the same sort that accompany non-regional universes. They would accompany a universe whose elements were overlapping and interactive practices (rather than individual instances of general forms) and which would therefore admit dialogic or interactive procedures for adjudicating truth claims (rather than strictly inductive/deductive procedures). These procedures would be rational, nonetheless, and would need to be serviced by the postcritical equivalents of logicians and philosophers.

A second consequence would be to collect a family of mutually supportive procedures for correcting social and religious institutions informed by non-dialogic models of rationality. Among the postcritical interpreters, Lindbeck, for example, noted that these models divide into "propositionalist" and "traditionalist"—what Fishbane called "personalistic" and "objectivistic"—alternatives. Peirce's logic provides a way of reducing these alternatives to the common ground of a dyadic semiotic.

A third consequence would be to encourage mutually supportive discussion among postcritical scholars of anthropology and philosophy, on the one hand, and of biblical interpretation and textually grounded theology on the other hand. The regional universe of postcritical inquiry emerges specifically out of traditions of biblical interpretation that enunciate the particular pattern of dialogic rationality examined in this project. The leading principles of this rationality are to be identified with biblical words themselves, as interpreted in these traditions. It would therefore be the task of postcritical biblical interpreters to identify the leading principles of postcritical rationality. It would be the task of postcritical philosophers and anthropologists to articulate the logic of inquiry that is informed by those principles.

## NOTES

1. The scholars whose work appears in this volume are merely representative of an expanding collection of scholars whose work displays the tendencies of postcritical interpretation. Here is a sampling of these works.

Additional works by Christian scholars: Ronald Thiemann, *Revelation and Theology: The Gospel as Narrative Promise* (Notre Dame: University of Notre Dame Press, 1985); Bruce Marshall, *Christology in Conflict: The Identity of a Saviour in Rahner and Barth* (Oxford: Basil Blackwell, 1987); Katherine Tanner, *God and Creation in Christian Theology* (Oxford: Blackwell, 1988); William C. Placher, *Unapologetic Theology* (Philadelphia: Westminster, 1989); Avery Dulles, *The Craft of Theology: From Symbol to System* (New York: Crossroad, 1992). Dulles introduces a Catholic postcritical theology, engaging Lindbeck's postcritical theology in a manner that illuminates and extends the discussion in this volume. Because Dulles' text appeared just as this volume went to press, I have space only to sample its postcritical program. In an introductory chapter, "Toward a Postcritical Theology," Dulles argues that "postcritical thinking does not reject criticism but carries it to new lengths," scrutinizing the errant tendencies of modernist criticism to overstate and decontextualize doubt. Complementing the postcritical philosophies of Michael Polanyi, Hans-Georg Gadamer and Paul Ricoeur, postcritical theology resituates criticism in its appropriately social and hermeneutical setting. Two features of Dulles' hermeneutics are of particular relevance to this volume: his semiotic model for theological discourse, and his advocating several potentially complementary approaches to scripture, including Lindbeck's "cultural-linguistic" approach.

Additional works by Jewish scholars: David Stern, "Midrash and Indeterminacy," *Critical Inquiry* 15 (1988): 132–61; Richard Sarason, "Toward a New Agendum for the Study of Rabbinic Midrashic Literature," in J. Petuchowski and E. Fleischer, eds., *Studies in Aggadah, Targum and Jewish Liturgy in Memory of Joseph Heinemann* (Jerusalem: Magnes Press, 1981): English section, pp. 55–73; Jacob Neusner's forthcoming descriptive theology of late rabbinic midrashim, presented in a series of studies beginning with *From Literature to Theology in Formative Judaism;* Michael Wyschogrod, *The Body of Faith: Judaism as Corporeal Election* (New York: The Seabury Press, 1983); David Novak, *Jewish-Christian Dialogue: A Jewish Justification* (New York: Oxford University Press, 1989); Michael Rosenak, *Commandments and Concerns: Jewish Religious Education in Secular Society* (Philadelphia: The Jewish Publication Society, 1987).

1a. Moshe Greenberg, "The Vision of Jerusalem in Ezekiel 8–11: A Holistic Interpretation," in *The Divine Helmsman: Studies on God's Control of Human Events, Presented to Lou H. Silberman,* ed. J.L. Crenshaw and S. Sandmel (New York: KTAV Pub. House, 1980), pp. 143–63. For related articles in English, see "What Are Valid Criteria for Determining Inauthentic Matter in Ezekiel?" in *Ezekiel and His Book,* Bibliotheca Ephemeridum Theologicarum Lovaviensium LXXIV, ed. J. Lust (Leuven: University Press, 1986), pp. 123–35; and "Can Modern Critical Bible Scholarship Have a Jewish Character?" *Immanuel* 15 (1982/83): 7–12.

2. *Ibid.,* p. 143.

3. *Ibid.* Greenberg cites this passage of Spinoza's: ". . . the

method of interpreting Scripture does not differ from the method of interpreting nature. . . . For as the interpretation of nature consists in drawing up a history (= a systematic account of the data) of nature and therefrom inferring definitions of natural phenomena, so Scriptural interpretation necessarily proceeds by drawing up a true history of Scripture and from it . . . to infer correctly the intentions of the authors of Scripture. . . . Everyone will advance without danger of error . . . if they admit no principles for interpreting Scripture . . . save as they find in Scripture itself." Baruch Spinoza, *Theological-Political Tractate,* trans. R.H.M. Elwes (New York: Dover, 1951), p. 99, adjusted to Wirzubski's Hebrew translation (Jerusalem: Magnes Press, 1961), p. 79.

4. *Ibid.,* p. 144, citing S.R. Driver, *An Introduction to the Literature of the Old Testament,* 9th ed. (Edinburgh: Clark, 1913), pp. viif, x.

5. *Ibid.,* pp. 145–46.

6. *Ibid.,* p. 146.

7. *Ibid.,* p. 148.

8. Hans Frei, *The Eclipse of Biblical Narrative: A Study in Eighteenth and Nineteenth Century Hermeneutics* (New Haven and London: Yale University Press, 1974), pp. 60ff.

9. *Eclipse,* pp. 62, 61.

10. *Eclipse,* p. 118.

11. Frei cites Erich Auerbach, *Mimesis* (Princeton: Princeton University Press, 1968).

12. "The Vision of Jerusalem in Ezekiel 8–11: A Holistic Interpretation," p. 146.

13. *Ibid.*

14. At the same time, Greenberg offers a mediating alternative in his method of reading the plain-sense as it would be received by what he calls an "ideal reader." See "The Vision of Jerusalem in Ezekiel 8–11," *op. cit.*

15. Kadushin's two most well-known works are *The Rabbinic Mind* (New York: Bloch Pub., 1972) and *Worship and Ethics* (Evanston: Northwestern University Press, 1964).

16. Among the essays I wrote on Kadushin's method were "Max Kadushin as Rabbinic Pragmatist," in *Understanding the Rabbinic Mind: Essays on the Hermeneutic of Max Kadushin,* ed. Peter Ochs (Atlanta: Scholars Press for South Florida Studies in the History of

Judaism, 1990); "A Rabbinic Pragmatism," in *Theology and Dialogue,* ed. Bruce Marshall (Notre Dame: University of Notre Dame Press, 1990); and "Rabbinic Text-Process Theology," in *Jewish Thought* 1, No. 1 (Fall, 1991): 1–36.

17. George Lindbeck, *The Nature of Doctrine, Religion and Theology in a Postliberal Age* (Philadelphia: The Westminster Press, 1984).

18. *The Nature of Doctrine,* p. 16.

19. *Ibid.*

20. *The Nature of Doctrine,* p. 31.

21. There is a reason for the choice of three Jewish and two Christian hermeneuts. Among postcritical interpreters, I have found that the Christians are moved, more than the Jews, by the ideal of a single, authoritative hermeneutic in the study of which individual hermeneuts would differ only through a division of scholarly labor. In this case, for example, Frei emphasizes historical study, Lindbeck interpretive doctrine and theory, but their work appears to serve a single goal. The Jews, on the other hand, may find unity in the fact of a shared text, but are less inclined to seek (or at least to achieve!) agreement on preferred methods of interpreting it. Jewish postcritical interpretations may cohere dialectically, therefore, rather than through similitude: in this case, Fraade, Halivni and Fishbane are joined by a division of modalities—moderate, conservative and radical modes of postcritical interpretation—rather than by a division of labor.

22. See, *inter alia, Collected Papers of Charles Sanders Peirce,* eds. Charles Harteshorne and Paul Weiss (Cambridge: Harvard University Press, 1934–35), Vol. 1, par. 338ff and Vol. 2, par. 228. Future references to this collection will be to CP, followed by volume and paragraph number (e.g., CP 1.338). For relevant discussions of Peirce's semiotics, see Vincent Colapietro, *Peirce's Approach to the Self* (Albany: SUNY Press, 1989), *passim,* and Michael Raposa, *Peirce's Philosophy of Religion* (Bloomington: Indiana University Press, 1989), pp. 117–23, and *passim.*

23. Cf. J.L. Austin, *How to Do Things with Words* (Cambridge: Harvard University Press, 1978). Note the relevant discussion of Austin in Edith Wyschogrod, "Works That 'Faith': The Grammar

of Ethics in Judaism," in *Cross Currents, Religion and Intellectual Life* 40.2 (Summer, 1990): 176–93.

24. "Literal Reading," in this volume, p. 58.

25. "Literal Reading," in this volume, p. 61.

26. "Literal Reading," in this volume, p. 78.

27. "Literal Reading," in this volume, p. 80.

28. *The Nature of Doctrine*, pp. 16, 24, *passim,* where the approach is exemplified by Peter Geach, G.K. Chesterton, C.S. Lewis and Malcolm Muggeridge.

29. *The Nature of Doctrine*, p. 31, citing Bernard Lonergan, *Method in Theology* (Herder and Herder, 1972): 101–24.

30. Citing Lonergan, pp. 120, 122.

31. *The Nature of Doctrine*, p. 16.

32. *Ibid.*

33. See CP 2.262; 3.419ff.

34. See CP 5.570; Cf. 5.140ff.

35. See CP 5.192.

36. George Lindbeck, "The Story-shaped Church: Critical Exegesis and Theological Interpretation," in *Scriptural Authority and Narrative Interpretation,* ed. G. Green (Philadelphia: Fortress Press, 1987), p. 164.

37. *The Nature of Doctrine*, p. 74. Cf. pp. 4, 12, *passim.*

38. Frei, "Literal Reading," p. 33.

39. *Ibid.,* citing Clifford Geertz, "From the Native's Point of View: On the Nature of Anthropological Understanding," in *Interpretive Social Science,* ed. P. Rabinow and W.M. Sullivan (Berkeley: University of California Press, 1979), pp. 240ff.

40. "Literal Reading," p. 36.

41. Delivered at the American Theological Society, Princeton, 1987; hereafter, "Doctrine."

42. "Doctrine," p. 2.

43. "Doctrine," p. 12.

44. "The Story-Shaped Church," pp. 169, *passim.* Elsewhere, Lindbeck argues, in fact, that Luther's conception of the creed is fundamentally homiletic, or "haggadic," because the gospel itself is *haggadah:* see "Martin Luther and the Rabbinic Mind," in *Understanding the Rabbinic Mind: Essays on the Hermeneutic of Max*

*Kadushin,* ed. P. Ochs (Atlanta: Scholar's Press, 1990), 141–64, at 146ff.

45. Albany: State University of New York Press, 1991.

46. *From Tradition to Commentary,* p. 24.

47. *From Tradition to Commentary,* pp. 1–2.

48. *Ibid.*

49. *Sifre Deuteronomy* § 310, cited in *From Tradition to Commentary,* pp. 75–76, with commentary following pp. 76–79 (Fraade translates from the MS Vatican).

50. *Sifre* interprets:

> "May my discourse come down as rain" (Deut. 32:2): Just as rain falls on trees and infuses each type with its distinctive flavor . . . so too words of Torah are all one, but they comprise *mikra* (Scripture) and *mishna* (oral teaching): *midrash* (exegesis), *halakhot* (laws) and *haggadot* (narratives). (§ 306, cited in *From Tradition to Commentary,* p. 96).

51. New York and Oxford: Oxford University Press, 1991.

52. Bloomington: Indiana University Press, 1989.

53. New York and Oxford: Oxford University Press, 1991.

54. Among the features of this account are his interpretations of the legal nullity of scriptural texts transmitted through the First Temple period and of Ezra's role in restoring the correct meanings of these texts and thereby initiating the rabbinic mode of midrashic exegesis.

55. *Peshat and Derash,* p. v.

56. *Peshat and Derash,* p. 92.

57. *Peshat and Derash,* p. ix.

58. *Peshat and Derash,* p. 103.

59. *Ibid.* Halivni notes that the Rashbam "could afford to adhere strictly to *peshat* even when it ran counter to practical halakha because," in these cases, he tended to ground his halakhic expositions on some redundancy of word or letter in the scriptural text (p. 27). Separating the realms of *peshat* and *derash* more radically, Halivni has no need to adopt this exegetical device.

One implication is that Halivni's work on the *peshat* of the Talmud might contribute to the process of halakhic decision-making, but not directly. Its contribution would come, if at all, only in the way its readings might in the long run filter into reformulations of centuries of accumulated patterns of legal argumentation. Halivni reminds us repeatedly that law is not guided by the text alone, but also by precedent and by the time-bound contingencies of social life. God, he says, has withdrawn from direct participation in the legal process; the eternal is the immediate subject-matter only of intellectual speculation (*hashkafa*), not of *halakhah*.

60. "Contemporary Methods of the Study of Talmud," *Journal of Jewish Studies* 30 (1979), pp. 192–201, at 193.

61. *Ibid.*

62. "Contemporary Methods," pp. 195, 198.

63. "Contemporary Methods," p. 198.

64. "Contemporary Methods," pp. 199–200. As indicated by the title of his critical scholarship on the Talmud, "Sources and Traditions" (*Mekorot Umasorot,* Jerusalem: The Jewish Theological Seminary of America, 1982), Halivni's most general hypothesis is that a distinction may be drawn between rabbinic sayings which preserve their original form ("sources") and those which have been changed in the course of transmission ("traditions"). Subsequent interpreters have attempted to rectify inequalities between the two through forced interpretations; Halivni has sought to rectify them, instead, by reconstructively distinguishing original forms from the transmitted ones.

65. This does not imply that the possibilities are endless, since an accurate intratextual reading would warrant discounting most possibilities.

66. Halivni may also attribute to the speculative scholar the capacity to display the ideal meaning of a text with respect to an ideal ("eternal") interpretant. If so, his approach in this regard either reflects a medieval-modern concern to privilege one context of meaning as transcendent or supra-contextual, or a postcritical scholar's context-specific effort to offset subjectivist tendencies.

67. *Peshat and Derash*, p. 50.

68. *Peshat and Derash*, p. 49.

69. The most striking illustration of the force of Halivni's critique is his study of *pilpul* ("farfetched casuistic deductions") in

halakhic scholarship of the sixteenth century and after (*Peshat and Derash*, pp. 42–44). He notes that when *peshat* is identified with natural sense, the pilpulists appear to deviate most problematically from rabbinic Judaism's progressive concern to protect the integrity of the *peshat*. *Pilpul* appears to ignore the text's literal reference. When *peshat* is identified, however, with extended intratextual context, the pilpulists appear to exemplify this concern! They fully respect the contextual integrity of their base-texts as stimuli for additional deductions.

70. Michael Fishbane, *The Garments of Torah, Essays in Biblical Hermeneutics* (Bloomington: Indiana University Press, 1989).

71. Michael Fishbane, *Biblical Interpretation in Ancient Israel* (Oxford: Oxford University Press, 1985).

72. Fishbane's words, in *Garments*, p. 45.

73. Oxford: Oxford University Press, 1989 (1985).

74. *Zohar* III. 152. Translation from *Zohar—The Book of Splendor: Basic Readings from the Kabbalah*, ed. Gershom Scholem (New York: Schocken Books, 1963), pp. 121f. Cited in *Garments*, p. 34.

75. *Ibid.*

76. *Garments*, p. 24, citing *Pesiqta de-Rav Kahana* II, ed. Mandelbaum, pp. 379–81.

77. *Garments*, pp. 27–28.

78. Cf. *Garments*, pp. 64–65.

79. *Garments*, p. 65.

80. *Biblical Interpretation*, pp. 271, 408–09.

81. Cf. Buber's discussion of God's hidden face (for example, "Job," *The Prophetic Faith*, New York: The Macmillan Co., 1949, pp. 187–97) and Arthur Cohen's notion of catastrophic moments as *caesuras* in the historical-hermeneutical continuum of Israel's life (in *The Tremendum: A Theological Interpretation of the Holocaust*, New York: Crossroad, 1981).

82. From *l'derosh*, "to search after."

83. *Garments*, p. 100.

84. Franz Rosenzweig, *The Star of Redemption*, trans. William Hallo (New York: Holt, Rinehart and Winston, 1970), p. 198.

85. For Peirce's original statement of this theory, see "The Fixation of Belief," *Popular Science Monthly* 12 (1877): 1–15; repr. CP

5. 358–387. See also "What Pragmatism Is," *The Monist* 15 (1905): 161–81; repr. in. CP 5. 411–37.

86.   These definitions of icon, index and symbol are adapted from CP 2.247–49.

87.   See above, "The Rules of Postcritical Interpretation."

# PART ONE: THE POSTCRITICAL TURN IN RECENT CHRISTIAN HERMENEUTICS AND THEOLOGY

The postcritical trend in recent Jewish and Christian scriptural and hermeneutical scholarship emerges out of a critique of the inadequacies of modern, critical Bible scholarship and of the theories of interpretation which have attended it. Theorizing about this critique has been more typically a Christian than a Jewish task. Articles by Christian scholars Hans Frei, of blessed memory, and George Lindbeck therefore introduce the concerns of this volume.

As discussed in the Introduction to this volume, Frei and Lindbeck offer a critique of ways in which historical-critical, hermeneutical and deconstructive methods of interpretation have been used to displace the Christian tradition of reading the "plain sense" of scripture. As an alternative to this displacement, they offer a modest theory of "intratextual reading," which theory they associate with Clifford Geertz's interpretation of religions as cultural and symbol systems. They say that to read the Bible intratextually is to read its plain sense with respect to a religious community's rules for reading-and-observing the text as sacred text.

At the same time, Frei and Lindbeck speak of a need to reappraise those tendencies in patristic religious communities that encouraged the delegitimization of Judaism and, with it, the mistreatment of Jews and the misrepresentation of Christianity's Jewish origins. The "midrashic method" of the rabbis serves as a prototype for their own method of intratextual reading.

## Chapter Two

# THE "LITERAL READING" OF BIBLICAL NARRATIVE IN THE CHRISTIAN TRADITION: DOES IT STRETCH OR WILL IT BREAK?

## HANS W. FREI
### (Abridged and edited by Kathryn Tanner)

I will comment on what I perceive to be a wide, though of course not unanimous, traditional consensus among Christians in the west on the primacy of the literal reading of the Bible, on its connections with narrative, on its present status and future outlook.

Much of the essay will be taken up with "hermeneutics," the theory of the interpretation of texts and of the character of understanding going into that activity. In the midst of a mounting crescendo of dissent from thematic readings of narratives as normative guides for living and believing as well as reading, hermeneutical theory is the most prominent contemporary champion of the embattled tradition. But I also believe that the defense is a failure, so that, in the words of the essay's title, the literal reading will break apart under its ministrations. One may well hope that the *sensus literalis* has a future. If it does, there will be good reason to explain what it is about with a far more modest theory—more modest both in its claims about what counts as valid interpretation and in the scope of the material on which it may pertinently comment.

## I. THE PRIMACY OF THE LITERAL SENSE
## IN CHRISTIAN INTERPRETATION

Most literate cultures have sacred stories and include them in their sacred texts. Contact and conflict among religions within the same demographic area or cultural family typically result in a parasitic takeover in altered form of the elements of one such text by a later, or even a contemporaneous, religious group as part of its own scripture. So it has between Hinduism and Buddhism, between Hebrew and Christian scripture, and between Hebrew and Christian scripture and the Qur'an. Sacred stories are obvious targets for such scriptural transformation. The adherents of Jesus did not obliterate the story of John the Baptist, assigning him instead the role of forerunner and witness in the story of Jesus and thus a secure, if subordinate, place in the Christian New Testament.

The most striking example of this kind of takeover in the history of western culture is the inclusion of Jewish in Christian scripture by means of "typology" or "figuration," so that not only "Old Testament" narrative but its legal texts and its prophetic as well as wisdom literature are taken to point beyond themselves to their "fulfillment" in the "New Testament." The Jewish texts are taken as "types" of the story of Jesus as their common "antitype," an appropriating procedure that begins in the New Testament, notably in the letters of Paul, the letter to the Hebrews, and the synoptic gospels, and then becomes the common characteristic of the Christian tradition of scriptural interpretation until modern times.

Two features in this process are especially striking. First, the story of Jesus has a unifying force and a prescriptive character in both the New Testament and the Christian community that, despite the importance of the Exodus accounts, neither narrative generally nor any specific narrative has in Jewish scripture and the Jewish community. Second, it was largely by reason of this centrality of the story of Jesus that the Christian interpretive tradition in the west gradually assigned clear primacy to the literal sense in the reading of scripture, not to be contradicted by other legitimate senses—tropological, allegorical, and anagogical. In the ancient church, some of the parables of Jesus—for example, that of the good Samaritan (Lk 10:25–37)—were interpreted allegorically as referring latently or spiritually to all sorts of types, and more especially to Jesus

himself, but this could only be done because the story of Jesus itself
was taken to have a literal or plain meaning: He was the Messiah,
and the fourfold storied depiction in the gospels, especially of his
passion and resurrection, was the enacted form of his identity as
Messiah. Thus, by and large, except for the school of Origen in
which the Old Testament received a kind of *independent* allegorical
interpretation, allegory tended to be in the service of literal interpretation, with Jesus the center or focus of coherence for such reading.
In that way, allegory remained legitimate up until the reformation,
even in its supposed rejection by the school of Antioch. Typological
or figural interpretation, which was applied not only to the Old
Testament but also to the meaning of extrabiblical life and events,
including one's own, stood in an unstable equilibrium between allegorical and literal interpretations.

The title of James Preus' important book on the history of
Christian Old Testament interpretation, *From Shadow to Promise,*[1]
points out a basic distinction between two kinds of allegorical and
typological interpretations in Christian "Old Testament" reading.
The "Old Testament" could be understood as "mere" letter or
shadow, a "carnal" figure in the most derogatory sense, to which the
"New Testament" stood in virtual contrast as the corresponding
"spiritual" or genuine reality, and the all but direct contrary of its
prefigured representation. Whenever the Old Testament is seen in
this way as "letter" or "carnal shadow," spiritual and literal reading
coincide, and figural and allegorical reading are one. "Spiritual
reading" in this context is that of those who are in the first place
privy to the truth directly rather than "under a veil," and who know,
secondly, that the reality depicted is "heavenly," spiritual or religious, rather than earthly, empirical, material, or political. But
since it is the story of Jesus taken literally that unveils this higher
truth, the "literal" sense is the key to spiritual interpretation of the
New Testament. In this as in some other respects, "letter" and
"spirit" turn out to be mutually fit or reinforcing in much orthodox
Christianity, despite the superficially contrary Pauline declaration
(2 Cor 3:6).

On the other hand, rather than as *shadow,* the Old Testament
could be understood as *promise,* that is, as pointing to a state of
affairs literally meant but only incompletely or not yet actualized at

the time it was written. Figure and fulfillment, or type and antitype, are related along a temporal as well as a literary or metaphorical axis. An earlier is followed by a later historical event in a chronological sequence; at the same time earlier and later are related as trope to true meaning. Much reformation and orthodox Protestant exegesis was governed by this outlook.

Interpretive traditions of religious communities tend to reach a consensus on certain central texts. The literal reading of the gospel stories was the crucial instance of this consensus in the early church. The "literal" reading in this fashion became the normative or "plain" reading of the texts. There is no prior reason why the "plain" reading could not have been "spiritual" in contrast to "literal," and certainly the temptation was strong. The identification of the plain with literal sense was not a logically necessary development, but it did begin with the early Christian community and was perhaps unique to Christianity. The creed, "rule of faith" or "rule of truth," which governed the gospels' use in the church, asserted the primacy of their literal sense. Moreover, it did this right from the beginning in the *ascriptive* even more than in the *descriptive* mode. That "Jesus"—not someone else or nobody in particular—is the subject, the agent, and patient of these stories was said to be their crucial point, and the descriptions of events, sayings, personal qualities, and so forth became literal by being firmly predicated of him. Not until the Protestant reformation was the literal sense understood as authoritative—because perspicuous—in its own right, without authorization from the interpretive tradition.

This rule use of the New Testament stories entailed the expropriative rules for the interpretation of Jewish scripture which we have noted, and all three cases of the procedure—shadow and reality, prophecy and fulfillment, metaphorical type and literal antitype —came to present modern Christian biblical reading with two enormous problems. First, how is one to acknowledge the autonomy of the Jewish scriptural tradition without a collapse of Christian interpretation? Even if you brutalized it, you needed Jewish scripture; for what is a fulfillment without antecedents that need to be fulfilled? Christians could neither do without Jewish scripture nor accord it that autonomous status that a modern understanding of religions calls for. The second problem is a natural extension of the first.

Suppose that the literal sense of the New Testament prefigures a still newer reading that displaces it in turn. A new set of inside interpreters transcends the now old (i.e. New Testament), exoteric, or carnal, to reach a new spiritual sense which, because it refers to the truth in this real and not veiled form, is identical with the *true* literal sense. That new reading could be a new religion. It could already be history, for example the Ottoman Turks carrying the Qur'an westward. The new reading could also be the product of a vision of a new humanity in which the previous difference between insiders and outsiders, esoteric and exoteric, or spiritual and carnal reading would disappear. All humanity would be the true new church.[2]

On the other hand, such a new reading could involve the discovery that we are all outsiders to the truth. The only point at which literal and true spiritual senses coincide therefore is not—as Christians have claimed—in the gospel narratives, nor in any later substitute, but in the shock of recognition that, the road to truth being barred, there must be an end to the literal sense. Rather than all humanity being insiders, we are all outsiders, and the only thing we know is that the truth is what we do not know.[3] The very notion of a true referent of the narrative texts of the New Testament and of the textual meaning as possible truth is for Frank Kermode a persistent and haunting illusion. Readers of narrative texts are forever caught up in their dialectical alternation of divinatory disclosure and foreclosing secrecy. For deconstructionists, by contrast, the discovery of the illusory character of linguistic meaning as truth is liberating. With that liberation comes a way of reading a text which reverses the prior belief that texts open up a world: the world must be seen as an indefinitely extended and open-ended, loosely interconnected, "intertextual" network, and kind of rhetorical *cosa nostra.*

## II. HERMENEUTICAL THEORY, DECONSTRUCTION, AND THE LITERAL SENSE

This destruction of "normative" or "true" reading means an end, among other things, to the enterprise called "hermeneutics," the notion of a unitary and systematic theory of understanding. According to the tradition of phenomenological hermeneutics, biblical narrative becomes a "regional" instance of the universally valid pattern of interpretation. In this view: (1) all texts are "discourse," even if, being inscribed discourse, they gain freedom from the person of the author; (2) the obverse side of "discourse" is "understanding." The basic condition of the possibility of understanding texts is the transcendentally grounded universal dialectic between understanding and the subject matter to be understood. Although the text is freed from its author and therefore possessed of its own meaning —"utterance" meaning in contrast to "utterer's" meaning, in Paul Ricoeur's terms[4]—utterance meaning is inherently related to an appropriating understanding.[5] Understanding (or interpretation) is an internal event; it is nothing less than the centered self or transcendental ego in that particular and basic mode. The dialectic in which this event is operational is when the understanding stands "before" a text, so that the text is its equal or superior and not a replaceable phenomenon controlled by the ego's own interests or cultural location. Language is, of course, indispensable to this discourse-and-consciousness process or event, but linguistic "sense," that is, the semiotic structures and semantic patterns of discourse, must also be related to its function as an expression of preconceptual consciousness or experience. There is therefore a thrust within language both in utterance meaning and its appropriation, by means of which it transcends itself *qua* semiotic structure and semantic sense (beginning with the sentence) through such instruments as symbol and metaphor and "refers" to a real world. Obviously it is actually *we,* the language users, who refer linguistically, so that the reality referent of language is at the same time a mode of human consciousness or of our "being-in-the-world." Language is the way of realizing or enacting self-presence in the presence of a world of meaning and truth, which is at the same time "distanced" from us having its own referential integrity. By a natural extension, metaphor and symbol (i.e. "poetic" language) are taken to be the modes in which language (and experience) can express the creative thrust of the centered self toward an absolute limit and the "world" espied at that limit. In other words, there is a "split reference" in symbol and metaphor, to self-presence and its being-in-the-world, and—through one of its modes, the mode of limit experience and language—to the disclosed presence of the transcendent as the limit or self-transcending instance of the "secondary" world accessible through poetic language.

The "objective" world of descriptive discourse is consigned to a decidedly peripheral and ambiguous status in the situation of "limit disclosure." The "limit" and "disclosure" situation in which transcendence and understanding come together is the class to which biblical writings belong, and to which the concept "revelation" is at least "homologous."[6] This view is in fact the hermeneutical equivalent of the "doctrine of revelation" of liberal and neoorthodox religious apologists a generation ago, who held that "revelation" is a "spiritual event" rather than an historical or metaphysical propositional claim.

One should note three consequences of this view when it is applied to a literal reading of the gospels. First, if the literal sense means that the story of Jesus is above all about a specific fictional or historical person by that name, then the hermeneutical position we have described entails a view of him as ascriptive subject chiefly in the form of consciousness, that is, of his selfhood as "understanding." Like anyone else, Jesus is here not in the first place the agent of his actions nor the enacted project(s) that constitute(s) him, nor the person to whom the actions of others happen; he is, rather, the verbal expresser of a certain preconceptual consciousness which he then, in a logically derivative or secondary sense, exhibits in action. For example, *that* Jesus was crucified is not a decisive part of his personal story, only that he was so consistent in his "mode-of-being-in-the-world" as to take the risk willingly. The personal world in the hermeneutical scheme is one in which the status of happenings is that of carnal shadows of the true "secondary" world of "meanings" "understood" in "disclosure."

On a technical and specifically hermeneutical level, what is wrong with this scheme is simply its claim to inclusiveness and adequacy for the interpretation of all texts depicting persons in a world. By and large, the Christian tradition of literal reading has resisted this reduction of the subject of the narrative to consciousness rather than agent-in-occurrence, and of descriptive to metaphoric discourse in the presentation of the way in which this subject was significantly related to a world about him.

Second, it seems that *any* kind of literal ascription of "meaning" to a personal subject within the narrative world is highly tenuous under this hermeneutical governance. The clearly and irreducibly personal focus within this scheme is constituted not by the "meaning" of the narrative but by the interpreter—that is, the "understanding" to which "meaning" is related. What narratives present (whether or not "literally") is not in the first place ascriptive selves that are the subjects of their predicates, not even really the self-expressive, centered consciousness or transcendental ego, but the "mode-of-being-in-the-world" which these selves exemplify and which is "represented" by being "disclosed" to "understanding." In the words of David Tracy, a theologian whose New Testament hermeneutics is a close reading and precise regional application of Ricoeur's general hermeneutics:

> One may formulate the principal meaning referred to by the historically reconstructed re-presentative words, deeds, and destiny of Jesus the Christ as follows: the principal referent disclosed by this limit-language is the disclosure of a certain limit-mode-of-being-in-the-world; the disclosure of a new, and agapic, a self-sacrificing righteousness willing to risk living at that limit where one seems in the presence of the righteous, loving, gracious God re-presented in Jesus the Christ.[7]

Not that one can have any such "mode" without personal ascription either within the story or in appropriation (is that perhaps the point of the solecism, "the principal referent disclosed . . . is . . . the disclosure . . ."?), but the ascription in the story is simply a temporary personal thickening within the free-flowing stream of a general class of describable dispositional attitudes. "Jesus" in the statement quoted names a meaning, namely (the disclosure of) a generalizable set of attitudes (self-sacrificing righteousness, etc.), rather than these attitudes being referred to, held, or actuated by "Jesus." What is being set forth here in technical language is a view of the gospel narratives which is far closer to traditional allegorical than literal reading: Certain virtues or dispositions are hypostatized, that is, they are the significant referents of certain statements, but to maintain the narrative rather than didactic shape of these statements there has to be a personal embodiment, an "archetype" Kant called it, to exemplify them. But the archetype is identified by the virtues, not they by him through his self-enactment in significant temporal sequence. In this view, the link between meaning-reference and ascription to a personal subject within the story is tenuous at best. At worst it is eliminated. The irreducibly personal element comes only in the "represented" "disclosure" situation, that is, in "understanding" appropriation of the text.

As with dispositional description and ascription, so with the "kerygmatic" verbal expression of consciousness "re-presented" by the gospels. To "limit" *experience* there corresponds to metaphoric "limit" *language,* and the two have the same "referent." Traditionally, "the kingdom of God" in Jesus' preaching and Jesus himself have been understood to identify or "refer" to each other. By contrast, in hermeneutical theory one subsumes Jesus' preaching, especially the parables of the kingdom of God, under a more general reference. In Ricoeur's terms, there is an "extravagance" in the denouement and the main characters that contrasts with the realism of the narrative and constitutes the parables' specific "religious" trait.[8] Religious language redescribes human experience: "The ultimate referent of the parables, proverbs, and eschatological sayings is not the Kingdom of God, but human reality in its wholeness. Religious language discloses the religious dimension of common human experience."[9]

In sum, then, the view that being human is inseparable from being an agent becomes highly problematic in a general anthropology of consciousness and its hermeneutics. The irreducibly *descriptive* as well as any irreducibly personal *ascriptive* character of literal reading is even more problematic in this hermeneutical setting. Yet one variant or another of this theory, more than any other, has been proposed as a general and foundational justification for a revised traditional reading of the narrative texts of the New Testament. Numerous warrants for doing so have been adduced by the theory's adherents: the applicability to these narratives of such concepts as revelation, uniqueness and (simultaneously) generality of meaning; the significance of personal understanding and appropriation; the claim to normatively valid interpretation which transcends, without ignoring, the cultural setting of both texts and interpreters; and the claim to diachronic continuity between presently valid interpretation and a tradition of interpretation reaching back to the text itself, in particular the tradition of interpretation that assigns a distinctive status to Jesus in these stories.

Indeed, this last consideration has been particularly important to those Christian theologians who have adopted this general theory for regional hermeneutical application to the New Testament. They have been motivated by a desire on the one hand to claim the unsurpassability of the New Testament narratives' ascriptive reference to Jesus, so that they do not become esoteric or carnal shadows, in principle surpassable by a later and fuller spiritual "reference" or "disclosure," but on the other to deny that this unsurpassability involves the invidious distinction between insiders and outsiders to the truth.[10] So they try to maintain that Jesus is the irreducible ascriptive subject of the New Testament narratives, while at the same time they make general religious experience (or something like it) the "referent" of these stories.[11] It is an uneasy alliance of conflicting hermeneutical aims. The theory simply cannot bear the freight of all that its proponents want to load onto its shoulders. Whatever may be the case in its other regional exemplifications, when it is applied to the New Testament narrative texts the result is that the tradition of literal reading is not merely stretched into a revised shape, but broken.

The very possibility of reading New Testament narratives in this way has to stand or fall with the viability of the theory in the first place. It is well to be clear on what this does and does not involve. Paul Ricoeur has drawn attention to certain distinctions that one may summarize as precritical, critical, and postcritical stages in reading or, in his own terms, first and second naiveté (with "criticism" in between). A similar distinction is that between the "masters of suspicion" and a "hermeneutics of restoration" or "retrieval." Ricoeur's postcritical reading with a second naiveté that corresponds to a hermeneutics of restoration is the kind of reading that might well be of a "revised literal" sort. It distances the text from the author, from the original discourse's existential situation and from every other kind of reading that would go "behind" the text and "refer" it to any other world of meaning than its own, the world "in front of" the text. Yet this kind of reading has been through the mill trying to transcend critically that (first) naive literalism for which every statement on the printed page "means" either because it refers to a true state of affairs, or because it shapes a realm of discourse whose vocabulary one can finally only understand by repeating it. If the general theory of hermeneutics is to stand, it must persuade us that its appeal to a second naiveté and to a hermeneutics of restoration constitutes a genuine option: neither this first naiveté nor a reading with that "suspicion" which regards the linguistic "world," which text and reader may share, as a mere ideological or psychological superstructure.

An indispensable assumption in explaining the possibility of reading with second naiveté is that there can be a coincidence, a "fusion of horizons," in H.G. Gadamer's phrase, between the world of the text and the present reader who, though doubtless part of its world, is also the subject transcendental to it. This position is a strong revision of the "romantic" hermeneutics of Schleiermacher, for whom "understanding" was a direct dialogue between the reader and the spirit of the author, present in the latter's language. "If," writes Paul Ricoeur,

> we preserve the language of Romanticist hermeneutics when it speaks of overcoming the distance . . . of appropriating what was distant, other, foreign, it will be at the price of an important corrective. That which we make our own . . . is not a foreign experience, but the power of disclosing a world which constitutes the reference of the text.
>
> The link between disclosure and appropriation is, to my mind, the cornerstone of a hermeneutic which could claim both to overcome the shortcomings of historicism and to remain faithful to the original intention of Schleiermacher's hermeneutics. To understand an author better than he could understand himself is to display the power of disclosure implied in his discourse beyond the limited horizon of his own existential situation.[12]

In this theory, the kind of language used to indicate the link between "disclosure" and "understanding" invariably appeals to the experience of "historicity" or time consciousness, and the dimension of the link is always that of the present poised between past and future. In interpretation of the New Testament narratives, this temporal outlook is very clear indeed. Their "meaning" is "*re-presented*" to the understanding. There is no proper understanding of texts from the past, "distanced" or released from their original moorings, except on the model (or, rather, more than the model) of a temporally present event, an event in or of contemporary consciousness.

Why this centrality of the link between disclosure and the temporally present event of understanding? No doubt there are many reasons, but surely one of the chief is simply a set of conceptual needs: one *needs* to have the text refer to or open up a (usually diachronic) world, if it is not merely to function as an instance of an internally connected general semiotic system or code in which the specific linguistic content or message is no more than a trivial surface phenomenon. Furthermore, one *needs* to have the text open up a world independent of the text's cultural origins and every other reductive explanation, if we are going to have a hermeneutics in which understanding a text entails normative and valid exegetical interpretations, in a word, a hermeneutics for "second naiveté." One *needs,* finally and foremost, to have a text both atemporally distanced from its moorings in a cultural and authorial or existential past and yet also re-entering the temporal dimension at the point of the present, if it is going to have the capacity to inform an understanding that is itself essentially characterized as present, in a work of hermeneutics of restoration. And yet this present re-entry of the text must not be a function or predicate of the presently understanding self—else it is illusory self-projection. "Disclosure" is a term satisfying these needs: the text is normative, in fact it transcends present understanding *ontologically,* but only in such a way that it is in principle *hermeneutically* focused toward the latter. Textual "disclosure" means that the language of the text "refers," but refers strictly in the mode of presentness. It also means that language, especially metaphoric language, refers creatively without creating what it refers to. "Disclosure" answers the need for and reality of coincidence of referential meaning and understanding.

The language of the text in opening up a world is simultaneously opened up by it. That simultaneity prevents language from turning either into simple descriptive, that is, falsely representational ("objectivist") language, or into being captured by purely "subjectivist" and self-projecting understanding. We *must* have "disclosure" if we are to have a hermeneutics that respects Heidegger's affirmation that language speaks because it indwells a world, instead of a hermeneutics that is a linguistic replica of the Cartesian error of separating out a self-contained, self-certain ego of "understanding" from the understood world. Here, then, is the claim to recovering that view in which texts can in principle be normatively or validly interpreted because they refer to a truly possible world—a world Kermode declared to be either inaccessible through the text or illusory in the first place, and one which Nietzsche and Derrida have taken, if anything, to be worse than illusory because of a wishful misuse of texts.

Deconstruction, a deliberate subversion of this theory as of many others, is not identical with the strictly anti-hermeneutical procedure of "suspicion," with which hermeneutical theorists have understood themselves to be in sharp contention. Deconstruction is an immanent subversion, rather than an external, all-embracing reductionist treatment of phenomenological hermeneutics.[13] "Language," whether as discourse or text, is to be caught out and tripped up in its own metaphorical character precisely at the point where philosophical theorists claim recourse to a close relation between metaphor and technical concept or true meaning. In the case of the hermeneutical theory under discussion, an example of such metaphorical usage would be the phrase " 'referent' basically manifests the meaning 'in front of' the text,"[14] a turn of phrase whose strikingly spatial character highlights, through its contrast to "meaning 'behind' the text," at once the distinction and the coherence between "sense" and "reference." The "referent" "in front of the text" is precisely that restorative "sense" of the reading of second naiveté, for which text and reader come to share a common referential world which they cannot share in critical reading of the "meaning behind the text." Meaning "in front of the text" is a centered world of meaning made accessible and viable to an equally centered self.

In the one case ("meaning behind the text") the spatial metaphor is intended to indicate mutual absence or distance between semantic sense, real referent, and the reader's world. By contrast, the other spatial metaphor ("in front of") is supposed to indicate the overcoming of that distance without a direct—either naive or

Romantic—*mergence* of the previously distanced partners. To someone like Derrida, it is clear that the one metaphor derives its meaning simply by oppositional affinity with the first. Insofar as it is supposed to indicate a significant *conceptual* pairing (distance between two linguistic "worlds" which remains while nonetheless being overcome, the reading of second naiveté), it simply spins its wheels. It is a case of "absence" supposedly being "presence" at the same time, a virtual admission of the fault that deconstructionists espy at the foundation of the edifice of the traditional "signifier/signified" relation. The natural affinity of the second metaphor is not that of a "signifier" with a normative "signified" but simply that of one signifier or metaphor with another, previous one. Any "meaning" that "in front of" may have is *deferred* along a loosely connected, potentially indefinite metaphorical axis, and in the meantime it is what it is simply by displacing that from which it differs ("meaning behind the text"). It is this displacement of a signified world into the intertextuality of an indefinite sequence of signifiers —a focal insistence of the deconstructionists—that is so apt in their critique of phenomenological hermeneutics: the "worlds" that are supposedly "disclosed" actually have the subversive, deconstructing non-referentiality of pure metaphoricity built into them. Phenomenological hermeneutics, to deconstructionists, is *malgre lui,* a celebration of that very non-referential purity of textual metaphoricity that it sets out to transcend. Second naiveté, far from being explained and justified, is an illusion, a verbal pirouette.

Such instances of the hermeneutical theory's built-in susceptibility to deconstruction are crucial to the deconstructionists' cumulative argument that the general bearing of hermeneutical theory is one for which "understanding" as self-presence is the indispensable and irreducible counterpart to textual "meaning" as linguistic presence, and vice versa. Language as signifier has life or spirit breathed into it by its immediate relation to self-presence, and that in turn allows it to take the shape of the signified, the means by which it attains meaning as referent or ontologically present truth. Conversely and simultaneously, "disclosure" is the bridge over which truth as presence in turn travels to present itself as meaning to self-presence now. If "meaning" implies absence and *difference* instead of centeredness or presence, then self-presence or "understanding"

—its indispensable polar correlate in the theory—is bound to be just as hollow. Not that deconstructionists necessarily deny the "reality" of centered selfhood, or even of experienced self-consciousness as its basic mode, after the fashion of the masters of "suspicion." Rather, as part of explaining and justifying "interpretive" textual reading, specifically in the mode of second naiveté, this ingredient simply dissolves; like "presence," self-presence turns into absence, the absence of centeredness and of its "now," in relation to textuality and intertextuality.

One may well be skeptical about Derrida's and his followers' consignment of the *whole* western linguistic tradition to the supposed metaphysical or "ontotheological" prioritizing of "phonocentric," and "logocentric," discourse over text and writing. Deconstructionist association of Christianity (in contrast to Judaism) with ontotheology *tout court* has all the appearance of overkill, as sweeping generalizations usually do. Christianity, especially in its reformation Protestant rather than liberal or neo-orthodox forms, is very much a "religion of the text," for which the textuality of the Bible is not systematically or metaphysically, but only in quite informal fashion, coordinated with linguistic meaning of a logocentric sort. In fact, the grammatical literalism of the "unfallen" biblical text, together with its textual autonomy from the priority over the *viva vox* of the interpretive tradition—all of which the reformers proposed—may bear a remote resemblance (doubtless no more!) to the deconstructionists' "textuality" and "intertextuality," which the latter have so far apparently not discerned. On the other hand, the integrity of textuality does not involve a systematic denial of ontotheology as one fit articulation among others for Christian doctrinal language. In other words, a Christian theological observer will want to resist the tendency toward global and foundational claims on behalf of inclusive theories that deconstructionists seem to share in practice, whatever the theory, with other theorists. Furthermore, it is obvious that deconstruction is anything but universally helpful to a Christian reading of Christian scripture, even though it may be useful *selectively,* just as hermeneutical theory may be similarly and modestly appropriate. (One thinks, for example, of aspects of experiential selfhood and self-understanding in the gospel of John, in the reading of which a phenomenological interpretive scheme might have limited but significant applicability). It is doubtful that *any* scheme for reading texts, and narrative texts in particular, and biblical narrative texts even more specifically, can serve globally and foundationally, so that the reading of biblical material would simply be a regional instance of the universal procedure. But deconstruction does provide a strong case against the theory at issue. The hermeneutical claim is, as we saw earlier, doubtful enough when it is judged by criteria of coherence and adequacy in regard to restorative or revised-literal reading of New Testament narratives. But now one also has to add that its very claim to adequate status as a universal and foundational theory justifying the restorative reading of "second naiveté" has been rendered highly dubious by the immanent subversion of its philosophical into a metaphorical turn at crucial points.

*Either* "second naiveté" is no concept but simply a misleading term, and restorative hermeneutics explains or justifies no way of reading, *or* if one is to hold out for anything like it, one had better invent a more adequate theory to support the claim. There is of course another option: one may want to claim that a notion similar to "second naiveté" is indeed meaningful, but not because it is part of, or justified by, any general theory. But that is a position which neither hermeneutical phenomenologists nor deconstructionists will tolerate.

Closely interwoven with hermeneutics is a position in modern liberal Christian theology, for which theological articulation has always to be the fruit of carefully coordinating present cultural self-understanding—that is, a phenomenology of the contemporary cultural life-world—with an interpretation of the normative self-understanding inherent in Christianity in its historically varying external manifestations.[15] A paradoxical challenge now awaits the attention of this theology: to consider seriously the possibility that the present cultural situation is among other things a *post-hermeneutical* situation.

Up to now this challenge has gone unmet among the theory's theological advocates; they have seen no need for serious modification of their views. Just as in hermeneutical and phenomenological theory "understanding" as an event of self-presence remains a basically unquestioned category, and a cultural world is always a particular collective understanding, so in the theory's cultural-theological version religious experience or something like it remains a serenely assured category with an ever pertinent, ever available cultural correlate in every situation, including that which is post-hermeneutical or post-religious. So, for example, in the words of David Tracy, "We must keep alive the sense of the uncanny—the post-religious, religious sense of our situation."[16] It seems never really to have been in question in the first place.

## III. PROSPECTS FOR THE LITERAL SENSE

What of the future of the "literal reading"? The less entangled in theory and the more firmly rooted not in a narrative (literary) tradition but in its primary and original context a religious community's "rule" for faithful reading, the more clearly it is likely to come into view, and the stronger as well as more flexible and supple it is likely to look. From that perspective, a theory confined to describing how and in what specific kind of context a certain kind of reading functions is an improvement over the kind of theoretical endeavor that tries to justify its very possibility in general.

Hermeneutical theory obviously belongs to the latter kind, but so also do those arguments for and against the historical factuality of the (perhaps!) history-like or literal and (perhaps!) historical narratives of the Bible that have generated so much religious and scholarly heat since the eighteenth century. As arguments claiming general validity they have usually been governed on both sides by the assumptions that "meaning" is identical with "possible truth," and that if a story belongs to the genre of history-like or "realistic" narrative, its meaning *qua* possible truth belongs to the class called "factuality." The necessary obverse is that if stories are *not* judgeable by this criterion, they are finally not realistic but belong to some other genre and therefore make a different kind of truth claim.

A recent proposal about the mutual bearing of realistic narrative and history represents a transition from a high-powered to a less ambitious kind of general theorizing. This proposal holds that the gospel stories as well as large portions of Old Testament narrative are indeed "realistic," but that the issue of their making or not making factual or, for that matter, other kinds of truth claims is not part of the scope of hermeneutical inquiry. "Meaning" in this view is logically distinct from "truth," even where the two bear so strong a family resemblance as the designations "history-like" and "historical" imply. The factuality or non-factuality of at least some of these narratives, important as it is no doubt in a larger religious or an even general context, involves a separate argument from that concerning their meaning.[17]

Two related assumptions are implied when this move is made as part of a plea on behalf of realistic or literal (as well as figural) reading. First, there is a suspension of the question whether "truth" is a general class to which all reasonable people have equal access as a set of proper conclusions drawn from credible grounds, by way of rational procedures common to all. But, second, "meaning," unlike "truth," *can* be affirmed to be such a general class allowing across-the-board access to all reasonable people who know how to relate genus, species, and individual case properly. One appeals first to a qualitatively distinct genus of text (and meaning) called "literary" and then argues both historically and in principle that within it there is a species called "realistic narrative" that is quite distinct from, say, romance or heroic epic. To this species the biblical narrative is said to belong; indeed it is often said to be its original and paradigm.[18]

The resemblance of this view to Anglo-American "new criticism" is obvious and has often been pointed out. Both claim that the text is a normative and pure "meaning" world of its own which, quite apart from any factual reference it may have, and apart from its author's intention or its reader's reception, stands on its own with the authority of self-evident intelligibility. The reader's "interpretation" can, and indeed has to be minimal, reiterative, and formal, so that the very term "interpretation" is already misleadingly high-powered. "Criticism" is a far more appropriate term because it is more low-keyed and leaves the text sacrosanct, confining itself to second-order analysis, chiefly of the formal stylistic devices which are the "literary" body of the text. In the case of the "realistic" novel these are devices such as temporal structuring, the irreducible interaction of character and plot, ordinary or "mixed" rather than elevated style, and so forth. These devices are said to be of the very essence of the text and of its quality as a linguistic sacrament, inseparable from the world that it is (rather than merely represents), but also the means by which that world is rendered to the reader so that he/she can understand it without any large-scale "creative" contribution of his/her own.

This outlook is less high-powered than hermeneutical theory, not only because it is confined to "meaning" as logically distinct from "truth" but because the formal features of realistic narrative about which it generalizes are so often as not implicit rather than explicit, so that they must be *exhibited* in textual examples rather than *stated* in abstract terms. But even though less high-powered, general theory it remains: the gospel narratives "mean" realistically because that is the general literary class to which they belong. But precisely in respect of generalizing adequacy this theory has grave weaknesses. First, the claim to the self-subsistence or self-referentiality of the text apart from any truth world is as artificial as it may (perhaps!) be logically advantageous. Moreover, the view is usually not held consistently, for "new critics" argue both for the integrity and the truth of their approach when challenged by contrary reductionist views such as historicism, structuralism, or deconstruction. Despite their anti- or non-philosophical bearing, in fact many of them espouse a theory of a purely aesthetic kind of truth in literature. Second, it is similarly artificial and dubious to claim a purely external relation of text and reading, which in effect sets aside the mutual implication of interpretation and textual meaning (as hermeneutical theorists would have it) or of reading and the textuality of the text (in terms of the deconstructionists). If a narrative or a poem should "not mean but be," avoiding paraphrase as the proper means to the realization of this ideal comes close to enthroning verbal repetition as the highest form of understanding.

In short, the less high-powered general theory that upholds the literal or realistic reading of the gospels may be just as perilously perched as its more majestic and pretentious hermeneutical cousin. There is a greater problem yet with the more modest view. The resemblance of "new criticism" to, indeed its partial derivation from, Christian theology (especially Aristotelian modes of that theology) has often and rightly been pointed out. Endowing the text with the stature of complete and authoritative embodiment of "truth" in "meaning," so that it is purely and objectively self-referential, is a literary equivalent of the Christian dogma of Jesus Christ as incarnate Son of God, the divine Word that is one with the bodied person it assumes. The irony of "new criticism" (and it is not the first instance of this kind) is to have taken this specific case and to have turned it instead into a general theory of meaning, literature, and even culture, in their own right. A whole class of general meaning constructs are all understood "incarnationally" or "sacramentally." As a result, the original of this process of derivation, the doctrine of the incarnation of the Word of God in the person and destiny of Jesus of Nazareth, has now become an optional member within the general class, in which those who subscribe to the class may or may not wish to believe. There may or may not be a class called "realistic narrative," but to take it as a general category of which the synoptic gospel narratives and the doctrine of the incarnation are a dependent instance is first to put the cart before the horse and then cut the lines and claim that the vehicle is self-propelled.

Whatever one may think of the phenomenologists' hermeneutical theory, it *is* a general theory; however, under its auspices the literal reading of the gospel narratives vanishes, both because in application the theory revises it into incoherence and out of existence, and because the theory *qua* theory cannot persuasively make good on its claim to the availability of the revisionary literalism of a "second naiveté." As for the "new criticism," a literal reading of the gospels is appropriate under its auspices, but only because and to the extent that it is in fact a disguised Christian understanding of them.

Rather than an example of theory of meaning, what we have in the *sensus literalis* is a reading that governs and bends to its own ends whatever general categories it shares—as indeed it has to share —with other kinds of reading (e.g. "meaning," "truth," as well as their relation). It is a case-specific reading which may or may not find reduced analogues elsewhere. Second, it is not only case-specific but as such belongs first and foremost into the context of a sociolinguistic community, that is, of the specific religion of which it is part, rather than into a literary ambience. Both considerations involve lowering our theoretical sights yet further to the level of mere description rather than explanation, to the specific set of texts and the most specific context, rather than to a general class of texts ("realistic narrative") and the most general context ("human experience"). That exercise in self-restraint should not be difficult to state, despite the complexity of the exposition up to this point. Nor does it preclude inquiry into either the fact or the character of possible truth claims involved in the literal reading of the gospels. It is simply an acknowledgment of the inescapably ambiguous or problematic *philosophical* status of such claims when they are analyzed under the auspices of general theories. The theoretical task compatible with the literal reading of the gospel narratives is that of describing how and in what context it functions. In that regard we need to do little more than return to the beginning of the essay: established or "plain" readings are warranted by their agreement with a religious community's rules for reading its sacred text. It is at best question-able that they are warranted, except quite provisionally, under any other circumstances: theories of realistic narrative for example are not likely to be highly plausible except in tandem with an informal cultural consensus that certain texts have the quasi-sacred and ob-jective literary status of "classics," which form the core of a broader literary "canon." The plausibility structure in this case is a literary imitation of a religious community's authority structure; it rests on a tradition, reinforced by communal, usually professional, agencies authorized to articulate the consensus about what is to be included within the canon and what is to be especially exalted within that privileged group as "classic." The pleas by advocates of phenomeno-logical hermeneutics that the status of a "classic" is warranted when a work provides a "realized experience of that which is essential, that which endures"[19] is little more than a tacit acknowledgment that the temporary cultural consensus is already on the wane, and agreed upon or "plain" readings with it. As a warranting argument it is a last-ditch holding operation, no matter how sound it may be as a report of how people are likely to experience works that already (or still) have the cultural status of classics.

In the tradition of Christian religion and its communal life, scripture has played many parts; it has been a guide to life, an inspira-tion to heart and mind, a norm for believing. The largely informal set of rules under which it has customarily been read in the commu-nity, in the midst of much disagreement about its contents, has been fairly flexible and usually not too constrictive. The *minimal* agree-ment about reading the scriptures (as distinct from their status or scope) has been as follows. First, Christian reading of Christian scripture must not deny the literal ascription to Jesus—and not to any other person, event, time or idea—of those occurrences, teachings, personal qualities and religious attributes associated with him in the stories in which he plays a part, as well as in the other New Testament writings in which his name is invoked. Second, no Christian reading may deny either the unity of Old and New Testament or the congruence (which is not by any means the same as literal identity) of that unity with the ascriptive literalism of the gospel narratives. Third, any readings not in principle in contradiction with these two rules are permissible, and two of the obvious candidates would be the various sorts of historical-critical and literary readings.

Whether or not there are exact parallels in other religions to this sort of governed use of scriptures for the edification, practical guidance, and orientation in belief of the members, it is at least a typical ingredient in a recognizably religious pattern.[20]

The descriptive context for the *sensus literalis* is the religion of which it is part, understood at once as a determinate code in which beliefs, ritual, and behavior patterns, ethos as well as narrative, come together as a common semiotic system, and also as the community which is that system in use. Clifford Geertz calls culture an "acted document," and the term applies also to religion.[21] A "culture" (including a religion) is like a language, a multi-level communicative network that forms the indispensably enabling context for persons to enact both themselves and their mutual relations. Geertz calls the low-level theoretical effort at describing culture, which we also affirm for religion, "thick description" (using a term of Gilbert Ryle's). It is, first, description of details as parts of "interworked systems of construable signs . . . within which they can be intelligibly . . . described."[22] Second, it is description from the actor's, participant's, or language user's point of view, yet without mimicry or confusion of identity on the part of the interpreter.[23]

Those who follow this low-level use of theory for "placing" religions as symbol systems are persuaded that the description and critical appraisal of a religion from within the religious community itself, and external "thick" description, while certainly not identical, are not wholly disparate. Yet their congruence does not require—on the contrary it eschews—the elaborate synthesizing requirements of a more general, explanatory theory. To understand a religion or a culture to which one is not native does not demand a general doctrine of the core of humanity, selfhood, and the grounds of intersubjective experience. There is of course the need for normal human sensitivity and respect. But beyond that, in Geertz's words:

> Whatever accurate sense one gets of what one's informants are "really like" comes . . . from the ability to construe their modes of expression, what I would call their symbol systems. . . . Understanding the form and pressure of . . . natives' inner lives is more like grasping a proverb, catching an allusion, seeing a joke—or . . . reading a poem—than it is like achieving communion.[24]

This is understanding without "empathy" or "transcultural identification with our subjects."[25] George Lindbeck has called this low-level theoretical deployment in the analysis of religions a "cultural linguistic approach" to the topic,[26] and has used the term "intratextual" to describe the kind of theology—the "normative explication of the meaning a religion has for its adherents"—that is not identical but congruent with it.[27] The congruence lies in the persuasion that

> Meaning is constituted by the uses of a specific language rather than being distinguishable from it. Thus the proper way to determine what "God" signifies, for example, is by examining how the word operates in a religion and thereby shapes reality and experience rather than by first establishing its propositional or experiential meaning and reinterpreting or reformulating its uses accordingly.[28]

"Intratextuality" in many of the "high" religions is used not only in an extended or metaphorical but in a literal sense, for they are in varying degrees "religions of the (or a) book." "They all have relatively fixed canons of writings that they treat as exemplary or normative instantiations of their semiotic codes. One test of faithfulness for all of them is the degree to which descriptions correspond to the semiotic universe paradigmatically encoded in holy writ."[29]
The direction in the flow of intratextual interpretation is that of

absorbing the extratextual universe into the text, rather than the reverse (extratextual) direction. The literal sense is the paradigmatic form of such intratextual interpretation in the Christian community's use of its scripture: the literal ascription to Jesus of Nazareth of the stories connected with him is of such far-reaching import that it not only serves as focus for inner-canonical typology but reshapes extratextual language in its manifold descriptive uses into a typological relation to these stories. The reason why the intratextual universe of this Christian symbol system is a narrative one is that a specific set of texts, which happen to be narrative, has become primary, even within scripture, and has been assigned a literal reading as their primary or "plain" sense. They have become the paradigm for the construal not only of what is inside that system but for all that is outside. They provide the interpretive pattern in terms of which *all* reality is experienced and read in this religion. Only in a secondary or derivative sense have they become ingredient in a general and literary narrative tradition. The latter is actually not only a provisional but a highly variable set of contexts for these texts; it is not foundational for their meaning, and there is no intrinsic reason to suppose that any given general theory for their reading in that context, be it hermeneutical or anti-hermeneutical, ought to be assigned pride of place—including that of "new criticism" with its logical dependence on Christian theology. Equally clearly, it is once more a case of putting the cart before the horse—but this time the wagon is theological rather than literary—if one constructs a general and inalienable human quality called "narrative" or "narrativity," within which to interpret the gospels and provide foundational warrant for the possibility of their existential and ontological meaningfulness. The notion that Christian theology is a member of a general class of "narrative theology" is no more than a minor will-o'-the-wisp.

"Meaning" in a cultural-linguistic and intratextual interpretive frame is the skill that allows ethnographer and native to meet in mutual respect; if they happen to be the same person, it is the bridge over which he/she may pass from one shore to the other and undertake the return journey; if they are natives from different tribes, it is the common ground that is established as they learn each other's languages, rather than a known precondition for doing so.

To return to the beginning. The third of these tasks is perhaps the most immediately pressing for Christian interpretation and for the future of its use of the literal sense. For the next-door neighbor to Christianity in all its various forms is Judaism with its own diversity, and they share those parts of a common scripture which Christianity has usurped from Judaism. The most pressing question from this vantage point is not the fate of the literal sense in the event of a new, perhaps more nearly universal, spiritual truth that would also constitute a new literal reading and threaten to reduce the Christian reading of the New Testament to exoteric, carnal status. This is unlikely, for we have noted that religions are specific symbol systems and not a single, high-culture reproduction of symbol-neutral eternal "truth."

A far more urgent issue for Christian interpretation is the unpredictable consequences of learning the "language" of the Jewish tradition, including the nearest Jewish equivalent to Christian literal reading. To discover midrash in all its subtlety and breadth of options and to understand *peshat* (the traditional sense)[30] may well be to begin to repair a series of contacts established and broken time and again in the history of the church, whenever linguistic and textual Old Testament issues became pressing in intra-Christian debate. Perhaps the future may be better than the past as a result of the intervening period of liberal scholarship and the persuasion that the two religions, even though closely interwined, are quite distinct, each with its own integrity. The convergence of distinctness and commensurability between them has yet to be discovered, and attention to midrash and to the literal sense may play a significant part in the discovery.

In addition to the inter-religious enrichment for which one may hope from such joint inquiry, certainly for Christianity, the secular gains may be surprisingly large, even if strictly speaking incidental or secondary. The Protestant theologian Friedrich Schleiermacher called Judaism a fossil religion, in part at least out of the animus which many rationalist, romantic, and idealistic thinkers bore toward Jewish particularism. And yet it is now conceivable that "fossil" may bear more of the future of the culture of the west in its hands than Christianity, and its traditional, particularistic forms may not be adventitious to the fact. Cultural, religious, and historical parallels are dangerous and speculative. Nonetheless there may be a lesson here, at least to the effect that the relation between Christianity and Judaism—including the complex issues of the relation between their scriptures and scriptural interpretations—may play an indispensable part in the process of Christian recovery of its own intratextual or self-description. With or without the aid of such a discussion, the most fateful issue for Christian self-description is that of regaining its autonomous vocation as a religion, after its defeat in its secondary vocation of providing ideological coherence, foundation, and stability to western culture. Beyond that, however, the example of Judaism in the modern western world might be a beacon to a reconstituted Christian community. One never knows what this community might then contribute once again to that culture or its residues, including its political life, its quest for justice and freedom—and even its literature. If the priorities are rightly ordered, the literal sense may be counted on to play a significant part in such a less pretentious event. It will stretch and not break.

## NOTES

1.  James S. Preus, *From Shadow to Promise: Old Testament Interpretation from Augustine to the Young Luther* (Cambridge: Harvard University Press, 1969).

2.  Cf. G.E. Lessing, "The Education of the Human Race," *Lessing's Theological Writings,* translated and introduced by Henry Chadwick (Stanford: Stanford University Press, 1967), p. 96. The same message is of course a large part of the parable of the rings in Lessing's *Nathan the Wise.*

3.  Cf. Frank Kermode, *The Genesis of Secrecy: On the Interpretation of Narrative* (Cambridge: Harvard University Press, 1979), pp. 18ff,143ff, *passim.*

4.  Paul Ricoeur, *Interpretation Theory: Discourse and the Surplus of Meaning* (Fort Worth: Texas Christian University Press, 1976), pp. 12ff.

5.  *Ibid.,* p. 12.

6.  Cf. Paul Ricoeur, "Toward a Hermeneutic of the Idea of Reve-

lation," *Essays on Biblical Interpretation,* ed. Lewis S. Mudge (Philadelphia: Fortress Press, 1980), pp. 73–118.

7. David Tracy, *Blessed Rage for Order: The New Pluralism in Theology* (New York: Seabury Press, 1975), p. 221

8. *Semeia 4: Paul Ricoeur on Biblical Hermeneutics,* ed. J.D. Crossan (Missoula: Scholars Press, 1975), p. 32.

9. *Ibid.,* pp. 127ff.

10. Tracy, *op. cit.,* p. 206. Cf. *supra,* pp. 102–15 for a statement of the issue.

11. Tracy's statement of the matter, *op cit.,* pp. 205–07, is quite typical. If the tenor of the passage quoted above (note 7) is to turn "Jesus" into an allegory of "universal meaningfulness" in the shape of an event or disclosure (cf. *ibid.,* p. 106), Tracy's subsequent *The Analogical Imagination: Christian Theology and the Culture of Pluralism* (New York: Crossroad, 1981), part II, chs. 6 and 7, tends to redress the balance and stress "Jesus" as the unsurpassable ascriptive subject of the narrative manifesting and proclaiming the "Christ event" as an event "from God."

12. Paul Ricoeur, "The Model of the Text: Meaningful Action Considered as a Test," P. Rabinow and W.M. Sullivan (eds.), *Interpretive Social Science* (Berkeley: University of California Press, 1979), p. 98.

13. Cf. Christopher Norris, *Deconstruction: Theory and Practice* (London and New York: Methuen, 1982), p. 31.

14. Tracy, *Blessed Rage for Order,* p. 51, *passim.*

15. Cf. Tracy, *The Analogical Imagination,* p. 340.

16. Cf. Tracy, *The Analogical Imagination,* p. 362. For Tracy's remarks about Derrida, cf. *ibid.,* pp. 117ff, 220ff (note 12), 361ff, *passim.*

17. This position is implied by the present writer in *The Eclipse of Biblical Narrative* (New Haven: Yale University Press, 1974), and made explicit in *The Identity of Jesus Christ* (Philadelphia: Fortress Press, 1975).

18. The classic statement of this case is Erich Auerbach, *Mimesis: The Representation of Reality in Western Literature* (Princeton: Princeton University Press, 1953).

19. Tracy, *The Analogical Imagination,* p. 108.

20. For an interesting parallel see Gerhard Bowering, *The Mystical Vision of Existence in Classical Islam* (Berlin and New York: Walter de Gruyter, 1980), pp. 140ff.

21. Clifford Geertz, *The Interpretation of Cultures* (New York: Basic Books, 1973), p. 10.

22. *Ibid.,* p. 13.

23. *Ibid.,* pp. 13, 27.

24. Geertz, "From the Native's Point of View: On the Nature of Anthropological Understanding," P. Rabinow and W.M. Sullivan (eds.), *op. cit.,* pp. 240ff.

25. *Ibid.,* p. 226.

26. George A. Lindbeck, *The Nature of Doctrine: Religion and Theology in a Postliberal Age* (Philadelphia; Westminster Press, 1984), pp. 32ff. I wish to acknowledge my profound indebtedness to this book and to its author.

27. *Ibid.,* p. 113.

28. *Ibid.,* p. 114.

29. *Ibid.,* p. 116.

30. Cf. Raphael Loewe, "The 'Plain' Meaning of Scripture in Early Jewish Exegesis," *Papers of the Institute of Jewish Studies in London I* (Jerusalem, 1964), pp. 140–85, esp, pp. 180ff.

# Chapter Three

# TOWARD A POSTLIBERAL THEOLOGY

## GEORGE LINDBECK

This essay outlines an understanding of theology that is consistent with what I have elsewhere described as a "cultural-linguistic" approach to religion.[1] In this approach, religions are seen as comprehensive interpretive schemes, usually embodied in myths and narratives, which structure human experience and understanding of self and world. Not every telling of one of these cosmic stories is religious, however. It must be told with a view, in the words of William Christian, to identifying and describing what is taken to be "more important than everything else in the universe."[2]

Stated more technically, a religion can be viewed as a kind of cultural and/or linguistic framework or medium which shapes the entirety of life and thought. Like a culture or language, it is a communal phenomenon that shapes the subjectivities of individuals rather than being primarily a manifestation of those subjectivities. It comprises a vocabulary of discursive and non-discursive symbols together with a distinctive logic or grammar in terms of which this vocabulary can be meaningfully deployed. Lastly, just as a language is correlated with a form of life, so too a religion's doctrines, stories and ethical directives are integrally related to the rituals it practices, the experiences it evokes, the actions it recommends and the institutional forms it develops.

The *cultural-linguistic approach* is to be distinguished from two others. As illustrated in at least four of the six theses of Lonergan's theory of religion,[3] the *experiential-expressivist approach* holds that:

(1) different religions are diverse expressions or objectifications of a common core experience; (2) the experience, while conscious, may be unknown on the level of self-conscious reflection; (3) it is present in all human beings; (4) in most religions, the experience is the source and norm of objectifications: it is by reference to the experience that their adequacy or inadequacy is to be judged. The *propositional approach* is the approach of traditional orthodoxies, but it also has certain affinities to the outlook on religion adopted by much modern Anglo-American analytic philosophy, with its preoccupation with the cognitive or informational meaningfulness of religious utterances. For this approach, religions, like philosophies and sciences as they were classically conceived, offer informative propositions or truth claims about objective realities.

Theology, when practiced in a manner that is consistent with the cultural-linguistic approach, is second-order reflection on first-order religious language and practice. Its tasks are to describe the conceptual grammar and vocabulary of this language and practice, to apply their rules and principles to concrete situations, and to understand them in their relations to other religions, ideologies, and domains of discourse, thought and action.

As is suggested by the reference to "grammar," the descriptive task is also a normative one; theologians seek to describe speech and conduct that make sense in terms of a given religion's own standards (for example, its "grammatical rules"). In the usual Christian terminology, this is the task of systematics or dogmatics, and the criterion of good description is "faithfulness" to the "sources" of the faith, especially scripture. Analogously, the task of applying rules and principles is the province of practical theology, and the criterion of assessment is applicability. The task of understanding first-order language and practice in relation to other discourses and practices is the province of apologetic or foundational theology; its criterion of assessment is intelligibility by general rather than religion-specific standards.

My central concern in these pages is with the dogmatic problem of faithfulness. It is to this I shall turn after some initial comments on the interrelations of criteria of assessment in the three functionally distinct theological disciplines.

## I. THE PROBLEM OF ASSESSMENT

Concern with all three types of criteria is present in every theological discipline. When, for example, dogmaticians attempt faithfully to describe the normative features of a religion, they are also interested in applicability and intelligibility. Similarly, practical and foundational theologians seek not only to apply and make the religion intelligible but also to be faithful.

Further specification of the meaning of these terms depends on the view of religion which is presupposed. For our present purposes, it is sufficient to distinguish three possibilities. We have already mentioned the cultural-linguistic one which, because it is recent, may be called postliberal. Theological liberals, in contrast, generally see religion as an expression of religious experience, and they may therefore be called experiential-expressivists. Third, the rationalistic outlooks which prevailed before the rise of modern liberalism emphasized propositional truth claims: religions were conceived primarily as collections or systems of true and/or false propositions. The distinction between preliberal, liberal, and postliberal theologies—corresponding to propositional, experiential-expressivist and cultural-linguistic views of religion—should not be confused with the quite different distinction between faithfulness and unfaithfulness, between doctrinal orthodoxy and heterodoxy. At least in Christianity, all three types of theology can take what are generally regarded as both orthodox and heretical forms. What happens, however, is that the understanding of orthodoxy or of faithfulness changes, as does the understanding of applicability and intelligibility.

This explains how theologies reflecting one or another of these views of religion can combine formal similarities with fundamental material differences. Spanish inquisitors and enlightenment theologians disagreed radically in creed and practice and yet agreed on the formal point that propositional truth is the decisive test of adequacy. Similarly, some doctrinally conservative Oxford Anglicans and their equally conservative Lutheran counterparts in the Erlangen school shared the liberal commitment to the primacy of experience with certain twentieth century "death of God" theologians, but they differed on the material question of what kind of experiences are religiously crucial. Analogously, a Christian postliberal consensus on the primarily cultural-linguistic character of religions would not by itself overcome substantive disagreements between conservatives and progressives, feminists and antifeminists, Catholics and Protestants. Nevertheless, common frameworks do make possible, though not guarantee, genuine arguments over the relative adequacy of specifiably different positions.

Such arguments are difficult, however, when theologies have formally different views of religion. The problem is that each type of theology is embedded in a conceptual framework so comprehensive that it shapes its own criteria of adequacy. Thus what propositionalists, with their stress on unchanging truth and falsity, regard as faithful, applicable, and intelligible is likely to be dismissed as dead orthodoxy by liberal experiential-expressivists. Conversely, the liberal claim that change and pluralism in religious expression are necessary for intelligibility, applicability, and faithfulness is attacked by the propositionally orthodox as an irrationally relativistic and a practically self-defeating betrayal of the faith. A postliberal might propose to overcome this polarization between tradition and innovation by distinguishing between abiding doctrinal grammar and variable theological vocabulary, but this proposal appears from other perspectives as the worst of two worlds rather than the best of both. In view of this situation, the most that can be done in this essay is to comment on how faithfulness, in particular, might be understood in postliberal theologies[4] and then to leave it to the readers to make their own assessments.

## II. Faithfulness as Intratextuality

The task of descriptive theology, whether dogmatic or systematic, is to give a normative explication of the meaning a religion has for its adherents. What I call an "intratextual" method of descriptive theology locates religious meaning within a religious system or text, while an "extratextual" method locates it outside a system or text, either in the objective realities to which it refers or in the experiences it symbolizes. The extratextual method is favored by those whose understanding of religion is propositional or experiential-expressive; the intratextual method is favored by cultural-linguists.

For them, meaning is constituted by the uses of a specific language rather than being distinguishable from it. In this view, the proper way to determine what "God" signifies, for example, is to examine how the word operates within a religion and thereby shapes reality and experience, rather than first to establish its propositional or experiential meaning and then to reinterpret or reformulate its uses accordingly.

In an extended sense, something like intratextuality is characteristic of the descriptions not only of religion but also of other forms of rule-governed human behavior, from carpentry and mathematics to languages and cultures. Hammers and saws, ordinals and numerals, winks and signs of the cross, words and sentences are made comprehensible by indicating how they fit into systems of communication or purposeful action, not by reference to outside factors. One does not successfully identify the 8:02 to New York by describing the history or manufacture of trains or even by a complete inventory of the cars, passengers, and conductors that constituted and traveled on it on a given day. Even if none of the cars, passengers, and crew were the same the next day, the train would still be the 8:02 to New York. Its meaning, its very reality, is its function within a particular transportation system. Much the same can be said of winks and signs of the cross: they are quite distinct from non-meaningful but physically identical eye twitches and hand motions, and their reality as meaningful signs is wholly constituted in any individual occurrence by their intratextuality, that is, so to speak, by their place in a story.

Meaning is more fully intratextual in systems of signs, or semiotic systems—composed, as they are, of interpretive and communicative signs, symbols, and actions—than in other forms of ruled human behavior, such as carpentry or transportation systems. Among semiotic systems, intratextuality, in an extended sense, is greater in natural languages, cultures, and religions that potentially embrace all aspects of life: the way one can speak of all life and reality in French, or from an American or a Jewish perspective. Intratextuality is greater, still, when these languages, cultures and religions redescribe this embrace reflexively, within second-order systems of representation: the way one can also describe French culture in French terms, American culture in American terms, and

Judaism in Jewish ones. Such reflexivity makes it possible for theology to be intratextual, not simply by explicating religion from within but also by describing everything as inside, as interpreted by the religion within the terms of its religiously shaped second-order concepts.

In view of their comprehensiveness, reflexivity, and complexity, religions require what Clifford Geertz, borrowing a term from Gilbert Ryle, has called "thick description."[5] Geertz applies the term to culture, but with the understanding that it also holds for religion. A religion cannot be treated as a formalizable "symbolic system . . . by isolating its elements, specifying the internal relationships among these elements, and then characterizing the whole system in some general way—according to the core symbols around which it is organized, the underlying structures of which it is the surface expression, or the ideological principles upon which it is based. . . . This hermetic approach to things seems to me to run the danger of locking . . . analysis away from its proper object, the informal logic of actual life." The theologian, like the ethnographer, should approach "such broader interpretations and abstract analyses from the direction of exceedingly extended acquaintances with extremely small matters." "As inter-locked systems of construable signs . . . culture [including religion] is not a power, something to which social events, behaviors, institutions, or processes can be causally attributed; it is a context, something within which they can be intelligibly—that is, thickly—described." Only by detailed "familiarity with the imaginative universe in which . . . acts are signs" can one diagnose or specify the meaning of these acts for the adherents of a religion. What the theologian needs to explicate "is a multiplicity of complex conceptual structures, many of them superimposed or knotted into one another, which are at once strange, irregular and inexplicit, and which he [or she] must contrive somehow first to grasp and then to render." In rendering the salient features, the essential task "is not to codify abstract regularities but to make thick description possible, not to generalize across cases but to generalize within them." If this is not done, one may think, for example, that Roman and Confucian *gravitas* are much the same, or that atheistic Marxism more nearly resembles atheistic Buddhism than biblical theism. This is as egregious an error as supposing that uninflected English is closer to uninflected Chinese than to German.

Thick description, it should be noted, is not to be confused with Baconian empiricism, with sticking to current facts. It is rather the full range of the interpretive medium which needs to be exhibited, and because this range in the case of religion is potentially all-encompassing, description has a creative aspect. There is, indeed, no more demanding exercise of the inventive and imaginative powers than to explore how a language, culture, or religion may be employed to give meaning to new domains of thought, reality, and action. Theological description can be a highly constructive enterprise.

Finally, in the instance of religions more than any other type of semiotic system, description is not simply metaphorically but also literally intratextual. This is true in some degree of all the world's major faiths. They all have relatively fixed canons of writings that they treat as exemplary or normative instantiations of their semiotic codes. One test of faithfulness for all of them is the degree to which descriptions correspond to the semiotic universe paradigmatically encoded in holy writ.

The importance of texts and of intratextuality for theological faithfulness becomes clearer when we consider the unwritten religions of non-literate societies. Evans-Pritchard[6] tells of a Nuer tribesman who excitedly reported to him that a woman in the village had given birth to twins, both dead, and that one was a hippopotamus and had been placed in a stream, and the other a bird and had been placed in a tree. There are in that society no canonical documents to consult in order to locate these puzzling events within the wider contexts that give them meaning. Is the equation of dead twins with birds and hippopotami central or peripheral to Nuer thought and life? Would the religion and culture be gravely disturbed if this equation were eliminated? Even the wisest of Evans-Pritchard's informants might not have understood these questions, and even if they did, they presumably would have had no idea of how to reach a consensus in answering them. In oral cultures, there is no transpersonal authority to which the experts on tradition can refer their disputes. This helps explain why purely customary religions and cultures readily dissolve under the pressure of historical, social, and linguistic change, but it also suggests that canonical texts are a condition, not only for the survival of a religion but also for the very possibility of normative theological description. In any case, whether or not this is universally true, the intrasemiotic character of descriptive theology is inseparable from intratextuality in the three western monotheisms—Judaism, Christianity, and Islam. These are preeminently religions of the book.

We need now to speak in more detail of how to interpret a text in terms of its immanent meanings—that is, in terms of the meanings immanent in the religious language of whose use the text is a paradigmatic instance. On the informal level this is not a problem; it becomes so, as we shall see, only when theology becomes alienated from those ways of reading classics,[7] whether religious or nonreligious, that seem natural within a given culture or society. Masterpieces such as *Oedipus Rex* and *War and Peace,* for example, evoke their own domains of meaning. They do so by what they themselves say about the events and personages of which they tell. In order to understand them in their own terms, there is no need for extraneous references to, for example, Freud's theories or historical treatments of the Napoleonic wars. Further, such works shape the imagination and perceptions of the attentive reader so that he or she forever views the world to some extent through the lenses they supply. To describe the basic meaning of these books is an intratextual task, a matter of explicating their contents and the perspectives on extratextual reality that they generate.[8]

These same considerations apply even more forcefully to the preeminently authoritative texts that are the canonical writings of religious communities. For those who are steeped in them, no world is more real than the ones they create. A scriptural world is thus able to absorb the universe. It supplies the interpretive framework within which believers seek to live their lives and understand reality. This happens quite apart from formal theories. Augustine did not describe his work in the categories we are employing, but the whole of his theological production can be understood as a progressive, even if not always successful, struggle to insert everything from Platonism and the Pelagian problem to the fall of Rome into the world of the Bible. Aquinas tried to do something similar with Aristotelianism, and Schleiermacher with German romantic idealism. The way they described extrascriptural realities and experience, so it can be argued, was shaped by biblical categories much more than was warranted by their formal methodologies.

Especially in the case of Aquinas, however, the shaping was in part methodologically legitimated. Traditional exegetical procedures (of which he gave one of the classic descriptions)[9] assume that scripture creates its own domain of meaning and that the task of interpretation is to extend this over the whole of reality. The particular ways of doing this depend, to be sure, on the character of the religion and its texts. One set of interpretive techniques is appropriate when the Torah is the center of the scripture, another when it is the story of Jesus, and still another when it is the Buddha's enlightenment and teachings. For the most part, we shall limit our observations on this point to the Christian case.

In classical Christianity, there was a special though not exclusive emphasis on typological or figural devices, first to unify the canon, and second to encompass the cosmos. Typology was used to incorporate the Hebrew scriptures into a canon that focused on Christ, and then, by extension, to embrace extrabiblical reality. King David, for example, was in some respects a typological foreshadowing of Jesus, but he was also, in Carolingian times, a type for Charlemagne and, in reformation days, as even Protestants said, for Charles V in his wars against the Turks. Thus an Old Testament type, filtered through the New Testament antitype, became a model for later kings and, in the case of Charlemagne, provided a documentable stimulus to the organization of the educational and parish systems that stand at the institutional origins of western civilization. Unlike allegories, typological interpretations did not empty Old Testament or postbiblical personages and events of their own reality;[10] these interpretations therefore constituted a powerful means for imaginatively incorporating all being into a Christ-centered world.

It is important to note the direction of interpretation. Typology does not make scriptural contents into metaphors for extrascriptural realities, but the other way around. It does not suggest, as is often said in our day, that believers find their stories in the Bible, but rather that they make the story of the Bible their story. The cross is not to be viewed as a figurative representation of suffering nor the messianic kingdom as a symbol for hope in the future; rather, suffering should be cruciform, and hopes for the future messianic. More generally stated, it is the religion instantiated in scripture that defines being, truth, goodness, and beauty, and the nonscriptural exemplifications of these realities that need to be transformed into figures (or types or antitypes) of the scriptural ones. Intratextual theology redescribes reality within the scriptural framework rather than translating scripture into extrascriptural categories. It is the text, so to speak, which absorbs the world, rather than the world the text.

There is always the danger, however, that the extrabiblical materials inserted into the biblical universe will themselves become the basic framework of interpretation. This is what happened, so the Christian mainstream concluded, in the case of Gnosticism. Here Hellenism became the interpreter rather than the interpreted. The Jewish rabbi who is the crucified and resurrected Messiah of the New Testament accounts was transformed into a mythological figure illustrative of thoroughly non-scriptural meanings. Nor did the mainstream wholly escape the danger. It insisted creedally that the Jesus of which scripture speaks is the Lord, but it often read scripture in so Hellenistic a way that this Jesus came to resemble a semi-pagan demigod. The doctrinal consensus on the primacy of scripture, on the canonical status of the Old as well as the New Testament, and on the full humanity of Christ did not by itself provide the scriptural framework for a Christian reinterpretation of the classical heritage. Better theological and exegetical procedures were needed.

Up to the reformation, this need was filled in part through the typological methods we have already noted. From Augustine, through Aquinas, to Luther and Calvin, there was an increasing resistance in the west to indiscriminate allegorizing and an insistence on the primacy of a specifiable literal intratextual sense. Whatever the failures in actual execution, and they were many, the interpretive direction was from the Bible to the world rather than vice versa.

Among the reformers, the resistance to allegorizing and the greater emphasis on intratextuality (*scriptura sui ipsius interpres*) heightened rather than diminished the emphasis on proclamation, or on the preached word. Scripture, one might say, was interpreted by its use,[11] by the *viva vox evangelii.* In the intratextual context, emphasizing the living word in this way involves applying the language, concepts, and categories of scripture to contemporary realities. This emphasis is different in its intellectual, practical, and homiletical consequences from liberal attempts, of which Ebeling's is the most notable,[12] to understand the reformation notion of the word of God as an experiential "word event."

As the work of Hans Frei shows,[13] the situation has changed radically in recent centuries, and new difficulties have arisen. Typological interpretation collapsed under the combined onslaughts of rationalistic, pietistic, and historical-critical developments. Scripture ceased to function as the lens through which theologians viewed the world and instead became primarily an object of study whose religiously significant or literal meaning was located outside itself. The primarily literary approaches of the past, with their affinities to informal ways of reading the classics in their own terms, were replaced by fundamentalist, historical-critical, and expressivist preoccupations with facticity or experience. The intratextual meanings of scripture continue informally to shape the imagination of the west (even atheistic Marxists think of history as the unfolding of a determinate pattern with an ultimately ineluctable outcome), but theologians do not make these meanings methodologically primary. Instead, if they are existentially inclined, theologians reinterpret the notion of providential guidance, for example, as a symbolic expression of confidence in the face of the vicissitudes of life; if they objectivize, theologians might, as did Teilhard de Chardin, interpret providence in terms of an optimistic version of evolutionary science. The possibility of regaining a specifically biblical understanding of providence depends in part on the possibility of once again reading scripture, theologically, in literary rather than non-literary ways.

The depth of the present crisis is best seen when one considers that even those who agree doctrinally that the story of Jesus is the key to understanding reality are often in fundamental theological disagreement over what the story is really about, that is, over its normative or literal sense.[14] Is the literal meaning of the story the history it is on some readings supposed to record, and, if so, is this history that of the fundamentalist or of the historical critic? Or is the real meaning, the theologically important meaning, the way of being in the world which the story symbolizes, or the liberating actions and attitudes it expresses, or the ethical ideals it instantiates, or the metaphysical truths about God-humanity it illustrates, or the gospel promises it embodies? Each of these ways of construing the story depends on a distinct interpretive framework (historical, phenomenological, existential, ethical, metaphysical, doctrinal) that specifies the questions asked of the text and shapes the pictures of Jesus that emerge. These pictures may all be formally orthodox in the sense that they are reconcilable with Nicea, but their implications for religious practice and understanding are radically divergent. Nothing better illustrates the point that, for most purposes, theological issues are more crucial and interesting than doctrinal ones.

The intratextual way of dealing with this problem depends heavily on literary considerations. The normative or literal meaning must be consistent with the kind of text it is taken to be by the community for which it is important. The meaning must not be esoteric: not something behind, beneath, or in front of the text; not something that the text reveals, discloses, implies, or suggests to those with extraneous metaphysical, historical, or experiential interests. It must rather be what the text says in terms of the communal language of which the text is an instantiation. A legal document should not be treated in quasi-kabbalistic fashion as, first of all, a piece of expressive symbolism (though it may secondarily be that also); nor should the Genesis account of creation be turned fundamentalistically into science; nor should one turn a realistic narrative (which a novel also can be) into history (or, alternatively, as the historical critic is wont to do, into a source of clues for the reconstruction of history). The literary character of the story of Jesus may be to utilize, in the fashion of realistic narratives, the interaction of purpose and circumstance to render the identity description of an agent. If so, then the literal and theologically controlling meaning of the story is Jesus' identity as thus rendered, and not his historicity, existential significance, or metaphysical status.[15] The implications of the story for determining the metaphysical status, or existential significance, or historical career of Jesus Christ may have varying degrees of theological importance, but they are not determinative.

The believer, so an intratextual approach would maintain, is not told primarily to be conformed to a reconstructed Jesus of history (as Hans Küng maintains),[16] nor to a metaphysical Christ of faith (as in much of the propositionalist tradition),[17] nor to an abba experience of God (as for Schillebeeckx),[18] nor to an agapeic way to being in the world (as for David Tracy).[19] The believer is, rather, to be conformed to the Jesus Christ depicted in the narrative. An intratextual reading tries to derive the interpretive framework that designates the theologically controlling sense from the literary structure of the text itself.[20]

This type of literary approach can be extended to cover all of scripture, and not simply the story of Jesus. What is the literary genre of the Bible as a whole in its canonical unity? What holds together the diverse materials it contains—poetic, prophetic, legal, liturgical, sapiential, mythical, legendary, and historical? These are all embraced, it would seem, in an overarching story that has the specific literary features of realistic narrative as exemplified in diverse ways, for example, by certain kinds of parables, novels, and historical accounts. It is as if the Bible were a "vast, loosely-structured, non-fictional novel" (to use a phrase David Kelsey applies to Karl Barth's view of scripture).[21]

It is possible, furthermore, to specify the primary function of the canonical narrative (which is also the function of many of its most important component stories from the Pentateuch to the gospels). This function is "to render a character . . . offer an identity description of an agent,"[22] namely God. The narrative does this, not through accounts of what God is in and of himself, but through accounts of the interaction of his deeds and purposes with those of creatures in their ever-changing circumstances. These accounts reach their climax in what the gospels say about the risen, ascended, and ever-present Jesus Christ whose identity as the divine-human agent is unsubstitutably enacted in the stories of Jesus of Nazareth. The climax, however, is logically inseparable from what precedes it. The Jesus of the gospels is the Son of the God of Abraham, Isaac, and Jacob in the same strong sense that the Hamlet of Shakespeare's play is Prince of Denmark. In both cases, the title with its reference to the wider context irreplaceably rather than contingently identifies the bearer of the name.

It is easy to see how, on this view, theological descriptions of a religion may need to be materially diverse even when the formal criterion of faithfulness remains one. The primary focus is not on God's being in itself, for that is not what the text is about, but on how life is to be lived and reality construed in the light of God's character as an agent as this is depicted in the stories of Israel and of Jesus. Life, however, is not the same in catacombs and space shuttles, and reality is different for, let us say, Platonists and Whiteheadians. Catacomb dwellers and astronauts might rightly emphasize diverse aspects of the biblical accounts of God's character and action in describing their respective situations. Judging by catacomb paintings, the first group often saw themselves as sheep in need of a shepherd, while the second group would perhaps be well advised to stress God's grant to human beings of stewardship over planet Earth. Similarly, Platonic and Whiteheadian differences over the nature of reality lead to sharp disagreements about the proper characterization of God's metaphysical properties, while antimetaphysicians, in turn, argue that no theory of divine attributes is consistent with the character of the biblical God.

All these theologies could agree, nonetheless, that God is appropriately depicted in stories about a being who created the cosmos without any humanly fathomable reason, but—simply for his own good pleasure and the pleasure of his goodness—appointed homo sapiens steward of one minuscule part of this cosmos, permitted appalling evils, chose Israel and the church as witnessing peoples, and sent Jesus as Messiah and Immanuel, God with us. The intention of these theologies, whether successful or unsuccessful, could in every case be to describe life and reality in ways conformable to what these stories indicate about God. They could, to repeat, have a common intratextual norm of faithfulness despite their material disagreements.

Intratextual theologies can also, however, disagree on the norm. They can dispute over whether realistic narrative is the best or only way to identify the distinctive genre and interpretive framework of the Christian canon, and, even if it is, on how to characterize the divine agent at work in the biblical stories. More fundamentally, they could disagree on the extent and unity of the canon. If Revelation and Daniel are the center of scripture, as they seem to be for Scofield Bible premillennialists, a very different picture of God's agency and purposes emerges. Further, as current debates over feminism vividly remind us, past tradition and present consensus can serve as extensions of the canon and deeply influence the interpretation of the whole. These extensions can on occasion go beyond the specifically Christian or religious realm. The philosophical tradition from Plato to Heidegger operates as the canonical corpus for much western reflection on God or the human condition; when this reflection is recognized as operating with a peculiarly western rather than transculturally available idiom, it begins to acquire some of the features of intratextuality.[23] In short, intratextuality may be a condition for the faithful description and development of a religion or tradition, but the material or doctrinal consequences of this depend, self-evidently, in part on what canon is appealed to.

It must also be noted that intratextuality in a postcritical or postliberal mode is significantly different from traditional, precritical varieties. We now can make a distinction (unavailable before the development of modern science and historical studies) between realistic narrative and historical or scientific descriptions. The Bible is often "history-like" even when it is not "likely history." It can therefore be taken seriously in the first respect as a delineator of the character of divine and human agents, even when its history or science is challenged. As parables such as that of the prodigal son remind us, the rendering of God's character is not in every instance logically dependent on the facticity of the story.

Furthermore, historical criticism influences the theological-literary interpretation of texts. A postcritical narrative reading of scripture such as is found to some extent in von Rad's work on the Old Testament[24] is notably different from a precritical one. Or, to cite a more specific example, if the historical critic is right in claiming that the Johannine "Before Abraham was, I am" (Jn 8:58) is not a self-description of the preresurrection Jesus but a communal confession of faith, then even those who fully accept the confession will want to modify traditional theological descriptions of what Jesus was in his life on earth. They may agree doctrinally with Chalcedon, but prefer a Pauline *theologia crucis* to the Christological *theologia gloriae* that is often associated with Chalcedon (and that one finds even in such great exponents of the theology of the cross as Luther).

Nevertheless, in an intratextual approach, literary considerations are more important than historical-critical ones in determining the canonical sense even in cases such as this. It is because the literary genre of John is clearly not that of veridical history that the statement in question can be readily accepted as a communal confession rather than a self-description.

Finally, and more generally, the postcritical focus on intratextual meanings involves a change in attitude toward some aspects of the text that were important for premodern interpretation. The physical details of what, if anything, happened on Mount Sinai, for example, are no longer of direct interest for typological or figurative purposes, as they often were for the tradition, but the basic questions remain much the same: What is the nature and function of Torah? In the New Testament, the Torah is custodial in Israel and fulfilled in Christ, but what does this imply for later Christianity and its relations to Judaism? Is not Torah by analogical extension both custodial and fulfilled for Christian communities in this age before the end when fulfillment is not yet final, and does this not make Christians much closer to Jews than they have generally thought? What, furthermore, does the holocaust have to do with Mount Sinai, on the one hand, and another mountain, Calvary, on the other? As these questions indicate, a postliberal intratextuality provides warrants for imaginatively and conceptually incorporating postbiblical worlds into the world of the Bible in much the same fashion as did the tradition. The consequences will often be very different, however, both because there are changes in the extrabiblical realities that are to be typologically interpreted and because the critical approach to history has necessitated a more rigorous intratextuality.

Before concluding this discussion, I must reiterate that the practice of intratextuality is only loosely related to explicit theory. Not only good grammarians or mathematicians, but also theologians may be quite wrongheaded in the understanding of what they in fact actually do. There is no reason for surprise if an apparent propositionalist, like Aquinas, or an undoubted experiential-expressivist, such as Schleiermacher, were more intratextual in their actual practice than their theories would seem to allow. Their performance would perhaps have improved if their theories of religion had been different, but this is true only if other conditions remained equal. Native genius and religious commitment are helpful, but in order to convert these into theological competence one also needs a supportive environment, the tutelage of expert practitioners, and assiduous practice in a complex set of unformalizable skills that even the best theoretician cannot adequately characterize. Where these conditions are lacking, even good theory cannot greatly enhance performance, and where they are present, poor theory may be relatively harmless.

The implications of these observations do not bode well, however, for the future of postliberal theology. The conditions for practice seem to be steadily weakening. Disarray in church and society makes the transmission of the necessary skills more and more difficult. Those who share in the intellectual high culture of our day are rarely socialized intensively into coherent religious languages and conformal forms of life. This is not necessarily disastrous for the long-range prospects of religion (which is not dependent on elites), but it is for theology as an intellectually and academically creative enterprise capable of making significant contributions to the wider culture and society. Furthermore, theology (in the sense of reflection in the service of religion) is being increasingly replaced in seminaries as well as universities by religious studies. There are fewer and fewer institutional settings favorable to the intratextual interpretation of religion and of extrascriptural realities. Reinhold Niebuhr may have been the last American theologian who in practice (and to some extent in theory) made extended and effective attempts to redescribe major aspects of the contemporary scene in distinctively biblical terms. After the brief neoorthodox interlude (which was itself sometimes thoroughly liberal in its theological methodology, as in the case of Paul Tillich), the liberal tendency to redescribe religion in extrascriptural frameworks has once again become dominant. Religions have become foreign texts that are much easier to translate into currently popular categories than to read in terms of their intrinsic sense. Thus the fundamental obstacles to intratextual theological faithfulness may well derive from the modern psychosocial situation rather than from scholarly or intellectual considerations.

The modern situation creates problems for all the world's great transcultural and long-enduring religions. Buddhism, Hinduism and Confucianism in the east, and the three "religions of the book" of middle eastern origin all have canonical textual traditions which have functioned intratextually to absorb diverse and changing worlds of thought and life. It seems unlikely that any of them can survive, much less be faithfully innovative, unless there is a body of adherents for whom the textual tradition functions, so to speak, as a conceptual mother tongue. It may be that such linguistic competence will be sustainable in the future only in relatively tight-knit minority communities. Some of the more impressive examples of such communities are to be found in rabbinic Judaism in its creative periods (though Christianity, perhaps especially during the first centuries, is not without instances). Whether any comparable manifestations of innovative intratextuality will be possible in the future remains to be seen, but one thing is clear. At least in biblical religions, intratextuality cannot be genuine, cannot be faithful, unless it is innovative. A condition for the vitality of these traditions is that they redescribe in their own distinctive idioms the new social and intellectual worlds in which their adherents for the most part actually live and into which humanity as a whole is now moving.

## NOTES

1. This essay is a somewhat modified version of the first two parts of Chapter 6 of my *The Nature of Doctrine: Religion and Theology in a Postliberal Age* (Philadelphia: Westminster, 1984), pp. 112–38. I also summarize aspects of Chapter 1, p. 16 and of Chapter 2, pp. 31–33.

2. William A. Christian, Sr., *Meaning and Truth in Religion* (Princeton: Princeton University Press, 1964), pp. 60ff.

3. Bernard Lonergan, *Method in Theology* (New York: Herder & Herder, 1972), pp. 101–24.

4. The type of theology I have in mind could also be called "postmodern," "postrevisionist," or "post-neo-orthodox," but "postliberal" seems best because what I have in mind postdates the experiential-expressive approach which is the mark of liberal method. This technical use of the word is much broader than the ordinary one:

methodological liberals may be conservative or traditionalist in theology or, often alternatively, innovative in theology and reactionary
in social or political matters (as were the pro-Nazi *Deutsche
Christen*).

5. Clifford Geertz, *The Interpretation of Culture* (New York: Basic Books, 1973), pp. 3–30. The quotations that follow in this paragraph are taken in order from pp. 17, 21, 13, 10, and 26.

6. E.E. Evans-Pritchard, *Nuer Religion* (Oxford: Oxford University Press, 1956), p. 84. This "notorious ethnographic example" is
cited by T.M.S. Evans, "On the Social Anthropology of Religions,"
*Journal of Religion,* 62/4 (1982): 376.

7. Unlike David Tracy, *The Analogical Imagination* (New York:
Crossroad Publishing Co., 1981), I am using "classic" to refer to
texts that are culturally established for whatever reason. Tracy's
model, in contrast to mine, is not cultural-linguistic. For him classics are "certain expressions of the human spirit [which] so disclose a
compelling truth about our lives that we cannot deny them some
kind of normative status" (p. 108).

8. This and the following descriptions of intratextuality were
composed without conscious reference to deconstructionism, but,
given the current prominence of this form of literary theory, some
tentative comments on similarities and dissimilarities may be desirable in order to avoid misunderstandings. First, intratextualism, like
deconstructionism, does not share the traditional literary emphasis
on a text as that which is to be interpreted, whether (as in the now-
old "new criticism") as a self-contained aesthetic object or "verbal
icon," or as mimetic, or as expressive, or pragmatic. (For the meaning of these terms, see Meyer H. Abrams, *The Mirror and the Lamp:
Romantic Theory and the Critical Tradition* [Oxford: Oxford University Press, 1953]; cited by M.A. Tolbert, *Religious Study Review*
8/1 [1982], p. 2.) Instead, intratextualism treats texts as "mediums
of interpretation" and thus shares the deconstructionist emphasis
on texts as constituting the (or a) world within which everything is or
can be construed. Related to this, in the second place, is a common
concern with what Christopher Norris, speaking of Paul de Man,
calls "the play of figural language," "the grammar of tropes," and
"the rhetoric of textual performance" (Christopher Norris, *Deconstruction: Theory and Practice* [Methuen & Co., 1982], pp. 106,

108). In the third place, however, the great difference is that for the deconstructionists there is no single privileged idiom, text, or text-constituted world. Their approach is *inter*textual rather than intra-textual: that is, they treat all writings as a single whole; all texts are, so to speak, mutually interpreting. One result is that what in the past would have been thought of as allegorizing is for them an acceptable mode of interpretation. In an intratextual religious or theological reading, in contrast, there is a privileged interpretive direction from whatever counts as holy writ to everything else. Other differences as well as similarities are discussed by Shira Wolosky in a treatment of Derrida's relation to Talmudic modes of interpretation ("Derrida, Jabes, Levinas: Sign Theory as Ethical Discourse," *Journal of Jewish Literary History* 2/3 [1982], pp. 283–301). It should incidentally be noted, however, that Derrida's understanding of Christian interpretive method as presented in this article is quite different from the typological approach, which I shall argue was historically dominant. It may be that Derrida's view of what is characteristically Christian in these matters has been influenced by the hermeneutics of Paul Ricoeur, whose student he once was.

9. Thomas Aquinas, *ST* I.1.10.

10. For the structure, though not all the details, of my understanding of typological interpretation, see Hans Frei, *The Eclipse of Biblical Narrative* (New Haven: Yale University Press, 1974), esp. pp. 1–39.

11. Charles Wood, *The Formation of Christian Understanding* (Philadelphia: Westminster Press, 1981), pp. 42, 101, and *passim.*

12. See my review of Gerhard Ebeling's *Dogmatik des Christlichen Glaubens* in *Journal of Religion* 61 (1981) pp. 309–14.

13. Frei, *The Eclipse of Biblical Narrative,* pp. 39ff.

14. For the general way of looking at the problem of scriptural interpretation presented in this paragraph, though not for all the details, I am indebted to David Kelsey, *The Uses of Scripture in Recent Theology* (Philadelphia: Fortress Press, 1975).

15. This way of putting the matter is dependent on Hans Frei, *The Identity of Jesus Christ* (Philadelphia: Fortress Press, 1975).

16. In addition to Hans Küng's *On Being a Christian,* tr. by Edward Quinn (New York: Doubleday & Co., 1976), see his "Toward a New Consensus in Catholic (and Ecumenical) Theology," in

Leonard Swidler (ed.), *Consensus in Theology?* (Philadelphia: Westminster Press, 1980), pp. 1–17.

17. This is the focus of attack in Hick (ed.), *The Myth of God Incarnate* (Philadelphia: Westminster Press, 1977). See Chapter 5, n. 1, above.

18. Edward Schillebeeckx, *Jesus: An Experiment in Christology,* tr. by Hubert Hoskins (New York: Seabury Press, 1979).

19. David Tracy, *Blessed Rage for Order* (New York: Seabury Press, 1975).

20. Karl Barth's way of doing this is described and critically but sympathetically assessed in David Ford, *Barth and God's Story* (Frankfurt: Peter Lang, 1981). See also D. Ford, "Narrative in Theology," *British Journal of Religious Education* 4/3 (1982), pp. 115–19.

21. David Kelsey, *The Uses of Scripture in Recent Theology,* p. 48.

22. *Ibid.*

23. Richard Rorty partly illustrates this possibility of doing philosophy intratextually, but the inevitable vagueness of his canon of philosophical texts makes him verge on a philosophical version of deconstructionism. See his *Consequences of Pragmatism* (Minneapolis: University of Minnesota Press, 1982), esp. essays 6 (on Derrida), 8, and 12, and the Introduction.

24. Gerhard von Rad, *Old Testament Theology,* tr. by D.M.G. Stalker, 2 vols. (New York: Harper & Row, 1962, 1965).

# PART TWO: RABBINIC PROTOTYPES OF POSTCRITICAL INTERPRETATION

Articles by David Weiss Halivni, Steven Fraade and Michael Fishbane display features of the rabbinic hermeneutic which may become central, as well, to the practice of postcritical interpretation. As discussed in the Introduction to this volume, these features include the authority of the biblical text, read intratextually as the foundation for all subsequent interpretation; the distinction between a biblical text's plain-sense and its performative and transformative, midrashic interpretations; the multiplicity of midrashic interpretation, whose character emerges through a dialogue between the plain-sense of scripture and its performative significance for the lives of contemporary communities of interpreters.

Halivni's study of *peshat,* or plain-sense, provides a rabbinic counterpart to Frei's discussion of literal reading. It is a demonstrably postcritical reading, offering at once a textual analysis of rabbinic literature and a pragmatic analysis of the performative significance of that literature for critical rabbinic scholars today. At the same time, Halvini's analysis separates contemplative and communal aspects of interpretation in a way we do not find in the works of Frei and Lindbeck; his reading may therefore represent an objectivistic variety of postcritical reading. Fraade offers a moderate form of postcritical reading, in which the dialogic relation between text and intended listener is mirrored in the dialogic relation between text and contemporary interpreter. He analyzes the performative force of rabbinic commentary as displayed in the *Sifre Deuteronomy.* Fishbane displays the interests of a radical or hermeneutical variety of postcritical reading, selectively attending to aspects of rabbinic interpretation which liberate the text from the univocal interpretations of past traditions.

Chapter Four

# PLAIN SENSE AND APPLIED MEANING IN RABBINIC EXEGESIS

DAVID WEISS HALIVNI
(compiled and edited by Peter Ochs,
in consultation with the author*)

[* Ed. Note: To introduce this book's readers to the scope of
Prof. Halivni's recent hermeneutical writings in English, I have, in
the following order, compiled selections from several of his writings:
"Contradictory Yet Complementary: The Dichotomy Between
Practice and Intellect,",which is Ch. 4 of what was then the manu-
script of his recently published book, *Peshat and Derash: Plain and
Applied Meaning in Rabbinic Exegesis* (Oxford: Oxford University
Press, 1990); " 'Chate'u Yisrael' ('Israel Sinned'): A Proposed Reso-
lution to the Conflict of Peshat and Derash," Ch. 5 of that manu-
script; "On Man's Role in Revelation," in *From Ancient Israel to
Modern Judaism, Intellect in Quest of Understanding: Essays in
Honor of Marvin Fox,* ed. Nahum Sarna (Atlanta: Scholars Press for
Brown Judaica, 1990): pp. 29–52; and "The Impact on Religious
Life of the Critical Examination of Rabbinic Sources," a mono-
graph from which Halivni delivered a lecture at Columbia in 1989.
The sequence of topics in the essay presented here roughly follows
that of the latter monograph, but is noticeably different from that in
Halivni's book. The difference is significant, since Halivni's order of
presentation is part of the performative meaning of his book, separating "scholarly" from "theological" argumentation. In order to pre-

sent the main features of Halivni's hermeneutic in one brief essay, I have had to abandon any attempt to reproduce that performative meaning and to omit many of the subtleties of his argument, as well as his detailed illustrations and footnotes. Overall, I focus on what he calls his theological argumentation. To adapt the selections to the style of this book, I have added some transitional passages and edited some others. Halivni has also added to this text several passages composed after the publication of *Peshat and Derash*. I append a summary of what I consider Halivni's main points.]

The fact that the rabbis of the Talmud occasionally deviated, in their interpretation of the Bible, from the literal meaning of the text provoked condemnation from those outside the rabbinic tradition and puzzlement from those inside it. Spinoza[1] criticized Maimonides for sanctioning deviation from the literal meaning and called such a practice "rash and excessive." Two hundred years later, A. Geiger[2] chastised the rabbis of the Talmud for having abandoned "the natural meaning" of the text, which he attributed to their "deficient sense of exegesis." Insiders since the time of Saadya[3] (882–942), one of the most important Jewish scholars of the early middle ages, agonized over the conflict between what the text seems to say and the way it was understood by the rabbis of the Talmud. The discrepancy was particularly pronounced when it affected a matter of law, when a mode of behavior was demanded based upon an interpretation that was not congruous with the literal meaning of the text. An aggadic, non-legal passage could easily be converted into a metaphor or an allegory, blunting the troublesome edges of the literal meaning. In legal matters, however, conversion into metaphor or allegory is inappropriate, indeed forbidden. One is left with the dilemma, in the words of a recent traditional scholar,[4] to choose between "assuming that the Torah expressed itself—God forbid—in an unsuitable manner and accept the binding result of the rabbinic interpretation, or accept the literal meaning of the text and reject the rabbinic tradition"—in neither case a very comforting alternative for the traditionalist.

Several examples will suffice to indicate the frequent disparity between the meaning of a scriptural verse and its rabbinic interpretation. The clash between *peshat,* or the plain sense of scripture, and *derash,* or its applied meaning, falls under two categories: either a rabbinic interpretation is at odds with the *peshat* of an individual scriptural verse, or two or more scriptural verses are at odds with each other and must be reconciled through reference to a third verse. A prominent example of the first category is the rabbinic interpretation of the phrase "an eye for an eye" in Exodus 21:24 to mean monetary compensation, when the simple, literal meaning of the phrase *ayin tachat ayin* is, most likely, physical retribution. This example may serve as the paradigmatic instance of a rabbinic interpretation displacing the *peshat* of a verse and replacing it with a wholly different, and contrary, meaning.[5]

A second example in which the divergence between *peshat* and *derash* is equally stark involves levirate marriage (Deut 25:5–6), in which the biblical law enjoins a woman whose husband has died without children to marry one of the deceased husband's brothers, prescribing that "the first son whom she bears shall succeed to the name of his brother who is dead, that his name may not be blotted out of Israel." The straightforward meaning of the verse indicated that the living brother is to become a surrogate father for the deceased brother, who is considered the "real," if not natural, father of the firstborn offspring of the levirate marriage. The rabbis altered the meaning of the verse by claiming that the phrase *asher teled* refers not to the firstborn child, as the *peshat* suggests, but to the firstborn brother, that is, the oldest brother of the deceased, who shall perform the levirate marriage. By interpreting the phrase *asher teled* in the past tense (in the sense of *asher nolad*), and thereby abandoning its *peshat,* the rabbis modified the halakhic composition of the verse.[6]

The second category of confrontations between *peshat* and *derash* is comprised of two subcategories. In the first, two verses contradict each other and one of them is stripped of its *peshat,* that is, interpreted contrary to its *peshat,* to "resolve" the contradiction. An example of this subcategory is the contradiction between Exodus 12:9, which states, "Do not eat it [the paschal lamb] raw or cooked in water, but roasted . . . over the fire," and Deuteronomy 16:7, which states, "You shall cook [i.e. with water] and eat it." An attempt to reconcile these two verses is already evidenced by 2 Chronicles 35:13, "and they cooked the passover [sacrifice] with fire" ["cooked," that is, as in Deuteronomy 16:17, but "with fire," as used in Exodus 12:9 to refer to roasting].[7] In the second subcategory, contradictions between verses are resolved through the aid of a third verse. In these instances, the weight of the third verse tips the exegetical balance in favor of the *peshat* of one of the original two verses, creating a two against one situation. Though the matter of the correct practical halakhah is settled through this accounting of verses, the *peshat* of the minority verse is virtually annulled in the process, for it is assigned an exclusively *derash* meaning. This hermeneutic method is embodied in the last of Rabbi Ishmael's thirteen exegetical principles: "If two biblical passages contradict each other, they can be determined only by a third passage."[8] An example of this type of interpretive methodology, in which rabbinic *derash* overrides and dislodges scriptural *peshat* while effectively mediating between conflicting verses, is the resolution offered to the contradiction between Exodus 12:5, "you may take it [the passover offering] from the sheep or from the goats" and Deuteronomy 16:2, "you shall slaughter the passover sacrifice for the Lord your God, from the flock and herd." A third verse, Exodus 12:21, "pick out lambs for your families, and slaughter the passover offering," is brought as the deciding factor in this halakhic controversy, with the rabbis determining that the passover sacrifice must come from the flock only and not from the herd. The word "herd" is designated for the *chagiga* offering, even though the context clearly involves the paschal sacrifice, and thus is also plainly interpreted contrary to its *peshat*.[9] The *peshat* of one verse is here ultimately abandoned in the cause of textual reconciliation or, rather, halakhic compromise. This solution is already implied in 2 Chronicles 35:7–9. In fact, we have seen that the solutions to both contradictions of the second category—in which one verse is delegated a midrashic interpretation which negates its *peshat*—are already outlined in 2 Chronicles, a late biblical text attributed by tradition to Ezra the scribe.[10] The antiquity of this type of midrashic resolution—the resort to *derash* in the face of problematic *peshat*—is thus well established.

Why is *derash* needed to "amend" *peshat* that is either inherently problematic or that contradicts a scriptural prescription found elsewhere? Why are there ever instances in the Torah in which the *peshat* of a verse is either unreliable or misleading? Recognizing that the conception of the Torah as the embodiment of God's will is vital to our guarantee that the *halakhah* corresponds to God's bidding, one is led to wonder why the divine text does not always employ the most straightforward and unambiguous language with which to communicate its directives. It is an enigmatic datum of the Torah that, in the case of levirate marriage discussed above, the words *asher teled* are used instead of *asher nolad,* when the latter is actually, upon rabbinic interpretation, the intended meaning of the verse. The rabbis' need to resort to *derash,* because the *peshat* of a scriptural verse is, in a sense, deceiving, must be theologically puzzling to the reader imbued with the belief that the Torah is divine and in no need of human "emendation." Why, in sum, would the Torah say *peshat* when it really meant to imply *derash?*

We propose here a theory to explain the occasional discrepancy between scriptural *peshat* and rabbinic *derash* and to solve the theological puzzle of why the Torah is sometimes in need of midrashic revision. We suggest that, in cases where *derash* seems to depart radically from *peshat,* an act of restoration has taken place, rather than an act of revision. That is, rabbinic *derash* actually restores the original meaning of the scriptural verse, recovering its divine authorial intention, in places where the text itself had been altered through the historical process of *chate'u yisrael* (lit., "the people of Israel sinned"): the sinning of the Jews through idol worship and their consequent neglect of the biblical text during much of the post-Mosaic and first temple periods. Those occasions when rabbinic *derash* supplants the *peshat* of a verse signify that the current text of the verse is faulty and that, in fact, the *derash* was originally the *peshat* of the verse. In these cases, the *peshat* is actually misleading precisely because it is the result of textual corruption. The *derash* recaptures the textural sense of the original revelation that had existed before the process of *chate'u yisrael* set in.

## EZRA AND *CHATE'U YISRAEL*

The historical basis of this theory is an interpretation of the restorative efforts of Ezra in the early second temple period. The unqualified acceptance of the Torah, free of idolatrous syncretism, took place under the leadership of Ezra and Nehemiah in the fifth century B.C.E. Israel's renewal of community and of faith covenant (*amanah*) concluded a period of halakhic delinquency that began soon after Moses received the Torah. As implied in the book of Nehemiah, the period of the prophets was characterized by halakhic or legal inconsistencies and instability, captured in the phrase *chate'u yisrael.*

> And now, our God . . . do not treat lightly all the suffering that has overtaken us . . . . Our kings, officers, priests and fathers did not follow Your Teaching (*ve'et melakheinu, sareinu, va-avoteinu lo asu toratekha*)[11] and did not listen to Your commandments or to the warnings that You gave them. (Neh. 9:32–34.)

During this period, two fundamental religious institutions were either not observed at all or not observed properly: making the *sukkah* and preparing the paschal lamb.[12] The syncretistic proclivities of the Jews led not only to sins of omission and commission in the realm of practical halakhah, but also to the debasement and alteration of the scriptural text itself. Ezra arrested this syncretism and inaugurated the process of authoritative text dissemination and interpretation that led to rabbinic Judaism. It is not coincidental that the first mention of *midrash* in the later, exegetical sense is found in Ezra 7:10: "For Ezra had dedicated himself to seek (*lidrosh*) the Torah of the Lord so as to observe it, and to teach laws and rules to Israel." The Torah emerged as the sole textual source of religious authority and thus had to be interpreted explicitly, and implicitly through the *midrash halakhah,* so that its scope could be broadened organically. Ezra was thus the principal architect of those aspects of oral law that were not already included in the fundamental meanings of the scriptural commandments.

According to our interpretation of the process of *chate'u yisrael,* Ezra received an altered text of the Torah. At the same time he also possessed the knowledge and authority to indicate how the misleading *peshat* of certain passages should be corrected— although he lacked the authority actually to emend the faulty text in most cases. He initiated a process of textual rehabilitation, partly by providing a system of marking certain words of the Torah as spurious, and, more comprehensively, by disseminating an oral tradition of restorative exposition, or *midrash*. We are thus left with a scriptural text whose *peshat* is not always authoritative or decisive, but whose tradition of midrashic interpretation *is*. This tradition is our guarantee that, despite some blemishes in the text of Torah, our tradition of halakhic practice, or *"halakhah le-maaseh,"* *does* express the divine will as embodied in the original revelation to Moses. Our *halakhah* is codified according to rabbinic *derash* because *derash,* and not *peshat,* always conforms to the dictates of Sinaitic revelation.[13]

Several passages in rabbinic literature allude to the historical sequence of *chate'u yisrael,* priestly neglect of the scriptural text and Ezra's restorative activity. According to *Mishnah Parah* 3:5, "Moses prepared the first [red heifer, *parah adumah*], and Ezra prepared the second, and five [were prepared] after Ezra." This means that no red heifers were prepared between the careers of Moses and Ezra: in effect, the historical period between Moses and Ezra must be bracketed as a source of halakhic authority. According to *BT Sanhedrin* 21b–22a, the locus of the axial concept of *chate'u yisrael:*

> Mar Zutra, or as some say, Mar 'Ukba said: Originally the Torah was given to Israel in Hebrew characters and in the sacred [Hebrew] language; later, in the times of Ezra, the Torah was given in Ashurith script and Aramaic language. [Finally] they selected for Israel the Ashurith script and Hebrew language. . . .
>
> It has been taught: R. Jose said: Had Moses not preceded him, Ezra would have been worthy of receiving the Torah for Israel. Of Moses it is written, "And Moses went up unto God" (Ex. 19:3), and of Ezra it is written, "He, Ezra, went up from Babylon" (Ezra 7:6). As the going up of the former refers to the [receiving of the] Law, so does the going up of the latter. . . . And even though the Torah was not given through him [Ezra], its writing was changed through him. . . .[14]
>
> It has been taught: Rabbi said: The Torah was originally given to Israel in this [Ashurit] writing. *When they* [Israel] *sinned [she-chate'u],*[15] it was changed into Ra'ats:

But when they repented, the [Assyrian characters] were *re*-introduced. . . .

R. Simeon b. Eliezer said on the authority of R. Eliezer b. Parta, who spoke on the authority of R. Eleazar of Modin: This writing [of the law] was never changed. . . .

This passage presents a series of provocative historical-theological claims. The first, though disputed, is that the script (*ketav*) and language (*lashon*) of the Torah underwent changes and reversals through history, the period of Ezra being particularly significant and dynamic. The second claim is that, with regard to his textual emendations, Ezra possessed a stature and status equivalent to that of Moses,[16] demonstrating that the process of accepting revelation was an historically protracted one. The third claim, brought in the name of Rabbi, and the one most crucially relevant to our discussion, causally links the historical data of Israel's sinning repentance to alterations made in the script of the Torah. Nonetheless, this passage offered by Rabbi is not adequate to our theoretical needs because the claim in Sanhedrin is advanced only in regard to the script and language of the Torah, and not to its actual phraseology. We must look elsewhere in rabbinic literature for a more exact theological prototype for our modern resolution to the problem of the occasional discrepancy between *peshat* and *derash*. This paradigm is to be found in Bamidbar Rabbah III 13 (and parallels)[17] in a passage that enumerates and explains the presence of the ten *puncta extraordinaria,* or *eser nekudot,* in the Pentateuch. (Of the ten cases brought in this passage, we note here those most pertinent to our discussion:)

## THE TEN *PUNCTA EXTRAORDINARIA*

There is a point of the "vav" of "ve-Aharon" (Num. 3:39) to indicate that he was not of the number. . . . Another instance: "And he kissed him"—"*va-yishakehu*" (Gen. 33:4). There are points over the whole word to indicate that he (Esau) did not kiss him (Jacob) with all his heart. . . . Another example: "Or be in a journey afar off"—"*rechokah*" (Num. 9:10). This teaches that it was considered a distant journey even if it was only without the threshold of the Temple courtyard. Some say that even if a person was already near and was unclean he could not participate in the Passover sacrifice. . . . Another instance: "And a tenth ("*issaron*"), a tenth part you shall offer" (Num. 29:15). There is a point over the second "*vav*" of the first "*issaron*" used in connection with the first day of the festival. It teaches that there was one tenth only. Another instance: "The secret things belong unto the Lord our God; but the things that are revealed belong to us ("*lanu*") and to our children ("*u-lebanenu*") for ("*ad*") ever" (Deut. 29:28). Why are there points over "*lanu,*" "*u-lebanenu,*" and over the "*ayin*" of *ad?* God said unto them: "You have performed the precepts that have been revealed, and I, on My part, will make known to you the things which are secret."[18]

After exhausting the list of ten dotted passages and interpreting the significance of each, the text concludes with this crucial addendum:

Some give another reason why the dots are inserted ("*veyesh omrim*"). Ezra reasoned thus: If Elijah comes and asks: "Why have you written these words?" [i.e., "why have you included these suspect passages?"] I shall answer: "That is why I dotted these passages." And if he says to me: "You have done well in having written them," I shall erase the dots over them.

While the phrase "*ve-yesh omrim*" ("Some give another reason . . .") indicates that we are dealing with two disparate opinions in this passage, both opinions imply that the *peshat* of the Torah in these ten instances is, at the very least, misleading and must be either deleted or superseded by *derash*. According to the first opinion, Ezra lacked the authority *actually* to delete suspect words, but was able to mark such words with dots. The dotted passages must be modified, in some cases through commonplace homiletical exposition, in others through *derash* which clearly deviates from the *peshat,* in still others through interpretations which effectively, if not actually, delete a dotted word. According to the second opinion, Ezra had the right to delete a word if he was sure of its spuriousness: Elijah's question to Ezra, "Why have you written these words?" implies that Ezra possessed, *in potentia,* the power of textual emendation. In these ten instances, however, he was uncertain of the reliability of the text and therefore resorted to dots.

Startled by this assertion of Ezra's textual license, some readers have raised questions about the authenticity of this passage in *Bamidbar Rabbah.*[19] Such questions are unwarranted, however, since the passage is found in several locations in the rabbinic literature.[20] One may safely assume that the many commentators who have, without protestation, passed over the *Bamidbar* and these other passages have not been troubled by them. In fact, Rabbi J.F. Lisser (d. 1807), author of *Binyan Yehoshuah,* the standard commentary on *Avot de Rabbi Natan,* explicitly endorsed the authority of the passage and its theological implication: "Ezra the Scribe corrected the Torah, in the manner of scribal correction, as needed."[21] R. Meir Ish Shalom (1831–1908) also repudiated claims that the passage falls under the category of "he who has despised the word of the Lord" (Num. 15:31)[22] and is thus theologically heretical. In his *Bet Talmud,* he draws a distinction between the heretical belief that a verse in the Torah was written independently of divine revelation or recommendation and the theologically acceptable notion that God occasionally either instructs the prophet to add words to the scriptural text or approves of such an addition.[23] Heresy is at issue only if one claims that human intervention in the text was autonomous: if, for example, one believes that a scriptural verse was composed by Moses *of his own volition* (*moshe mi pi atsmo*).[24] Thus, R. Joseph b. Eliezer Tob Elem (Bonfils, b. 1335) offered a theological defense of Ibn Ezra's hint that certain verses in the Torah were authored after Moses.

> As he [Ibn Ezra] shows, Moses did not write this word, but Joshua or one of the other prophets wrote it. And since we must believe in the words of tradition and prophecy, what difference does it make whether Moses or some other

prophet wrote it, since the words of all of them are truth
and given through prophecy (i.e., divine revelation). . . .
The Torah warned "You should not add to it" (*bal tosif*)
only in regard to the number of commandments and their
fundamental principles, but not in regard to words.[25]

Another medieval scholar, Moses Alashkar (1466–1552), added, "It
makes no difference whether the Torah was given via Moses or via
Ezra in terms of whether sages can exposit upon it."[26] Thus, we
should interpret the *Bamidbar* passage to mean that Ezra made his
textual "corrections" with the approval of the divine author of
the Torah.

There is an historical development in the rabbinic account of
the *eser nekudot*.[27] In the earlier period, the *puncta* were considered
marks of erasure, indicating that a text is spurious and should be
deleted. By the time of Reb Yose, however, in the latter half of the
second century, some dots were understood to connote semi-*derashot*. In the period of the Gemara, the dots were understood almost
exclusively as marks of full-fledged *derashot*. As indicated in *Menachot* 87b, finally, the Stammaim—the anonymous authors of sections of the Talmud, who flourished soon after R. Ashi[28]—apparently considered *derashot* derived from dots to be idiosyncractic
expositions that need not be honored universally. They declared
that R. Meir did *not* utilize dots for the purpose of *derash*.[29]

This development is illustrated in the exegesis of the dot over
the *vav* of *issaron* ("one-tenth") in Numbers 29:15 [". . . and *onetenth* (*issaron issaron*) for each of the fourteen lambs"]. For *Sifrei*,
the dot marks a spurious word; one *issaron* should be excised. For
*BT Menachot* 87b, however, the dot marks a robust midrash (that
one may not measure with a three-tenths measure the meal offering
for a bullock or with a two-tenths measure for a ram). To take
another example, Reb Yose's interpretation of *rechokah* in Numbers 9:10 ["When any of you or of your posterity who are defiled by
a corpse or are on a *long* (*rechokah*) journey would offer a passover
sacrifice to the Lord . . ."][30] is not a *derasha* at all, but an emendation of the *peshat*. R. Yose's claim—that the diacritical mark over
the last letter, *he,* indicates that *rechokah* refers not to actual distance but to anywhere from "the threshold of the Forecourt and

beyond"—effectively deletes the entire word in Numbers 9:10, consistent with its absence in Numbers 9:13.

## A SOLUTION TO THE CONFLICT OF *PESHAT* AND *DERASH*

To advance our proposed solution to the textual conflict between *peshat* and *derash,* we follow the original, rather than the later rabbinic interpretation of the *puncta extraordinaire.* We read the dots exclusively as scribal symbols of erasure. Fearing the theological implications of there having been a "corrupt" text, the rabbis of the Talmud grew increasingly reluctant to interpret the dots in this way and resorted, instead, to sophisticated midrashic methods of "improving" the text. Restoring the original tradition of erasure leads us to draw a distinction between two cases of discrepancy between *peshat* and *derash.*

We say that the dots mark those texts whose errors could be repaired through the simple scribal mechanism of erasure. This leaves another class of texts whose more complex errors could have been repaired only through the restoration of missing information, and not through erasure alone. Among these are the cases cited at the beginning of this essay, "an eye for an eye" (Ex 21:24) and levirate marriage (Deut 25:54–56). Dots placed over these texts would not have conveyed sufficient information about how to restore the original *peshat.* Since he lacked sufficient authority to restore these texts, Ezra disseminated orally the method of exegesis through which the texts should be repaired. This is the oral tradition of *midrash halakhah.*

In sum, to advance our theory, we have integrated and extended the theological principles displayed in the texts of *Bamidbar Rabbah* and of *Sanhedrin 22a.* From the text of *Bamidbar Rabbah* comes the principle of the *puncta extraordinaire:* that, with divine approval, Ezra indicated where the text of the Torah should be emended. From *Sanhedrin* comes the additional principle of *chate'u yisrael:* that Ezra needed to emend the text in order to repair corruptions introduced during the period from Moses to Ezra.[31] Extending these principles, we conclude that, in *all* cases of discrepancy between *peshat* and halakhic *derash,* the *derash,* following Ezra's directives, restores the *peshat* that had been altered during the days of the First Temple. In simple cases, Ezra provided diacritical marks of erasure. For more complex cases, he initiated the tradition of *midrash halakhah.*

The notion of *chate'u yisrael* provides an historical foundation for our theory by stripping the First Temple period of halakhic authority. Of course, as the era of the prophets and of the emergence of Judaism's foundational principles, this period remains an integral link in "the chain of tradition" (*shalshelet ha-kabbalah*). The prophets predisposed the people to the undiluted and unattenuated service of God. Nonetheless, the prophets were not law-givers, and their efforts to elevate the religious standards of the people were not halakhic *per se.* The concept of *chate'u yisrael* thus enables a religious Jew to desacralize the First Temple period halakhically and regard it as a time of religious vacillation and scriptural mutability. In turn, from a rabbinic theological perspective, it imbues Ezra—to whom the activity of canonization is attributed by many critical Bible scholars[32]—with corrective and, indeed, revelatory authority. Even from a religious viewpoint, Ezra may legitimately be granted the power of canonization, or, in terms of our theory, of restoration.[33]

In response to our theory, readers may propose an alternative solution to the conflict of *peshat* and *derash.* Why not posit that the rabbis possessed the religious authority purposefully to revise the meaning of the biblical text through their creative exegesis? Why not recognize that even traditional Jewish scholars have asserted that the glory of the oral law rests in its capacity to "uproot" the written Torah and thus manipulate the authorial intention of the biblical text?[34] Such an attempt to dissolve the conflict between *peshat* and *derash* is theologically unacceptable for three reasons. First, it illegitimately blurs the systemic distinction between the written Torah and the oral law. Despite the occasional, hyperbolic extolment of the *torah she be'al peh* in the *aggadah,*[35] the written Torah is clearly granted superior and unchallengeable status within the Jewish legal system, particularly within its penal hierarchy. Second, whether one claims that the rabbis possessed divine license to amend the plain meaning of the written Torah, or that they adeptly adjusted the law to suit their changing socioeconomic conditions, this type of unrestrained and assertive halakhic revisionism, even on the part of the rabbis of the Talmud, sets a dangerous halakhic precedent. On the basis of such a precedent, every generation could claim the prerogative to amend the divine law in response to changing conditions and taste.[36] Such a misunderstanding of the character of rabbinic exegesis could result—and has resulted—in unwelcome and unfortunate halakhic decisions. Third, this alternative would lead to the unfeasible conclusion that the *halakhah* that governs our behavior today bears but slight resemblance to that commanded by God at Sinai. A religious Jew must believe, rather, that rabbinic *derash* preserves the continuity of tradition and safeguards the content of the Sinaitic revelation which is the fountainhead of all *halakhah*.

## A NON-MAXIMALIST THEORY OF REVELATION

There exist three rabbinic positions on the nature of the revelation of the oral law. Authors dealing with this subject have tended to blur the distinctions between the different positions by juxtaposing the relevant quotations from the Talmud without noting their mutually exclusive character. There seems to be a reluctance on the part of post-Talmudic scholars to admit to divided and varied opinion on such a sensitive issue as the nature of revelation. For understandable reasons they prefer a monolithic, uniform position which more and more has come to be defined by the extreme maximalist stance. In fact, however, no such rigid uniformity of opinion on the nature of revelation exists in rabbinic literature.

The three rabbinic positions may be classified as maximalist, intermediary and minimalistic. The *maximalist* position claims that God revealed to Moses on Mount Sinai the entire oral Torah consisting of all the legitimate arguments of, and all the legitimate solutions to, every issue that may arise, including "the comments that an astute student will someday make in the presence of his teacher."[37] Humanity merely needs to uncover them. True learning is rediscovering the given and the revealed.

The *intermediary* position claims that God revealed to Moses on Mount Sinai all the legitimate arguments of every issue that may arise but not their solutions. The solutions were left for human beings to offer, and whatever they offer becomes a part of "the words of the living God." This intermediary position is expressed quite forcefully in the following rabbinic midrash: "R. Yannai said: The words of the Torah were not given a clear-cut decision. For with every word which the Holy One, blessed be He, spoke to Moses, He offered him forty-nine arguments by which a thing may be proved clean, and forty-nine other arguments by which it may be proved unclean. When Moses asked, 'Master of the universe, in what way shall we know the true sense of a law?' God replied, 'The majority is to be followed—when a majority says it is unclean, it is unclean; when a majority says it is clean, it is clean.' "[38] Contradictions are thus built into revelation. Revelation was formulated within the framework of contradiction in the form of argumentation pro and con. No legitimate argument or solution can be in conflict with the divine opinion, for all such arguments and solutions constitute a part of God's opinion.

The *minimalistic* position claims that God revealed to Moses on Mount Sinai directions for humanity to follow and principles to implement, but not detailed stipulations. This minimalistic approach to revelation is advanced in *Midrash Tanchuma.*[39] Employing a *derash* on the word *kehaluto,* the midrash states that only principles, *kellalim,* and not all the details of the oral law, were revealed to Moses at Sinai. In contrast to the intermediary conception of revelation, in which only ultimate halakhic rulings were left for man to determine, the minimalistic position presents humanity with the opportunity, and authority, for the fleshing out of halakhic arguments and details from directional principles.

The minimalistic conception of the organic relationship between divinely-revealed principles and humanly-determined details is best reflected in the following, frequently quoted, but often misunderstood, rabbinic story: ". . . Moses went [into the academy of Rabbi Akiba] and sat down behind eight rows [of R. Akiba's disciples]. Not being able to follow their arguments he was ill at ease, but when they came to a certain subject and the disciples said to the master, 'Whence do you know it?' and the latter [R. Akiba] replied, 'It is a law given to Moses at Sinai,' Moses was comforted."[40] Though this story is sometimes interpreted to support the claim that each succeeding generation has an equal share in revelation, and that contemporary exegesis is not beholden to the past, it actually expresses the contrary notion that the arguments and details worked out by scholars like R. Akiba were grounded upon principles that had been revealed to Moses at Sinai.[41] Though Moses could not follow the argumentation in R. Akiba's academy, because these specific legal details had not been revealed to him, he was relieved to discover that the divinely-revealed principles were still being utilized as the wellspring of the legal system. The continuity and integrity of the revelatory process are affirmed, in this *aggadah,* within the conceptual framework of the minimalistic position. The halakhic arguments of R. Akiba, though unfamiliar to Moses, are the legitimate offspring of the original, foundational principles of revelation.

A diversity of views regarding the nature and scope of revelation underlies many statements throughout the Talmud. A prominent example is that of R. Zera in the name of Rava bar Zimuna: "If the earlier [scholars] (*rishonim*) were sons of angels, we are sons of man; and if the earlier [scholars] were sons of man, we are like asses."[42] R. Zera's reference to *rishonim* is to the earlier scholars who were the expositors of tradition and therefore the carriers and bearers of revelation. R. Zera's statement is, for one, a classic exposition of the concept of the inevitable decline of generations (*nitkatnu ha-dorot*). At the same time, the statement displays an uncertainty —unique in the Talmud—about how to characterize the earlier generations. Were they angelic or merely human? R. Zera's choice of metaphors suggests that his question may illustrate the rabbis' more typical uncertainties about how to characterize humanity's role in the revelatory process. According to the maximalistic position, even the earlier generations played a passive role, as mere recipients of God's revelation. In this case, their deserved title is "sons of man," and "we are like asses." According to the minimalistic position, however, the earlier generations were active participants: God gave humanity "a kab of wheat (from which to produce fine flour) and a bundle of flax (from which to produce cloth)";[43] humanity must, allegorically, strive to complete the process of baking and weaving, or, in real terms, contribute to and complete the process of revelation. On this view, humanity is both God's partner in the act of creation and God's associate in the task of revelation. In this case, the earlier generations must be "sons of angels," and "we are sons of man."

The notion that God's revelation permits and requires human argumentation is captured in the rabbinic *midrash* quoted earlier in the name of R. Yannai.[44] The governing principle of *acharei rabim le-hatot,* of following majority opinion in matters of dispute, reflects humanity's—here, the rabbis'—divinely-sanctioned role in halakhic decision making. If, however, revelation is therefore concretized in accordance with majority opinion, why should minority positions ever be recorded, rather than simply discarded and forgotten? Why maintain for posterity a textual record of rejected opinions?

According to R. Samson ben Abraham of Sens, one of the great French Tosafists (late twelfth to early thirteenth centuries), the Mishnah in *Eduyot* 1:5–6 offers two answers, corresponding implicitly to contrasting conceptions of revelation.[45] The first answer explains that the preservation of minority opinion justifies and legitimates the reversal of past decisions by future courts. An uncontested opinion could never be reversed. Therefore, the presence of a dissenting opinion creates an avenue of reopening the case and repealing a previous decision. A recorded minority position, though currently rejected, is thus not consigned permanently to halakhic oblivion. The second answer, presented by R. Judah, curtails the potential future usefulness of dissenting opinions. R. Judah explains that minority opinions are registered so that if a man shall say, "I hold such a tradition" (in opposition to the majority), another may reply to him, "You have but heard it as the view of so-and-so." The "tradition" in question can thus be labeled a minority position, nullifying its claim to halakhic legitimacy. For R. Judah, the label of "minority position" renders a dissenting opinion not potentially halakhically viable, but halakhically disabled and disqualified.

For R. Samson of Sens, the first answer corresponds with what we may call a non-maximalistic conception of revelation (encompassing both the intermediary and the minimalistic rabbinic positions). He explains that even though the minority position was not accepted previously, a later court may arise whose majority agrees with the minority position, and the dissenting position would then become legally binding. In each case, following the midrash in the name of R. Yannai, "the majority is to be followed." The avenues of judicial discretion must remain open because humanity's participation in the process of revelation is a continual one. For R. Samson of Sens, the second answer, of R. Judah, corresponds to a maximalistic conception of revelation. Once the divine will has been clearly determined according to majority opinion, all divergent positions are rendered null and void. Minority opinions are preserved precisely so that they will be recognized as halakhically invalid, or as non-revelatory. In this view, revelation is comprehensive, and humanity's role in the juridical process is therefore merely *pro forma.*

Our solution to the conflict of *peshat* and *derash* reinforces the non-maximalistic position. To be more precise, we adopt the intermediary conception of revelation. However, we believe that, because it does not limit interpretation to any finite set of principles, this intermediary conception offers more freedom of interpretation than the minimalistic one and may, in many cases, encompass it. We therefore present our position more generally as a non-maximalistic one. This position allows, on the one hand, for more flexibility than the strictly minimalistic one, since the latter reduces revelation to explicit, if general, principles that may themselves remain rigid. On the other hand, it provides a more adequate account of the role of controversy in the oral tradition than does the maximalistic position. It also provides a means of accounting for the halakhic status of minority opinion and, thereby, of the limits of majority rule. No human judgment, even if it follows the dictates of majority opinion, can be unequivocally true or certain. Thus, for example, an authoritative opinion in the Talmud claims that "one does not follow the majority in matters (disputes) of money,"[46] since the time-honored principle that the one who holds an object is presumed to own it is stronger than the evidence obtained from a majority of preceding cases. Another example is the celebrated rabbinic law that "with regard to saving life, one does not follow the majority."[47] At the same time, since it maintains the overarching principle of following consensus in matters of dispute (*acharei rabim le-hatot,*), the non-maximalistic conception of revelation still acknowledges the systemic halakhic boundaries that limit the abrogation of majority views. A consensus view on a legal issue, which had not been challenged by dissenting views when the issue originally arose, cannot validly be declared inoperative by a later generation. Unanimous positions of a previous generation cannot simply be abolished. Only when a new legal issue arises, which had not been addressed in previous halakhic discourse, does the requirement of recourse only to extant minority opinion become irrelevant.[48] Even then, however, the parameters of the original revelation exercise a systematic restraint on halakhic innovativeness.

The right of minority opinion is most dramatically expressed in two stories. The first is that of the dispute between R. Eliezer and R. Joshua, in which the Heavenly voice sides with R. Eliezer, but the law is decided according to R. Joshua, who declares that the Torah "is not in heaven!"[49] The second story is that of the dispute between God and His Heavenly Academy: a lesser known but more dramatic *aggadah,* in which God and His Heavenly Academy are disputing a halakhic question and summon Rabbah, a fourth century *amora,* to decide the case; Rabbah sides with God, but the law, as codified at the end of *Mishnah Negaim* 4, follows the Heavenly majority.[50] In *Peshat and Derash,* I argue that none of the customary interpretations of the story of R. Eliezer and R. Joshua[51] also account for the story of God and His Heavenly Academy.[52] I then suggest that the purpose of both of these stories was to promote the right of the minority to advocate its opinion by endowing the minority opinion with a divine imprimatur even as it is being rejected as a standard of practice. In both stores, God's opinion could not prevail in practice, since it was the opinion of the minority. Nevertheless, since "the stamp of God is truth," the minority opinions were in these cases true and thus divine opinions and, therefore, had to be tolerated intellectually as subjects of study. In the story of the Heavenly Voice, when the majority excommunicated R. Eliezer and prevented him from communicating with his students, God, as it were, became angry and "the world was smitten." R. Eliezer's minority opinion coincided with divine truth and, thus, could not be suppressed.

As these stories indicate, the practical meaning of revelation may not be consistent with its "objective" meaning, or the one stamped with God's approval. In this case, the practically non-binding meaning remains intellectually binding, as an objective truth, or truth-for-study. A non-maximalist view of revelation thus leads to dichotomous standards of exegetical truth: one standard reserved for practical law and one for intellectual endeavor. Halakhic homogeneity and intellectual latitude can thus be embraced simultaneously.

## A DICHOTOMOUS AND EVOLUTIONARY STANDARD OF TRUTH

Since, in Judaism, humans obey God's commandments most effectively through their behavior in the world, and since God's word is identified with absolute truth, it follows that any dichotomy between practice and scriptural exegesis leads necessarily to a two-tiered or dichotomous standard of truth, one pertaining to behavior and one to the activities of exegesis or study. This suggestion seems to contradict the traditional rabbinic stance, since the rabbis never explicitly affirmed a dichotomous standard of truth. They never explicitly divorced study from practice. Nevertheless, there are occasions where their discussions make more sense in terms of a two-tiered than of a single-tiered standard of truth.

The clearest example is the law pertaining to the *zaken mamreh,* "the elder that rebels against the decision of the court." *Mishnah Sanhedrin* 11:2 states, "If the elder has returned to his city" (after a visit to the [highest] court, situated in the chamber of hewn stone in the temple in Jerusalem, where he heard a decision against his opinion) "and again taught as he was wont to teach, he is *not* yet culpable; but if he gave a (practical) decision [*pesak*] concerning what should be done, he is culpable." I take that to mean that "the elder that rebels against the decision of the court," even after his visit to Jerusalem, could continue to teach very much the same way he was wont to. When the Mishnah says "he is not culpable," it does not mean that he is only capitally not culpable, but also that he is not culpable of censure, that he can freely advocate his position.[53] What he cannot do is to behave according to his position and, more importantly, to instruct others to follow him. It appears, then, that although the view of the elder went against both the majority of his colleagues and the judges of the highest court situated in the temple, he was free to express his opinion—as a matter of study, but not as a matter of practice.

In the celebrated case presented in *Mishnah Rosh Hashanah* 2:8–9, R. Joshua still insisted on the correctness of his position, even after he celebrated the holy days according to the calendar reckoning of his opponent, R. Gamliel. He merely followed R. Gamliel's reckoning in practice, while remaining opposed to it in theory. The simplest interpretation of this passage is that the rabbis hinted at a dichotomy between the standards of truth that pertain to practice and to study. The same interpretation applies to several other passages: for example, Akabya ben Mahalalel's clinging steadfastly to his own tradition, against the opinion of the majority (*Mishnah Eduyot* 5:7); and the dramatic dispute between R. Eliezer and R. Joshua (*BT Baba Metsia* 59b).[54]

As we noted earlier, the Talmud retains minority opinions, even though halakhic disputes are decided by majority opinion, according to the principle of *acharei rabim le-hatot*.[55] Following the non-maximalistic conception of revelation, these minority opinions remain potentially viable in some other context of legal decision making. In a system governed by a two-tiered standard of truth, the minority opinion could, in fact, be true according to one standard, the majority opinion true according to another. I believe such a standard is implied by all the stories we have just mentioned, as well as the previously mentioned, and even more dramatic, story about the dispute in Heaven between the Holy One, blessed be He, and the entire Heavenly Academy.[56] In these cases, the law ultimately went according to the majority and against God. Nonetheless, "the stamp of God is truth" (*BT Shabbat* 55a); God's own opinion in this case could not be untrue. The simplest way to account for the apparent paradox is to refer to a two-tiered standard: one truth for the opinion of the majority, who determine the *halakhah,* and another truth for the opinion of God, whose truth is the truth of study as opposed to practice. This is the standard of truth which guides those who study *Torah lishmah,* "for its own sake." Guided by such a standard, the Rashbam (d. 1174), one of the greatest *poskim* (adjudicators) of his time, often explained the text against the practical *halakhah* to which he strictly adhered. He believed that this type of commentary, free of the restraints of practical *halakhah*, epitomized the study of Torah, which is, in rabbinic law, a commandment by itself and therefore ought not to be reduced to a means of fulfilling other commandments.

The notion of a standard of truth for study, independently of practice, accredits critical textual scholarship—that is, examining both the Bible and the Talmud independently of traditional or *halakhic* interpretations—as a *bonafide* religious activity. As I have argued elsewhere, "when one studies the Bible critically, that is, according to the *peshat*, with no intention of changing practical *halakhah*, one is fulfilling the commandment to study Torah to a higher degree than when one is studying the same law according to traditional interpretation. This is especially true if the *peshat* proves to be in contrast with traditional interpretation (as, for instance, interpreting "an eye for an eye" literally, as opposed to [its referring to] monetary compensation). This learning is fuller, purer, having no vested interest other than the welfare of learning."[57]

If the rabbis failed to enunciate such a two-tiered standard, it is because they did not inhabit a universe of discourse in which this standard was an explicit option. We do inhabit such a universe, however, and for those of us who adopt a non-maximalistic conception of revelation, such a standard is not only an option, but requisite. The universe of discourse to which I refer is our evolutionary rather than synchronic conception of the contexts in terms of which interpretation has meaning. With the evolutionary conception comes a diminished conception of textual yield. Let me explain these notions briefly.

Our attentiveness to a "conflict" between *peshat* and *derash* is itself an index of the difference between our exegetical posture and that of the rabbis of the Talmud. When confronting a legal text whose *peshat* needed to be revised, they "read-in" to the text a different meaning, which they generally considered the true meaning of the text.

This technique of "reading-in" is evident in the cases we considered at the outset of this essay: for example, the rabbis' interpreting "an eye for eye" (Ex 21:24) to mean monetary compensation, or identifying the "first son" in the levirate marriage of Deuteronomy 25:5–6 with the "firstborn brother" rather than the "firstborn child." The rabbis did not share our belief that the simple meaning is necessarily superior and did not believe "reading-in" violated the integrity of a text, as long as the whole verse was involved and no part of it was taken out of its rhetorical context.[58] In the famous Talmudic statement "no one text can be deprived of its *peshat*" (*ein mikra yotseh midei peshuto*),[59] *peshat* should not be understood as "literal" meaning, as opposed to "applied" meaning, or *derash,* but as "context": a text cannot be torn out of its context.[60] Concerned with textual context, rather than historical context, the rabbis adopted a synchronic rather than a diachronic, or time-bound, conception of the context of exegesis: in our terms, they were not averse to contemporizing or anachronistic readings.

For the medieval rabbis, however, "reading-in" strains the text and, even when it resolves problems of superfluity or contextualism, it cannot exhaust the text's full meaning; the "plain meaning" must also be retained. Open to the influence of Arabic philosophy, these scholars began, in the tenth century, to argue for the superiority of *peshat* over *derash,* reinterpreting the term *peshat* to refer to "plain meaning," as opposed to "context." Some of the scholars read this interpretation back into the rabbinic literature, claiming that the rabbis of the Talmud were usually aware that "reading-in" altered the plain-meaning in favor of rabbinically instituted or traditional interpretations. They claimed that, in such cases, the rabbis cited biblical texts merely as *asmakhtot,* or "supports" brought in after the fact. Contrary to the claims of the medieval scholars, however, the word *asmakhta* is never employed in Talmudic sources in this way. In the early fifth century, relatively late in the Talmudic period, the Amoraim reacted to the increasing number of rabbinic ordinances that appeared with biblical prooftexts. They introduced the word *asmakhta* at that time to indicate that, in such situations, a law contained a biblical prooftext, yet behaved like a law which was rabbinically, rather than biblically, instituted. Prior to that time, rabbinic ordinances or their equivalents were considered biblically charged since, according to the general understanding of Deuteronomy 17:8–12, the Bible permitted the sages to institute new laws.

A decided preference for *peshat* was therefore a medieval phenomenon. Nonetheless, there were intimations of this preference, faint stirrings, as early as the first century, when the sages contemporary with R. Joshua drew a clear distinction between biblical and rabbinic injunctions (see *Mishnah Yadaim* 3:2),[61] and when R. Joshua used the term *vadai* in the sense of literal meaning.[62] Subsequently, the number of rabbinic ordinances increased, not only because the rabbis added new ordinances, but also because many laws previously considered biblical were gradually redesignated rabbinic. The practice of "reading-in" declined during the time of the Amoraim. Rava, a fourth century Amora, determined that certain laws, although contained within biblical expositions, were nonetheless traditions which the rabbis later attached to verses of the Bible. In the fifth century, R. Ashi introduced the term *asmakhta,* as previously noted, but used it only once. The Stammaim, the anonymous authors of sections of the Talmud, utilized the word close to twenty-five times. By five hundred years later, the term had acquired its medieval meaning.

Throughout these years of rabbinic scholarship, there was thus a gradual evolution in the direction of greater respect for textual integrity and, at the same time, of diminished textual yield.[63] Modern scholarship continues this evolution, excluding "reading-in" altogether and insisting that the plain meaning alone is reliable—or, now, in its "postmodern" phase, questioning the reliability of the plain meaning itself. For the modern, rabbinic scholar, the conflict between *peshat* and *derash* is therefore problematic in a way it was not for the rabbis of the Talmud. At the same time, the modern rabbinic scholar's conception of evolutionary, or time-bound, exegesis helps resolve the problem by offering an evolutionary context for a two-tiered standard of truth. As I wrote on another occasion,

> a modern religious Jew must study Bible in a dual manner, according to the perception fitting the evolutionary rung of his/her ancestors and according to the perception fitting the evolutionary rung of its own. . . . Pertaining to observance, the modern religious Jew has to follow the interpretation of those to whom the initial revelation was given. God spoke to them in their language, according to their

mode of interpretation. Pertaining to exegesis, he or she remains a child of her age, following the standards of his or her time.[64]

## AN EDITORIAL SUMMARY OF HALIVNI'S ARGUMENT

Modern rabbinical scholars may resolve the conflict they perceive between *peshat* and *derash* by adopting the following interpretive conceptions and theories:

● *an evolutionary conception of rabbinic text interpretation.*

The conflict between *peshat* and *derash* is problematic for the modern rabbinic scholar, for whom exegesis is time-bound and thus specific to some particular context within the evolution of rabbinic text interpretation. For the rabbis of the Talmud, exegesis was not time-bound, and the contexts of interpretation were synchronic, rather than evolutionary. For that reason, the rabbis were able to practice "reading-in" as a means of identifying, rather than distorting, the *peshat* of a biblical text. For them, the *peshat* referred to the "contextual" meaning of a text, rather than the "plain," as opposed to the "applied" meaning. Particularly after the third, and again after the fifth centuries, the rabbis displayed some concerns about potential conflicts between such levels of meaning. Until the tenth century, however, rabbinical commentators failed to adopt the distinction between *peshat* and *derash* as a normative hermeneutical criterion.

● *a theory about rabbinic exegesis: that, in cases of explicit conflict between peshat and midrash halakhah, the midrash halakhah is to be seen as restoring the original text of Torah.*

● *a theory about scriptural exegesis: that the puncta extraordinaire are to be seen as signs of erasure and as indices of Ezra's role in the revelatory process.*

According to selected rabbinic sources, the previously noted claim of the rabbis has its *scriptural basis* in a theory about the *puncta extraordinaire.* They are to be interpreted exclusively as signs of erasure, instituted by Ezra and effected in the rabbis' restorative *midrash halakhah.* This leaves us with those cases of restorative *derash* for which there are no corresponding *puncta.* We say that, in those cases, Ezra instituted changes which were too complex to be noted merely by signs of erasure; he transmitted the changes through the oral tradition.

● *as an explanatory corollary, an historical theory of chate'u yisrael.*

According to selected rabbinic sources, Ezra's role in the revelatory process was made necessary by *chate'u yisrael:* the sins of Israel in the First Temple period, which sins nullified the halakhic force of the scriptural texts transmitted through this period. Ezra's responsibility was to correct the corrupted text of scripture he received, restore the original *peshat,* and, in these ways, participate in the revelatory process. Halivni[65] summarizes his theory as follows:

> For the religious Jew, God's revelation to Moses on Mount Sinai establishes two principles: that there is one God and that, to know God, the Jew must observe the *halakhah.* For the critical scholar, literary-historical evidence shows that, during the period of the First Temple, the children of Israel could not, in fact, accept these principles and were given, instead, to idolatrous practices. These practices were curtailed only in the time of Ezra. From their failure to maintain the *halakhah,* we infer that the Israelites of the First Temple period would also have neglected to maintain the texts of the Torah assiduously. From the fact that he restored the Mosaic principles of monotheism and *halakhah,* we infer that Ezra would also have restored the correct text of the Torah. Part of his restorative activity was to institute the tradition of *midrash halakhah.* Since Ezra's restorative activities were divinely authorized, we conclude that the institution of *midrash halakhah* was divinely authorized as well. The rabbis' midrashic activity continues and perfects this institution.

● *a two-tiered standard of exegetical truth.*

The problem of a conflict between *peshat* and *derash for medieval and modern rabbinic scholars* is to be resolved by noting the different standards of truth—intimated in some Talmudic passages, but never enunciated—which guide the study of Torah *lishmah* and the study of Torah for the sake of *halakhic* practice. The latter is informed by the principle of *acharei rabim lehatot,* of the rule of the majority opinion; the former, by the ideal of a single *peshat,* emblem of that truth which is the seal of God. (In terms of the evolutionary conception of rabbinic interpretation, each generation sees itself as arbiter of halakhic standards; its judgments bracket the question of evolution. On the other hand, the scholarly standard is of a single truth, with respect to which ideal it measures the evolution of both halakhic and scholarly exegeses.)

● *a non-maximalistic conception of revelation.*

The theory of a two-tiered standard of truth supports a non-maximalistic conception of revelation. According to the preferred, intermediary statement of this conception, God revealed to Moses all the legitimate arguments of every issue that may arise but not their solutions, which are left for future interpreters to determine, nor the principles to be adopted in arriving at those solutions. This statement enables us to account for the potential, future, halakhic viability of minority positions. According to the theory of a two-tiered standard of truth, a minority opinion could represent the scriptural *peshat* ("God's truth"), as opposed to interpretations offered in the interest of *halakhah* (the truth of the majority).

## NOTES

1. Benedict de Spinoza, *A Theologico-Political Treatise,* trans. R.H.M. Elwes (New York: Dover Publications, 1951), pp. 114–19. See also I. Husik, "Maimonides and Spinoza on the Interpretation of the Bible," in *Philosophical Essays,* ed. M.C. Nahm and L. Strauss (Oxford: B. Blackwell, 1952), pp. 141–59.

2. A. Geiger, "Das Verhältnis des naturlichen Schriftsinnes zur talmudischen Schriftdeutung," in *Wissenschaftliche Zeitschrift für jüdische Theologie* 5 (1844): 234–59. See also D. Weiss Halivni, *Midrash, Mishnah, and Gemara* (Cambridge: Harvard University Press, 1986), p. 122 n17.

3. See in particular Saadya ben Joseph, *The Book of Beliefs and Opinions,* trans. S. Rosenblatt (New Haven: Yale University Press, 1948), pp. 157–58.

4. K. Kahana in the introduction to D.Z. Hoffman's *Commen-*

*tary on Deuteronomy* (Tel Aviv: Netzach Press, 1960), p. 15 (Hebrew).

5. See *Mekhilta,* vol. 3, Tractate *Nezikin* (in reference to Ex 21:24), trans. Lauterbach, pp. 67–88; and BT *Baba Kama* 83b–84a.

6. See *Sifrei Deut.* 289, p. 307 in Finkelstein's edition and *B.T. Yevamot* 24a.

7. See *Mekhilta,* vol. 1, Tractate *Pischa,* parsha 4, pp. 28–33.

8. For details on the implementation of this principle, see my *Mekorot u-Mesorot* (Jerusalem: Jewish Theological Seminary, 1982), *Shabbat,* pp. 110–13.

9. See *Mekhilta,* vol. 1, Tractate *Pischa,* parsha 4, p. 32.

10. See *BT Baba Bat.* 15a.

11. In this context, the word *koheinu* refers to the priests in their role as teachers or guardians of the Torah (cf. Jer 2:8; Mal 2:7; Hag 2:11). They are held accountable for neglecting their duty to preserve the text of the Torah. Further evidence about the neglect of the scriptural text is implied by Neh 8. The absence of public, communal reading of the Torah meant that it was in the guardianship of various parties, whose separateness may have fostered textual multiplicity and adulteration. Ezra's efforts were thus aimed at communal and scriptural consolidation and uniformity.

12. For the former, see Neh 8:17, and for the latter, see 2 Kgs 23:22.

13. A case in point is the fast of the seventeenth of Tamuz which, according to *Mishnah Taanit* 4:6, is based, for one, on the date of the breaching of the city (*havka ha-ir*). However, in the text of Jer 52:6–7, the ninth of Tamuz is given as the date of the breaching. The Palestinian Talmud *Taanit* refers to this discrepancy as *kilkul chesbon,* "a mistaken calculation." The Tosafot (the collections of supercommentaries to Rashi's Talmudic commentaries, compiled principally during the twelfth through fourteenth centuries) and even more strongly the Rashba (Rabbi Solomon ben Abraham Adret, 1235–1310), explain the Palestinian Talmud to mean that, while the actual breaching took place on the 17th (making our fast day consistent with the actual occurrence), people mistook the date (identifying it with the 9th) and that our text follows the mistaken notion of the people (see, for example, the Tosafot to *BT Rosh Hashanah* 18: *zeh tisha b'tammuz*). In this view, the Yerushalmi

tacitly acknowledged that our text is not always halakhically binding.

14. The *Tosefta* and *PT* mention here, in accord with the statement of Mar Zutra, that both script and language were changed by Ezra.

15. Having been idolatrous throughout the First Temple period —Rashi. See, however, Neh 9:32, *Otsar ha-Geonim,* and the comments of the Ran [R. Nissim ben Reuben Gerondi, d. 1380].

16. There are also rabbinic passages, such as in *BT Sukkah* 20a, which implicitly minimize Ezra's role vis-à-vis the text of the Torah by comparing it to the roles of Hillel and R. Chiya and his sons, rather than to that of Moses (see, however, *Tosefta Sotah* 13:4 and parallels). See also *BT Zevachim* 62a and Josephus, *Antiquities,* vol. XI, pp. 136–59, where Ezra is called the reader of the laws of God.

17. The passage is quoted from *Bamidbar Rabbah* because this text is the preferred one. Cf. *Avot de Rabbi Natan,* n. I, ch. 34, 50b and II, ch. 37, 49a, ed. Schechter; *Sifrei Numbers,* piskha 69, pp. 64ff, ed. Horovitz; *Midrash Mishlei* XXVI 24, 50a, ed. Buber. See also *Batei Midrashot,* vol. II, ed. Wertheimer (Jerusalem 1959, p. 490).

18. There are five more instances of dotted words in the Hebrew Bible, but these lie outside the Pentateuch: 2 Sam 19:20; Ez 41:20 and 46:22; Is 44:9; and Ps 27:13. In Ez 41:20–21, *ha-heichal* is mentioned twice and the dot over the first indicates erasure. In Ez 46:22, as well as in Is 44:9 and Ps 27:13, the words *could* be deleted and the sense of the verse still be retained, but the deletion of the dotted word in 2 Sam 19:20 (*yatsa*) would disturb the flow of the verse.

19. For example, Azariah de Rossi (1511–1578) concluded, in his *Meor Enayim* (ed. Cassel, ch. 19, p. 232), that this text must have been written by a deviant student without his teacher's knowledge and therefore lacks authority and credibility. More recently, Rabbi Moshe Feinstein has declared, even more unequivocally, that this rabbinic passage represents an unadulterated heresy in attributing to Ezra such freedoms with the text of the Torah. He concluded that the text was added by *maskilim* [secularizers] and must be excised. See *Iggeret Moshe,* Yoreh Deah, vol. III, nos. 114–15. R. Feinstein was apparently not aware of the location of this rabbinic passage in several parallel sources, including the *Bamidbar Rabbah* version

noted above. His reaction can be contrasted fruitfully with that of the Netsiv, Rabbi N.Z.Y. Berlin (1817–1893) who, in his *Emek ha-Netsiv* on *be ha'alotekha,* p. 219, only described the passage as "peculiar," and not heretical. He was familiar with its location in parallel sources and thus realized that its excision was not a legitimate option.

20. See *Pirkei de Rabbenu ha-Kadosh,* vol. III, ed. L. Greenhut (Jerusalem, 1989), p. 86; *Midrash Chaserot ve-Yeterot,* ed. A. Marmorstein (London, 1918), pp. 32–33; *Arukh, c.v., "nakud"; Machzor Vitry,* ed. S. Horowitz (Nurnberg, 1933), p. 685; and also *Hadar Zekenim* (Livorna, 1849), which consists of *Baalei ha-Tosafot* and *Perushei ha-Rosh,* for two references to the passage in Tosafistic literature.

21. J.F. Lisser, *Binyan Yehoshuah* (Dyhernfurt, 1788). Lisser based his own commentary on what R. Meir Eisenstadt (1670–1744), the author of *Panim Meirot,* wrote in his book *Kotnot Or,* where the relevant passage from *Avot de Rabbi Natan* is quoted and explained.

22. *BT Sanhedrin* 99a and parallels.

23. *Bet Talmud,* vol. I, eds. I.H. Weiss and M. Friedmann (Vienna, 1881), p. 234–38. See also Chaim Hirschensohn, *Malki ba Kodesh,* vol. II (Hoboken, 1921), p. 215.

24. Cf. the eighth principle of Maimonides' thirteen principles of faith, as stated in his commentary to the *Mishnah Sanhedrin,* ch. 10.

25. R. Joseph b. Eliezer Tob Elem, *Tsofnat Pa'aneakh* (Berlin, 1912), pp. 91–92, in his supercommentary on Ibn Ezra's commentary on Gen 12:6 ("The Canaanites were then in the land").

26. Moses Alashkar, *Responsum No. 74.*

27. This accounts for the inconsistencies that can be discerned within the biblical and Talmudic commentaries concerning the significance of the *eser nekudot.* For examples of such inconsistencies, compare Rashi's comments on *BT Pesachim* 93b, s.v., *"nakod,"* with his comment on *BT Baba Metsia 87a,* s.v., *"limdah";* and the *Mizrachi* and *Gur Aryeh* on the respective verses.

28. After 427 C.E.

29. Cf. the commentary of Ramban to Num 9:10.

30. From Mishnah *Pesachim* 9:2, on one of the ten instances of *puncta extraordinaria.*

31. The principle of *chate'u yisrael* is also alluded to directly in *b.Ned.* 22b ("had not Israel sinned, only the Pentateuch and the book of Joshua would have been given to them") and indirectly in *Mishna Parah* 3:5 (indicating that no red heifers were prepared between the careers of Moses and Ezra, the Mishnah implies that the intervening period was one of ritual carelessness and impurity).

32. For the latest scholarly treatment of Ezra's role, see John Barton, *Oracles of God* (Oxford: Oxford University Press, 1986), p. 23: "Nearly all modern scholars agree that the . . . Torah was the first of three divisions to be accorded canonical status, and in this, many would think Ezra may well have been at least partially instrumental, though naturally the authority of most of the Pentateuch was agreed upon before this work."

33. Rabbinic sources such as *BT Baba Batra* 14b acknowledge Ezra's role in canonizing the prophetic books (including, for example, the decision to confine the prophecies of Obadiah to only a page and a half of written text). For the religious Jew, Ezra must therefore be credited with prophetic insight.

34. For an example of this type of traditionalist theology, see the commentary of the Gaon of Vilna at the beginning of "*mishpatim.*"

35. See *PT Berakhot* 1:4 and parallels.

36. Indeed, early leaders of the reform movement in the nineteenth century perceived themselves as heirs and successors to the rabbis of the Talmud. Thus the most perceptive and learned reformer, Abraham Geiger, saw in the work of the reformers "the most organic continuation of the activities of the Rabbis" (I. Heinemman, *Ta'amei ha-Mitsvot,* vol. II, Jerusalem, 1956, p. 171).

37. *PT Peah* 17a.

38. *Midrash Tehillim* 12:4.

39. *Ki Tisah* 16.

40. *BT Menachot* 29b.

41. That this story reflects a minimalistic, and not a maximalistic, conception of revelation has already been noted by R. Zev Einhorn in his commentary on *Midrash Rabbah, Chukat* (Num 19:6).

42. *BT Shabbat* 112b; *PT Demai* 1:3.

43. *Tana DeBei Eliyahu Zuta,* Ch. 2.

44. Cf. above, p. 12.

45. *Tosafot Shanz.*

46. *BT Baba Kama* 27b and parallels.

47. *BT Yoma* 84b.

48. For the *posek* (jurist) who espouses a maximalistic position, the solution to a new halakhic issue must already have been revealed and can thus be found within the compass of previous halakhic discourse. For the non-maximalist, the solution to a new halakhic issue has not been revealed and is thus not predetermined.

49. *BT Baba Metsia* 59b. For readers unfamiliar with these stories, a fuller account follows:

> . . . It has been taught: On that day R. Eliezer brought forward every imaginable argument, but they did not accept them. So he said to them: "If the halakhah agrees with me, let this carob tree prove it!" Thereupon the carob tree was torn a hundred cubits out of its place—others affirm, four hundred cubits. "No proof can be brought from a carob tree," they retorted. Again he said to them: "If the halakhah agrees with me, let the stream of water prove it!" Whereupon the stream of water flowed backwards. "No proof can be brought from a stream of water," they rejoined. Again he urged: "If the halakhah agrees with me, let the walls of the schoolhouse prove it," whereupon the walls inclined to fall. But R. Joshua rebuked them, saying, "When scholars are engaged in a halakhic dispute, what concern is it of yours?" Hence the walls did not fall, in honor of R. Joshua, nor did they return to their upright position, in honor of R. Eliezer; and they are still standing thus inclined. Again he said to them, "If the halakhah agrees with me, let it be proved from Heaven!" Whereupon a Heavenly Voice cried out: "Why do you dispute with R. Eliezer, seeing that in all matters the halakhah agrees with him?" But R. Joshua arose and exclaimed: "It is not in heaven" (Deut. 30:12). What did he mean by this? Said R. Jeremiah: "That the Torah had already been given

at Mount Sinai [and is thus no longer in heaven]. We pay no attention to a Heavenly Voice, because You have long since written in the Torah at Mount Sinai, "One must incline after the majority" (Ex. 23). . . .

50.  *BT Baba Metsia* 86a:

Now, they were disputing in the Heavenly Academy thus: If the bright spot preceded the white hair, he is unclean; if the reverse, he is clean. If the order is in doubt—the Holy One, blessed be He, ruled, "He is clean," while the entire Heavenly Academy maintained, "He is unclean." "Who shall decide it?" they asked.—Rabbah b. Nachmani; for he said, "I am pre-eminent in the laws of leprosy and tents." A messenger was sent for him, but the Angel of Death could not approach him, because he did not interrupt his studies [even for a moment]. In the meantime, a wind blew and caused a rustling in the bushes, and he imagined it to be a troop of soldiers. "Let me die," he exclaimed, "rather than be delivered into the hands of the State." As he was dying, he exclaimed, "Clean, clean!" Then a Heavenly Voice cried out, "Happy are you, O Rabbah b. Nachmani, whose body is pure and whose soul has departed in purity!"

51.  For example, some commentators claim that the purpose of the story was to extol the greatness of R. Eliezer. Others claim its purpose was to preserve the independence of the judicial system, including majority rule, by safeguarding it against outside encroachment, even that of divine intervention. Still others see in the story a triumph of the human over the divine.

52.  The latter story does not explicitly mention that the law was decided according to the majority.

53.  Cf. R.M. Hakohen, *Yad Malakhi,* passage 526.

54.  Also at the beginning of the third chapter of *PT Moed Katan.* See above, p. 125. For the literature on this story, see Y. Englard, *Shenaton ha-Mishpat ha-Ivri* (Jerusalem: The Institute for the

Study of Mishpat Ivri, 1974), vol. 1, pp. 45–56. See also R.D. Lurya's *Introduction to Pirkei D'Rabbi Eliezer.*

55. See above, p. 123.

56. In *BT Baba Metsia* 86a. See above, p. 125.

57. "An Unscientific Postscript," in *The Seminary at One Hundred,* Centennial Volume of the Jewish Theological Seminary of America (New York, 1987), p. 276.

58. This, then, is the reason for the lack of unambiguous Talmudic *proof* for our proposed solution to the conflict of *peshat* and *derash.* Equipped with our modern exegetical sensibility, we perceive more acutely than did the rabbis of the Talmud the problem of the occasional discrepancy between *peshat* and *derash.* If they had shared this perception, there probably *would* have been more explicit Talmudic reference to the historical sequence we have outlined. Recognizing the dynamic of time-bound exegesis, we must be satisfied with the evidence for our theory yielded by analogical reasoning.

59. *Shabbat* 63a, *Yevamot* 11b and 24a.

60. A good example is *BT Ketuvot* 111b, where the Talmud asks, after R. Dimi expounded non-literally the two verses of Genesis 49:11–12 minus the last word, "What is the *peshat* of the verse?" The Talmud then proceeds to give an even more non-literal exposition, but one which includes also the last word. There, *peshat* clearly refers to a "continuation" of the last word. Etymologically, the root *psht* means "extension, continuation, context."

61. ". . . . They [the sages] answered, You may infer nothing about the words of the Law from the words of the Scribes, and nothing about the words of the Scribes from the words of Law . . . ."

62. Cf. W. Bacher, *Die exegetische Terminologie der jüdische Traditionsliteratur* (Leipzig: J.C. Hinrichs, 1905), *s.v. vadai,* p. 60. See also the gloss of R.S. Strashun to *Midrash Rabbah,* Genesis, Vilna ed, 98:4.

63. That is, for the earlier scholars, the text displayed a multiplicity of warranted meanings, while, for the more recent scholars, warranted meanings may be reduced to one.

64. "An Unscientific Postscript," p. 276. To a religious Jew, evolution, too, is a divine creation ("in the beginning, God created

heaven and earth"—he created everything, including the means of creation). God created the evolutionary, or time-bound, mode of perception, indicating to humanity that he wants his word to be intellectually understood by them in accordance with their respective evolutionary rungs.

65. In a recent conversation.

# Chapter Five

# THE TURN TO COMMENTARY IN ANCIENT JUDAISM: THE CASE OF *SIFRE* DEUTERONOMY[1]

## STEVEN FRAADE

Although scriptural interpretation is as old as scripture itself,[2] the turn to scriptural commentary as a medium of such interpretation was first evidenced, both in Palestine and in the Jewish diaspora, only near the end of the Second Temple period (first century B.C.E.–first century C.E.), and even then not very extensively. Thus, when several rabbinic scriptural commentaries first appeared in literary form in the mid-third century C.E., they had few formal antecedents, even as they drew on a wealth of interpretive traditions extending far back into Second Temple times, perhaps even as far back as when biblical formation and interpretation were as yet indistinguishable. In this essay, I examine this rabbinic turn to commentary, as evidenced in the *Sifre,* the first extant commentary to the biblical book of Deuteronomy and one of our earliest compilations of rabbinic exegesis. I examine the *Sifre* against the backdrop of its only known antecedents as biblical commentary: the prophetic *pěšārîm* of the Dead Sea sectaries and the allegorical commentaries of the Jewish philosopher-exegete Philo of Alexandria. Since, in antiquity as today, there were many other ways to interpret a text, I wish to ask: Why might one choose commentary as the medium for such communication? In asking this question in specific relation to the *Sifre,* I wish to examine the nature, function, and purpose of such a work of ancient commentary: What, how, and with whom does it seek to communicate? To ask the question in this way is to inquire after the literary form and sociohistorical function of a commentary, and especially after the interrelation of this form and function. Since, as I shall argue, modern critical commentary to such texts of ancient traditional commentary is an appropriate medium for seeking to understand their performative dynamics, the above questions will ring doubly.

I begin with a working definition of commentary as "a systematic series of explanations or interpretations (as of a writing)."[3] Of course, this definition tells us nothing of the methods or forms employed by such interpretations; how closely and in what manner they adhere to the text being interpreted or to one another; or the attitude of their authors toward that base-text, or toward their intended audience. For all of these we can imagine many possibilities. But all commentaries so defined may be said to exhibit the following structural traits: they begin with an extended base-text, of which they designate successive subunits for exegetical attention, to each of which they attach a comment or chain of comments distinct from the base-text, to which the commentary sooner or later returns in order to take up the next selected subunit in sequence. Thus, depending on how much of the base-text it comments upon, the overall movement of the commentary follows to some degree the progression of the base-text to which it attends. Herein lies what might be viewed as commentary's paradoxical nature: it atomizes its base-text, even as that base-text provides the overall structural framework by which a collection of otherwise discrete and sometimes discordant comments acquire a *degree* of progressive continuity and external coherence.

Although today we might take for granted the commentary form as a way of interpreting a text, especially of scripture, it does not appear to have been the favored mode of scriptural interpretation in postbiblical but prerabbinic varieties of Judaism. The majority of that interpretation took the form of what has been called "rewritten Bible,"[4] which paraphrased the biblical text, blurring the distinction between that text and its interpretation. It was as if the biblical text itself were replaced by its interpretive retelling. In some cases the "rewritten Bible" followed the order of the biblical text upon which it appears to be based, filling in what are understood to be its gaps and clarifying what are understood to be its ambiguities.[5] But in other cases the "rewritten Bible" substantially reworked the biblical order, blending together biblical texts from different locations and mixing together biblical citation with biblical paraphrase in such a way as to conceal both the words of the biblical text and its order within its retelling. The authority for such retelling was often pseudepigraphically attributed to an inspired biblical figure (e.g. Enoch) or to God himself (as in the *Temple Scroll*), thereby claiming the status of actual revelation for what to us appears as a retelling.

Another form which also needs to be distinguished from the commentary is that of the homily or sermon. A preacher or teacher would begin with a particular biblical verse, story, or motif and weave around it a web of biblical citations, allusions, and interpretations, the organizing and unifying principle of which would be the thematic message he sought to convey. While such a homily might depend heavily on biblical language and image for its rhetorical force, it would not direct its audience's attention to any successive biblical text per se.

Similarly, the books of the New Testament contain extensive interpretations of the Hebrew Bible. However, their outer structure is not that of commenting on scripture, but rather, in the case of the gospels, of telling the story of Jesus' life and death, or, in the case of Acts and the Pauline letters, of relating how his teachings were spread and the church established after his death. This is not to minimize the role of scriptural interpretation in these writings but rather to stress that fragmented biblical interpretation and imagery are here incorporated into the structure of a story, rather than fragmented stories being incorporated into the structure of scriptural commentary, as is often the case in rabbinic commentary.

Against this backdrop and in preparation for our discussion of the *Sifre*'s commentary, it is important to examine briefly what I have previously designated as the *only* two extant historical antecedents to rabbinic biblical commentary as such. Even if these did not directly influence rabbinic commentary, they may serve as models for two aspects of commentary which are creatively combined in the *Sifre:* the prophetic *pĕšārîm* among the Dead Sea Scrolls, which may be termed deictic in their mode of commentary, and the allegorical commentaries of Philo, which may be termed dialogical.[6] The continuous *pěšārîm* are commentaries to prophetic texts of scripture (Habakkuk, Nahum, and Psalms being the most extensive and important).[7] They interpret the actual words of those books, sentence by sentence or phrase by phrase in succession, as signifying the events, groups, and personages that play key roles in the sacred history of the Dead Sea sect, some part of which presumably produced and studied these texts. The group's understanding of the revealed nature of these commentaries is best expressed in the following piece of *pēšer* commentary:

> And God told Habakkuk to write down the things that are going to come upon the last generation, but the fulfillment of the end-time he did not make known to him. And when it says, "So that he can run who reads it" (Hab. 2:2), the interpretation of it concerns (*pišrô 'al*) the Teacher of Righteousness, to whom God made known all the mysteries of the words of His servants the prophets.[8]

From this we see why the *pěšārîm,* as continuous commentaries, apply to prophetic scriptures. Understood to communicate God's salvific plan for future history, these scriptures were thought to be veiled in a mysterious language whose full meaning had not been disclosed to the prophets and their contemporaries but only subsequently to the Teacher of Righteousness. He in turn, it is presumed, revealed their hidden meanings in the form of *pēšer* commentaries to his sectarian followers. These commentaries enabled the sectaries to understand recent history as a confirmation rather than denial of their elect self-understanding and to prepare for the "end of days," in which they thought themselves to be living and during which they expected, as God's chosen, soon to be vindicated for their exile and sufferings. To give just one example (1QpHab 9.3–12):

> [A]  When it says, "For you have plundered many nations, but all the rest of peoples will plunder you" (Hab. 2:8a), the interpretation of it concerns (*pišrô 'al*) the last priests of Jerusalem, who amass wealth and profit from plunder of

the peoples; but at the end of days their wealth together
with their booty will be given into the hand of the army of
the Kittim [= the Romans]. For they are "the rest of the
peoples."

[B] "On account of human bloodshed and violence done
to the land, the city, and all its inhabitants" (ibid., 8b). The
interpretation of it concerns the [W]icked Priest, whom—
because of wrong done to the Teacher of Righteousness
and his partisans [or, council]—God gave into the hand of
his enemies to humble him with disease for annihilation in
despair, beca[u]se he had acted wickedly against his
[= God's] chosen ones.

By dividing the verse (Hab 2:8) into two halves and providing different significations for each, the *pēšer* has the verse refer both to the
officiating Jerusalem priests of its own time ("the last priests of Jerusalem") and to the Wicked Priest in the time of the sect's "founder,"
the Teacher of Righteousness. By adjoining these two interpretations according to the scriptural order (the preceding interpretation
took 2:8a to refer to the [Wicked] Priest as well), the *pēšer* implicitly
enchains them, thereby associating, if not equating, (1) the wicked-
ness of the present priests with that of the Wicked Priest, (2) the
expected punishments of the present priests with the already realized punishment of the Wicked Priest, and, more implicitly, (3) the
sufferings of the *pēšer*'s audience with those of the Teacher and his
associates. Thus, the sectaries' present self-understanding is justified
both in relation to scriptural prophecy and in relation to their own
intermediate past as these are exegetically re-presented.

Many scholars have noted that both the term *pēšer* and the
exegetical methods employed by the *pĕšārîm* suggest an activity similar to that of dream, vision, or oracle interpretation, in which each
symbolic detail in sequence is assigned its concrete signification in
the life of the dreamer or society for whom the oracle is intended.[9] In
other words, the enigmatic terms of the original "narrative," here
the words of the prophet, are "translated" into the manifest language of a new narrative, here the life of the sect. Each of these
narratives is fragmented so as to be *interrelated,* but not successively

integrated with the other. The commentary form serves this decoding function well: it *performatively* demonstrates, over and over again, the complete and continuous correspondence between the *words* of the original prophecy and its fulfillment in the details of the sect's "story." It does so through a terminology that repeatedly connects the one to the other without collapsing the space between them. Although the formal movement is from scripture to the sociohistorical world of the sect, it is as much the latter that is given deeper meaning by this interconnection as the former. This commentary structure would have the effect of repeatedly shuttling its sectarian students between the scriptural prophecies and their fulfillment in the life of the community. Such engagement in the very work of commentary would effectively reinforce the message that the *pĕšārîm* repeatedly convey: that the sectaries be justified in viewing and experiencing themselves as God's elect, for whose sake history, as foretold in the scriptural prophecies, was rapidly approaching its messianic vindication and consummation. This is rhetorically very different from the converse procedure, whereby the sacred story of the sect might have been continuously told, spiced with prophetic citations to lend that story teleological significance as the fulfillment of biblical prophecies.

Given this function of the *pĕšārîm,* it is not surprising that these commentaries usually keep their interpretations short, returning without too much digression to the next unit of the prophetic baseverse. Also related to the oracular nature of the *pĕšārîm* is the fact that secondary verses, taken from entirely different parts of scripture, are *not* drawn into the commentary, either to prove the interpretation of the prophetic lemma or to provide the exegetical basis for an associated point. The exegetical focus is entirely on the prophetic base-verse and its equally prophetic decoding. This is in striking contrast with scriptural interpretation found elsewhere in the Dead Sea Scrolls, where the citation and interpretation of one verse may be enchained with that of another, often from a different part of scripture.[10] Finally, and perhaps most importantly, the oracular nature of the *pĕšārîm* requires that each phrase of the prophetic basetext receive a single, authoritative, declarative interpretation, for it is in that interpretation alone that the ancient prophecies are understood to find their *completion.* Thus, the *pĕšārîm* may be said to exemplify a deictic mode of commentary: characterized by a demonstrative terminology that links, in direct correspondence, each discrete segment of the prophetic base-text to its decoded signification.[11]

Although the Dead Sea Scroll *pěšārîm* are often adduced as the closest antecedents to midrashic (rabbinic) commentary,[12] in many ways the commentaries of Philo of Alexandria (ca. 20 B.C.E–ca. 50 C.E.) offer a more important corpus for purposes of comparison and contrast, in part because of their greater volume, but also because they attend, as do our earliest rabbinic collections of commentary, not to prophetic books but to the Torah (Pentateuch). That Philo was our most prolific early Jewish writer of biblical commentaries is most likely related to the fact that Alexandria was in his time a major center of textual scholarship, much of which took the form of running commentaries (*hypomnēmata*) to classical Greek texts, as it had been for at least two centuries earlier.[13] That Philo focused entirely on the books of the Torah is related to his high regard for the divinely inspired, philosopher-lawgiver Moses, in whose writings lay the original and most complete imprint of the divine logos.

I would like to focus briefly on three structural features of Philo's commentaries which distinguish them from the *pěšārîm* and which are shared, mutatis mutandis, by early rabbinic scriptural commentaries.

(1) Philo's commentaries are dialectical in style and form. Often, after the lemma is cited, a rhetorical question or problem is raised regarding one of its "literal" (relating to the physical world) meanings. The body of the commentary then advances one or more allegorical (relating to the life of the soul) interpretations of the lemma as either an answer to the question or an obviation of the problem. This form is especially evident in Philo's *Questions and Answers on Genesis* and *Exodus,* but forms the underlying structure of the more complex allegorical commentaries as well. This is not to deny that Philo employs deictic exegesis, that is, linking a biblical word or phrase with its meaning ("this is," "this means," etc.). Rather, it is to stress that this form does not define the structure of his commentaries overall as it does the Qumran *pěšārîm.* The question and answer structure, even if wooden, at least creates the impression of dialogue between the author and scripture, as well as

between the author and his readers. It serves to open the lemma to interpretation and to draw the reader into that activity.

(2) Philo's allegorical commentaries, but not his more succinct *Questions and Answers on Genesis* and *Exodus,* frequently cite other verses from the Pentateuch in addressing an exegetical question or problem initially raised with respect to the lemma, or in supplementing an initial interpretation of the lemma. The link between the lemma and another verse may be verbal or thematic. But unlike contemporary philosophical texts, where Homer may be cited to interpret Homer or Plato to interpret Plato, these secondary verses themselves often become the objects of Philo's interpretation, sometimes in the form of another question or problem. Such concatenation of interpretations can at times be extreme, appearing to lead the reader far from the base-verse and its initial interpretation(s). But this practice is understood by Philo as necessary to uncovering, if not completely, the deeper chain of encoded meanings to which each scriptural verse points, in combination with others. While this procedure of interpreting scripture with scripture is completely absent from the continuous *pĕšārîm,* it is a common feature of early rabbinic commentary.

(3) Philo's allegorical commentaries commonly give multiple interpretations of the lemma. In his most basic form of commentary, these multiple levels of meaning are first literal, then allegorical. Very often an adduced literal meaning is either mundanely clear and hence insufficient, or problematic and hence improbable, in either case requiring Philo, in his commitment to the scripture's revelatory purpose, to uncover the text's deeper, under-sense (*hyponoia*). Sign posts to this under-sense are to be found in the scriptural text itself. In other words, the lemma's literal meaning is often considered by Philo not to tell the whole story but to point beyond itself to the whole story. Therefore, the search for the symbolic or allegorical level of meaning cannot begin until the biblical text is first engaged and questioned at its literal level of signification. In the more complex forms of his allegorical commentary, Philo often suggests multiple meanings, *both* at and beyond the literal level, often enchaining them in hierarchical order, ascending as might the soul from most physical to most metaphysical levels. But Philo sometimes simply sets such alternative literal and symbolic meanings

alongside one another as equal, even contradictory alternatives, attributing them sometimes to different *anonymous* exegetes ("some say," "others say").[14] However, even with such concatenation of interpretations, Philo never claims to have exhausted the biblical text's possible meanings. Even when he clearly favors his own, allegorical interpretation over those that have preceded it, he leaves open the possibility of there being still other, deeper meanings to be uncovered, or better ways to express what he has uncovered. Both of these concessions are related not so much to Philo's personal modesty as to his view of the inadequacy of language to represent directly the truth which the inspired soul, whether that of Moses or of Philo as the interpreter of his words, can apprehend.[15] This open-ended practice of multiple interpretations and levels of interpretation, the product of a succession of biblical interpreters to whom Philo acknowledges his debt even while claiming superiority for his own added level of other-worldly interpretation, contrasts sharply with what we witnessed of the Dead Sea *pĕšārîm,* with their presumption that the words of the biblical prophets had been directly, univocally, and finally decoded so as to point to a particular set of "historical" (sectarian) referents.

The following passage provides as good an exemplification of these characteristics as is available in one text. It comments on Genesis 15:15, wherein God promises to Abraham: "Thou shalt depart to thy fathers nourished with peace, in a goodly old age."

> After "thou shalt depart" come the words "to thy fathers."
> What fathers? This is worth inquiring. For Moses could
> not mean those who had lived in the land of the Chal-
> deans, who were the only kinsfolk Abraham had, seeing
> that the oracle had set his dwelling away from all those of
> his blood. For we read, "the Lord said unto Abraham 'de-
> part from thy land and from thy kinsfolk and from the
> house of thy father unto the land which I shall shew thee,
> and I will make thee into a great nation' "(Gen. 12:1, 2).
> Was it reasonable that he should again have affinity with
> the very persons from whom he had been alienated by the
> forethought of God? Or that he who was to be the captain
> of another race and nation should be associated with that

of a former age?[16] . . . . No; by "fathers" he does not mean those whom the pilgrim soul has left behind, those who lie buried in the sepulchres of Chaldaea, but possibly, as some say, the sun, moon and other stars to which it is held that all things on earth owe their birth and framing, or as others think, the archetypal ideas which, invisible and intelligible *there,* are the patterns of things visible and sensible *here*— the idea in which, as they say, the mind of the Sage finds its new home. Others again have surmised that by "fathers" are meant the first principles and potentialities, from which the world has been framed, earth, water, air and fire. For into these, they say, each thing that has come into being is duly resolved. Just as nouns and verbs and all parts of speech which are composed of the "elements" in the grammatical sense are finally resolved into the same, so too each of us is composed of the four mundane elements, borrowing small fragments from the substance of each, and this debt he repays when the appointed time-cycles are completed, rendering the dry in him to earth, the wet to water, the cold to air, and the warm to fire. These all belong to the body, but the soul whose nature is intellectual and celestial will depart to find a father in ether, the purest of the substances. For we may suppose that, as the men of old declared, there is a fifth substance, moving in a circle, differing by its superior quality from the four. Out of this they thought the stars and the whole of heaven had been made and deduced as a natural consequence that the human soul also was a fragment thereof.[17]

What is of interest here is the way in which the commentary dialectically progresses from the first rejected meaning ("fathers" as Abraham's biological ancestors), through a series of more symbolic but not yet allegorical meanings suggested by other exegetes ("fathers" as, successively, the heavenly bodies, the archetypal ideas, and the physical elements), and finally to what we must presume is Philo's own allegorical preference ("fathers" as the heavenly ether from which the perceptible world was born and to which the soul seeks to return). This exegetical progression through multiple interpretations parallels, in a sense, the journey of the soul itself as it leaves its physical confines in order to return to its spiritual source. Put differently, the "breaking-open"[18] of the text of the lemma, initiated by a questioning of its literal probability, is necessary in order to begin the process whereby its deeper sense will eventually be disclosed, just as the final dissolution of the body at death into its constitutive elements is necessary in order to release the soul for return to its ethereal source. In both cases the progression is of necessity by stages. Philo does not so much reject the interpretations of his predecessors as ascend them as steps to his own interpretation. Even in this progression the chain of interpretations oscillates between physical and spiritual poles until it finally reaches its destination: from heavenly, but still physical, bodies to archetypal ideas, and from the mundane elements to the purest of elements, ether. It is not, in the end, that Abraham is promised a return to the heavenly bodies, but that his soul alone should return to its ethereal origins, the origins as well of the heavenly bodies. If there is something circular in this interpretation, beginning and ending with the heavenly bodies, then commentary is circular in yet another way, for the return of the soul to its ethereal source is suggested but not quite realized when Philo returns to the text of scripture, so as to confront in the next verse its literal sense once again.

Here we see something of the performative aspect of Philo's employment of commentary: the overall progression in each unit of commentary from literal to allegorical, whatever its internal delays, is facilitated by the succession of alternative interpretations. This exegetical movement is by a series of steps, like the spiritual progression from fleshly trappings to ethical and spiritual perfection, with each such step requiring attentive effort. This interpretive struggle must be repeated over and over again, even if on the broader plane of scriptural commentary there is net progress, as symbolized for Philo by the chronological progression of biblical characters, each of whom represents an ever higher virtue and state of the soul.

Even though Philo clearly favors the allegorical level of interpretation, it cannot be attained without first engaging the text of scripture and its literal meanings. This is the exegetical equivalent of the tension Philo acknowledges between the observance of the commandments and the apprehension of their metaphysical significance. In a famous passage in which he criticizes those whose preoccupation with the allegorical interpretation of laws leads them to neglect their literal sense as requiring observance, Philo counsels dual aims: "[to give] a more full and exact investigation of what is not seen [=the allegorical] and in what is seen [=the literal] to be stewards without reproach." Exactly as we have to take thought for the body, because it is the abode of the soul, so we must pay heed to the letter of the laws (*phētoi nomoi*).[19]

According to Philo, it is impossible for one to *bypass* the body, or observances, or the literal meanings of scripture while striving to move beyond them in pursuit of virtue and wisdom; in a sense, one must move *through* them. Observing the commandments is as necessary to the virtues as engaging the literal meanings of scripture is necessary to deeper understanding. Such literal engagement is better achieved through the structures of commentary, with their fragmentation of the scriptural text and subsequent concatenation of interpretations, than through more distilled forms of exegesis, which Philo practices as well. Scriptural commentary as a practice stands parallel to observance of the commandments in its performative power and necessity, seeking to make of Philo's readers "stewards" of the text even as they looked and moved beyond it.

The *sociohistorical* functioning of Philo's commentary structures needs also to be considered. Philo seeks to convince his fellow Alexandrian Jews that the two cultures, Jewish and Greek, which compete for their attention are in essence one. Moses alone, the supreme philosopher and lawgiver, had the divine logos imprinted upon his soul, which he in turn has imprinted within the text of his Torah, which in turn can leave its imprint not only on the soul of the individual but also on the life of the community which exegetically and performatively engages it.[20] But since this might not be obvious to those who have no guide in uncovering these teachings hidden beneath the letters of scripture's laws and narratives, Philo offers himself as the supremely qualified guide for his time, endeavoring to demonstrate to his audience that whatever surrounding Greek culture has to offer can be obtained in purer and more original form in Israel's own scriptural heritage.

To sustain this argument, Philo undertakes what amounts to a major translation project, rendering scripture into the best cultural vernacular of his Hellenistically educated or exposed public. And since his argument is not simply about the contents of scripture, but also about the status of its text as that central symbol which defines Israel and distinguishes the Jewish community from its neighbors, that translation had to take, at least in part, the form of a dialogical engagement with that text—and not simply a distilled paraphrase of it. In other words, Philo sought in the dialogical structure of commentary, itself *adapted* from wider Greek usage, a performative instrument with which to link for his readers the language of Jewish scripture to the philosophical language of high Greek culture as he understood it, without dissolving the difference between them and while asserting the primacy of the former and the *derivativeness* of the latter. Through a rhetorical give and take not only with the plurality of scripture's text, but also with a plurality of post-biblical interpretive voices, Philo's commentaries might draw his community into a dynamic engagement and identification with both Moses' Torah and its philosophically attuned, allegorical translation.

Returning to our earliest rabbinic commentaries, we see that when compared to their *only* two Jewish antecedents—the commentaries of *pēšer* and Philo—they display the characteristic commentary modes of each: deictic and dialogical. For example, the *Sifre*'s commentary may definitively proclaim what a scriptural word or phrase signifies, and then question that assigned meaning or set another, even discordant, meaning dialectically alongside it. Still, overall, it is the dialogical mode that characterizes the *Sifre*'s commentary.[21] In this way the structure of the *Sifre*'s commentary is closer overall to that of Philo than to that of *pēšer*. Not surprisingly, therefore, two other dialogical features of Philo's (and non-Jewish philosophical) commentaries, absent from the *pēšārîm* commentaries, are also found in the *Sifre,* albeit with important differences: the interpretation of scripture with scripture and the concatenation of multiple interpretations. But it is precisely with regard to multiple interpretations that the *Sifre*'s commentary, and early rabbinic commentary more generally, are significantly different from those of Philo. In the *Sifre,* multiple interpretations or their sub-groupings may be ordered editorially so as to be encountered in progression, but not according to any standard hierarchical principle or plan. Before turning to this difference, however, there is something else to be learned from our brief look at the commentaries of *pēšer* and Philo as antecedents to that of the *Sifre*.

Ancient scriptural commentaries—and others may wish to extend this point to other kinds of commentary—even as they closely scrutinize the particles of the text to which they attend, are always about that text as a *whole*. By this I mean that they seek both for the text as a whole to be held in high regard by its interpretive community, and for the interpretive community to view *itself* in relation to that text as mediated by its commentary. Such a commentary is, therefore, not simply a series of declarative assertions about the meanings of words in a text, but also an attempt to *effect* a relationship between that text overall and those for whom it is "scripture." Ancient scriptural commentaries are not simply constative conduits of meaning but also performative media by which the polymorphic "world" of the text and that of its students are transformatively brought toward each other, while never fully merged, so as to confront one another through the double-dialogue of commentary.[22] In this "double-dialogue," the commentary simultaneously faces and engages the text that it interprets and the society of "readers" for whom and with whom it interprets.

By focusing attention on this *double-facing* character of ancient scriptural commentary, I wish to avoid two tendencies in scholarly understandings and employments of such commentaries: what I would call the "hermeneuticist" and "historicist" fallacies. The former tendency is to see the commentary primarily in its facing toward scripture and to view hermeneutical practice as if conducted within a sociohistorical isolation booth into which only the commentator and his chosen text, or self-contained corpus of texts, are allowed entrance. The latter tendency is to see the commentary primarily in its facing toward the events and/or circumstances of its time and to view its response to and representation of those events as being only slightly veiled by the formal guise of the scriptural exegesis in which it is wrapped. The former claims to have explained the commentary when it has identified hermeneutical pressures within scripture and the commentary's responses to those. The latter claims to have explained the commentary when it has identified historical pressures outside of scripture and the commentary's responses to those.

These two tendencies, even as they face, and view commentary as facing, opposite directions, are really two sides of the same coin. That is the coin which presumes that the hermeneutics and historicity of scriptural commentary can conveniently and neatly be detached from one another, in the first case by viewing the hermeneutics of commentary's *interpretations* apart from the sociohistorical grounding of its performance, and in the latter case by viewing the historicity of commentary's *representations* apart from the hermeneutical grounding of its performance. One consequence of this common position is the view that such a text, whether as a whole or in its parts, is either hermeneutical or historiographic, facing either in upon itself and the texts with which it intersects or out upon history and society. Rather than reject either of these two facings, I wish to assert their inextricable interconnection. Their bifurcation, while perhaps useful for maintaining our disciplinary boundaries, reductively distorts the hermeneutical and historical aspects of a commentary such as the *Sifre*'s by viewing them in isolation from one another. Such a text of scriptural commentary may be seen as reflecting on and responding to its sociohistorical setting no less significantly, even if less directly and more complexly, than a continuous narration of the same. Likewise, bits of historical narrative set within a text of scriptural commentary must be understood in rhetorical relation to their more explicitly exegetical contexts, and not simply extracted as direct historical representations.[23]

Let us look now at one small example from the *Sifre* that exhibits the congruence of deictic and dialogical modes of interpretation. The verse to be commented upon is Deuteronomy 32:7, part of the "song" that Moses delivered to the people shortly before his death, in which he rehearsed their sacred history in order to prepare them for entering the promised land. The verse comprises two parallel doublets:

Remember the days of old (ʿolām),
consider the years (šĕnôt) of each and every generation;

ask your father and he will inform you,
your elders and they will tell you.

The *Sifre* divides the verse in order to explicate its parts, and does so twice. Here is its first set of comments:

[A] "Remember the days of old": [God said to them:] Take heed of what I did to the earliest generations: what I did to the people of the generation of the Flood, and what I did to the people of the generation of the Dispersion [the Tower of Babel], and what I did to the people of Sodom.

[B] "Consider the years of each and every generation": You can find no generation without people like those of the generation of the Flood, and you can find no generation without people like those of the generation of the Dispersion and like those of Sodom, but each and every individual is judged according to his deeds.

[C] "Ask your father and he will inform you": These are the prophets as it says, "When Elisha beheld it he cried out [to Elijah], 'Father, father' " (2 Kgs. 2:12).

[D] "Your elders and they will tell you": These are the elders, as it is said, "Gather for Me seventy men of the elders of Israel" (Num. 11:16).[24]

At the most basic level, the commentary distinguishes between the verse's parallel elements: "days of old" and "each and every generation"; "your father" and "your elders." The commentary begins by identifying "days of old" (literally, "days of eternity") with the earliest generations of human history, in particular with three generations that are understood by the rabbis to have been thoroughly wicked and rebellious in their behavior.[25] It is these specific generations which God Himself urges Israel to recall in the commentary's paraphrastic restatement of the lemma. This interpretation of "days of old" as referring to the early rebellious *generations* anticipates the interpretation of the next clause, with its "each and every generation." According to that interpretation, Moses urges his audience to differentiate (*bînû*) between the earliest rebellious generations whose members were entirely wicked, and later generations, including that of the present, whose moral make-up is more mixed. These later generations are no longer judged en masse, but their individual members are judged each according to his or her own deeds.

Next, the terms "father" and "elders," appearing in parallel construction in the biblical text, are understood as signifying not one's own biological father and the elderly of one's family or community as sources of wisdom, as would seem to be the scriptural sense, but *inspired biblical leadership classes.* The word "father" is deictically interpreted, with the aid of another verse, to signify "prophets." The word "elders" is similarly interpreted as signifying "elders," but now, again with the aid of another verse, not those of advanced age within one's community but those non-priests who were divinely authorized to share in Moses' leadership and judiciary functions (Ex 18:13–26; Num 11:16–25; Deut 1:9–18). In the *Sifre,* as in other rabbinic collections, the rabbinic sages view themselves as the extension of this biblical class of lay elders, especially in their appointment to positions of judicial and administrative responsibility over the larger Jewish community. The commentary's juxtaposition of "prophets" and "elders" may also serve subtly to associate the two, as they are associated elsewhere in early rabbinic tradition. Thus, according to the rabbinic "chain of tradition," Joshua transmitted the Torah to the elders, who passed it on to the prophets, who, in turn, passed it on to the proto-rabbinic elders of Second Temple times.[26]

Returning to the *Sifre*'s commentary to Deuteronomy 32:7, we see that if the first set of interpretations (A–D) focuses on the biblical past, the second set focuses on the ultimate future:

Another interpretation:

[A'] "Remember the days of old eternity (ʿolām)": He [=Moses] said to them: Whenever God brings sufferings to you, remember how many good and consoling things he will give you in the world (ʿolām) to come.

[B'] "Consider the years of each and every generation": This is the generation of the Messiah, which will last for three generations, as it is said, "Let them fear You as long as the sun shines and the moon lasts, for a generation and generations" (Ps. 72:5).[27]

[C'] "Ask your father and he will inform you": In the future Israel will be able to see and hear as if hearing from the Holy One, as it is said, "Your ears shall hear a word behind you" (Isa. 30:21), and it says, "Your teacher [=God] shall not hide himself any more, and your eyes shall see your teacher" (Isa. 30:20).

[D'] "Your elders and they will tell you": What I [=God] revealed to the elders on the mountain, as it is said, "And to Moses He said, 'Ascend to God [you and Aaron, Nadab, Abihu, and the seventy elders of Israel]' " (Exod. 24:1).

This second set of interpretations, demarcated by "another interpretation," begins with the sufferings of the present and then shifts our attention to the distant, messianic future. In the midst of such present sufferings, the righteous (we may presume) are told by Moses to consider the *future* "days of eternity," wherein they will finally be rewarded. Similarly, the generations referred to in the verse's second clause, earlier interpreted as signifying the three earliest rebellious generations, are now deictically interpreted as signifying the three generations of the Messiah at the end of time. Thus, in both sets of comments the "days of eternity" are defined in relation to the next biblical clause as referring to three generations, primeval and messianic. Similarly, the verse's "father," first interpreted as signifying the prophets, is now interpreted less directly as signifying God, who in the messianic future will be the teacher of *all* of Israel, obviating the need for mediating prophets. Note how the order of the prooftext verses from Isaiah has been reversed (30:21 followed by 30:20): not only will Israel hear the word of their teacher but they will see him. This reversal permits the commentary to ask implicitly: What will be the nature of that direct vision of God? This implicit question is answered by the citation and interpretation of the final clause of the lemma, once again in God's own voice: In the future *all* of Israel will directly behold me, as did the inspired biblical elders upon Mount Sinai (as related in Exodus 24:9–11).[28]

Because each of these two commentaries to Deuteronomy 32:7 comprises a set of four interpretations, how we perceive the effect of their overall juxtaposition is related to how we perceive the nature of the internal linkages between their parts. At the outermost level, the fact that the first set of interpretations moves from the distant past to the present, while the second moves from the present to the distant future, suggests that the editorial ordering of these two commentaries is not as accidental as might first appear: textual order as encountered in the chronology of "reading" bears some relation to "historical" chronology. The three "pre-historical" rebellious generations are set opposite the three messianic generations. In the former the wicked are punished while in the latter the righteous will be rewarded. In the delicately suspended "time-between," the righteous are punished for their own deeds, even as they look forward in consolation to their future rewards. Whereas in biblical times Israel obtained knowledge of God's will through the intermediacy of their divinely authorized prophets and elders, in the messianic future Israel will hear and behold God directly. But how is God's will to be known and his presence experienced in the here-and-now, when there are neither prophets in the biblical sense nor possibilities for direct knowledge of God? This question, implicitly asked by the commentary's juxtapositions, is also implicitly answered: the rabbinic successors to the biblical elders presently fulfill this mediating function. In this regard it is significant that the elders alone remain constant both between the lemma and its interpretation and between the two sets of interpretations. Thus, "father" is taken to signify first prophets and then God, "days of eternity" is taken to signify first the beginning of time and then its end, and "each and every generation" is taken to signify first early rebellious generations and then the final messianic generations. But "elders" are always the elders—the inspired class of elders, that is—whose biblically assigned roles in revelation and in its societal adjudication remain operative throughout time, or until such time as Israel's direct hearing and seeing of God will make their mediating functions unnecessary.

Finally, it may be noted that the two-part commentary is framed overall by one other recurring feature: in the very first interpretation (A) and the very last (D'), God himself addresses Israel directly, whereas in the intermediary interpretations (as in the "time-between") either Moses (A') or the anonymous voice of the rabbinic commentary does the speaking.

Thus, the commentary's editorial juxtaposition of otherwise deictic significations of scriptural meaning draws its students into a collective, interpretive dialogue with the divine voice in scripture. This feature, in many different forms, is characteristic of the *Sifre*'s anthological structure at its multiple levels of composition. Not only are multiple interpretations often provided for a given lemma, but even within a single interpretation diverse types of materials (another verse, a parable, a story, a rule) are often combined in such ways that the unspecified nature of their interconnections is unclear. Even where a verse is minutely divided and a different brief interpretation is offered for each of its atomized parts (as in the above example), the student of the text is left with several questions whether or not, and if so how, those interpretations should be understood in relation to one another, and how are a sequence of interpretations to successive verses to be viewed in relation to one another: discretely or interdependently? In sum, to what extent do we have a collection of independent exegetical assertions and traditional recollections that have been strung together for no apparent reason other than to preserve them, and to what extent do we have, as we saw in *pēšer* and in Philo, the editorial enchaining of traditions and interpretations for other purposes, presumably rhetorical, as well? Our difficulty in answering this question lies in part in our frequent lack of an authorial voice to tell us how to proceed from one such assertion to the next: how, as interpreters of the commentary, to fill the connective gaps between the traditions set before us.

In this regard, let us return briefly to our two Jewish commentary antecedents. The Dead Sea *pēšārîm,* as we saw, present themselves as the authoritative decodings of scriptural prophecies, having been revealed by God to the Teacher of Righteousness, who in turn passed them on to his followers. Even if we cannot discern what precisely in the lemma is "producing" its interpretation, the overall relation of prophetic scripture to its commentary, and of that commentary to its community of students, is self-evident: together the commentary's interpretations add up to the prophetically prefigured sacred history of the sect as God's elect in the end of days. Philo's allegorical commentaries are also presented as the work of a single author, even though he incorporates the interpretations of "others." We may wonder often why Philo leads us so far afield, and how to interconnect our tour of one verse with that of the next, but at least we know that it is he who is leading us. Once again, there is a degree of predictability, albeit less so than with the *pĕšārîm,* as he repeatedly takes us from lemma, to its literal meaning, to a chain of symbolic meanings, often in ascending order. The overall route of the commentary is that of the journey of the soul to moral and spiritual perfection.

By contrast, the *Sifre*'s commentary presents itself, implicitly to be sure, as the *collective* and *cumulative* teachings of the class of rabbinic sages, even as those teachings are understood to originate in the revelation at Sinai. Already in the *Sifre,* Sinaitic revelation is re-presented as being twofold: that which was immediately inscribed as scripture and that which as oral teaching only achieved its socially available expression over time.[29] Between Sinai and the time of the text's redaction (mid-third century C.E.), there stands no single individual who is said to have authored the commentary or to have authorized its interpretations. In other words, the commentary lacks overall a single subsuming narrative voice or hermeneutical mastercode.

The collective nature of the *Sifre*'s text is not just a matter of its authoring or redacting, but also of its implied audience: the collectivity or class of rabbinic sages and their disciples of mid-third century Palestine, in addition to whatever audiences extended well beyond such time and place. The *Sifre* uses several metaphors to describe the study activity of such sages and their disciples. They are to attend constantly to "words of Torah" (both scriptural and rabbinic), cultivating them again and again like a farmer does his field or vineyard.[30] Thus, the first task of the sage is to maintain the words of Torah that he has learned by continually reviewing them, pouring over them, to the point of fully absorbing them into his person, that is, memory.[31] Then, having them ever ready in his "mouth," he can disseminate them as needed.[32] In this activity the sage is compared to a well that constantly gathers waters (Torah teachings) from all sides, so that once full he can disperse those waters to his disciples.[33] Note the two-step procedure: gathering and disseminating, joining and dividing. Similarly, the collectivity of rabbinic teachings is compared to a mixture of flour, bran, and meal, which the disciple sorts out with a sieve. The disciple according to this tradition does not so much correspond to the person who does the sorting as to the *sieve* itself, refining teachings as they pass *through* him.[34]

These metaphors for rabbinic study can be taken to describe the "production" of the text of commentary, wherein diverse rabbinic traditions have been gathered, arranged and often subtly reshaped in the process. But to the extent that these gathered, arranged, and reshaped traditions still do not fully cohere or concord with one another, or with the verses of Deuteronomy to which they are attached, the above descriptions of rabbinic study can be taken to describe as well the dialogical "consumption" of the text of commentary by the plurality of its students. They, in working their way through the collected traditions of the commentary, continue the interpretive process of connecting and differentiating that the redacted text itself has set in motion *but not completed.* These students advance its unfinished work by filling-out, but never finally, the anonymous narrative voice which is only partially present in the text itself. The dialectical dynamic of such study leads to the transformative internalization and actualization of the commentary's network of traditions (and perspectives) within its students. In a sense, as they work through the commentary, the commentary works through them.

We gain here a literary glimpse of the dialogical system of study and teaching by whose illocutionary force disciples became sages and sages became a class that could extend their teachings, practices, and vision of the world into Jewish society more broadly.[35] But that larger world was neither simple nor static, comprising itself a dangerous complex of discordant strands or voices in need of sense-making configuration. The rabbinic work of dynamically configuring the heterogeneity of tradition is related to the rabbinic work of positively positioning Israel as a whole within the heterogeneous web of history and nature. Commentary could provide the society of sages not only with a performative medium for their own shared self-understanding, but also with one by which they could effectively fashion and refashion larger Israel's supple self-understanding within the world and through time.

Such a medium requires that heterogeneous traditions, whose oral origins we can only guess, be contained but not congealed within the structural framework of ongoing scriptural commentary. Thus rendered accessible but remaining fluid, these traditions might be dynamically absorbed by the students of the commentary as they pore over it in their own repetitive acts of interpretive study. These students, in turn, might return orally the rabbinic "words of Torah" that they have so absorbed back out into rabbinic society and beyond in new combinations and reshapings, which might eventually be collected and configured once again to form another literary work of commentary.

This dialogical view of the *Sifre*'s commentary requires that our own critical interpretation of its texts adopt two converging perspectives: that of their formation and that of their reception. By the first I mean attention to how otherwise discrete and sometimes discordant traditions have been redactionally combined and to varying degrees configured so as to form a running commentary to the text of Deuteronomy. There are two ways to discern such activity. The first looks *within* the immediate text for editorial signposts, such as linguistic, structural, or thematic links and repetitions that serve to interconnect adjacent traditions beyond the mere fact of their physical juxtaposition. The second looks *without* the text to other rabbinic texts of the same vintage in which related traditions have been differently combined and subtly reshaped so as to produce different rhetorical effects. Through such comparison and contrast it is possible to see both the relative freedom and the limits to that freedom by which the *Sifre*'s editors were able to fashion commentary out of tradition.[36]

The second perspective from which to view the *Sifre*'s work of commentary is that of the rabbinic student of its text, putting ourselves in the position of one who, in progressively working through the text of commentary, seeks to understand its contained traditions in relation both to one another and to the text of scripture upon which it comments. In a sense, such students of our text are drawn into the work of its commentary so as to provide the missing voice that variously joins together *and* differentiates what has already been gathered and arranged before them. If we assume that, in describing the study of activity of the sages and their disciples, the *Sifre* also describes how its own text of Torah teaching ought to be studied by its students, then we cannot understand the social work of that commentary without attempting to pose ourselves in such students' places, even as we employ the distancing tools of the first perspective of intra- and inter-textual critical analysis as controls.

This is a dangerous task, but no less so than the task of any historian who tries to understand an ancient society by viewing it from "within," even while acknowledging and maintaining his or her distance from it. Here I wish to strike a cautionary note. By heuristically posing ourselves in the position of the ancient students of the text, we cannot pretend to *be* such students, exhaustively uncovering in any simple way what would have been its single "original" meaning to them. Our distance from the ancient text of the *Sifre* and its cultural setting, as well as the ambiguities of its own anthological multivocality, precludes such certainty and closure. What we *can* seek is a self-consciously modest understanding of what and how that text might have communicated within the broader parameters and paradigms of meaning and discourse defined by the ancient linguistic and cultural matrices of which that text was a part. Even so, we must admit the hermeneutical circularity of our *reconstructing* of those matrices through our reading of such texts. This is simply to acknowledge that any discrete text of tradition and commentary might "mean more than it says" once it is encountered within such broader interassociative frames, beginning with those of the surrounding *Sifre* commentary and extending to other proximate rabbinic collections and configurations of tradition, midrashic as well as non-midrashic.[37] This is not to suggest a harmonizing approach, but simply one that recognizes that no discrete text is ever understood monologically "in its own terms," but always dialogically in terms of the larger matrices of signification in which it is set and to which it contributes. For us foreigners that setting—in all its diversity, complexity, and discordancy—is accessible to us mainly in the wider range of rabbinic texts, which like a succession of concentric yet interlocking circles frame the discourse of any particular text, even as they may be challenged by it.

I am proposing that the critical analysis of a rabbinic scriptural commentary take the form of commentary, that in its own way is dialogical, alternating between the perspectives of the text's formation and reception, as well as between those of the ancient student of the text and the modern critic of it. Such a commentary would seek to make both hermeneutical and historical sense of a rabbinic commentary in relation to its ancient setting without claiming reductively to have exhausted or mastered either. If, as I have argued, such a commentary's chief "intent" was to engage dialogically its ancient rabbinic students in the reconstructive and redemptive work of its interpretation, then my own intent is not only to disclose something of how the *Sifre*'s commentary interprets scripture, but also to demonstrate how it involves the interpretive collaboration of its students in the ongoing advancement of that work in such a way as to advance their own socioreligious self-understanding. I see no way out of the methodological difficulties of this task, at least not if we wish to ask how the *Sifre*'s commentary might have *functioned* as such, that is, how it would have performed its transformative work of interpretation not only in relation to the text of Deuteronomy but also in relation to the society of interpreters whom we know as the rabbinic sages and their disciples. The social construction and solidification of that sub-culture, in significant measure through its collective self-representing work of Torah study, was regarded by the rabbinic shapers of the *Sifre*'s commentary as a necessary precondition for their command, in turn and in time, of a similar transformation of Israelite culture and society overall.

Rabbinic shapers of such commentary sought not simply to transmit correct interpretations of scripture, but to shape and ultimately to redeem Jewish society through its dialogically and performatively engaging encounter with a polyphony of "words of Torah." As modern critical students of ancient rabbinic commentary who seek not simply to master its forms and messages but also to understand and even experience a modest something of how it works, we ourselves need to become practitioners of commentary.

## NOTES

1. This is a revised version of the introductory chapter of my book, *From Tradition to Commentary: Torah and Its Interpretation in the Midrash Sifre to Deuteronomy* (Albany: State University of New York Press, 1991). For fuller bibliographic support and finer nuancing of the arguments set forth here, the reader should refer to that chapter, especially to its notes.

2. See Michael Fishbane, *Biblical Interpretation in Ancient Israel* (Oxford: Clarendon Press, 1985).

3. *Webster's Ninth New Collegiate Dictionary* (Springfield: Merriam-Webster, 1983), p. 264. Compare Roland Barthes' characterization of commentary as "the gradual analysis of a single text." *S/Z*, trans. Richard Miller (New York: Hill and Wang, 1974), p. 12.

4. For this term see Geza Vermes, *Scripture and Tradition in Judaism,* rev. ed. (Leiden: E.J. Brill, 1973), pp. 228–29.

5. Examples would be the so-called *Genesis Apocryphon* and Pseudo-Philo's *Biblical Antiquities.*

6. These terms "deictic" and "dialogical" will be explained through exemplification below.

7. For the texts, translations, notes, and overall discussion, see Maurya P. Horgan, *Pesharim: Qumran Interpretation of Biblical Books* (Washington, DC: Catholic Biblical Association of America, 1979). The extant *pĕšārîm* exist in single copies dating from the late first century B.C.E., even though they are thought to refer to events and personages of the mid-second century B.C.E. How much older these commentaries are than the time of their extant copies is a matter of debate, and probably speculation.

8. 1QpHab 7.1–5. Here and in what follows, the translations of *pĕšārîm* are from M. Hargan, *Pesharim.*

9. For more detailed discussion, see in particular Michael Fishbane, "The Qumran Pesher and Traits of Ancient Hermeneutics," in *Proceedings of the Sixth World Congress of Jewish Studies*, vol. 1

(Jerusalem: World Union of Jewish Studies, 1977), pp. 97–114; Lou Silberman, "Unriddling the Riddle: A Study in the Structure and Language of the Habakkuk Pesher (1QpHab)," *Revue de Qumran* 3 (1961):323–64; M. Horgan, *Pesharim,* pp. 252–59 (with further bibliography).

10. For example, see in particular CD 7.9–8.2; 4QFlorilegium; and 4QTestimonia.

11. Such declarative terminology (like "this is") may be compared to that employed in the interpretation of dreams, visions, and oracles. On such usage in Jewish and Christian apocalyptic genres, see Martha Himmelfarb, *Tours of Hell: An Apocalyptic Form in Jewish and Christian Literature* (Philadelphia: University of Pennsylvania Press, 1983), pp. 45–67. Michael Fishbane, in *Biblical Interpretation in Ancient Israel* (Oxford: Clarendon Press, 1985), pp. 44–55, uses the term "deictic" for such terminology (e.g., the demonstrative pronoun *zeh*) when used by scribal glossators to scripture. This sort of procedure of direct interpretive correspondence also characterizes most ancient near eastern commentaries, on which see J. Krecher, "Kommentare," in *Reallexikon der Assyriologie und vorderasiatischen Archaeologie* 6.3/4 (1981):188–91.

12. For a discussion of the extent to which this comparison has been overdrawn, see M. Horgan, *Pesharim,* pp. 250–52 (with bibliography in the notes). See also David Stern, "Midrash and Indeterminacy," *Critical Inquiry* 15 (1988):142–43.

13. For discussion and references, see my *From Tradition to Commentary,* pp. 176–78 (nn. 24, 25).

14. An example will be given below. It has always been a crux of Philonic scholarship to identify the unnamed authorities whose interpretations he so frequently cites. See David M. Hay, "Philo's References to Other Allegorists," *Studia Philonica* 6 (1979–80):41–75; Thomas H. Tobin, *The Creation of Man: Philo and the History of Interpretation.*

15. Thus, Philo will sometimes qualify his interpretations with "perhaps" (mēpote). However, he is not adverse to claiming for his "highest" interpretations divine inspiration, even as he is uncertain whether his words can properly express them. See *Cher.* 27.

16. Philo continues here in the same vein.

17. *Her.* 277–83 (LCL 4:424–29).

18. The expression is from David T. Tunia, "The Structure of Philo's Allegorical Treatises: A Review of Two Recent Studies and Some Additional Comments," *Vigiliae Christianae* 38 [1984]:237.

19. *Mig.* 89 (LCL 4:182–3).

20. For a discussion of this language of textual imprint in Philo, see John David Dawson, "Ancient Alexandrian Interpretation of Scripture," pp. 160–65.

21. My distinction between deictic and dialogical should not be drawn too sharply, for even commentaries that are deictic, to the extent that they structurally differentiate between the lemma and its interpretation, may be said to be dialogical, in that they draw their readers into the shuttle between the two. The difference is simply that in raising the dialogical aspect of all commentary to a more explicit level, what I have termed dialogical commentary draws its audience into a more dynamic and open-ended participation in the work of interpretation.

22. I have adapted the heuristic distinction between the constative and performative aspects from Jerome J. McGann, *Social Values and Poetic Acts: The Historical Judgment of Literary Work* (Cambridge: Harvard University Press, 1988), esp. pp. 19–31, and Stanley Fish, *Doing What Comes Naturally: Change, Rhetoric, and the Practice of Theory in Literary and Legal Studies* (Durham: Duke University Press, 1989), pp. 57–67, both of whom refer back to John Searle, "The Logical Status of Fictional Discourse," in *Expression and Meaning: Studies in the Theory of Speech Acts* (Cambridge: Cambridge University Press, 1979), pp. 58–75; and ultimately to J.L. Austin, *How To Do Things With Words,* 2nd ed. (Cambridge: Harvard University Press, 1975).

23. For convenient entrances to the larger discussion of the possibilities of historical pursuit following the loss of hermeneutical innocence, see David Simpson, "Literary Criticism and the Return to History," *Critical Inquiry* 14 (1988):721–47; John E. Toews, "Intellectual History after the Linguistic Turn: The Autonomy of Meaning and the Irreducibility of Experience," *American History Review* 92 (1987):879–907; Hayden White, "The Question of Narrative in Contemporary Historical Theory," *History and Theory* 23 (1984):1–33. For further bibliography, see my book, *From Tradition to Commentary,* pp. 193–94.

24. *Sifre Deut.* 310. The text can be found in the edition of Louis Finkelstein on pp. 350–51. Where my translation differs from Finkelstein's text, it is because I follow better witnesses.

25. On the rabbinic exegetical portrayal of a chain of early rebellious generations, and its historiographic implications for rabbinic self-understanding, see my book, *Enosh and His Generation: Pre-Israelite Hero and History in Postbiblical Interpretation* (Chico: Scholars Press, 1984), esp. pp. 216–25, 226–27, 231–34.

26. For the sequence Joshua-elders-prophets, see *m. Abot* 1:1, with the Joshua-elders sequence deriving from Joshua 24:31 and Judges 2:7. For the idea that the prophets were succeeded, once classical prophecy ceased, by the elders, who are associated in their authority with the rabbinic sages, see *m. Yad.* 4:3 and *Seder Olam Rabba* 30 (ed. Ratner, pp. 140–41), which cites Deuteronomy 32:7 in a way similar to the *Sifre,* but more clearly identifying the elders in that verse with the sages.

27. The phrase "generation and generations" is interpreted as three generations since "generation" is one and "generations" is two, the minimum plural.

28. Thus, Exodus 24:9–10 states that "Moses went up with Aaron, Nadab and Abihu, and the seventy elders of Israel, and they saw the God of Israel."

29. See especially *Sifre Deut.* §313 (ed. Finkelstein, p. 355); §351 (p. 408). The oral Torah was nonetheless revealed at Sinai, and even perceived, at least in part, by those standing there.

30. See *Sifre Deut.* §48 (ed. Finkelstein, p. 109).

31. See especially §306 (ed. Finkelstein, p. 336).

32. §13 (ed. Finkelstein, p. 22); §34 (ed. Finkelstein, p. 60).

33. §48 (ed. Finkelstein, pp. 109–10).

34. §48 (ed. Finkelstein, pp. 109–10).

35. My view of the dialogical interrelation of textual formation and reception may be compared to Paul Ricoeur's dialectic of a text's configuration by its author and refiguration by its readers, in *Time and Narrative,* vol. 3, esp. pp. 157–79. The relationship between the practice of commentary and the class of sages in third century Palestine, a time of significant rabbinic expansion and solidification, is explored in greater detail in Chapter Three of my book, *From Tradition to Commentary.*

36. For a fuller description and justification of this method, see my earlier, "Sifre Deuteronomy 26 (ad Deut. 3:23: How Conscious the Composition?") *Hebrew Union College Annual* 54 (1983):245–57.

37. For a fuller discussion, framed in relation to the historical study of earlier political discourse, see J.G.A. Pockock, *Politics, Language, and Time: Essays on Political Thought and History* (New York: Athenean, 1971), pp. 23–33.

Chapter Six

# EXTRA-BIBLICAL EXEGESIS:
# THE SENSE OF NOT READING
# IN RABBINIC MIDRASH

## MICHAEL FISHBANE

On November 24, 1644, John Milton responded to a parliamentary ordinance passed on June 14 of the previous year. Control of printing was the issue, and the result was his famous *Aereopagitica*. In due course, the following ironic rhetoric occurs. Milton writes that, since the "knowledge and survey of vice" is necessary for "the constituting of human virtue," fear of the "infection" which might arise from such study could encourage the suppression of all works which "scout into the region of sin." Among these, the Bible is particularly worrisome,

> for that [work] ofttimes relates blasphemy not nicely, it describes the carnal sense of wicked men unelegantly, it brings in honest men passionately murmuring against Providence through all the arguments of Epicurus: in other great disputes it answers dubiously and darkly to the common reader: and ask a Talmudist what ails the modesty of his marginal Keri, that Moses and all the prophets cannot persuade him to pronounce the textual Chetiv.

This is a point worth pondering. Among the manifest dangers of scripture, Milton listed not only its brute descriptions of brutish men and sundry accounts of blasphemy and desire. He also stressed the occasional paradoxes of its pronounciation, the "marginal Keri" and the "textual Chetiv." By this, Milton alluded to the rabbinic practice of substituting special (though traditional) readings for various forms found in sacred scripture. Thus certain words are read (the *qeri*) differently from the way they are written (the *ketiv*), while, in rare instances, words may be read when nothing is written in scripture at all. One therefore reads scripture according to a fixed tradition that is recorded in old Masoretic lists and the margins of printed (rabbinic) Bibles but never in the holy scrolls themselves. In a true Derridean sense, one might say that the *qeri-ketiv* difference of the Masoretic masters is a defiant *différance:* a point where the written text of the eye diverges significantly from the traditional articulation of it. Drawing on the ancient account preserved in *Sifre Deuteronomy* (356) and elsewhere,[1] Rabbi David Kimchi, several centuries before Milton, wrote the following about this phenomenon in the preface to his commentary on the book of Joshua.

> It seems that these words (i.e., the *qeri* and *ketiv*) have come about because the books (of Scripture) were lost and scattered during the first exile; and the sages who were knowledgeable in Scripture had died; and the men of the Great Assembly, who restored the Torah to its previous state, found divergent readings in the books, and followed those which were supported by the majority of readings, according to their understanding (of them). But wherever they could not decisively resolve the reading, they wrote one down but did not vocalize it, or they wrote it down in the margin but not in the text. Similarly, they sometimes inserted one reading (lit., 'one way') in the text and another in the margin.[2]

Modern scholars have not left Kimchi's formulation as written, but have "read" its details in different ways.[3] The veracity of such historical reconstructions is not at issue here. What I wish to consider is the fact that, already in antiquity, rabbinic scholars based some of their exegetical constructions of the Bible, or *midrash,* on scribal differences (some later formalized as *qeri-ketiv* variations). Two instances of this creative exchange between textual forms and exegetical formulations may suffice here.

The first instance derives from a legal *derashah* (or scriptural exposition) by R. Eleazar ben R. Jose on Leviticus 25:30. The biblical context deals with the sale of a dwelling in a walled town. According to the law, the original owner has the right to redeem the property until the end of the year of sale. If the property is not redeemed after this period, the regulation states that "the house in the walled town shall rest in perpetuity in the buyer and his descendants," *veqam ha-bayit asher lo'* (the *ketiv*) *homah*. The operative portion of this rule is clearly the clause *asher lo' homah*. In translating it as referring to a "house in a walled town" I have followed the traditional *qeri*, which substitutes *lo* (preposition plus pronominal suffix, i.e. "to it") for the negative particle *lo'* of the *ketiv* (i.e. "not"). Thus the received wording is "the house which is *not* in a walled town." This orthographic variation (*lo'/lo*) is fairly common in the Hebrew Bible (e.g. Ex 21:8; Is 63:9) and must in many cases be due to aural errors. But given the legal or theological implications of such variants, as well as the relative contextual plausibility of one reading or another, it is striking that R. Eleazar has used *both* variants (the traditional *qeri* and *ketiv*) in his *derashah*. In *BT Megillah* 3b he states: "even though it (the town) has no (wall) now, it did have one previously." Thus the orthographic difference between *lo'* and *lo* preserved at Leviticus 25:30 is not suppressed by the sage; it serves as the basis for a complex legal formulation in which both scribal values are valorized. R. Eleazar manifestly interprets scripture both with *and* against an official synagogal reading. The dynamic role of midrash as both a conserver and converter of tradition is thus manifest.

A second instance of exegetical hermeneutics rooted in textual variants comes from the aggadic, or non-legal sphere of midrash. Here again, the scriptural exposition in *Mishnah Sotah* V.5 turns on a *lo'/lo* variation. R. Joshua ben Hyrkanos teaches, "Job served God only out of love, as Scripture says: 'Yea, though He slay me, *lo 'ayachel*, yet will I trust in Him' (Job 13:15)." "However," he continues, "the (exegetical) meaning (of the verse) still hangs in the balance (*ve-'adayin haddabar shaqul*):[4] (should one understand the phrase as meaning) 'for Him, *lo*, do I wait,' or 'I do not, *lo'*, await Him'?" He questions whether the positive assertion of the one, or the negative grapheme of the other (the traditional *qeri* and *ketiv*), should be followed. If one opts for the positive assertion, then R. Joshua's teaching about Job's piety is biblically supported. But if one opts for the negative *ketiv,* then R. Joshua's statement seems groundless. R. Joshua resolves the matter in favor of the positive theological assertion, relying for support on the theological remark in Job 26:5, "I shall not lose my integrity until I die." He uses a second scriptural verse from Job to support the primary claim of the *derashah.* On the face of it, this is an unexceptional midrashic maneuver; and one suspects that R. Joshua has stacked his rhetorical deck for just this end. Nevertheless, the very fact that the negative formulation was raised as a serious theological possibility should not pass unnoticed. Presumably, both readings were traditional, and no one manuscript tradition was more authoritative to determine the theological issue at hand. It was only the pull of a midrashic move (the invocation here of another Joban verse) which resolved the exegetical stalemate. It would appear that R. Yohanan ben Zakkai never thought of this prooftext when he asserted (earlier in the text) a contrary evaluation of Job. "Job," he said, "served God only from fear (of punishment)."

These two instances of scribal variation were subsequently canonized in the official *qeri-ketiv* lists of the Masoretes. But the ancient midrash also preserves homilies based on more unofficial textual variants. Indeed, this phenomenon explains the famous teaching of R. Haninah in *BT Baba Batra* 64a—recited to this day near the close of the traditional sabbath service. Referring to the post-exilic prophecy of Isaiah 54:13, "and your sons (*banayikh*) shall enjoy great peace," he said: "Do not read 'your sons (*banayikh*),' but '*bonayikh*—your builders.' " In its full context, this new reading provides a scriptural basis for a homily asserting that "the sages increase peace (*marbim shalom*) in the world," and "there will be great peace (*shalom rav*) for the lovers of Torah." There is little doubt that these two phrases about the increase of peace reutilize the scriptural lemma "great peace (*rav shalom*)." But on what basis does R. Haninah turn the whole discussion from "sons" to "builders"? Is this merely a natural association, something akin to the verbal pun found in Genesis 16:2?[5] Or is the exegetical exchange between *banayikh-bonayikh* based rather on a scribal variant? The fact that the large Isaiah scroll found at Qumran has a hanging *vav* after the initial *beth,* so that its *banaykhi* was pronounced *bonaykhi,* argues for the second alternative. The link between Massoretic "sons" (*banayikh*) and midrashic "builders" (*bonayikh*) may therefore be assumed to be both phonetic and orthographic in nature.[6] But R. Haninah does not just propose his new reading *bonayikh* for *banayikh.* He invokes it imperiously, saying, "Do not read (*'al tiqre*) 'your sons (*banayikh,*)' but (*'elah*) 'your builders (*bonayikh*).' " Indeed, with this exegetical formula (*'al tiqre . . . 'elah*) we have crossed to a new hermeneutical frontier. For if, in the case of genuine manuscript variants, there is a traditional imperative to read what is not written (in scripture), then we may say that the *'al tiqre* imperative is a midrashic instruction *not* to read what is the traditional reading. An oral tradition is thus written down as scripture.[7] Midrashic teachings like R. Haninah's (and they are legion) do not replace the traditional reading with a new authority; they rather suspend it playfully for the sake of the exposition, introducing difference where none was expected, and swerving a passage along a new contour of thought. And yet for all their exegetical delight, when we catch the midrashist *in flagrante delicto,* as it were, it is not so much his hermeneutical passion that excites our interest as his *passepartout:* his justification of a theological point on the basis of a biblical passage which conforms neither to the orthography nor to the sense of the original. In a word, the scriptural support is flagrantly non-scriptural in the most precise sense, for the midrashist shouts: *'al tiqre . . . 'elah,* "Do not read (this) but (that)." The theological justification thus appropriates scriptural authority *mirabile dictu,* that is to say, through the exegetical articulation of a midrashic *différance.*

I

Working at the surface of scripture, the *'al tiqre* technique paradoxically reconstructs the received letters of the Bible for the sake of providing a given teaching some biblical justification. Working at a deeper level, the technique also provides the means for articulating some relatively radical rabbinic theology. The following bit of midrashic exegesis demonstrates the point. My example comes from *BT Hagiga* 13a, where it is reported that the elders of Pumbeditha once requested Rab Joseph bar Hiyya to instruct them in the esoteric "Account of the Divine Chariot." "Said he to them: 'Concerning this we were taught (in Song 4:11): "Honey and milk under your tongue;" (that is,) words sweeter than honey and milk should be (kept) under your tongue.' " This said, the Talmudic text continues: "R. Abbahu inferred this (teaching prohibiting the public instruction of esoterica) from (Proverbs 27:26): 'lambs (*kevasim*) for your garments'; (that is,) things which are the secret of the world (*kivshono shel 'olam*) should be (kept) under your garment."

In the printed editions of the Talmud, the hermenuetical exchange made by R. Abbahu—from "lambs for your garment" to "secrets of the world"—is not explicit. It is only the manifest pun between "lambs" (*kevasim*) and "secrets" (*kevshono*) which suggests that the underlying biblical support for the instruction is *via* an implicit *'al tiqre* procedure. That is to say, R. Abbahu cited the word *kevasim* ("lambs") from scripture but implied the midrashic reading *kevushim* ("hidden things"), a simple enough transformation. This supposition is variously confirmed, by a manuscript tradition of this tractate,[8] by the citation of the *logion* in the *Ein Ya'akov* (ad loc.), and by the commentary of Jehuda ben Barzilai al Barceloni to the *Sefer Yetzira*.[9] For, alongside our printed Talmud text, the following reading is preserved after the citation from Proverbs: "Do not read '*kevasim*' but '*kevushim*' "; that is, " '*al tiqre* lambs, *'elah* secret things."[10]

I bring up this example for two reasons. First and foremost, it is typical of the implicit *'al tiqre* technique. Second, it introduces the rabbis' use of hermeneutical strategies of substitution to disclose more hidden scriptural meanings. In the present context, I shall limit myself to two examples of substitution, each of which discloses a mythic theology embedded in rabbinic midrash: divine empowerment through ritual praxis and divine pathos in response to human suffering.[11]

To sharpen the context, some pertinent reflections of Gershom Scholem may be recalled at this point. Speaking of Jewish mysticism, Scholem once observed that "[t]he whole of Aggadah," or the non-legal aspects of rabbinic midrash, "can in a way be regarded as a popular mythology of the Jewish universe." He further added that the "mythical element which is deeply rooted in the creative forms of Aggadic production" operates on a wider, cosmic plane in the Kabbalah.[12] This development is most clearly observed, he believed, in the sphere of ritual. Thus, as in the Bible, where (he said) the "history-saturated ritual was accompanied by no magical action" and the "rites of remembrance produce no *effect,*" "the ritual of Rabbinical Judaism [also] makes nothing happen and *transforms* nothing."[13] Both its rituals of remembrance and its rites of sanctification are "completely divorced from the solemnity of action on the mythical plane." By contrast, stressed Scholem, "nowhere does the Jewish literature of the Middle Ages bear the mythical character of these rites—except among the Kabbalists."[14]

If all this is true, it is only partially so. I say this not because I wish to reaffirm that the Aggadah is a "popular mythology of the Jewish universe." It certainly is. But such a characterization is, I think, an altogether weak reading of a certain portion of the midrashic corpus. To be sure, Scholem's characterization does not entirely demote the anthropomorphic and anthropopathic imagery of midrash to mere metaphor, but it underreads the bold production of mythical exegesis in the Aggadah. Such mythologizations of scripture are often composed in support of a mythical-magical view of God and the commandments. Something of this production and its poetics now follow.

## II

The first sermon in *Pisqa* 25 of the *Pisiqta de-Rav Kahana* was composed for sometime during the "Days of Penitence" before Yom Kippur.[15] The sermon, concerned with divine mercy and human praxis, opens with Job 17:9, "But the righteous one holds fast to his way, and the pure of hands will increase (his) strength (*yosif 'ometz*)." The preacher initially applies the passage to God, and therewith inverts the sense of the verse. Referring to Job's rebutting Eliphaz' claim (in 15:4) that his condition weakens other men's faith, the preacher now interprets the passage, theologically, to mean that God, who is both righteous and pure of action, gives strength (*koach*) to the righteous in order "that they may do His will." This construction concluded, the preacher then applies the Joban passage to both Moses and the righteous, citing R. Azariah's interpretation: "Whenever the righteous do the will of the Holy One, Blessed be He, they increase strength (*mosifin koach*) in the *dynamis*," that is to say, they empower the divine principle of immanent power through their performance of the commandments.[16] Quite certainly, "*some* thing" quite mythical (even magical) is presumed to obtain through the righteous performance of the commandments (*mitzvot*). The preacher reinforces this impression through the scriptural prooftexts he invokes to justify this assertion, as well as in the corresponding assertion that God is disempowered as a result of Israel's failure to do the commandments.

To support the ritual empowerment of God through performance of the *mitzvot,* the preacher adduces Numbers 14:17, "Let the strength (*koach*) of the Lord be made great." This text was first invoked in the sermon to support the attribution of the opening Joban verse to Moses. This would suggest that Moses, a righteous one, was able to empower (*ma'atzim koach*) God's attribute of mercy through this particular prayer. This interpretation conforms to a consistent Targumic and midrashic tradition on this verse.[17] The overall notion recurs dramatically in several Talmudic sources as well. For example, just this theological idea is the basis for the remarkable prayer which God is said to recite to himself and which the divine power Akhatriel asks the high priest Ishmael to recite *on God's behalf* when he enters the holy of holies on the Day of Atonement (*BT Berakhot* 7a).[18] On the basis of this and related evidence, we may surmise that our homily's reference to divine empowerment through the faithful performance of the commandments was also understood to mean the empowerment of God's attribute of mercy. Such a possibility is strengthened by the fact that this discourse was designed for the days of penitence before Yom Kippur.[19] In any event, this *theologoumenon* of ritual empowerment is complemented by the following equally remarkable statement: "and if not (i.e. if the commandments are not performed), (then the verse) 'You have forgotten the Rock which bore you' (Deut. 32:18) applies, as it were (*kivyakhol*)."

The prooftext is an apparent puzzle. It is not directly obvious how this deuteronomic verse supports the assertion which precedes it. In fact, the Masoretic citation *tzur yeladekha teshi,* "you have forgotten the Rock (viz. God) which bore you," seems to have no relation to this context. What possible scriptural justification could this passage provide for the assertion that failure to perform the commandments results in a diminishment of God? Is there an exegetical connection between this "forgetting God" and the diminishment of divine power? The answer lies in the implicit *'al tiqre* technique at play. Although nothing is added to the deuteronomic prooftext in this sermon, homiletical glosses found in *Leviticus Rabba* (XXIII.12) and *Sifrei Deuteronomy* (319) suggest that the verb *teshi* ("you have forgotten") was midrashically construed as if it was derived from the stem *nashash* ("to weaken") or *natash* ("to destroy"), but *not* from the stem *nashah* ("to forget"). Accordingly, while the assertion of divine empowerment through ritual praxis is exegetically established by reinterpreting Job 17:9 and Numbers 14:17, the corresponding notion of divine depletion through ritual lassitude is scripturally justified by means of an implicit rereading of the Masoretic prooftext. One must therefore not read *teshi* ("you have forgotten"), but *hetashta* ("you have weakened") God who bore you!

A profound theology of the commandments, with mythic-cosmic implications, is presupposed here. It hints at a theurgy of ritual praxis which undoubtedly enlivened the concrete commitment to the *mitzvot* in ancient Judaism. Yet the biblical justification of the foregoing rabbinic theology is in effect not a biblical justification at all but, rather, a midrashic one. In the *'al tiqre* hermeneutic, the exegetical imperative is not to read scripture as received, but as revised. Midrash is thus not so much a rewritten Bible, in the manner of the Book of Jubilees or pseudo-Philo's *Liber Antiquitatum Biblicarum*. It is rather a reread bible: a drama of readerly collusion. If this is so, one may wonder about the scriptural authority for the midrashic instructions. Indeed, one may even feel a bit like Alice in Wonderland, who objects to Humpty Dumpty's imperious substitution of the phrase "a nice knock-down argument" for the word "glory." In a rather scornful tone, Humpty Dumpty retorts, "When *I* use a word, it means just what I choose it to mean—neither more nor less." When Alice asks whether one "*can* make words mean different things," the resourceful Humpty counters that "the question is which is to be master—that's all."

To echo Mr. Dumpty's retort, one must ponder about the rabbis' method. Granting that no rabbinic midrashist intended his interpretative act to dispossess the scriptural authority of the Bible, how did the sages assert their exegetical authority over the text? The answer for the case at hand (Deut 32:18) lies, I think, in the word *kivyakhol*—translated earlier by "as it were." On the face of it, this term appears to be a pious gloss on the mythical midrash at hand, a kind of rational disclaimer, signifying that the acute anthropopathic assertions about God should not be taken literally. Recalling the exposition in Deuteronomy 32:18, one might therefore claim that the pointed use of *kivyakhol* serves to weaken the bold notion that ritual failure diminishes God: to say that this theology is only adduced *als ob,* "as if" one could suppose such a thing. In fact, and for understandable reasons, this has been the explanation of the word *kivyakhol* in the long history of its exegesis, from Rashi's Talmudic glosses (for example, *BT Yoma* 3b) to the researches of N. Bruell,[20] and W. Bacher.[21] But if *kivyakhol* is in fact a rational disclaimer for exegetical daring, we must still wonder why such mythical midrash was invoked in the first place. Why assert (about God) with one breath what one feels constrained to withdraw with another? Why open the mouth to temptation at all?

The solution to the exegetical issue is less convoluted than the solution to the theological issue. The use of *kivyakhol* in classical midrash is in fact no poor man's piety but the heroics of rabbinic hermeneutics. It provided a way of becoming master of the text and its theology while simultaneously acknowledging the independent authority of scripture. Indeed, a full review of the evidence suggests that whenever the word *kivyakhol* was used—and it was used primarily in assertions about God—it functioned to indicate that *if* one read the biblical passage midrashically, then such and so is the sense which *could be* construed.[22] That is to say, the formula *kivyakhol* literally means "as it were" or "if one may suppose," but it served to introduce a reading of scripture built by a midrashic construction, usually of the (implicit) *'al tiqre* type. Let us return to the midrashic exposition of Deuteronomy 32:18 cited earlier. Freely paraphrased, the passage reads, "If you do not perform the commandments, then the scriptural phrase *tzur yeladekha teshi* ("you have forgotten the

Rock which bore you") applies to you; for it can be understood to mean, *as it were:* 'you have weakened God (the Rock) who bore you.' " In this and many other examples, scripture justifies the midrashic instruction at hand. We must only stress that it does so *kivyakhol:* only on the strength of the exegete's bold rereading of it.

## III

I have thus far isolated two modalities of mythical midrash: those expressing theologies of divine empowerment, and those dealing with divine pathos. As with the preceding example, the following expositions also utilize the term *kivyakhol* in conjunction with the (implicit) *'al tiqre* method. I shall start with an example of historical pathos.

*Exodus Rabba* (XXX.24) preserves a dense but expressive exegesis of the phrase *ki qerova yeshu'ati lavo',* "for My salvation is near to come" (Is 56:1). Within the scriptural context of this phrase, God simply announces the imminent advent of his salvation. Accordingly, the pronoun suffix of *yeshu'ati (/ti/)* functions as a straightforward objective genitive; that is to say, "My salvation" means the act of salvation which God (the speaker) will bring about. This sense is inverted in the course of the exposition. With deceptively naive literalism, the midrashist construes the suffix as a subjective genitive, so that the text now projects an image of God's own salvation. The midrashist begins with a philologist's observation: "Scripture does not say *'your* salvation' (2nd person plural) but *'My* salvation.' " And he adds: "May His Name be blessed! For were it not (so) written (in scripture), one could not say it *('ilulei she-haddavar katuv 'iy 'epshar le-'omero).*"

What is the point? Why does the midrashist belabor the grammatical *différance* between "My" and "your" salvation if the sense is semantically straightforward? The answer unfolds in the continuation of the *derashah,* where God is made to say: "If you (Israel) do not have merit, I shall perform (the salvation) *bishvili,* for My *own* sake; for, *kivyakhol,* as long as you are in trouble I am with you, as it says (in scripture): *'imo 'anokhi betzarah,* 'I am with him (Israel) in trouble' (Ps. 91:15). And, I will redeem Myself, as it says . . . 'Rejoice greatly, O daughter of Jerusalem . . . (for) behold your king comes unto you: He is righteous and *nosha'*, victorious (Zech. 9:9).' " After citing this last prooftext, the midrashist adds another textual observation. "Scripture does not write *moshi'a* ('a savior') but *nosha'* ('is saved')." With this philological flourish, the rhetor rounds-off his exegetical proof that the Isaianic verse (*ki kerova yeshu'ati lavo'*) means "*My* salvation is near to come."

If "salvation is near to come," the hermeneutical process of this midrash is far from forthcoming. A clue to its meaning lies in the conjunction of the formula *'ilulei she-haddavar katuv* ("were it not [so] stated in scripture") with the term *kivyakhol.* When this occurs, the midrashic sense of the lemma is derived by reinflecting the written grapheme (the *davar katuv,* "scripture" in the literal sense) in anthropomorphic or anthropopathic ways. The received letters or vowels of scripture remain intact. As a result, new sense is not construed through a semiotic refiguration of the forms of scripture, but by their semantic re-emphasis. By stressing the significance of the pronominal suffix /*ti*/ and by also emphasizing God's involvement in Israel's suffering and salvation, the midrashist indicates that his reinterpretation of the Isaianic verse hinges upon reading *yeshu'ati* as a noun plus a *subjective* genitive. Thus one is expected to read "*My own* salvation is near to come," not "*My* salvation is near to come." The midrash on Isaiah 56:1 thus unfolds by means of an implicit *'al tiqre* procedure which semantically rereads "what is written in scripture" in a daring theological way.

The same hermeneutical logic underlies the other prooftexts in this homiletical unit. For example, whereas the passage from Psalm 91:15 (*'imo 'anokhi betzarah*) would ordinarily be construed to mean "I (God) shall be with him (Israel) in his suffering," now, under the pressure of the midrashic rereading of *yeshu'ati,* these words are reinflected to mean, "I (God) will be with Israel *betzarah,* sufferingly," that is, in shared pathos. A similar exegetical pressure affects the final proof of the exposition, which cites Zechariah 9:9 and adds the observation that "Scripture does not write *moshi'a* but *nosha'.*" Since one would have naturally expected an active participle like *moshi'a* ("savior") to correspond to the first noun *tzaddik* ("righteous"), the specific use of the passive-reflexive participle *nosha'* ("is saved") can only confirm for the midrashist that God's own salvation is textually marked in scripture. Thus, once again the hermenuetical term *kivyakhol* signals a daring reinflection of the traditional sense and sensibility of scripture. And once again the Bible is turned against itself to produce a myth of divine pathos.

In other midrashic texts, this co-suffering of God and Israel is personalized through a *mythos* of divine compassion for human pain. A striking example occurs in *Mishnah Sanhedrin* (6.4). This text reports an historical episode about capital punishment by hanging. Added to it is the practice of removing a hanged corpse before nightfall, in fulfillment of the negative commandment (Deut 21:23): "His body shall not remain all night upon the tree; but thou shalt surely bury him the same day, for he that is hanged is a curse against God (*ki qilelat 'elohim talui*)." The precise meaning of this rule was a matter of ancient legal discussion, as is attested by the exegetical discussions of it preserved in the so-called *Temple Scroll.* In part, the issue turned on whether the regulation prescribed death by hanging or hanging (for show and shame) after the death penalty was administered (by some other means).[23] Our *mishnah* concludes with successive midrashic expositions of the deuteronomic text, each one elicited by the motivation clause that is appended to the biblical rule ("for he that is hanged is a curse against God"). The first of these expositions, following the aforementioned case of capital punishment (for witchcraft), interprets the biblical phrase "for he that is hanged is a curse against God" to mean that he that is hanged (is so punished) because he cursed (the name of) God. This comment is itself the result of a bold hermeneutical maneuver. But, for present purposes, our attention is drawn to the very next *mishnah* (6.5) where another more remarkable interpretation is provided. We read, "Rabbi Meir said: 'When a person is in grave trouble (*mitzta'er*), what does the Shekhinah say? (It says) *kivyakhol:* "My head is in pain, my arm is in pain (*qallani me-roshi, qallani mi-yadi*).' "

What is involved here? What is the relation between the human suffering in the first part of Rabbi Meier's remark and the divine sympathy subsequently asserted about the Shekhinah, God's indwelling presence? The clue lies once more with the term *kivyakhol.* This term introduces a blatant anthropopathism into the midrash and signals an implicit *'al tiqre* hermeneutic. The result is that our scriptural verse ("for he that is hanged is a curse against God, *ki qilelat 'elohim talui*") is radically reappropriated to support a theology of divine pathos. Between the lemma and the teaching is a midrashic reading which runs something like this: "for a hanged one (viz. a human in distress) is a *qilelat* of God; (however) do not read *qilelat 'elohim*, a curse of God, but *qallat 'elohim*, the pain of God."

It is a secondary matter here that the key verb *qalal* must be euphemistically construed in order for the midrash to make sense. The central hermeneutical fact is rather that Deuteronomy 21:23 serves to express a midrashic *mythologoumenon* of divine suffering. Remarkably, by the merest exegetical allowance, we find that scripture enfolds a myth of divine care in an old casuistic construction. So delicate, indeed, is the thread of discourse that the merest move of the midrashic shuttle weaves a texture of compassion around a stern legal rule. In this way, a motivation clause which advocates the removal of a hanged corpse because of the horrific blasphemy involved reveals the shudder of divine anguish at human suffering. The readerly collusion between midrashist and audience thus stands exposed for all its hermeneutical power. More precisely, through his punning allusion to a shared lemma (*qallani* alludes to *qilelat 'elohim*), the exegete involves the reader in the active process of midrashic production. Accepting the intertextual invitation, the addressee may re-enact the exegete's own rereading of the biblical text in the manner of a midrashic mimesis, moving from a shared scripture to its shared reauthoring. In this process also lies the reauthorization of Torah for the community as a whole.

Our final example of mythical midrash further extends the discussion of readerly collusion one step more. The text is found in *Sifrei Bemidbar* (*Beha'alotekha*), *Pisqa* 84.[24] Starting with the biblical phrase *veyanusu misaneykha*, "And may Your enemies (O Lord) be routed" (Num 10:35), the comments successively turn on the pivot of God's enemies. The midrash opens with the comment that "anyone who hates Israel, as it were (*ke'ilu*), hates the Creator"; the point is concluded with appropriate prooftexts. The midrash then adds, "and anyone who rises against Israel, as it were (*ke'ilu*), rises against God." After several prooftexts, the following verse from Zechariah (2:12) is adduced: "for whoever hurts you (viz. Israel) is like one who hurts his own eye (*kenoge'a be-vavat 'eyno*)." Of this verse, Rabbi Judah said, "Scripture does not say *be-vavat 'ayin* (who hurts an eye,) but *be-vavat 'eyno,* his (very own) eye." And he added, "Scripture is directed, *kivyakhol,* against God, but it has been euphemistically modified (*'elah she-kinah ha-katuv*)." There then follows a whole list of cases where scripture has been putatively changed because, otherwise, the formulation about God would appear unseemly. These are the famous cases of scribal corrections, also known as *tiqqunei sopherim.*[25]

Just what about Zechariah 2:12 was theologically disrespectful? The exegetical mote is apparently the anthropomorphic simile that is used: "for whosoever hurts you *is like* one who hurts his own eye (*'eyno*)." But as you can see, as it were, there is really nothing in this phrase which even remotely requires euphemistic correction. The simile seems quite neutral: "his eye" refers to the eye of the avenger, who, by hurting Israel, hurts himself as well. It is only the mythic theology of the midrash which produces a hypothetical reconstruction of an assumed uncorrected text, one in which God presumably said, "Whoever hurts Israel is like one who hurts *My* eye (that is, *'eyni* for *'eyno*)." In fact, the midrashist acknowledges this rabbinic reconstruction by invoking the word *kivyakhol,* his index of a hypothetical reading, before citing the prooftext from Zechariah.

Since none of the other biblical texts adduced as euphemistic revisions deals with this theme of divine pathos, and since none of them uses the word *kivyakhol,* I am inclined to suppose that they are all intrusive in this midrash. My supposition is further supported by the existence (in different forms in the different manuscripts) of a repetition of R. Judah's midrash (along with the word *kivyakhol*) after the list of texts, in the manner of an editorial resumption which brackets a literary interpolation.[26] I therefore contend that, among other prooftexts, at least our Zecharian passage is a midrash, and no scribal correction in the exact sense.[27] R. Judah's comment presupposes that we do not read *'eyno,* "his eye," with the received Masoretic text, but *'eyni,* "My eye," as the midrashic subtext. In comparison with other examples of the *'al tiqre* phenomenon, the brazenness of the midrashic maneuver here is that the hermeneutical construction does not hypothecate a *new* text but dares to assert an *original* scripture. It would seem that midrashic authority and textual authorship get confused in this instance. But let us not be doubly duped. We were duly warned, *kivyakhol.*

IV

In the course of these reflections, I have referred to a readerly collusion between the exegetical speaker and the addressee. *Do not read* this *but* that, we hear (*'al tiqre . . . 'elah*). Repeatedly, a will to theological power through textuality has reformed and reimagined scripture. The markings of *kivyakhol* are nothing if they are not also the signs of hermeneutical desire, the imaginative shaping of the letters of scripture in accordance with theological will. Midrashic projection thus seems to qualify as a majestic mimesis, an exegetical tracing of thought along the curve of God's letters for the sake of divinizing human desire. Slowly, one reading after another, the words of scripture are reformed and reunited into a new corpus: midrash.

To what may this be compared? To the scattered fragments of Osiris, which were gathered up by Isis in her patient wanderings over the land. This old myth, probably in the form retold by Plutarch, was itself compared by Milton (also in the *Areopagitica*) to the destruction of virgin Truth, whose "lovely form" was hewed "into a thousand pieces, and scattered to the four winds. From that time ever since, the sad friends of Truth, such as durst appear, imitating the careful search that Isis made for the mangled body of Osiris, went up and down gathering limb by limb, still as they could find them." Strange to say, this account of Isis and Osiris is almost certainly the basis of the wonderful midrash in the *Mekhilta de-Rabbi Ishmael* (*Va-yehi Be-shallach* 1) dealing with Moses' recovering the bones of Joseph buried in the Nile.[28] According to this legend, the casket containing Joseph's bones arose from the hidden depths after Moses inscribed a gold tablet with God's holy name (the *Shem Ha-Meforash*) and threw it into the river while reciting an adjuration.[29] However, do not read *Shem Ha-Meforash,* the explicitly articulated name of God, but the *shem ha-meforash,* the nouns and words which are articulated by the descendants of Moses. These are the words of midrash, which are joined to scripture as bone is joined to bone, so that a new creation be formed, *kivyakhol.*

## NOTES

1. See *Sifrei Deuteronomy,* ed. L. Finkelstein, p. 423; also *Aboth de-Rabbi Nathan,* B, ch 46, ed. S. Schechter, 65a, and *PT Ta'anit* iv 2.68a.

2. For the reading "one reading" and "another (reading)," emending *biderash 'ehad* and *biderash 'aher* to *biderekh 'ehad* and *biderekh 'aher,* respectively, see S. Lieberman, *Hellenism in Jewish Palestine* (New York: The Jewish Theological Seminary of America, 1962), 21 n 9.

3. For an overall introduction to the *qeri-ketiv* phenomenon, see the discussion of C.D. Ginsburg, *Introduction to the Massoretico-Critical Edition of the Hebrew Bible* (1897), part II, chap. vii; also chap. xi (iii–iv). This work has been reprinted with a critical prolegomenon by H. Orlinsky (New York: Ktav Publishing House, 1966). For a critique of earlier views, and a fresh proposal, see J. Barr, "A New Look at Ketibh-Qere," *Oudtestamentische Studien* 21 (1981), pp. 19–37.

4. In addition to this phrase, cf. the equivalent expression *ve-'adayin ha-davar talui* in *Sifrei Deuteronomy,* ed. Finkelstein, p. 393. On the more complicated idiom *ve-ad akshav ha-moznayim me'uyin* ("and thus far the scales are balanced"), see *Tanhuma, ki tissa'* 34; also cf. *Tanhuma* Buber, *Shelah,* Add. from Ms Rome 39b–40a. This idiom has been the subject of much recent discussion, for which see M. Friedman in *Tarbiz* 54 (1984–85), with previous literature and texts indicated.

5. In the remark "Perhaps *'ibbaneh* from her" there is a play on the verb *banah* ("to build") and the noun *ben* ("son"). One can understand *'ibbaneh* to mean "I shall be built up" *and* "I shall be provided a son."

6. See the discussion of E.Y. Kutscher, *Ha-Lashon Ve-Hareqa'Ha-Leshoni Shel Megillat Yeshayah* (Jerusalem: Magnes Press, 1959), p. 171. There are many other cases where the vowel *qametz qaton* is marked by a *vav* at Qumran. A Massoretic parallel

occurs at Jeremiah 1:5. The traditional *ketiv* for "I created you" is *'etzarekh,* while the *qeri* is *'etzorekh*—with a *vav* used to mark the second vowel. Medieval speculations to the contrary (Rashi and R. Joseph Kara construed the *qeri* from the stem *tzur* ("to circumscribe"), it would seem that the *qeri-ketiv* variants here are simply orthographic alternatives of the same verbal stem *yatzar* ("to create").

7. See the compendium and discussion of A. Rosenzweig, "Die Al-Tikrei Deutungen," *Festscrift . . . I. Lewy* (Breslau, 1911), pp. 204–53. A rich range of examples may be culled from the often remarkable (traditional) study of R. Samuel Waldberg, *Sefer Darkei Ha-Shinnuyim* (Lemberg, 1870, reprinted by Makor, Jerusalem, 1970). Many thanks to Prof. David Weiss Halivni for this reference and for providing me with a copy.

8. See H. Strack, *Talmud Babylonicum cod. Monacensis,* 95 (Leiden, 1912), fol. 71b.

9. See his *Commentary* on the *Sefer Yetzirah* (Berlin: Z.H. Itzkovski, 1885), 23.

10. For a striking use of Proverbs 27:26 in connection with *sitrei torah,* see *Song of Songs Rabba* I.i.2.

11. For present purposes, I make use of the term "mythic theology" in the sense of *historia divina,* that is to say, the actions and feelings of God in the heavenly realm.

12. See *Major Trends in Jewish Mysticism* (New York: Schocken Books, paper ed., 1961), p. 31.

13. *On the Kabbalah and Its Symbolism* (New York: Schocken Books, 1965), p. 121.

14. *Ibid.,* pp. 121f.

15. See ed. Mandelbaum, II, 379–81, for the text.

16. Greek *dynamis* here translates Hebrew *gevurah.* Cf. the wide-ranging discussion of E.E. Urbach, *The Sages* (Jerusalem: Magnes Press, 1969), ch. 5 (Hebrew).

17. See Targum Ps.-Jonathan I, *ad loc.;* and the tradition in *Yalqut Shim'oni, Ve'ethanan* 814.

18. For an analysis of the divine power who figures in this passage, see G. Scholem, *Jewish Gnosticism, Merkabah Mysticism, and Talmudic Tradition* (New York: The Jewish Theological Seminary of America, 1965), pp. 751–55; and for a striking prayer of the type

suggested by our passage, see M. Cohen, *The Shi'ur Qomah* (Landham: University Press of America, 1983), 246, 11. 182–85.

19. More precise speculations regarding the occasion of this discourse are offered by A. Goldberg in *Qiryat Sefer* 43 (1967–68), 77.

20. *"kivyakhol,"* in J.J. Kobak's *Jeschurun* 4 (1871), 1–6.

21. *Die exegetische Terminologie der jüdischen Traditionsliteratur* (Leipzig, 1899), I, 72.

22. A. Marmorstein, *The Old Rabbinic Doctrine of God. II. Essays in Anthropomorphism* (London, 1937; reprinted by KTAV; New York, 1968), 131, recognized that *kivyakhol* is no mere disclaimer for rabbinic anthropomorphisms, and that it is found near scriptural passages. But he left the point hanging and, in a sense, ambiguous. In addition, his fanciful explanation of the term as an acronym thoroughly blurred a precise appreciation of the dynamics at hand.

23. See *Megillat Ha-Miqdash*, ed. Y. Yadin (Jerusalem, 1977), I: 285–90, II: 202–04. The particular construction found there, where the *vav* of (*vehumat*) *vetalita* is understood as explicative (viz. "and you shall hang him on a tree, *that* he die) is also preserved in the beraitha at *BT Sanhedrin* 46b, and in textual readings found in the Peshitta and some manuscripts of the Septuagint. On these readings, see M. Wilcox, " 'Upon the Tree'—Deut. 21:22–23 in the New Testament," *Journal of Biblical Literature* 96 (1977):90 and L Rosso, "Deuteronomio 21,22. Contributo del Rotolo Alla Valutazione di una Variante Medievale dei Settanta," *Revue de Qumran* 9 (1977):231–36.

24. In the edition of H.S. Horovitz, *Siphre D'Be Rab* (Leipzig, 1917; reprinted by Wahrmann Books; Jerusalem, 1966), pp. 81f.

25. On this, cf. Ginsburg, *op. cit.,* pp. 347–67. For early examples of this phenomenon in the Bible, see my *Biblical Interpretation in Ancient Israel* (Oxford: The Clarendon Press, 1985), pp. 66–77.

26. For this phenomenon, see H. Weiner, *The Composition of Judges II 11 to 1 Kings II 46* (Leipzig: J.C. Hinrichs, 1929), and C. Kuhl, "Die 'Wiederaufnahme'—ein literarisches Prinzip?" *Zeitschrift fur die alttestamentlicher Wissenschaft* 64 (1952), pp. 1–11.

27. For an even stronger conclusion, see W.E. Barnes, "Ancient

Corrections in the Text of the Old Testament (*Tikkun Sopherim*)," *Journal of Theological Studies* 1 (1900):413: "the *tikkun* tradition is not Massoretic (i.e., textual) but Midrashic (i.e., exegetical or, more accurately, homiletic)." This position is rejected by Lieberman, *op. cit.*, pp. 28–37.

28. See the observations of M. Gudemann, *Religionsgeschichtliche Studien* (Leipzig, 1876), pp. 26ff, and B. Heller, "Die Saga von Sarge Josephs . . . ," *Monatschrift für die Geschichte und Wissenshaft des Judentums* 70 (1926): 271ff.

29. For an examination of the textual and recensional variants of this text with an eye to their treatment of the "magical" content involved, see J. Goldin, "The Magic of Magic and Superstition," in *Aspects of Religious Propaganda in Judaism and Early Christianity*, ed. E. Schüssler Fiorenza (Notre Dame: University of Notre Dame Press, 1976), pp. 127f (and notes).

# PART THREE: PRAGMATIC TRENDS IN MEDIEVAL AND EARLY MODERN PHILOSOPHY

Postcritical scholars tend to be suspicious of traditional philosophy. They view philosophy's presumption of a privileged role among the sciences as either a challenge to the authority of revealed scripture or as a vain attempt to locate a single canon of knowledge outside of the plurality of communities in which knowledge finds its contexts. The canons of knowledge are intracommunal or intratextual, and there is no getting àt.these canons without intimate acquaintance with the practices through which they are displayed.

This postcritical critique of philosophy is warranted but overstated. It is warranted by the fact that classical and modern philosophers tended to ignore the intratextual or intracommunal contexts of knowledge. They tended either to privilege one context over another, without saying so, or to launch major reforms of a given community of knowledge under the guise of a search for the purported foundations of knowledge itself. The postcritical critique is overstated, however, because it extends its critique of specific traditions of philosophic practice to an unwarranted critique of philosophic practice *in general.* In fact, postcritical scholarship is well served by postcritical developments in philosophy itself, as illustrated by the pertinence of Wittgenstein's *Investigations* to the Christian theory of intratextuality and of Peirce's pragmatism to the theory of rabbinic semiotics.

As suggested in the Introduction to this volume, philosophy has at least two major contributions to make to the development of postcritical inquiry. The first is to provide the logical discipline required for articulating the rules of interpretation that are embedded in specific practices of scriptural interpretation. In their day to day work, text scholars do not need to think self-consciously about these rules; indeed, attempts at such self-consciousness would, more likely than not, interfere with their attentiveness to the work at hand. Self-consciousness has its function, however, at times of significant change, or of "paradigm shifts," in the practice of interpretation. At these times, former practices no longer seem to work, and scholars find themselves, willy-nilly, debating specific rules of interpretation and arguing on behalf of specific ways of reforming these rules. The essays collected in Parts One and Two of this volume present context-specific, reformatory arguments of this kind. These arguments are already philosophic, to the extent that they attempt to bring embedded rules to self-consciousness. And each of them could be strengthened—that is, brought under more complete self-control—through the use of logical procedures developed in postcritical philosophy. The goal of this philosophy is, specifically, to strengthen the procedures that are available for articulating and evaluating intratextual or intracommunal rules of interpretation.

The second contribution of postcritical philosophy is to facilitate dialogue among reformers from different canons of interpretation, that is, among practitioners who are attempting to articulate, evaluate and reform some of their respective communities' rules of interpretation. The postcritical approach is not, in the fashion of traditional philosophy, to search for some single, extracommunal criterion for arbitrating among the various sets of rules. It is, instead, to disclose ways in which one community's methods of repairing rules may be pertinent to another community's methods, and vice versa. The Introduction to this volume illustrates the postcritical approach. There it is suggested that certain Christian scholars offer theories of interpretation pertinent to the reformatory efforts of certain Jewish scholars, while the Jewish scholars offer studies of rabbinic midrash pertinent to the reformatory efforts of the Christian scholars. The paradigm of "postcritical scriptural interpretation" is itself a philosophic construction, introduced as a means of identifying whatever reciprocal interests may link these two communities of scholars. Whether or nor this particular paradigm succeeds as an instrument of dialogue, it illustrates the kinds of paradigm that will be needed to facilitate dialogue among disparate communities of knowledge.

The essays of Part Three of this volume show that the postcritical model of philosophy is not altogether new in western tradition. Certain medieval and early modern philosophers already began to criticize the classical conception of knowledge as privileged cognition or privileged experience and to replace it with an understanding of knowledge as knowledge-in-use. They claimed, furthermore, that the process of knowing is completed only in the nurturance of human character, as displayed in publicly recognizable signs. And they tended to illustrate their claims through studies of scriptural traditions.

The Bible scholar Moshe Greenberg examines the uses of scripture in Moses Maimonides' law compendium, the *Mishneh Torah.* As suggested by the series of hermeneutical devices he employed to reread scripture, Maimonides claimed that we know a revealed text through our interpretive responses to it and through the ways those responses guide our conduct in the world. In this view, Maimonides' philosophic study of scripture need not be read as a merely allegorizing attempt to reread scriptural texts as types of which some *a priori* metaphysics provided the anti-type. The anti-types of his scripture were, instead, *pragmata:* that is, forms of practice, or fundamental ways of living in the world, of which the rabbinic virtues were paradigmatic. Maimonides' philosophy was in this sense an instrument for disclosing and reforming the rules of interpretation-and-conduct embedded in his community's discourse.

The theologian David Burrell offers a comparative study of ways in which early modern representatives of the three scriptural faiths understood the relation between religious practice and theological discourse. According to Burrell, Maimonides' agnosticism was paradigmatic of the concern of all three faiths to respect the ontological difference between God and creation. Thomas Aquinas claimed that we know the unknown and perfectly simple God through the way our understanding of God's names leads us into a process of interminable spiritual development or perfection. Aquinas' notion of perfection terms provided a linguistically sophisticated paradigm of the three faiths' performative, as opposed to merely mimetic, knowledge of God. Al-Ghazali, finally, offered a paradigmatic account of the spiritual training necessary for the proper knowledge-in-use of God's names.

The rabbinic semiotician José Faur examines the contributions of the *converso* thinker Francisco Sánchez to modern philosophic skepticism, in particular to what he considers the overthrow of scholastic authoritarianism in the sciences of nature and of ecclesial authoritarianism in scriptural hermeneutics. According to Faur, Sánchez inherited Maimonides' rabbinic skepticism, according to which our knowledge of nature and of revealed texts always remains a knowledge-in-use. In Sánchez' work, this pragmatic conception yielded an early doctrine of scientific experimentalism and a critique of the intrusions of ecclesiastical political authority into religious practice. While otherwise critical of Spinoza's self-separation from the rabbinic community, Faur finds him in one ironic sense a worthy disciple of the tradition of Maimonides and Sánchez: he helped liberate Bible reading from the impositions of metaphysical as well as political *a priorisms*.

The pragmatic philosopher John E. Smith examines Jonathan Edwards' attempt to redirect the course of American Puritanism, from introspective soul-searching to a pragmatic concern with the signs of holiness, in particular, with holy practice. In Smith's reading, Edwards claimed that we know the world through our affective and transformative responses to it and that we know ourselves through the manifestation of these responses in our spiritual development and conduct. Displayed through "signs" of the Spirit's indwelling, these manifestations acquire, ultimately, a public face. As Smith has argued elsewhere, Edwards anticipated the pragmatists' identification of our intellectual conceptions with what Peirce called "conditional dispositions to act."

Like Edwards, all the medieval and early modern thinkers described in these essays may be dubbed *proto-pragmatists*. Their identification of knowledge with knowledge-in-use brought them just one step away from the postcritical claim that knowledge-in-use means knowledge within the context of intracommunal practice.

Chapter Seven

# THE USES OF SCRIPTURE IN CLASSICAL, MEDIEVAL JUDAISM: PROOFTEXTS IN MAIMONIDES' CODE

## MOSHE GREENBERG

In the cultural tradition of the west, the Jews are the oldest extant example of a people constituted throughout most of its history by allegiance to a written document, the Torah: referring, in its larger sense, to all of Hebrew scriptures as well as to its authorized interpretation. The canonical scriptures defined Israel as a people, prescribed its norms of conduct and described its place in the past and future of humanity. The tradition of authorized interpretation lent the Torah its social efficacy by (1) enacting a program of mass education as prescribed in the canon and thereby providing the Torah a popular base, and (2) maintaining and vigorously expanding the canon's own procedures and traditions of exegesis, thereby assuring the canon's continuous adjustment to contemporary needs.

Both these factors are displayed in Maimonides' great digest of Jewish law and theology, the *Mishneh Torah* ("a second to the Torah," or, more popularly, the "Code").[1] Ostensibly imitating the *Mishnah* of Rabbi Judah the Prince, Maimonides presents his Code for popular edification, summing up the beliefs and practices of Judaism topically, in categorical, non-argumentative form, as they may be gathered from talmudic, midrashic and geonic[2] literature. The Code is to be, literally, a "second to the Torah":

A person who will first read the written Torah and after-
wards this work, through which he will learn the oral law
entire, will not need to read another book besides.[3]

Juxtaposing written and oral law, Maimonides incorporates into the
Code a great number of biblical prooftexts, many more in fact than
in Rabbi Judah's *Mishnah*.[4] These prooftexts establish the Code's
scriptural authority. At the same time, they appear to employ scriptural citations in other than their contextual or plain sense. In this
way, the prooftexts also establish the authority of the hermeneutical
procedures that the Code's readers must employ in order to reason
from the plain sense of scripture to its use in the Code.

In this article I describe the results of an exercise in interpreting
the hermeneutical operations exhibited in the prooftexts used in the
first book of Maimonides' Code: the *Sefer Ha-Madda'*, or "Book of
Knowledge," the most theological book of the Code.[5] I compared
the plain sense of each scriptural citation in its primary or scriptural
context with the meaning Maimonides attributes to it when used as
prooftext. For each citation, I then identified a hermeneutical procedure according to which the meaning-in-use may be evolved from
the plain sense. These are the hermeneutical procedures the Code's
readers must recognize in order to acknowledge the Code's scriptural authority. I have identified fifteen hermeneutical procedures,
accounting for virtually all of the prooftexts in *Sefer Ha-Madda'*.[6]
Many prooftexts display more than one of the procedures; very few
merely embellish Maimonides' claims, and fewer still are enigmatic.

While Maimonides does not disclose his sources, most of the
prooftexts are drawn from the talmudic and midrashic literature. To
this extent, the Code offers a representative sampling of the hermeneutical procedures of classical Judaism in its maturity. A smaller
group of prooftexts displays Maimonides' philosophical interests
independent of the central tendencies of talmudic Judaism. It may
be said that the Code calls into play hermeneutical principles which
contemporize the scriptural sources according to the understanding
of the intellectual elite of twelfth to thirteenth century Jewry.

Such a reading of the biblical prooftexts in *Sefer Ha-Madda'* is
"holistic" rather than historical. Elsewhere,[7] I have described the

holistic reading of scripture as the attempt to identify a scriptural text's plain or contextual sense for an "ideal reader." For interpreting the primary, biblical text, I define the ideal reader as a personification of the full range of interpretive possibilities inherent in the text at the time when it reached its present disposition.

In this exercise, the ideal reader is defined in terms of Maimonides' declared purpose to provide a book which would suffice by itself to complement the Bible. The ideal reader, then, possesses but two books, the Bible and the Code. The Code, however, supplies not only a vast elaboration of the Bible's normative content, but also a great number of specific interpretations of biblical passages. Ignorant of the varied historical origins of these interpretations, our reader perceives their products as synchronous and as displaying a large range of hermeneutical extensions of the plain sense. I assume that the reader will distinguish between the plain sense of a passage of scripture and its meaning-in-use in the Code and will therefore understand the Code as authorizing the hermeneutical procedures implicit in its use of prooftexts.

The following pages are divided into two sections. In Section One I present the results of my exercise in interpretive reading. I identify each hermeneutical procedure with a letter of the alphabet, a descriptive label and a brief summary of its principal features. For each procedure, I provide several illustrations from the Code, generally placing one in the body of the paper and the rest in end notes. Where appropriate, I append a comment explicating the gap between the plain sense of the scriptural citation and its meaning-in-use in the Code. While Maimonides has drawn most of the Code's prooftexts from rabbinic sources, I adopt the convention in Section One of referring to "M" as the author responsible for the use to which the prooftext is put. In Section Two I summarize the results of this exercise.

## SECTION ONE: HERMENEUTICAL PROCEDURES IN
### *SEFER HA-MADDA'*

**A. Plain sense:** M. cites a verse according to its contextual sense, at times supplying a commentary.

A.1 The sage does not run in public or behave in a frenzied manner . . . but walks equably, like one preoccupied. Even by one's manner of walking it is manifest whether he is a sage or a fool, as Solomon said, "On the road also, when a fool walks, his mind is wanting, and he says to all that he is a fool" (Eccles. 10:3)—he proclaims to everyone concerning himself that he is a fool. *De'ot* 5.8.

A.2 God did not determine what any individual would do when he foretold how the Egyptians or the Israelites would behave in the future; he only described in general terms how people customarily act, as in the verse, "for the poor shall not cease being in the land" (Deut 15:11), which is not a decree of fate but a description of the way things are (*minhago shel 'olam*). *Teshuvah* 6.5.

*Comment:* M. observes correctly that Deuteronomy 15:11, though it sounds like a prediction of what has been determined to be, merely predicates the habitual presence of the poor in society as the ground of an exhortation to be open-handed. This serves M. as a warrant to interpret similarly other passages in which God predicts human behavior and thus to avoid the conflict between determinism and human responsibility. Knowing how things are, God predicts the general course of events; this puts no constraint on the conduct of any individual, leaving him free to choose his actions.

**B. Generalization:** what is true for a particular case (the cited passage) is true for others or generally; this includes stereotyping and may entail abstraction from the context.

B.1 Whoever transgresses willfully any one of the commandments . . . desecrates God's name; that is why we read, in the case of a false oath, "You must not swear falsely by my name and thus desecrate the name of your God. I am the Lord" (Lev 19:12). *Yesode Torah* 5.10.

*Comment:* The citation refers only to a false oath that uses God's name, where the resulting desecration of the name is obvious;

M. generalizes this result to every case of willful transgression of a commandment.

> B.2 Gentiles, coarse in nature, nurse their anger forever, as the text says of the Gibeonites, inasmuch as they refused to forgive and be conciliated, but demanded the death of Saul's sons, "Now the Gibeonites were not of the Israelites" (II Sam 21:2). *Teshuvah* 2.10

*Comment:* The clause cited belongs to a parenthesis supplying the background of Saul's massacre of the Gibeonites, a remnant of the indigenous Amorites; it recalls the oath of protection that the Israelites gave them at the conquest and that Saul violated. M. abstracts the clause and construes it as a deliberate attempt to contrast the Gibeonites with the Israelites in order to explain the former's ruthlessness. This trait is then generalized to all Gentiles.

**C. Specification:** a generality is concretized in a particular; a general admonition is institutionalized.

> C.1 Repentance is always in order, but during the ten days between the New Year holy day and the Day of Atonement it is most appropriate, and is immediately accepted, as it is said "Seek the Lord when he makes himself available; call on him when he is near" (Isa 55:6). *Teshuvah* 2.6.

*Comment:* The biblical context is a prophecy of salvation from exile. The prophet's admonition is couched in general terms of seasons of special grace; M. applies it in particular to the annual ten days of repentance.[8]

**D. Rubricization or proverbization:** a citation (often a fragment of a verse) is abstracted from its context to serve as a rubric (a title, a name) for a value or a principle or to serve as a proverb.

D.1 If a sage behaved scrupulously, spoke pleasantly to people, acted in a conciliatory manner, received people graciously, did not answer insult with insult . . . conducted his business honestly . . . went beyond the letter of the law . . . so that everybody praised him, loved him and tried to emulate him, such a person sanctifies the name of God; of him Scripture says, "You are my servant, Israel, through whom I get glory" (Isa 49:3). *Yesode Torah* 5.11.

*Comment:* In its scriptural context, this is a quotation, by "the servant of the Lord," of God's declaration to him; the quotation climaxes a brief account of the "servant's" preparation from birth to be an instrument in God's hand for returning Israel to him and for bringing his salvation to the ends of the earth (vss. 5–6). M. abstracts the verse-fragment from its scriptural context and employs it to express a relation between human and God whereby the human is an instrument of God's glorification. The fragment thus functions as a proverb defining a value embodied in a specific situation, or as a rubric of that value. M. then identifies the specific situation: through the Torah-sage's exemplary conduct, the Torah and God who gave it are praised.[9]

**E.  Use of a story to illustrate a rule or principle:** as an example to emulate or to shun; this may entail adjusting the story to fit the rule or principle.

E.1  When one has offended his fellow, the offended party must not harbor hatred silently as it is said of a villain, "Absalom did not speak hostilely or amicably to Amnon, for Absalom hated Amnon" (II Sam 13:22); rather he is commanded to advise the offender, saying to him, "Why did you do thus and so to me?" . . . And if the offender relented and begged his pardon, he must pardon. Nor may the pardoner be hardhearted, as it is said, "Abraham prayed to God, and God healed Abimelech" (Gen 20:17).

*Comment:* In the first citation, Absalom's silent hatred is an explicit scriptural illustration of condemned behavior (cf. F.1. below); the citation is used according to its plain sense (cf. A above). The second citation (Gen 20:17) is a problem. In the story Abimelech—a Philistine king—hearing from Abraham that Sarah is his sister (a device to protect Abraham's life), takes Sarah to wife, only to be plagued by God for it. God reveals to Abimelech his offense and is told to return Sarah to her husband, at which time (God tells the king) Abraham would pray on his behalf to cure him. The king complies, and Abraham indeed intercedes on behalf of the king, illustrating the principle that a pardoner should not be hardhearted, but should graciously accept the relenting offender's bid for pardon.

The difficulty with the prooftext is the typing of Abimelech as the offender and Abraham as the one offended, who, in the role of reprover, graciously accedes when begged to pardon. In the biblical story, Abimelech appears more offended than offending; rather than begging pardon, he remonstrates with Abraham almost in the very words M. dictates to the offended for reproving: "What have you done to us, and how have I sinned against you that you have involved me and my kingdom in a grievous sin?" (Gen 20:9). M. reads the story through the medium of a ready-made pattern of behavior posited by the rules of conciliation: namely, the sequence of offense, open reproof, regretful bid for pardon, and gracious acceptance of the bid. This pattern is imposed on a different sequence in our story. According to the pattern, Abimelech's unwitting near-adultery owing to Abraham's deceit is construed as an offense against Abraham; God's reproof of Abimelech as Abraham's reproof; Abimelech's coerced return of Sarah as his bid for pardon; and Abraham's intercession as his gracious grant of pardon. M.'s view has, to be sure, a scriptural basis: God does treat the king as an offender, and the king's retreat is answered by a favor from Abraham. This is a good example of a hermeneutical maneuver whose result reacts on our perception of the original text.[10]

**F. Ascription of multiple meanings to a given text:** out of conviction that the biblical text is supercharged.

F.1 God has commanded us not to read those books (composed by idolators describing their worship). . . . Concerning this is it said, "Lest you inquire after their gods saying, 'How do these nations worship?' " (Deut 12:30). You must not inquire after the manner of idol-worship, even though you do not worship, for this will cause you to turn your mind to it, and to do as they do, as the verse continues, "I would do so too." *Avodah Zarah* 3.2.

[Different idols have differing modes of worship; Jews are forbidden to worship an idol according to its proper mode] as it is said, "How do these nations worship their gods—I would do so too." *Avodah Zarah* 3.2.

*Comment:* The same passage yields two meanings: one must not study the manner of worship of the idolators, asking how they do it, for that might lead to imitating them. Nor must one worship the idol according to its proper mode, for that is prohibited by the same language; indeed scripture defines culpable idol-worship as only that which is performed according to the proper rites of the idol. Neither interpretation accords with the plain sense of Deuteronomy 12:30, whose concern is to ban studying the worship of the idolators in order to imitate them in the worship of Israel's God: to introduce idolatrous ways of worship into the rites of God such as child sacrifice (see vs. 31).[11]

**G. Decontextualization and Atomization:** constructing additional meanings by interpreting a verse-fragment apart from its context; recombining such fragments into new wholes.

G.1 Whoever obliterates one of the sacred, pure names by which God is called incurs the penalty of flogging. In connection with idolatry it is said, "You must obliterate their (=the idols') names from that place (of idol-worship). You must not do so to the Lord your God" (Deut 12:3–4). *Yesode Torah* 6.1.

*Comment:* The full text of these verses prohibits worshiping the God of Israel at the many sites at which the pagans worship their gods; the Israelites must, rather, confine their worship to a single site to be chosen by God: "You must obliterate all the places at which the nations whom you are dispossessing worshiped their gods, on the high mountains and the hills and under every leafy tree. You must demolish their altars and break their pillars . . . and obliterate their names from that place. You must not do so for the Lord your God; but to the place where the Lord your God shall choose out of all your tribes to set his name there—to his dwelling you shall resort and come there" (Deut 12:2–5). M. combines the final clause of vs. 3 with the initial clause of vs. 4—both abstracted from their context—creating the new interdiction and commandment: a command to obliterate the names of the pagan gods, that is, to erase their names, and a ban on "doing so to/for the Lord your God," that is, on erasing his name. This hermeneutic maneuver raises to a symbolic level the coarser physical injunctions of the biblical texts separating Israel from pagan ways (cf. L below). It discloses new levels of meaning without at the same time supplanting the texts' primary, contextual meaning.

**H. Inference from juxtaposition:** drawing inferences from the juxtaposition of passages.

> H.1  It is the custom of sensible people to acquire a gainful occupation first, then to build a home, and afterward to take a wife, as it is said, "What man has planted a vineyard but not yet desacralized it . . . has built a house but not yet dedicated it . . . has betrothed a woman but has not yet taken her to wife?" (Deut 20:50–7). But the fool marries first, and afterward, if he can afford it, he buys a house, and later yet, when he is along in years, he tries to acquire a trade or lives off the dole; and so we read in the (covenant-) curses, "You will betroth a woman, you will build a house, you will plant a vineyard" (Deut 28:30); i.e., your actions will be backwards so that you will not prosper in your efforts. *De'ot* 5.11.

*Comment:* The first trio comprises three classes of conscripts declared exempt from military service by the priest who accompanies the army; the order seems hierarchical, with marriage the highest value. For M. the collocation of items in the series has an additional meaning: it suggests the recommended sequence of adult life-stations. M. has inverted the first two items in the citation—the scriptural order being "built a house" then "planted a vineyard"—to suit his didactic purpose. He was probably influenced by the (reverse) order in the curse passage, for there (Deut 28) the items of Deuteronomy 20 appear in the sequence "take a wife, build a house, plant a vineyard." The ominous context—punishment for breach of covenant—dictates that the added significance be negative: this is the sequence of a fool's life-stations.[12]

**I. Exploitation of alternative lexical and syntactical options:** usually accompanied by decontextualizing and abstracting a segment of text.

> I.1 One who lives off his own labor is highly meritorious. . . . Thereby he earns all honor and good in this world and in the world to come, as it is said, "When (*ki*) you eat of the toil of your hands, you are happy and it shall be good for you" (Ps 128:2)—"you are happy" in this world "and it shall be good for you" in the world that is wholly good. *Talmud Torah* 3.11.

*Comment:* The psalm details the happiness of "all who fear the Lord, who walk in his ways" (vs 1). Hence our verse 2 can no more be conditional (*ki* = "when") than the rest of the verses of the psalm that assert categorically the blessings of the God-fearer. The *ki* of verse 2 is asseverative, "indeed" (as in Lam 3:23: "The kindnesses of the Lord indeed (*ki*) have not ceased, his mercies indeed (*ki*) have not ended"), and the verse means: (as a God-fearer) you shall indeed eat the products of your toil, you shall be happy, etc. This contrasts with the wicked, who are cursed thus: "The yield of your soil and the produce of all your toil shall be consumed by a people whom you do not know" (Deut 28:33).

M. has abstracted and interpreted the verse according to the temporal/conditional sense of *ki,* namely "if, when": when are you happy? when you eat what your own hands, not another's, have produced. Moreover, M. suppresses the parallelism of the clauses, "You are happy and it shall be good for you" in favor of maximal distinction between them: the first a reference to this world, the second, to the next.[13] By exploiting alternative lexical and syntactical options, M. is able to use the verse as the scriptural peg on which to hang a talmudic value—the virtue of being gainfully employed. In effect, M. has rubricized the abstracted verse (see D.).[14]

**J. Maximization:** drawing extreme consequences, beyond a text's normal range of meaning.

J.1 But when the Jews control the gentiles we are prohibited from allowing an idolatrous gentile among us. Even if he is only a temporary resident or a transient for the purpose of trade, he may not pass through our country until he has accepted the seven Noachide commandments [minimal religio-moral precepts of humanity], as it is said, "They shall not dwell in your land" (Exod 23:33)—even for a moment. *'Avodah Zarah* 10.6.

*Comment:* The citation is taken from a warning not to come to terms with the inhabitants of Canaan: "They shall not dwell in your land lest they lead you to sin against me, when you worship their gods, for that will ensnare you." The sense is to rid the country of its settled population of idolators. M. maximizes the ban by investing the durative "dwell" with momentary meaning—"stay for a moment"—thus excluding even transients, those whose commerce requires them to pass through the land, who can hardly be in a position to lead Jews into error.[15]

**K. Literalization or prosification:** interpreting a figure of speech at face value or restricting the sense of an expression more narrowly than is required by the context.

K.1 It is stated explicitly in the Torah and the Prophets that God is not corporeal, as it is said, "For the Lord your God is God in the heaven above and on the earth below"

(Josh 2:11), and no body can be (at once) in two places. *Yesode Ha-torah* 1.8.

*Comment:* When Rahab exclaims that the fame of Israel's God and his invincibility have demoralized her townspeople and convinced them of his omnipotence, she does not enunciate a physical law or intend such to be inferred. To be "God above and below" means to exercise dominion everywhere, and it is pressing the language to draw the logical conclusion that M. draws from Rahab's merism—a figure by which a whole is expressed through division into two; for example, "young and old" = everyone; "heaven and earth" = everywhere.

K.2 Women and servants are exempt from the study of Torah, but a male minor, his father is obligated to teach him Torah, as it is said, "You shall teach them (God's commandments) to your sons to speak of them" (Deut 11:19). But a woman is not obligated to teach her son, since only one who is obligated to study is obligated to teach. *Talmud Torah* 1.1.

*Comment:* The citation is from a general admonition to observe God's commandments and love him, addressed to the nation at large and bolstered by the promise of agricultural prosperity for obedience, and threat of famine and exile for disobedience. Teaching children the Torah is necessary so that they know their responsibility as members of the covenant people. In Deuteronomy 29:10 "little ones" (male and female) and women are included among the Israelite covenant partners, and in 31:12 women and little ones are among those convoked in the septennial re-enactment of the Sinai "day of assembly" (in which God proclaimed the decalogue, the basis of his covenant with Israel, in the hearing of the whole people). The purpose of the convocation is that the adults "hear (the rehearsed Torah) . . . and learn to fear the Lord . . . and their sons (=children, equivalent to the preceding "little ones") who are ignorant hear and learn to fear the Lord." In those rites, then, the obligation of hearing the covenant stipulations (=Torah) lies on all adults and all little ones regardless of sex. Hence it is to be inferred that, in our citation, the obligation of teaching "sons" embraces daughters as well, and those addressed include all adults, women as well as men. Be it noted, too, that respecting the arch-sin against the covenant, incitement to idolatry, women are explicitly named among those liable ("Should your . . . daughter or the wife of your bosom incite you"—Deut 13:7), even though in the sequel only masculine forms are used. Now it is clear that women are liable only because they are supposed to know the covenant stipulations; but if they are not included in those who must be informed of those stipulations, they cannot be held responsible for violating them. (There seems to be a certain tension between the halachic exemption of women from learning the Torah and the general halachic rule that "all negative commandments in the Torah obligate men and women equally" (*Avodah Zarah* 12.3); but if women are exempt from learning, how are they to know these negative commandments that obligate them?)

For M., the obligation to learn is associated with liberty; servants and women are exempt because they are not sovereign over their time, and the study of Torah must be accorded set times (*Talmud Torah* 1.8). Since a married woman is subjugated to the needs of her husband and family, she is exempt from the duty to learn Torah; and since the education of minors is preparation for adult responsibility, a minor female too is exempt from learning Torah. On the other hand, since adult males are obligated to study Torah at set times (a democratization of God's injunction to Joshua, "You shall study—or: recite—it day and night," Josh 1:8, see below N), fathers are obligated to train their sons in the duty of fixed study of Torah.

The halakhically strict construction of "You shall teach them to your sons" (and not to your daughters) is thus the outcome of two factors: (1) the conception of Torah study as a routine, fixed in schedule and curriculum; and (2) a definite assignment of roles to adult males and females, whereby males retain some control over their time while females are so subject to the calls of familial responsibility and tasks as to lack such control. Through the combination of these two factors, study of Torah in rabbinic Judaism is a "liberal art" (an art that requires some degree of liberty). This is not a biblical conception.

K.3 Some sins deserve punishment in this life, on one's body or property or minor children; for a person's minor children, such whose mind has not yet been formed and who have not yet become liable to commandments, are considered his possessions. The text says, "A man for his own sin shall be put to death (Deut 24:16)—the rule applies to grown men. *Teshuvah* 6.1.

*Comment:* The biblical injunction addresses a court, forbidding it to punish vicariously across generations: "Fathers shall not be put to death on account of sons, nor sons on account of fathers; a man (*'ish* = each person) for his own offense shall be put to death." Both parts of the verse, the negative and the positive, deal with this single issue; the emphasis was deserved in the light of ancient practice.[16]

M. isolates the last clause and ascribes it to the working of divine punishment. That each person dies for his own sin is contradicted by infant mortality. A degree of rationalization is obtained by the literal construction of *'ish* as "a (grown) man": only adults are judged as autonomous moral individuals. That leaves open the status of the morally unformed person, the minor who has not yet a full mental capacity and cannot therefore be responsible for what he does. Such a minor has not yet emerged into individuality and is not to be regarded as a moral, autonomous entity. His moral guardian is his parent, who is held answerable for his child's liabilities. The other side of the coin is the child's inclusion in the moral state of its parents: parents condemned by their conduct implicate their minor children in their punishment. By this conception, Deuteronomy 24:16b, originally guarding minors from vengeance taken on their parents (by earthly agency), is understood as subjecting minors to the divine retribution dealt to their parents. Hermeneutics defeats the plain sense in the interest of theodicy.

**L. Refinement:** rationalizing or spiritualizing the primary sense of scripture.

L.1 Don't think that repentance is only of sins in which there is some act, such as fornication or robbery or theft.

Just as one must repent of these so he must examine his bad traits and repent of them—anger, hate, envy, competitiveness, mockery, pursuit of gain and glory, gourmandizing, and the like; of all such he must repent. Indeed, these offenses are worse than those in which there is some act, for when one becomes addicted to one of these he forsakes them only with difficulty, so the text says, "Let the wicked one forsake his way, and the base man his devisings" (Isa 55:6). *Teshuvah* 7.3.

*Comment:* In biblical Hebrew "the way" of someone refers precisely to his actions; in Ezekiel 33:11 "the evil man's turning from his way" is spelled out in verses 14–15 to mean "doing what is just and right: returning (a poor borrower's) pledge, making good what he has robbed (another of), following statutes of life and not acting crookedly." "Devisings" refers similarly to planning specific actions, as the word implies. M. appears to exploit the vagueness of "way" and the inwardness of "devisings" to refer the entire verse to general traits of character and penchants (underlying specific acts of wrongdoing): a refinement of the idea of repentance for the purpose of thoroughgoing and fundamental self-correction.

L.2  Cognition of this matter (that the prime cause is God) is a positive commandment, as it is said, "I, the Lord am your God" (Ex 20:2). Whoever thinks that there is a God besides this One transgresses a negative commandment, as it is said, "You shall have no other god besides Me" (ibid. vs. 3), and denies the basic principle, for that is the basic principle on which everything depends. *Yesode Torah* 1.6.

*Comment:* The first two statements of the decalogue, here cited, are related as motive and command: "Since I, the Lord, am your God who liberated you from the land of Egypt, from the house of bondage, you shall have no other god besides Me." The divine claim on Israel for exclusive worship is historically grounded; the infinite benefaction God conferred on Israel by liberating them created an infinite obligation on them to be loyal servants of him alone.

For M., recognizing God's existence is first of all an intellectual obligation, established independently of historical events. For M., the first statement of the decalogue—separated from the second already in talmudic literature and thus sundered from its connection to the exodus—implies a conclusion arrived at by reason; moreover, it includes a command to know this conclusion. "I the Lord am your God" means: you are to acknowledge my being God (= the prime cause) as a postulate of reason. The next statement flows out of the first as a logical conclusion: having recognized my Godhood as a postulate of reason you may not imagine the existence of an equal, a rival, god (this is argued in detail in the following paragraphs).

The empirical, experiential motive in scripture for Israel's obligation of exclusive acknowledgement and allegiance to its God is transformed by M. into an obligation to recognize the rational necessity of God's existence (as the prime cause of all that is), and a prohibition of conceiving the existence of another like him. The biblical expressions of the empirical ground of loyalty to God and the consequential ban on the worship of other gods are converted into positive and negative injunctions concerning intellection and ratiocination. The language of faith based on events is boldly and baldly transmuted into language of faith based on reason.

**M. Metaphorization:** reading scriptural passages as metaphors, specifically, of philosophical or spiritual-ascetic values. Metaphors may serve theological, ethical, or pedagogical purposes.

M.1 Prophets cannot prophesy at will, but our master Moses was otherwise: whenever he willed it the holy spirit of prophesy rested upon him . . . as it is said, "Wait, that I may hear what the Lord commands concerning you" (Num 9:8). God assured him of this, as it is said, "Go say to them (the Israelites), 'Return to your tents,' but you stay here with me" (Deut 5:27–28) from which you learn that other prophets return to their "tents," namely their physical needs, when their prophecy is finished, just like other people; hence they do not withdraw from their wives. But

our master Moses did not return to his former "tent,"
hence he withdrew permanently from his wife, and from
the like of her. . . . *Yesode Torah* 7.6.

*Comment:* The ability of Moses to obtain divine responses (i.e.
to prophesy) at will is shown by the passage in Numbers 9:8, in
which he directs inquirers to stand by until he receives an oracle in
reply to their inquiry. M. says no more than what is implicit in the
plain sense of scripture.

The Deuteronomy 5:27–28 passage is treated differently. In
context, the passage refers to God's acquiescing in the people's re-
quest, after the Sinai theophany, to be spared further exposure to the
terrifyingly direct contact with him; they ask Moses to be their mediator in future communications from God. God concurs: the people
are to return from their place of assembly at the foot of the mountain to their tents, away from the presence of God, while Moses is to
remain at the mountain to receive further word on behalf of the
people. For M., the surface meaning points to a deeper theological
doctrine of the uniqueness of Moses' prophecy. Whereas other
prophets had to ready themselves spiritually in order to receive the
holy spirit and, after prophesying, relapsed into mundane preoccupations, "the mind of Moses attached itself to the Rock Everlasting;
the 'splendor' (Num 27:20) never left him, the skin of his face ra-
diated (Ex 34:30–35), and he became as holy as the angels" (*Yesode
Torah* 7.6 end). To ascend to such spiritual heights, Moses had to
withdraw his intellect from mundane affairs, particularly from the
grossly corporeal and sensory. This withdrawal is foreshadowed in
scripture's injunction that the sexes separate three days prior to the
Sinai theophany, readying the entire people for a prophetic experience (Ex 19:14–15). On the basis of this injunction, M. offers two
"storeys" of metaphorization. On the "first storey," following the
midrashic commentary, "return to your tents" (Deut 5:27) is a metaphor for God's permitting the people after theophany to resume
normal (sexual) relations with their wives, while requiring Moses to
continue his abstinence (vs 28, "but you stay here with me"). The
"second storey" is built on the first. "Tents = wives" is itself a metonym for "physical needs," or attention to corporeal, mundane af-

fairs ("his wife and . . . the like of her"). In M.'s view, Moses never diverted his mind from Godly thoughts after Sinai; he separated himself from his wife (the "first storey" metaphor, which M. considers the historic, plain sense of scripture) and "stayed" forever "with" God, that is, he dedicated his mind to contemplating divine matters for the rest of his life.

This complex metaphorization illustrates the simultaneous levels of scriptural sense: the literal meaning of "return to your tents" is but a metaphor for: resume sexual relations with your wives. And this is a metonym for: relapse into attention to worldly matters, as is the wont of all prophets beside Moses. The last sense is the timeless theological teaching of the passage that yields itself only to one capable of proper metaphorization.

> M.2 One should regard himself as always on the verge of death; perhaps he shall die within the hour and be permanently settled in his sins; therefore he should repent on the spot and not think, "When I get old I shall repent," lest he die before he grows old. That is what Solomon [meant when he] said, in his wisdom, "At all times let your clothes be white (clean), And oil on your head not be wanting" (Eccles. 9:8). *Teshuvah* 7.2.

*Comment:* The Kohelet verse is part of a passage (9:7–10) urging the reader to enjoy the pleasures of this life, for the ability to do so is a manifest sign of divine approval; moreover, if one misses pleasures, nothing after death can make up for them. This hedonistic advice, of a piece with Kohelet's view of the vanity of existence, is converted by M. into exalted ethical teaching by metaphorization: laundered clothing and oiled head are metaphors for a person cleansed of sin by repentance. The sage urges one to hold himself "at all times" in a cleansed spiritual state lest he be suddenly overtaken by death and thus lose forever the chance of expunging his sins.

> M.3 A disciple who has not attained competence to render decisions yet renders them is foolish, wicked, and arrogant; of him it is said: "She has felled (*hippila*) many

(*rabbim*) corpses" (Prov 7:26). Likewise a sage who has attained competence to render decisions and does not render them withholds Torah and puts stumbling-blocks before the blind, and of him it is said, "and numerous (*'atsumim*) are all her slain" (*ibid.*). *Talmud Torah* 5.4.

*Comment:* In context, the verse sums up the menace of the "alien woman" who seduces simple youths and sets them on a road to perdition. But the chapter opens with a contrast of Dame Wisdom (whom the young disciple is urged to embrace) and "the alien woman" (whom he must shun), a contrast that hints at the possible metaphorization of the latter, like that which occurs in Proverbs 9 where Dame Folly (vss 13–18)—opposed to Dame Wisdom (vss 1–6)—is described as a seductress of youth in terms recalling an "alien woman." The possibility is fully exploited by M.: if Dame Wisdom is Torah personified, then the "alien woman" is ignorance personified. Of her Proverbs 7:26a says that she has "aborted" (*hippila,* "caused to fall," in a postbiblical Hebrew sense), that is, brought forth before their time, rabbis (a play on *rabbim*) who are corpses. In other words: ignorance has produced abortions—unripe births—in the form of worthless teachers.

The second part of vs 26 describes metaphorically another ill effect of ignorance: *'atsumim* evokes *'atsam* "shut (the eye)" and is heard as "blinded" or "shut off, withheld from (light = Torah)." The whole second clause then will mean: blinded, or withheld from Torah are all the victims of ignorance. This is taken as a contrary of the preceding clause, in that it speaks not of the feckless teachers produced by ignorance, but of an erring public who are left in the dark owing to the refusal of competent teachers to enlighten them.

By a metaphorization that has a foothold in the biblical text, M. converts a worldly teaching into precepts of academic ethics.

**N. Contemporization:** adjusting to current circumstances ideas and ordinances that were predicated on different and obsolete conditions.

N.1 It is a grave offense to despise the sages or hate them. Jerusalem was destroyed only because they despised the disciples of the sages that were in her, as it is said, "They made light of the messengers of God and despised his words and mocked at his prophets" (II Chron 36:16)—that is, despised the teachers of his words. *Talmud Torah* 6.11.

*Comment:* The biblical citation is part of an indictment of Jerusalem, to the effect that its doom was sealed because its inhabitants refused to heed the warnings continuously given to it by generations of prophets, sent by God to prod them into repenting. M. contemporizes the lesson by equating the biblical messengers of God (=prophets) with sages ("disciples of the sages") through his interpretation of "(despise) his words" as "(despise) the teachers of his words." Functionally the contemporary sages are equivalent to the biblical prophets and so may be understood as the referent of the biblical term; the contemporization anachronistically interprets the biblical text according to present-day functionaries.[17]

## SECTION TWO: INTERPRETATIONS

These fifteen hermeneutical operations account for almost all of the meanings of scripture found in *Sefer Ha-Madda'*. As a rule, the cited passage moves beyond its original sense in its new Maimonidean setting; only in very few cases is the citation static, a scriptural flourish adorning M.'s statement, as in *De'ot* 1.1:

Then there is the avaricious person, who cannot be satisfied by any amount of money, in accord with the verse, 'Who loves money will never be sated with money' (Eccles 5:9).

The vast majority of citations are interpreted in a transparent manner: the hermeneutical maneuver is typically self-explanatory and requires no special knowledge in order to follow it. There are some rare exceptions when the maneuver may be enigmatic, as for example in the following passage:

Likewise if one made an idol with his own hands for others even if for a gentile, he is flogged, as it is said, 'Molten gods you shall not make for yourselves' (Lev 19:4). *Avodah Zarah* 3.9.

In this case, however, only a glance at the midrashic source of this ruling discloses its underlying hermeneutical operation:

> From the verse 'Molten gods you shall not make for your-selves,' may I infer that if others make them for you it is allowed? No; the text reads 'not for yourselves' (under any circumstances). If so, may I infer that if you make them for others it is alright? No; the text reads "you shall not make not-for-yourselves' (i.e., you shall not make for others). *Sifra Qedoshim,* end of Sect. 1.

M. has abstracted the last hermeneutical step from its context in the *Sifra.*

The relation of the original scriptures to the scriptures as presented in *Sefer Ha-Madda'* illustrates Jonathan Z. Smith's insight:

> Where there is a canon (a closed list of authoritative texts), it is possible to predict the *necessary* occurrence of a hermeneut, of an interpreter whose task it is continually to extend the domain of the closed canon over everything that is known or everything that exists *without* altering the canon in the process.[18]

For the "ideal reader" of *Sefer Ha-Madda'*—one who possesses only the Bible and M.'s Code[19]—M. represents such a hermeneut, and his use of scripture in *Sefer Ha-Madda'* displays the hermeneutical procedures through which the closed canon of scripture is extended "over everything that is known." To conclude this exercise, let us spell out the general lessons our ideal reader would learn by observing M.'s hermeneutical activity.

First, from the sheer abundance of citation, our ideal reader would have gathered that rabbinic Judaism, as exemplified in part in *Sefer Ha-Madda',* is derived from, or is indeed an elaborated expression of, the Bible. Both its theological and legal precepts are rooted in scripture, and this is what lends rabbinic Judaism its authority as an exposition of a divinely ordained canon. The frequency of citation and its distribution over several fields of religious life are implicit retorts to the Karaite accusation that rabbinic Judaism is a human figment.[20]

Second, the relation of scripture to rabbinic Judaism is by no means static. While there are some cases in *Sefer Ha-Madda'* in which a biblical citation retains its contextual sense, the citations are used more typically in an innovative fashion. The primary sense of scripture may be extended by such logical moves as generalization and specification, or it may be left behind more radically as a citation is abstracted from its setting in scripture and its semantic cargo released from the bounds of its original context. Underlying this dynamic interpretation is a view of the scriptural text as supercharged with meaning: beyond its primary contextual sense, a text continues to discharge its meanings when it is abstracted, fragmented, or combined innovatively with other texts, all in accord with the varying circumstances and purposes with respect to which it is addressed.

Third, the ideal reader, unlike M., cannot be aware of the various ideological settings out of which dynamic interpretations emerge. Chief among these settings are (a) the talmudic-midrashic value world; (b) philosophical and theological speculation; (c) ascetic trends.[21] This variety of settings represents a layering of Jewish thought, in which the biblical foundation was successively overlaid by more or less systematically developed ideational and value structures, each claiming biblical derivation. Harmoniously consolidating these layers in his interpretation, M. denies his readers such an historical perspective. He portrays the cosmos of talmudic Judaism as both uniquely organized and uniquely enriched by subsequent developments. As such, it is contemporary for its reader and not obsolete, capable of absorbing the best thought of the age. Since M. insisted on the biblical origins of contemporary Judaism, the effect is to portray the Bible as an enduringly adequate guide and inspiration for living through all time. Better said, it is to portray the Bible as an adequate and enduring guide when interpreted by the rabbinic sage who knows how to evoke its multifaceted meanings.

Contemplating the great freedom of interpretation exhibited in M., our ideal reader may well ask, "Is there any control over that freedom? Are there limits to the liberty exercised by the exponents of rabbinic Judaism in their scriptural exegesis?" There is no explicit answer in Maimonides' Code, nor is there in the Code's talmudic-midrashic-rabbinic sources. These sources include lists of herme-neutical rules, but it is clear from the practice of the talmudic-midrashic sages that, in the vast majority of their scriptural interpretations, they were neither guarded nor constrained by rules. It would therefore seem that the only bounds to hermeneutic liberty were considerations of harmony with existing norms and values, the conception of harmony itself restricting the scope of those norms and values. One of the most powerful impressions made by the Code on the reader is that of the harmony and coherence of the Judaism it portrays. To that impression the constant citation of the Bible con-tributes no little part.

The attempt to trace all wisdom to the Bible is not an attempt on our part to draw out what is objectively in it; it is an attempt on our part to unify our knowledge by reference to a single source of authority, and there are good philosophical and psychological rea-sons why we should attempt to do so.[22]

It is unlikely that our ideal reader could have taken so detached a view of the hermeneutical enterprise we have described, but he or she surely would have endorsed this perceptive justification of it.

## APPENDIX:
### THE LOGIC OF RABBINIC SCRIPTURAL INTERPRETATION
### (P. OCHS)

Moshe Greenberg's study of Maimonides' Code isolates the variety of interpretive procedures available in medieval rabbinic hermeneutics. In the context of this volume, his study also provides an occasion for extending Max Kadushin's logic of rabbinic scrip-tural interpretation. In the Introduction to this volume, I suggest that Greenberg's own holistic method of reading the Bible belongs to the same postcritical family of scriptural hermeneutics as Kadu-shin's value-conceptual method of reading rabbinic *midrash*. In this appendix, I extend the comparison by redescribing Greenberg's reading of Maimonides in terms of Kadushin's reading of the rabbis.

According to Greenberg's study, Maimonides' Code identifies the meaning of scripture with its meaning-in-use. The plain sense of scripture functions here as the sense that recommends all warranted meanings-in-use. The plain sense includes but does not prescribe any such meanings. In this view, the general purpose of scriptural interpretation is guided by the community's heritage of interpretive presuppositions and methods and by a concern to address the community's behavioral needs, to prescribe requisite, context-specific meanings-in-use for the plain sense of scripture. In Kadushin's terms, these meanings-in-use may be identified with rabbinic value-statements.

Value-statements may be defined technically as typological statements (or statements of general norms or laws) of which both a selected scriptural passage and a statement of (oral) law are considered tokens (or context-specific determinations of those norms). The scriptural passage represents a determinate or unchanging token, since its meaning is defined intratextually. The statement of law represents a variable or contingent token, occasioned by a particular socio-historical context as well as by its place within the tradition of oral law.

Hermeneutical procedures are procedures for identifying or constructing such value-statements. The character and relative complexity of these procedures vary contextually, but all procedures share the following elements. The hermeneut assumes that scriptural passages of any literary sort implicate statements of value and that the fundamental range of possible values is indicated in the rabbinic literature. Postrabbinic values will, for the most part, be described as sub-sets of identifiably rabbinic values. The hermeneut will abstract—or claim to abstract—a given value from a given scriptural passage. This value is a concept which signifies some sort of behavioral virtue or vice and which, when predicated of some subject—some person or event or entity—produces a value-statement. In the value-statement, the value, or what Kadushin calls a value-concept, functions as a value predicate. Thus, the value-statement = value-predicate + subject. The primary hermeneutical step is to prescribe, as the meaning of a given scriptural passage, a value-predicate + some set of subjects particular to the textual context of the passage. The next step is to elide the subjects and thus abstract a general value about which the scriptural passage offers a token statement in the context of scripture. The final step is to demonstrate that the oral law in question simply predicates the same value-predicate of different subjects particular to the context of the law. In this procedure, the value-statement represents a *type,* of which any linguistically determinate expression is a token. This means that there is no determinate or privileged expression of a value-statement and that value-statements are identified only by way of their context-specific tokens (illustrations to follow).

The different hermeneutical procedures in the Code represent different ways of abstracting value-concepts from scriptural passages—or, conversely, of attributing value-concepts to those passages. For heuristic purposes, it is convenient to group the procedures into four sets, ordered according to the degree to which the members of each set transform the plain sense of scripture.

**Set I:** Here, the general context of scripture is considered generalizable, extending to the context of the Code. Without transforming its plain sense, the scriptural passage is read as if it were a token or instance of a general statement of value. The context of the passage contributes some particular subject.

In Greenberg's list, the one procedure that belongs to this first set is, **A. Plain sense.** This procedure appears to be strictly a case of hermeneutical abstraction, in which the hermeneut seeks to identify a value-predicate for which the scriptural context provides some particular subject. For example, according to A.1 (in Greenberg's study), the text "On the road also, when a fool walks, his mind is wanting . . ." (Koh 10.3) is a token of the value-statement suggested by this formula: "displays foolishness" (=value-predicate) + behavior (some particular case as subject). In this case, the subject is "walking." M. expresses the value-statement in these words, "Even by one's manner of walking it is manifest whether he is a sage or a fool."

**Set II:** Here, the scriptural context is considered inadequately generalizable. In order to adjust the scriptural passage to the context of the Code, the procedures of the second set transform either the subject or the predicate of the value-statement that would, we surmise, be abstracted from the plain sense. The transformations are effected by rudimentary procedures. For example, in B.1, Leviticus 19:12 would suggest such a value-statement as: "desecrates" (value predicate) + "swearing" (value subject). M. reads the value subject as specifying only one of a larger set of subjects, "swearing = transgressions in general," thus transforming the value-statement into this one: "transgression desecrates." The transformation is effected by a hypothetical reading, according to which it may, but need not, be true that, if swearing desecrates then all transgressions desecrate. In C.2, on the other hand (note 8), M. appears to reason deductively when he transforms the value-statement "Excessive righteousness is destructive" into the value-statement "Excessive fasting is destructive." He assumes that fasting is a case of righteousness. Greenberg offers four illustrations of this set:

> **B. Generalization:** the interpreter attends only to the logical subject or extension of the value statement of which the scriptural passage is a token. In this case, the passage is read as if specifying only one of a larger set of subjects.

> **C. Specification:** attending, again, only to matters of extension, the interpreter claims to identify a particular instance of a larger set of possible subjects.

> **D. Rubricization or proverbization:** the interpreter attends exclusively to the valuational predicate of a reconstructed value statement. For example, the interpreter reads a citation as if it were a rubric for a valuational predicate of which the Code supplies the logical subjects.

> **E. Use of a story to illustrate a rule or principle,** which may entail adjusting the story to suit the rule or princ-

iple. Attending, as in D, only to the valuational predicate, the interpreter reads a narrative as if it provided logical subjects for a valuational predicate identified only in the Code.

**Set III:** In this second transformational stage, the scriptural passage is read as if it were the token, equivocally, of two or more value-statements, that is, as if the passage were polysemic. Transformations are effected by atomizing passages into discrete elements, any one of which may signify a value, independently of the significations of the passage as a whole. In F.1, the entire passage, "Lest you inquire after their gods . . ." (Deut 12:30) suggests two value-statements: "idolatry" (value predicate) + "studying the ways of idolatry" (value subject) and "idolatry" + "worshiping in the way of idolatry." In I.1, a single text-fragment, *"ki,"* is defined out of context to introduce a conditional voice into Psalm 128:2; then the two clauses "you are happy" and "it shall be good for you" are atomized to produce the two value-statements: "this worldly happiness" (value predicate) + "gainful employment" (value subject) and "next-worldly happiness" + "gainful employment." The elementary procedure for Set III is: **F. Ascription of multiple meanings:** that is, reading a given text as a token of multiple value-statements. Greenberg notes five other procedures for reconstructing additional value-statements: **G. Decontextualization and atomization; H. Inference from juxtaposition; I. Exploitation of alternative lexical and syntactical options; J. Maximization;** and **K. Literalization or prosification.**

**Set IV:** Otherwise similar to Set III, this third transformational set introduces philosophic as well as literary devices for transforming the plain-sense into its meanings-in-use. In particular, this set displays the rationalistic and ascetic tendencies which mark the post-rabbinic, or uniquely "Maimonidean" aspect of M.'s interpretations. The set thereby displays most fully the hermeneutical principle that guides all of the procedures employed in the Code: that the scriptural canon retains its authority over all conduct because the canon anticipates all possible developments in the social, intellectual and spiritual lives of the people Israel. Accordingly, M. reconstructs scriptural value-statements on the assumption that they anticipate both the behavioral dilemmas and the authoritative methods of inquiry of his day. Commenting on N.1, for example, Greenberg writes that M. contemporizes the lesson of 2 Chronicles 36:16 "by equating the biblical messengers of God (= prophets) with sages ("disciples of the sages") through his interpretation of "(despise) his words" as "(despise) the teachers of his words." Functionally the contemporary sages are equivalent to the biblical prophet and so may be understood as the referent of the biblical term. M. thus makes the value conceptual substitution, "honor + prophets" = "honor + sages." Greenberg offers three illustrations of this set: **L. Refinement; M. Metaphorization; N. Contemporization.**

While listed here last, as the set whose procedures transform the plain sense of scripture most radically, Set IV could also be listed first, as the set whose procedures display M.'s hermeneutical assumptions most overtly. While presented in the form of rhetorical corrections, the Code's scriptural interpretations display the *value-conceptual judgments* that emerge when the rabbis' hermeneutical discourse is brought into dialogue with a philosophic, or rationalizing and spiritualizing, discourse. We need not assume that Kadushin's hermeneutic is any less philosophic, only that his philosophy belongs to a postcritical, rather than a medieval, discourse.

## NOTES

1. For references, see below, n. 5.
2. Or posttalmudic legal.
3. From the Introduction to the Code.
4. *Sefer Ha-Madda',* for example, comprising 455 paragraphs, has about 400 citations, or a citation for approximately every one and one-eighth paragraph. The highest density of citation occurs in *Teshuvah,* averaging two citations per paragraph; the lowest fre-

quency of citation occurs in *'Avodah Zarah* (treatise on idolatry), averaging one citation in every one and three-quarters paragraphs. But even this is higher than the corresponding Mishnaic tractate of *'Avodah Zarah* with its one citation for its every five and a half paragraphs; or—an even closer analogue to *Sefer Ha-Madda'*—the ethical and pedagogic Mishnaic treatise of *Avot,* with one citation for every three paragraphs.

5. *Sefer Ha-Madda'* is cited according to the edition of Simon Rawidowicz (Jerusalem: Rubin Mass, 1974), essentially the same as the standard editions. Translations of Maimonides and of the Bible are mine. The talmudic-midrashic sources of Maimonides are conveniently available in *Sefer Hamada',* ed. Saul Liberman, with annotations of sources, notes and elucidations by Jacob Cohen (Jerusalem: Mossad Harav Kook, 1964).

*Sefer Ha-Madda'* comprises five treatises (*hilkhot,* "laws concerning"): 1. *yesode torah,* "Foundation of Torah (= religion)," mostly theology and the doctrine of prophecy; 2. *de'ot,* "Ethical Characteristics"; 3. *talmud torah,* "Study of Torah"; 4. *'avodah zarah ve-huggot ha-goyyim,* "Idolatry and the Customs of the Gentiles"; 5. *teshuvah,* "Repentance."

The concept of citation prevailing in this essay accords with the careful definition of Stefan Morawski: "Quotation is the literal reproduction of a verbal text . . . wherein what is reproduced forms an integral part of some work and can easily be detached from the new whole in which it is incorporated. . . . The crucial features of the quotation are its literalness and its discreteness. . . . To the former is related the question of accuracy or fidelity, the latter is responsible for its appearance in inverted commas. Thus the quotation is a semantic portion designed to perform a certain function in a new and extraneous semantic structure of a higher order . . . through it one can examine the relationship between the original to which it properly belongs and the work which has borrowed it" ("The Basic Function of Quotation," in ed. A.J. Greimas, *et al., Signs., Language, Culture* (The Hague: Mouton, 1970), 690–705: p. 619.

The commonest quotation marker in *Sefer Ha-Madda'* is a phrase with the verb "said" (*'amar*), most frequently, "(as) it is said" —(*she-*) *ne'emar.* Such phrases are "as David said (in Psalms)," or "that is [the meaning of] what Solomon said in his wisdom (in Ecclesiastes)." In series, the much less used Aramaic form "and it is written" (*uketiv*) may appear. I have not included rhetorical allusions to scriptures; I have included a very few references to stories significantly interpreted (e.g. E.2, below).

6. Here is a tabulation of the prooftexts in *Sefer Ha-Madda'*: *Citations*

| Biblical Books | No. of Cit. | Distribution in *Sefer Ha-Madda'* |
|---|---|---|
| Deuteronomy | 112 | 48 in *'Avodah Zarah* |
| | | 31 in *Yesode Torah* |
| Leviticus | 35 | 13 in *'Avodah Zarah* |
| Exodus | 33 | 10 in *Yesode Torah* |
| | | 14 in *'Avodah Zarah* |
| Isaiah | 31 | 22 in *Teshuvah* |
| Proverbs | 30 | 10 in *De'ot* |
| | | 7 in *Talmud Torah* |
| Psalms | 29 | 16 in *Teshuvah* |
| Numbers | 23 | Evenly distributed in all treatises except *De'ot* |
| Kohelet | 15 | Mostly in *Teshuvah* and *De'ot* |
| Jeremiah | 15 | Mostly in *Teshuva h* and *De'ot* |
| Genesis | 13 | Mostly in *Yesode Torah* and *Teshuvah* |
| Samuel | 11 | Mostly in discussion of prophecy in *Yesode Torah* |
| Other books | 72 | Six or less citations per book |

The distribution of biblical books from which M. drew citations correlates well with the ethical and theological concerns of this first book of his Code.

7. "The Vision of Jerusalem in Ezekiel 8–11: A Holistic Interpretation," in ed. James Crenshaw and Samuel Sandmel, *The Divine Helmsman: Lou H. Silberman Festschrift* (New York: Ktav, 1980), pp. 143–64.

8. Additional examples:

C.2  Our sages forbade self-affliction through fasting; concerning such practices Solomon commanded, "Do not be excessively righteous; and do not be over-clever, lest you destroy yourself" (Eccles. 7:16) *De'ot* 3.1.

C.3  Everyone is obliged to love each and every Jew like oneself, as it is said, "You shall love your fellow as yourself" (Lev. 19:18). Accordingly, one must speak well of his fellow and care for his property as one cares for one's own property and is solicitous of one's own honor. *De'ot* 3.3.

9. See the illuminating article by Galit Hazan-Rokem, "The Biblical Verse as Proverb and Quotation," *Jerusalem Studies in Hebrew Literature* (Heb) 1 (1981):155–66.

As an additional example:

D.2  An elementary school teacher who leaves his pupils, or does other work while he is with them, or is careless about their learning, is in the category of "Cursed be whoever does the work of the Lord slackly" (Jer 48:10). *Talmud Torah* 2.3.

*Comment:* The continuation of this verse, of which this is the first half, is, "Cursed be whoever withholds his sword from shedding blood"; the context is a prophecy of Moab's devastation by divinely appointed executioners. The verse lays a curse on any of them who do God's bloody work slackly. In M. the verse fragment is abstracted from its scriptural context and its essence is extracted, to wit: damnable is the person who executes a sacred task incumbent upon him in a slovenly manner. This essence defines, as a rubric or a proverb, a category of behavior; as such M. applies it to the specific case of the unreliable teacher.

10. Additional example:

E.2  One may not divine as the gentiles do. . . . What constitutes divination? . . . Also the setting of signs: "If such and such a thing happens to me, I will do this or that, and if it does not happen I won't do it"—as Eliezer the servant of Abraham did (Gen 24:12–14). *Avodah Zarah* 11.4.

*Comment:* The sign set by Abraham's servant (identified with Eliezer of Genesis 15:2) to identify the future wife of Isaac is represented in the biblical story as legitimate (God signals his choice through it). M.'s rejection of it illustrates the occasional tension between the values of scripture and of rabbinic Judaism.

11. Additional example:

F.2 When a person has been offended, he must not harbor hatred silently . . . but he is commanded to advise the offender, saying to him, "Why did you do thus and so to me, and why did you sin against me in such and such a matter," as it is said, ["You shall not hate your brother in your heart] you shall surely reprove your comrade" (Lev 19:17) *De'ot* 6.6.

If one sees his fellow sinning, or following an evil course, he is obliged to set him aright and advise him that he is sinning against himself through his bad deeds, as it is said, "You shall surely reprove your comrade." *De'ot* 6.7.

*Comment:* The clause "You shall surely reprove your comrade" is interpreted twice: once in connection with the preceding clause, thus: "You shall not hate your brother in your heart, but (*waw* adversative) you shall surely reprove your comrade," and once as independent of it, a discrete injunction to intervene when seeing one's fellow behave in a reprobate manner.

12. Additional example:

H.2 If a woman shaved her sidelocks she is not liable, since it is said, "You shall not cut the sidelocks of your heads and you shall not destroy the edges of your beard" (Lev 19:27). Only one who is liable for transgressing "You shall not destroy" may be held liable for "You shall not cut," and a woman is not liable for "You shall not destroy" for she has no beard. *Avodah Zarah* 12.2.

*Comment:* In addition to the specific prohibitions in this verse, conveyed by the two clauses, information on those subject to them is conveyed by their juxtaposition. Both men and women have sidelocks, but only men have beards; by ascribing significance to the conjoining of these two prohibitions new information is elicited from the text, limiting the scope of the former ban to those affected by the latter. Collocational meaning is a supercharge on the verbal meaning of the verse.

13. James L. Kugel has described well the rabbinic "forgetting" of parallelism in favor of distinctions between parallel clauses in *The Idea of Biblical Poetry* (New Haven: Yale University Press, 1981), pp. 96–109.

14. Additional example:

I.2 Those who cause a town in Israel to apostacize are subject to the penalty of stoning, even if they did not apostacize but only incited their fellow townsmen to apostacize and worship (an alien deity). . . . What passage warns against inciting to apostasy (without stating its penalty)? "(The name of another god) shall not be sounded by ('al) your mouth" (Exod 23:13). *Avodah Zarah* 4.1.

*Comment:* The full verse reads, "You shall not mention the name of another god; it shall not be heard in ('al) your mouth"; the two clauses are parallel and prohibit uttering the name of an alien god (e.g. in a prayer or an oath). M. cites the second clause only and, by means of an alternative sense of 'al-pi- "at the bidding of," arrives at the sense "the name of an alien god must not be heard at your instigation"—a warning without penalty against incitement to idolatry. This answers the requirement of rabbinic legal exegesis that every penal law (here Deut 13:13–19) have a non-penal warning passage corresponding to it.

15. Note the same purpose in the following example:

> J.2 We are not to follow the customs of the gentiles, we are not to assimilate to them neither in costume nor in hairstyle or the like, as it is written, "And you shall not conduct yourselves according to the norms of the nation(s)" (Lev 20:23), and it is said, "and by their norms you shall not conduct yourselves" (Lev 18:3), and it is said, "Be careful not to be ensnared by them" (Deut 12:30)." *Avodah Zarah* 11.1.

*Comment:* All the above-cited passages deal with the natives of Canaan, whose immorality and idolatry Israel is warned away from. M. extends the prohibition to the external cultural features (costume, hair-style) of all Gentiles. Fear of assimilation (conversion to the religion of the Gentiles) commends a policy of total cultural separation, supported by maximizing exegesis.

Another example:

> J.3 If one's neighbors were scoundrels and sinners who would not let him dwell in the town except if he became like them and followed their evil conduct, he should depart for the caves and the brambles and the deserts rather than lead the life of a sinner, according to the tenor of, "Would that I were in the desert, a wayfarer's lodge, that I might leave my people and go away from them; for they are all adulterers, a band of faithless men" (Jer 9:1). *De'ot* 6.1.

*Comment:* The prophet conjures up a state he is not in, a course he did not follow, namely to remove himself from civilization in order to separate himself from his sinful neighbors. M. regards the passage as a recommendation—indeed a model—for proper behavior, by which he means, however, not the wish to withdraw to the desert but the act. What the prophet yearned for but did not do becomes maximized into a mandate for action.

16. See my discussion in *Yehezkal Kaufmann Jubilee Volume,* ed. Menahem Haran (Jerusalem: Magnes Press, 1960), pp. 20–27.

17. Additional examples:

N.2 One is obliged to be considerate of widows and orphans, because they are dejected and meek, even though they may be wealthy. We must be considerate even of a king's widow and his orphans, as it is said, "Every widow and orphan you (plural) shall not afflict" (Exod 22:21). *De'ot* 6.10.

*Comment:* The context enjoins the community to care for each and every widow and orphan, the plural subject and the two objects in the singular indicating collective responsibility for even a single case of violation. The continuation of the cited verse (21) reads: "Should you (plural) afflict him (singular, effectively "her or him"), for if he should cry for help to me I shall surely heed his cry, my anger will be kindled and I shall slay you (plural) by the sword, so your (plural) wives shall be widows and your children orphans" (vss 22–23). "Every (kol)" of verse 21 means "any, even one."

M. takes "every" to mean "even a wealthy man's, a king's." Beside obliterating the biblical point that punishment will be visited for even a single orphan and widow's cry, M. effaces the correlative collective responsibility indicated by the biblical plural subject by his opening formulation "One (*'adam*) is obliged." This formulation in the singular converts a collective obligation into an individual one, and it adjusts the biblical communal moral entity to the contemporary reality of a nation splintered and scattered over the earth. M. has in fact reversed the biblical emphasis: the individual is under obligation to be considerate of every class of orphan and widow.

N.3 Every man in Israel (Jewry) is obliged to study Torah . . . even if he is a beggar, even if saddled with wife and children he is obliged to set aside times for study of Torah by day and by night, as it is said, "You must study it day and night" (Josh 1:8). *Talmud Torah* 1.8.

*Comment:* At the head of the polity of Israel, Joshua is commanded in the cited verse to study—and observe—the Torah for as long as he lives continuously ("day and night"). M. democratizes the obligation, laying it on every Jewish male adult, as though the command to Joshua were grounded on his being a Jewish male adult (and needed special emphasis only because Joshua was a "king"; cf. Deut 17:19 where a similar obligation is laid on the king in order to keep him humble). Moreover, he derives a specification from the citation by taking a merism ("day and night" = continuously) literally; the study must be performed at set times by day and night. By democratizing the injunction to Joshua, M. gives it contemporary significance (as well as setting a royal standard of study and observance for the rank and file of Jewish men).

18. Jonathan Z. Smith, *Imagining Religion* (Chicago: University of Chicago Press, 1982), p. 48.

19. Earlier we defined the ideal reader as a "personification of the full range of interpretive possibilities inherent in the text at the time when it reached its present disposition."

20. Cf. Isadore Twersky, *Introduction to the Code of Maimonides,* Yale Judaica Series Vol. 22 (New Haven: Yale University Press, 1980), pp. 45, 145.

21. *Ibid.,* pp. 459–65.

22. Bernard Jackson, "Legalism," *Journal of Jewish Studies* 30 (1979), 1–22: pp. 13f.

## Chapter Eight

# MAIMONIDES, AQUINAS, AND GHAZALI ON NAMING GOD

## DAVID B. BURRELL, C.S.C.

After having prudently waived off his precocious student Joseph from beginning an instruction with metaphysical issues and especially from presenting such matters to common people (1.34), Maimonides goes on to make an exception for issues touching "God's incorporeality and His exemption from all affections" (1.35), since this doctrine bolsters our "belief that God is One, and that none besides Him is to be worshipped"—the core of Jewish faith.[1] For the intellectual underpinning of such a confession requires a conceptual apparatus able to show that "the difference between Him and His creatures is not merely qualitative but absolute."[2] Here we have stated the Rambam's primary motivation for his celebrated agnosticism regarding qualitative statements about God: "anything predicated about God is totally different from our attributes; no definition can comprehend both; therefore His existence and that of any other being totally differ from each another, and the term 'existence' is applied to both homonymously . . ." (1.35). The conceptual apparatus will be the thesis on divine simpleness elaborated by Ibn-Sina (and later honed by Aquinas), according to which that which distinguishes the First from all else—its "necessary existence" [*al-wujūd al-wajīb*]—prevents us from saying that such a One could have any attributes at all. So although the point of our attributing to God "whatever we regard as a state of perfection [is to express] that He is perfect in every respect, and that no imperfection or deficiency whatever is found in Him" (1.26), nevertheless the very activity of attribution so ill-matches the one thing we can know about the divine essence that its literal use will undermine the intent.

Despite his explicit objections to the manner in which Maimonides states his teaching, we shall see that Aquinas concurs completely with the premises composing his arguments, and even follows Maimonides' lead in his own creative resolution of this thorny issue. That his final resolution differs from the Rambam is due to a more sophisticated interweaving of metaphysics with language, which will allow Aquinas to speak coherently of certain terms signifying truly yet imperfectly. The upshot may sound a good deal more palatable than Maimonides' "sheer equivocity," yet Aquinas' champions have often forgotten that *analogy* was for him a species of *equivocity* (homonymity).[3] Al-Ghazali's parallel preoccupations about securing the divine unity (*tawḥīd*) required for the Muslim confession of faith (*shahada*) led him to presume an agnosticism regarding attributes as complete as the Rambam's, without however adopting (indeed explicitly rejecting) the Muslim philosophers' account of God's unity which required collapsing all attributes into an utterly simple divine essence. By distinguishing *names* from *attributes,* however, by reason of their origin in the Qur'an, as well as acknowledging considerable overlapping in our use of the divine names, Ghazali managed to attenuate the effect of his conceptual agnosticism, and show how our use of the Qur'anic names (and within limits, other perfection-terms as well) can be responsible and meaningful, and so qualify as well as any human speech is able to do, as discourse about God. Moreover, as we shall see, grounds can be adduced for assimilating Maimonides' final position to that of Ghazali, if one were to insist on the practical goal of the *Guide:* to harness philosophical reasoning to the "chief aim of man [which] should be to make himself, as far as possible, similar to God" (1.54).

The aim of these preliminary statements is to provoke readers to follow the contours of the following comparative study. The order of presentation breaks with chronology, where Ghazali (1058–1111) would come first, followed by Moses ben Maimon (1135–1204) and

Thomas Aquinas (1225–1274). Yet Maimonides states the issue—both religious and philosophical—so well that clarity suggests beginning with him. Moreover, his way of stating the issues is virtually shared by all three interlocutors. All participated in a common philosophic culture, symbolized by Avicenna. All shared a common religious imperative to distinguish the one God from everything else that is, while avowing all of it to be that God's creation. Those considerable commonalities allow us to speak of them as "interlocutors," even though some twenty years separated each from his successor, and the only direct link we can establish is that of Aquinas with Maimonides.

The west had little access to Ghazali, and what they had—his exposition of the positions taken by Muslim philosophers preliminary to refuting many of them—was so fair-minded that they grouped him with the *falāsifa:* those Muslim thinkers concerned to assimilate Greek philosophy. While the Rambam's temper and priorities suggest he would have agreed with Ghazali on critical questions (like the origin of the universe), there is no evidence, despite his virtual immersion in Islamic culture, that he had read Ghazali's writings. Averroes [Ibn-Rushd] could have provided a link, but his writings proved more influential in the west than in the east, and in any case, his face-off with Ghazali—the *Tahafut al-Tahafut,* which incorporates the text with which it takes issue: Ghazali's *Tahafut al-Falasifa*—would not have been written before 1180.[4] While the *Guide* was completed by 1194, it is questionable whether Averroes' writings were available to Maimonides or whether the demands on his time in Fostat would even have permitted fresh philosophical reading. His reference betimes to positions of Ibn-Sina as Aristotle's (in the *Guide*) leads one to believe he was expounding from memory philosophical positions he had assimilated for some time. So we must presume that any congruence between his view of these matters and that of Ghazali is due to a similarity of temper, both religious and philosophical, as well as the embracing context. Indeed it is that larger context which must explain how Aquinas found himself drawn to Maimonides as a guide in the delicate task of making philosophy over into a handmaid of faith, without violating her integrity. The intellectual openness of an age which also sponsored the crusades is astounding, and it is precisely that climate, which we might describe as *interfaith* and *intercultural,* which renders a comparative project like this one less suspect and perhaps even plausible.

### MOSES BEN MAIMON:
### ON SAYING WHAT WE COULD NEVER MEAN

The root of the Rambam's agnosticism, as has been suggested, lies in his understanding of what one is stating in confessing that God is one: "Hear, O Israel, the Lord our God is one Lord" (Deut 6:4). The One from whom comes everything that is: such a one must enjoy a unity and simpleness which could never obtain for a creature, and it will be the task of philosophy to secure that status conceptually. It will not be enough to quote the rabbis; furthermore, Islamic philosophy had a similar goal in bolstering divine unity, or *tawḥīd.* Moreover, a philosophical theologian, like Maimonides, will also need to defend what philosophy concludes, and such a role came quite naturally to him who was so long entrusted with the religious leadership of his faith community in Fostat. So looking beyond the propositions of philosophical debate, he needs to locate the *animus* which shaped certain positions: "the circumstances which caused men to believe in the corporeality of God" (1.53). It is the very language of revelation—for Maimonides and Aquinas, the Bible; for Ghazali, the Qur'an—which, taken literally, leads people to believe that God has the body presupposed by certain descriptions, and "that God *possesses* attributes" (emphasis added). What he is suggesting by the parallel is that many of those who would quickly see that a bodily God was sheer foolishness in the face of the revelation of the Lord of heaven and earth were not so quick to see the incongruities in attributing less tangible things to God, and so found themselves embroiled in recondite philosophical discussions of divine attributes.

For two centuries Islamic philosophical theologians had been debating whether the presence of multiple attributes attenuated God's unity. That is the trap which Maimonides wants to help his student Joseph elude.[5] He does this by building on his extensive discussions in the initial chapters of the book on biblical terms and their proper uses: (in summary) "we apply to all such passages the principle, 'the Torah' speaks with language of man, and say that the object [i.e., the point] of all these terms is to describe God as the most perfect being, not *as possessing* those qualities which are only perfections in relation to created living beings" (1.53, emphasis added). He objects to any form of speech which attributes even perfections to God—however just its intent—because it cannot help but be misleading, both semantically and ontologically. Semantically, because we can never know the divine reach of such perfections, and ontologically, because the very form of attributed discourse will lead both speaker and hearer into presuming that God *possesses* qualities—and so dilute the metaphysical simpleness required to secure philosophically the confession of faith in one God. Had he been skilled in the "formal mode," he would have noted how the incoherent compromise adopted by mainstream Islamic religious thought—that God's attributes "are eternal, subsisting in [the divine] essence, and that 'they are not He, nor are they other than He' "[6]—might be explained by their propensity to speak of attributes as though they were things: indeed the referents of adjectives (as substances were taken to be the referents of the nouns in the subject place of an attributive statement).

His understanding of the metaphysical presuppositions of attributive statements, then, requires him to locate the "ontological difference" between our discourse (with its inescapable implications) and the utterly simple being of the one God:[7] "if we, therefore, perceive in God certain relations of various kinds—for wisdom in us is different from power, and power from will—it does by no means follow that different elements are really contained in Him . . ." (1.53). The undifferentiated divine essence (*dhāt*) of the *falāsifa* anchors the Jewish confession of God's uniqueness. So far as scriptural reports of God's actions are concerned, "it is . . . intelligible how, in reference to God, those different actions can be caused by one simple substance . . . [and] the attributes found in Holy Scripture are either qualifications of His actions [i.e., God acts mercifully] . . . or indicate absolute perfection, but do not imply that the essence of God is a compound of various elements." We are tempted, of course, to infer divine character traits from the actions which revelation attributes to God, as we do with human beings; yet it is easy to avoid that presumption by reminding ourselves of the divine simpleness, and noting that it is intelligible (though hardly conceivable to us) that such a One may perform many actions without the Aristotelian infrastructure of powers which creatures need. What we took to be attributes, then, in the invocations of the psalmist—"eternal his merciful love, He is faithful from age to age"—remind us how it is that God acts, and gesture rhetorically to the absolute perfection of the One.

Such is Maimonides' position in brief. It can be a coherent one; whether he violated his own austere strictures in going on to talk about a God characterized by these perfections is a further question. Moreover, someone anxious to render him consistent would doubtless attempt to translate such statements into qualifications of God's action or rhetorical indications of divine perfection, as his rule prescribes. What is germane to our discussion is the way Maimonides' position reflects his placement of the "ontological difference." *Pace* Gersonides, this point is more fundamental than his difficulties with reconciling divine knowledge with the strong presumptions of the Torah regarding human freedom.[8] It is in fact his earlier position regarding statements which presume to be attributing features to God which allows him to locate "the cause of the error of [those who reach an intellectual impasse here in] their belief that God's knowledge is like ours," for the group he takes most to task are the philosophers who have already "demonstrated that there is no plurality in God . . . how can they imagine that they comprehend his knowledge, which is identical with his essence . . ." (3.20)? It is primary to Maimonides to cancel our unreflective presumption that talk about God's powers and perfections thereby attributes any multiplicity to the One.

## THOMAS AQUINAS: ON MEANING WHAT WE SAY

Aquinas' discussion of the "names of God"[9] is dominated by a cognate concern about God's unity. The immediately preceding questions in the *Summa Theologiae* had secured the uniqueness of the divine essence (1.3–11), culminating in the query "whether God is one?" (1.11). The upshot of his sophisticated philosophical theology regarding "what God is not," then, is to give coherent shape to the first article of the creed: "We believe in one God."[10] Although

Christian theologians are prone to refer to this as "divine transcendence," their preoccupations parallel Jewish concerns about the confession that God is one, as the structure of Aquinas' treatment displays, culminating in an untrammeled assertion of divine oneness.

In the face of so transcendent a characterization of the One, how can anything we say about God be said of God? That is the problematic which question 13 on "the names of God" proposes to address. The psalmist's invocations of God are taken to yield *names* —merciful, loving, faithful—in the medieval grammarians' (Latin or Arabic) sense of verbal nouns (or adjectives): "God is merciful." The Latin *nomen* (like the Arabic *ism*) must be rendered in English, according to the context, as "name," "noun," "term," or even "adjective," since they worked with but two major grammatical categories for terms: those which imply time (verbs) and those which do not (everything else: "particles" [*hurūf*] in Arabic, *nomina,* and syncategorematic terms in Latin). Unlike Ghazali, Aquinas does not underscore the scriptural origin of these "divine names," but his daily chanting of the psalms cannot be gainsaid. He treats them, whatever their provenance, as attributions to God of mercy, love, and fidelity, yet his final reason for objecting to Maimonides' form of agnosticism regarding our use of them is that his semantic resolution does not match "what we intend to say when we speak of God" (1.32.2). This is where one may infer, I believe, an allusion to the faithful's recitation of the psalms.

The other reason he adduces against "the position of Rabbi Moses," as he recapitulates it summarily, is better known: that so thoroughly negative a treatment of human attributions to divinity leaves us no principle of discriminating terms attributed appropriately to God from anything else. For if "God is merciful" can only *mean* "God is not merciful" then we could just as well say that God is bodily, meaning "God is not bodily." (Of course, Maimonides' reference to "the attributes found in Holy Scripture . . . indicat[ing] absolute perfection" [1.53] shows that he *presumed* a class of perfection-terms; Aquinas' argument clarifies how the position he took deprives him of any semantic reason for focusing on such terms.) Aquinas' example shows that he grasped the underlying motivation for the Rambam's position and that it is one he shared—as if to say: "neither of us wants to say God is bodily"; so he will propose a resolution faithful to that motivation yet more semantically coherent. That means he must locate the "ontological difference"—which they also share—in a different place, where it does not render even reflective human discourse about God nugatory.

The task is a formidable one, however, given Aquinas' parallel formation of the "ontological difference" as uncompromising divine simpleness (1.3). His position is every bit as opposed to attributive discourse about divinity as Maimonides', since the very form of a subject-predicate statement will misrepresent the unity of God. That is why Aquinas characterizes his treatment of the divine essence in questions 3 to 11 as "inquiring into what God is not" (1.3 Intro.). For this nature cannot be located (on the Aristotelian pattern of scientific inquiry) by genus and specific difference; as Avicenna insisted: God's essence (*dhāt*) is not a quiddity (*mahiyya*).[11] What allows us to locate divinity ontologically, however, is also what makes God to be one. God must be simple, that is, not composed. Such simpleness lies quite beyond our discourse, which is invariably composed, and so beyond our knowledge, so it behooves us to describe this inquiry as pursuing "what God is not." Aquinas manages to give a positive characterization of this uniqueness using a distinction of Avicenna to articulate divine simpleness as the absence of any distinction between God's essence and God's existing (1.3.4).[12] Maimonides had employed the same distinction to characterize God uniquely: "God alone is that being [in whom] existence and essence are perfectly identical" (1.57). This indeed is what shows that God's existence (and so everything else that can be said of God) is utterly unlike ours (1.56), as it gives us an appropriately transcendent way of noting the divine unity: "He is one but does not possess the attribute of unity" (1.57). This remark should also remind us of the inherently negative character of Aquinas' treatment of divinity, however "positive" the characterization of divine simpleness or unity as the identity of essence and existence in God. For such a oneness is, as Maimonides puts it, quite beyond characterization ("one [without] possessing the attribute of unity"), and can only point to the mystery which is the eternal unoriginated God.[13]

Yet this is the very One to whom we pray, and our praises attribute perfections—mercy, love, fidelity—to God. Aquinas proposes to bridge the gap between God's lack of articulation (or simpleness) and the inescapable articulation of our invocations and discourse by making us so acutely aware of that gap that our *use* of language toward and about God will respect and reflect it. He can be more sanguine than Maimonides about such reflectiveness working because he has a richer picture of the workings of language when it comes to sensitive interlocutors.[14] Displayed in his own writing, Aquinas regards language as a tool of human understanding, reflecting its own reaches as well as its impasses, for human understanding is itself linguistic. (Part of his argument, for example, that God's eternity is beyond our grasp reminds us that our discourse is inescapably tensed [1.8.1].) So language cannot be grasped by its syntax alone, as an object, but can only be understood in use. One of the cardinal ways in which Thomism misrepresented Aquinas was its persistent demand that his writings be "systematized," reflecting Cajetan's conviction that Aquinas *semper formaliter loquitur*—"always spoke formally." The test lay in his propensity for making distinctions: Thomists had to attempt a consistent mapping of them; in fact, Aquinas used them to understand the issue at hand. Congruence with distinctions made elsewhere was beside the point, in fact, contrary to the point of his practice.[15]

Question 13, "on the names of God," best illustrates this view of language and human understanding each at the service of each other, since one is called upon to stretch language both to and beyond its ostensible limits. The principal device which Aquinas uses, distinguishing the thing signified (*res significata*) from the manner or mode of signifying (*modus significandi*), is adapted from its modest employment in speculative grammars of his time, where lexical changes in a term might be thought to alter its meaning, especially in syllogistic argument.[16] A minor alteration to adjectival form (*modus significandi*) need not detract from the fact that this use bears the same meaning (*res significata*) as its noun form. If, however, Aquinas is after much bigger game here, the humble origins of this distinction will keep one from a ready misunderstanding —namely, that one might understand what mercy is (*res significata*) independently of our actual use of the term (*modus significandi*). Again, Aquinas' *use* of the distinction is not misleading; he reminds us repeatedly throughout question 13 that no *res* can be grasped without a *modus*—no meaning without a use, in more contemporary jargon. In fact, what he is using it to show is the real key to his treatment: the possibility of our *using* certain expressions to "imperfectly signify" an object beyond our grasp.[17]

There are three elements to this resolution: (1) only certain expressions qualify—specifically those whose proper use *demands* that we distinguish manner of signifying from what is signified, (2) that the syntax of these expressions contain resources for displaying the "ontological difference," and (3) that we be able to use them properly. Aquinas' resolution is significant because the third element cannot be taken for granted. The set of terms are, of course, intrinsically analogous expressions, but Aquinas does not offer a *theory* of analogy nor can his judicious display of the analogous resources of language be codified as one. The practice of the speaker is crucial here, so training in proper practice must be part of understanding how one can "imperfectly signify." We are reminded of Aquinas' judgment that theology is a practical as well as a theoretical mode of knowledge, and of the insistence of some of our contemporaries that an understanding of the individual that involves practices is required for proper ethical knowledge—how much more so in matters religious.[18] Let us see why this must be so.

Maimonides presumed that the terms used of God would be such as to intimate perfection; Aquinas specified that only such terms may properly be used. The reason he finds them suitable is their inherently analogous character, as exhibited in Socrates' enlightenment regarding the wisdom imputed to him by the oracle. Unwilling or unable to accept such praise, his own inquiry finally forced him to acknowledge that he, at least of all whom he had encountered, was the wisest—yet he was so precisely because he recognized that he was not wise.[19] A generalized form for this appreciation could be given as: "They alone are (*x*) who realize they are not (*x*)," where only perfection terms make sensible substitutions. Moreover, such a differential realization is ingredient to their proper use, so the formula offers a semantic rule, such that one who uses such terms unaware of their potential misuses them. Hence the derogatory expression "conventional morality"; whatever morality is, it cannot be mere convention, since its terms alone provide us with the leverage to criticize conventional or accustomed arrangements.

Aquinas characterizes this difference by adapting the received distinction of the manner of signifying from the thing signified to insist that a class of terms—perfection terms—require an active appreciation of that distinction for their proper use. One who assesses a political economy as *just* must be prepared to argue with another whose view of politics, economics, and the human good would call his presuppositions into question: the terms which Aquinas calls analogous have also been dubbed "essentially contested expressions."[20] Anyone who uses them as though they were not is either naive or self-deceived. We shall see that the proper use of such expressions requires a rich and discriminating experience, as well as a capacity for self-criticism long associated with spiritual disciplines of detachment—for the common human response, disappointingly enough, is defensiveness. Yet those same spiritual disciplines confirm one's being on a path of enhancement in understanding; the most trustworthy conversions have a continuing quality rather than a once-for-all completeness rejecting all that went before.[21] The sign that we understood how to use such expressions, and so succeed in meaning what we are saying (*res significata*), lies precisely in our recognizing that our manner of using the term (*modus significandi*) was inadequate to the task which we were using it to do—a task involving some kind of assessment. We can therefore speak properly of just arrangements, so long that we realize our grasp of justice is an imperfect one. This paradox, woven into our ordinary use of perfection-terms, offers the first element in Aquinas' account of how our praise of God's mercy may truly speak of God—by signifying the divine imperfectly.

The second element uses the *res/modus* distinction in its more purely grammatical form to heighten our awareness of the "ontological difference," and to use that same awareness to justify our statements signifying God—albeit "imperfectly." Each perfection term has two modes of expression: *concrete* (adjectival)—"merciful," and *abstract* (nominal)—"mercy." In characterizing these two modes as "concrete" and "abstract," Aquinas is faithful to Aristotle's view of language and reality, whereby qualities only exist in subjects, so the adjectival form "_____ is merciful" reflects their actual ("concrete") ontological status, while the noun form "mercy" is misleading since its capacity to stand on its own might lead one to imagine that qualities subsist. We can only properly speak of mercy by a conscious abstraction from merciful individuals.[22]

Applying this to our attributive statements about God, Aquinas makes the observation (which I would elevate to a semantic rule) that we use the concrete (adjectival) form to call attention to God's subsistence (as in "God is merciful") while we use the abstract (nominal) form to call attention to divine simpleness: "God is mercy" (1.13.1.2). The second form underscores divine simpleness because the use of the noun-form to complete the verb turns the statement into an identity rather than a proper predication like the first. I would turn this observation into a rule for proper use of perfection-terms *in divinis* because the abstract form alone is compatible with deism, while the concrete form alone fails to indicate that God's being merciful is not a factual observation but a normative statement. It is the abstract identity statement which reminds us of this dimension: if God is mercy, then it is God's mercy which offers the norm for being merciful. So a proper use of perfection-terms of God *presumes* their ability to assume both concrete and abstract forms, as well as *demands* that we use both modes of expression in speaking of God (the *res significata*). In short, I cannot properly say that God is merciful without realizing that such a One is also mercy—and vice versa. That simply reflects what it is for God to be merciful: the "concrete" formula offends against divine simpleness as a composite predication, but using it guards against anyone's reading the identity as though mercy might substitute for God—the enlightenment fallacy found in some forms of deism.

Aquinas insists that we can factor the "ontological difference" into our use of perfection-terms for God, and so succeed in signifying divinity, even if imperfectly. We compensate for the manifest lack of fit between our expressions and a simple divine being by using both forms of expression in a complementary manner. This observation-become-rule moves us already into the third element needed to explain how we might successfully but "imperfectly" signify a transcendent God by our expressions of praise or of clarification: our ability to use them properly. That involves an awareness that the object exceeds our grasp, as well as a capacity to exploit the resources of language itself—notably as exhibited in perfection terms, which we use quite ably in other contexts—to factor that very awareness of God's transcendence into our discourse (if not into individual statements, then into larger units of discourse, as evidenced in the rule of complementarity for concrete and abstract forms of the same term). Coupling this awareness with this capacity never presumes we have access to the thing signified—in this case, God's mercy, or God's being merciful—independent of our manners of signifying things being merciful. In fact, our very ignorance of the thing signified, or, if you will, of the manner in which God is merciful, is signaled by the rule of complementarity for abstract/ concrete expressions, which is itself a reflection of the analogous character of perfection-terms.

Rather than leading us to despair of ever knowing God's mercy, however, or threatening us with a crippling "relativism," the expressly analogous character of perfection-terms challenges our critical understanding and our self-understanding to make us ask whether or not we are using the terms correctly. This is to ask if we are using them in a manner that invites criticism leading to a purified understanding of mercy (*res significata*), or if we remain arrested in a specific conventional grasp of it. I suspect the conviction that there is a progressive understanding to be had stems from a believer's conviction that these expressions are in fact "names of God" delivered in revelation. This is a dimension which Ghazali will accentuate. Yet one cannot deny one's own experience either, which indicates how a progressively critical appropriation *can* lead to a more accurate and responsible use of such terms—in short, to a growth in wisdom. Religious folk who constantly worry about "relativism" may certainly be voicing a genuine concern, yet when coupled with a need for certitude and an endemic obliviousness to the manifestly analogous structure of perfection-terms, one suspects them of undervaluing to the point of overlooking the intellectual dimensions of what the Christian tradition has called *sanctification*—accounts of which are called *spirituality*.[23]

In any case, Aquinas, who could hardly be charged with "relativism" or logical imprecision, celebrated the analogous resources of language for enhancing our awareness of how to speak properly of God: by acknowledging the intricate impropriety of our language and, in this way, succeeding in "imperfectly signifying," say, God's mercy. Such spiritual disciplines are not restricted to Christianity. Maimonides veers in this direction when he acknowledges the way in which "negative attributes . . . are necessary to direct the mind to the truths which we must believe concerning God" (1.58), and goes on to show how, by working with what we know to be negations, we "learn that there is no other being like unto God, and we say that He is One . . ." (emphasis added). There seem to be degrees in the confession of divine oneness, and one way to learn how to say it properly is by a progressive grasp of the negations we say about God. What is barely intimated in Maimonides, however, will be an articulated path (*tariq*) for Ghazali, whose treatment of "divine names" subtly incorporates elements of the progressive understanding of self and of God so carefully elaborated in Sufism. In this sense, Ghazali's conversion to the Sufi path allows him to elaborate elements left quite implicit by Aquinas and Maimonides.

## AL-GHAZALI: ON NAMING WHAT WE CANNOT MEAN

In his treatise proposing to explain the meaning of each of the ninety-nine traditional names of God, Ghazali must first ascertain the status of these "names" culled from the Qur'an and then determine how we use them properly.[24] We will want to know how even a proper use of such names can lead us to know about God, who remains, for Ghazali, radically unknowable.[25] While Ghazali's problematic is not identical with that of Maimonides or Aquinas, he does treat many of the same issues.

Addressing himself first to the status of the divine names, Ghazali acknowledges that each name expresses an attribute and that our access to them will invariably be "by way of comparison" with human characteristics. Yet, he reminds us that they are presented only as *names*. How, then, are we to distinguish names and attributes? In a characteristically modern way: names are given, by one's parent or guardian or by oneself (the last alternative being best exemplified by God), whereas attributes are discovered. Now we may, of course, try to impose the name corresponding to an attribute—as we do in nicknames like "Stretch" or "Whitey." Ghazali shrewdly notes, however, that such nicknames are more often resented than appreciated—perhaps because they accentuate only one feature (192–3). Moreover, the Arabic custom of naming children by names which express complimentary attributes is just that—a custom. The names undoubtedly reflect parents' hopes and aspirations, but they are unreliable as descriptions of the child: youth or adult.

Having made the distinction, Ghazali would hardly propose that God wishes to mislead us about the character of divinity, so there must be some connection between *name* and *attribute* when it comes to the names God gives us to refer to God's own self. The Qur'an is punctuated by expressive verses intended as pointed commentary on the assertions just made, like: "Lo! Thy Lord! He is the All-Wise Creator" (15.86), "Lo! He, only He is the Hearer, the Seer" (17.1), or "Thy Lord is the Forgiver, Full of Mercy" (18.59). The ninety-nine traditional names are culled from these and enjoy divine authority, but how are we to understand them? Ghazali presumes the common thesis that like is known by like, so he can see but two ways in which we could use these names to gain some knowledge of God: comparison with the attributes as we understand them, or assimilating them ourselves. The first he will show to be inadequate, and the second impossible (51, M344). As we saw with Aquinas, however, inadequacy need not remove hope of a progressively less inadequate grasp, although Ghazali's more thoroughgoing experiential view of knowledge does not lend itself to a reach so ample as Aquinas'. Assimilation, in Ghazali's context, addresses some Sufi pretensions regarding identification of man with God (or ways of understanding their evocations) which he must explode in the face of "the distinction" of creator from creature.

But can there be no middle ground? No way of inquirers coming closer to divinity while recognizing that they will never adequately grasp "the one truly existing in itself, from which every true [thing] gets its true reality" (137-*al-Ḥaqq*)? Ghazali offers a slim thread, though it is better displayed than expressed in the *Maqsād*. The way it is displayed is by offering a *counsel* as part of the exposition of each name: how it is that one might become more merciful, say, as a creature—the "creature's way of sharing" in the attribute expressed by each name. Even though Ghazali will insist that this can only be a "creature's share," in the face of some Sufi claims of inherence (*ḥulūl*) or assimilation (or better, identification: *ittiḥād*), his own experiential view of knowledge would have to acknowledge an epistemic dimension to such a sharing. Moreover, that path embodies the mainline Sufi tradition which Ghazali is anxious to promote. But let us see how it might be articulated, by contrast to what he calls the "way of comparison."

Comparison is manifestly inadequate, since it can only recall us to the unbridgeable difference in *modes* of realizing and hence of understanding the names as attributes—the basis of Maimonides' radical agnosticism. Ghazali's example is charming: should one try to present the pleasures of sexual intercourse to an impotent person or a small boy by way of the pleasure of sweets, one would be answering his question but misleading him "since there is no correspondence between the sweetness of sugar and the pleasure of intercourse" (51, M344). Similarly, "in so far as we know ourselves to be powerful, knowing, living, speaking, and then hear them in [hearing] the attributes of God . . . we understand them with an inadequate comprehension" even more misleading than the example offered—for "our life, power, and understanding are farther from the life, power, and understanding of God . . . than sugar's sweetness is from the pleasure of intercourse." Hence "the outcome of defining God . . . by these attributes is also an illusory likeness, sharing [only] in the name"—echoes of the Rambam.

Should one hope for illumination of another sort, such as that claimed by the Sufis for "those who know," Ghazali faithfully renders that context by insisting: "the ultimate knowledge of the 'knowers' lies in their inability to know, and their realizing in fact that they do not know Him, that it is utterly impossible for them to know Him, and that it is impossible for anyone except God to know God with an authentic knowledge comprehending the [true nature] of the divine attributes" (54, M344).[26] Nevertheless, he does go on to admit a differentiation in the kinds of knowledge attained by "angels, prophets, and holy men" (55, M345). This consists in the varying degrees of understanding available to those who witness

> the wonders of His signs in the realms of heaven and earth,
> in creating spirits and bodies, and examine the wonders of
> the kingdom and the prodigies of workmanship: closely
> scrutinizing the details, inquiring into the fine points of

> wisdom, receiving in full the subtleties of organization, and being characterized by all of the angelic attributes which bring them close to God—great and glorious—and who by attaining these properties is in fact characterized by them.

Meditation on the fine points of the Most High's workmanship can lead to an appreciation of divine wisdom that leads one to act in a way more consonant with it—and so be characterized by a share in those properties expressed by the "beautiful names." There is no metaphysical identification here—creatures remain creatures—but there is a kind of divinization nonetheless, leading to a heartfelt confession of divine unity of a sort which only God can effect in us and which the "love of God" does effect because the human spirit is already a "divine thing, beyond that—of created intelligences."[27] Perhaps it is this conviction of divine power at work in those who seek to conform their lives to what they conceive the names of God to express, and thereby come progressively closer to God, that allows him to assert (in commenting on the name *al-Awal* [The First]) that "every knowing experienced this side of knowledge of Him is a step towards knowledge of Him" (147). The context is the Sufi way (*tarīq*), those journeying on it and the stages (*manāzil*) to which they attain. It is only in virtue of being on that way that one can be confident of a progressive understanding of the unknowable God, yet to the extent that one can be said to "draw closer," then Ghazali presumes a process whereby our use of the divine names would "imperfectly signify" God.

Ghazali falls short of making anything like Aquinas' claim about our use of language. The reason, I wager, is that his experiential view of human knowing is framed by a conception of "like knowing like." He must insist that "no one knows the essential reality of God's knowledge . . . without having a likeness of His knowledge" (56, M345), and since "the knowledge of God . . . is totally unlike the knowledge of creatures, so the knowledge creatures have of Him will neither be perfect nor authentic, but illusory and anthropomorphic." No middle ground here: creature and creator are so *unlike* that our knowledge allows us no access to what God's is like. Yet he will also reiterate that "the more a man comprehends of the details of the powers and wonders of making in the kingdom of the heavens, the more abundant his share will be in knowing the attribute of power" (57, M346). That claim presumes a progression, and, as we have seen, virtually presupposes the context of the Sufi way toward becoming a "knower." While that way offers no easy progression in knowledge—since their "ultimate knowledge . . . lies in their inability to know" (54)—nonetheless, the stages on this path reflect "an unending difference" (57, M346). That is, one may progress indefinitely in one's knowledge of God, since "the human potential for knowledge is unlimited" (58, M346). And one does so precisely by meditating on "His works in so far as they are His works," seeing them not "in as much as they be sky or earth or trees, but in so far as He made them." The knowledge so attained "would not leave the divine presence to one side, hence it would be possible for [such a one] to say: 'I know only God and I see only God.'"

Yet such an affirmation would have to be made in the light of Ghazali's earlier insistence that "only God knows God." Perhaps the truth is, however, that both may be said, and indeed must be said, for "each reflects a particular intention" (59, M347). He likens these complementary assertions to the celebrated Qur'anic verse associated with the battle of Badr: "You did not throw when you threw, but God threw." No contradiction here, "since there are two interpretations of throwing: on one it is attributed to man, while on the second to the Lord most high." That is more like the beginning of an endless controversy than it is the last word; however, Ghazali leaves us with it as his final word on the matter. In effect, he offers more suggestions than a resolution of this ticklish subject. Perhaps, however, he has given us more than he knows how to say, by displaying in the structure of his commentary the demand that each learner become a participant. According to this demand, that gradual assimilation to the ways of God entails a progressive knowing that, while aware of its inadequacy, would thereby become less and less so. Such a characterization remains faithful to Ghazali, and indeed offers his commentary on Aquinas' notion of "signifying imperfectly," however different their views of knowing and of language may be.

## SUMMARY

I have tried to show how these religious thinkers, each operating within a shared problematic but out of different traditions, may shed light on the other, by the strategies each adopts to meet the issues as he sees them. Even the most "intellectual" of them all—Thomas Aquinas—acknowledges a dimension of practical knowing in his way of exploiting the analogous dimensions of language, and if we were to underscore Maimonides' practical goal of the *Guide,* Ghazali offers some ways to overcome the Rambam's extreme agnosticism by adopting spiritual disciplines directing seekers to a way of life bringing them closer to God. This resolution of the matter underscores aspects left quite implicit by Aquinas and barely alluded to by Maimonides, yet certainly operative in their own lives and in their respective traditions. The model of theology-as-science, which Aquinas worked to give a determinate shape in the west, tended to rely on argument to further its understanding, relegating the realm of practice to individual spiritual direction and to religious rule. Contemporary readings of Maimonides underscore his final resolution in the *Guide* to intelligent and heartfelt observance.[28] It may be significant that a comparative treatment like this one signals the Islamic interlocutor as providing a more telling role for spiritual disciplines in our continuing quest for understanding in matters religious. Perhaps some such "interfaith complementarity" might illuminate other tangled issues in philosophical theology.

## NOTES

1. References to Moses Maimonides' *Guide for the Perplexed* (New York: Dover, 1956) will be given in the text by book, chapter. I have selected Friedlander's 1904 translation since his philosophical lexicon is more standard than Pines', and I have found it generally a faithful rendering to the Arabic. When alterations are made, they will be noted. (The title "Rambam" derives from *R*abbi *M*oses *b*en *M*aimon.)

2. This celebrated "distinction" of God from the world has been given acute philosophical expression in Robert Sokolowski's *God of*

*Faith and Reason* (Notre Dame: University of Notre Dame Press, 1982).

3. This essay reflects positions worked out in greater detail in my *Knowing the Unknowable God: Ibn-Sina, Maimonides, Aquinas* (Notre Dame: University of Notre Dame Press, 1986); the best treatment on Aquinas on analogy remains Ralph McInerny, *Logic of Analogy* (The Hague, 1961).

4. For the dating I am indebted to Roger Arnaldez' article in the *Encyclopedia of Islam* (Leiden: Brill, 1979) 911a; Averroes' *Tahafut* has been translated by Simon van den Bergh: Averroes' *Tahafut al-Tahafut* (Oxford: Oxford University Press, 1954).

5. See Michel Allard, *Le Problème des Attributs Divins* (Beirut: Librairie Catholique, 1965).

6. Cf. "sifa" in *Shorter Encyclopedia of Islam* (Ithaca: Cornell University Press, 1953), p. 545.

7. "Ontological difference" is a shorthand for the strategies which Soren Kierkegaard uses to differentiate a genuinely Christian conceptuality from pretenders (like Hegel)—cf. *Philosophical Fragments* (Princeton: Princeton University Press, 1967) *passim.* The import matches Sokolowski's "distinction"—see note 2.

8. See Norbert Samuelson, *Gersonides' Wars of the Lord—Treatise Three: On God's Knowledge* (Toronto: Pontifical Institute of Medieval Studies, 1977), pp. 182–224.

9. The primary locus can be found in *Summa Theologiae* 1.13, where references to more extended discussions are given. We shall use Herbert McCabe's excellent translation: *Summa Theologiae,* Vol. III: *Theological Language* (London: Eyre and Spottiswoode, 1965). Reference code: Part I, Q. 13, art. 2, reply to obj. 2 = 1.13.2.2.

10. I have developed the two levels of Aquinas' treatment of God—ontological, by way of "formal features" (1.2–11), and semantic, concerned with "attributes" (1.13)—in *Aquinas: God and Action* (Notre Dame: University of Notre Dame Press, 1979).

11. *Avicenne: La Metaphysique du Shifa,* tr. G.C. Anawati (Paris: Vrin, 1985), 8.4.

12. For Aquinas' transformation of Avicenna's distinction between *essence* and *existence,* see my *Knowing the Unknowable God,* ch. 3.

13. By understanding this fact, recent work on Aquinas has suc-

ceeded in "deconstructing" his Thomist *persona*, which presented the identity of essence and existence in God as a *thesis* grounding an ascending knowledge of God by way of analogy—a pattern of thought severely castigated by Karl Barth (as the "analogy of being") as falsifying the revelation of God as "totally other." Barth amended his criticism, however, when Przywara and others informed him of Aquinas' own treatment of these matters—see Hans Urs von Balthasar, *The Theology of Karl Barth* (New York: Holt, Reinhart, Winston, 1971). Moreover, Aquinas will insist that "eternity" properly belongs to God alone, so effectively distinguishing God's eternity from *timelessness* (1.8.3).

14. Maimonides' treatment of *similarity* (1.56) seems to presuppose a more conventional "template" understanding of meaning than Aquinas' thoroughly linguistic view.

15. Cf. Robert Sokolowski: "On Making Distinctions," *Review of Metaphysics* 32 (1979): 652–61.

16. For this dimension of Aquinas' thought, see M.-D. Chenu, *Théologie au Douzième Siècle* (Paris: Vrin, 1957), ch. "Grammaire et Theologie."

17. See the appendix to McCabe's version (note 9) of question 13: "Signifying Imperfectly." Since "imperfectly signify" becomes a quasi-technical term in this context, its meaning differs enough from "signify imperfectly" to justify the split infinitive!

18. I am thinking here of Alasdair MacIntyre and Martha Nussbaum, as exemplified in his *After Virtue,* 2nd ed. (Notre Dame: University of Notre Dame Press, 1986), and her *Fragility of Goodness* (New York: Cambridge University Press, 1986).

19. *Apology* 21d; Kierkegaard helps us once again by formulating Socrates' realization as the difference between "to understand [and] to understand"—*Sickness unto Death* (Princeton: Princeton University Press, 1941), p. 221.

20. W.B. Gallie, "Essentially Contested Concepts," *Pro. Aris. Soc.* 56 (1955–56), reprinted in Max Black, ed., *Importance of Language* (Englewood Cliffs: Prentice-Hall, 1962), pp. 121–46.

21. Thomas Merton's life, which he could not resist documenting, illustrates this admirably, especially as articulated by Elena Malits in *The Solitary Explorer: Thomas Merton's Transforming Journey* (San Francisco: Harper & Row, 1980).

22. Needless to say, those of a more "Platonist" persuasion think otherwise, and seem to find it natural ("concrete") to speak first of qualities, and then of their "instantiation." The differences here are utterly basic, and bear crucially on discourse about God, and especially on one's acceptance of the fact of analogous discourse and its significance.

23. Cf. Gary Gutting, "The Catholic and the Calvinist—A Dialogue on Faith and Reason," *Faith and Philosophy* 2 (1985), 236–56.

24. Abu-Hamid al-Ghazali: *Al-Maqsad al-Asna fi Sharh Maani Asma' Allah al-Husna* (= "The Sublime Intentions Present in Explaining the Meanings of the Beautiful Names of God"), Fadlou A. Shehadi, ed. (Beirut: Dar el-Machreq, 1971). Page citations will be given to the Arabic text, soon to appear in translation by University of Notre Dame Press. Portions have already been translated by Richard McCarthy in Appendix IV of his *Freedom and Fulfillment* (Boston: Twayne Publisher, 1980), which will be preceded by "M." McCarthy's book presents Ghazali's journey in an annotated translation.

25. Cf. Fadlou Shehadi, *Ghazali's Unique Unknowable God* (Leiden: Brill, 1964), and my "The Unknowability of God in al-Ghazali," *Religious Studies* 23 (1987), 171–82.

26. The "knowers" is a Sufi allusion to a manner of knowing God by a certain familiarity. The parallels with Maimonides and Aquinas are palpable; cf. *Guide of the Perplexed* 1.58: "Glory then to Him who is such that when the intellects contemplate His essence, their apprehension turns into incapacity . . . and when tongues aspire to magnify Him by means of attributive qualifications, all eloquence turns into weariness and incapacity!" (trans. Shlomo Pines; Chicago: University of Chicago Press, 1963); and *Expositio super librum Boethii de Trinitate* 1.2.1: "Since our understanding finds itself knowing God most perfectly when it knows that the divine nature lies beyond whatever it can apprehend in our present state, we can be said to know God as unknown, once we sum up what knowledge we have of Him" (ed. Decker; Leiden, 1959).

27. The citation is from Ghazali's masterwork: *Ihya' 'Ulum ad-Din,* Book 21 [*Kitab Sharh 'Aja'ib al-Qalb*] (Cairo, 1928), p. 14; a similar reference can also be found in Book 3, Bayan 1, translated in

Appendix 5 of McCarthy (see note 24), p. 366. The allusion is to 17:85: "They will ask you concerning the Spirit. Say: The Spirit is by command of my Lord"—but *min amri rabbi* could also be rendered: "is something divine," as Ghazali glosses it here.

28. Cf. Menachem Kellner's contribution to Lenn Evan Goodman, *Neoplatonism and Jewish Thought* (Albany: State University Press, 1992).

## Chapter Nine

# SÁNCHEZ' CRITIQUE OF *AUTHORITAS:* *CONVERSO* SKEPTICISM AND THE EMERGENCE OF RADICAL HERMENEUTICS

### JOSÉ FAUR

#### INTRODUCTION

In the west, hermeneutics traditionally concerned the interpretation of authoritative texts, which meant texts that could not be approached directly, but only through a hierarchy of authorities empowered to determine their "true" meaning. Originally, only the scriptural canon acquired such authority. Through the scholastic period, however, this authority was extended to texts representing all forms of learning, from universal history to medicine and the physical sciences. Iberian Christianity thereby inherited and perfected a method in which knowledge was subservient to ecclesial authority.

As is well known, sixteenth and seventeenth century skepticism challenged the scholastic concept of authority. As is not sufficiently well known, however, the rabbinic intellectual tradition contributed significantly to the development of European skepticism. This contribution came by way of the *conversos.* Knowingly or unknowingly these "new Christians" (*cristianos nuevos*) projected into the Christian environment principles and ideas that were intrinsic to rabbinic thought.

The *conversos* ("converts") were the Jews from Spain and Portugal and their descendants who were "forced" (thus their Hebrew name, *anusim*) to convert to Christianity in order to survive the massacre of Jews and subsequent expulsions that took place in fourteenth and fifteenth century Spain and Portugal. They were not a homogenous class and were ideologically divided into four groups. Some were devout Christians and became hateful of Jews and Judaism. Others wanted to preserve their Judaism at all cost and deeply abhorred the religion that was forced on them. Some, however, wished to be both, trying to form a syncretism between their old and new religions and ideals. Finally, there were those who wanted to be neither Jew nor Christian. This group, maligned by both Christian and Jewish scholars as nihilist and amoral, was the most significant from the point of view of European cultural history. Disappointed with the religious ideologies dominating Europe at the time, they sought a secular society, free from religious compulsion and ecclesiastical dominance. This concern was shared by all four groups, who were united by family and economic ties and, above all, by the racial persecutions they suffered in common.

The importance of the *converso* community in the shaping of modern Europe has not been yet systematically investigated. Americo Castro and his disciples have explored the enormous contributions made by the *converso* community to the scientific and intellectual life of Spain. Similarly, Marct Bataillon, in his classic *Erasmo y España*,[1] has shown the participation of the *conversos* in shaping new religious ideas and movements in Spain. The influence of the *conversos* spread beyond Spain, however. As a direct consequence of the expulsion (1492), and of Spain's and Portugal's racist policies of *pureza de sangre* ("purity of blood"), the *conversos* were scattered throughout Europe and the Mediterranean basin. Their influence thereby spread beyond the boundaries of the Iberian Peninsula, into the center of European culture and civilization. They were particularly instrumental in the dissemination of new, radical ideas that helped change the spiritual and intellectual horizons of the west.[2]

Of the *conversos* who fled the Iberian Peninsula in the fifteenth century, a large contingent settled in Bordeaux, in the southwest of France. Among these refugees were some of the most brilliant humanists and scientists of the time, who would soon contribute to the establishment of the Collège de Guyenne. The head of this college was the famous *converso* André de Gouveia (1497–1548) who until 1533 had been the rector of the Université de Paris. He remained head of the college until 1547, when he accepted the invitation of the King of Portugal to found the University of Coimbra. Gouveia brought into the faculty of Guyenne many of his relatives and other *conversos,* including many scholars imbued with the spirit of skepticism. Among them was Jehan Gelida, known for his critical views on scholasticism, who succeeded Gouveia in 1547. It was at Guyenne, under the philosophical direction of Gelida, that Francisco Sánchez acquired his skeptical spirit and religious outlook.

Sánchez (1550/51–1623) was the son of *conversos* and the father of modern skepticism.[3] He lived in Bordeaux (1562–1569), where his aunt was married to Antonio López, member of a powerful *converso* family, and where he attended the famous Collège de Guyenne. Although overtly Christian, Sánchez harbored deep feelings for Judaism and for the plight of Jews and fellow *conversos.* In fact, it appears that the aim of his major work, *Quod nihil scitur* ("That Nothing is Known," 1581), was to expose and develop a uniquely *converso* philosophy.

Despite his ostensive Christianity, there are strong indications of Sánchez' intention to offer his book in the interest of Jews and *conversos.* In his first book, published three years earlier—*Carmen de Cometa anno MC LXVII* (1578), a poem designed to refute the astrological notions associated with comets and other celestial events—Sánchez offered a dedication "To the very humane and erudite Diego de Castro," a distinguished professor of medicine at the University of Coimbra, and a man of letters.[4] He then dedicated *Quod nihil scitur* to "The most integral and eloquent man, Jacob de Castro." *Conversos* used "Diego" to translate the name "Jacob" (*Iahacob*). It appears, then, that Sánchez had dedicated both books to the same man and that, as indicated by the change of name, this man had during these three years openly returned to Judaism. The fact that Sánchez chose to risk his life by dedicating his most important philosophical work to such an individual indicates that he had no intention of severing his ties with the Jewish people.

At the end of his dedicatory letter, Sánchez tells Castro: "Accept it [this book] with a happy face, and enlist it in the number of yours, and to me with it." To "enlist" the book among those of his meant to include it among those special works that Jacob Castro regarded as particularly significant for "his" cause. Similarly, by asking to be "enlisted" among those who belonged to the intimate circle of Castro's friends, Sánchez was indicating that he wanted to be identified with those who believed in Castro's cause. There are more allusions to battles and confrontations. Explicitly, Sánchez writes that he trusted that his book should go forth "as a soldier who goes to battle against a lie." He makes it clear that he would not be able to direct the battle himself, and that such a task was incumbent upon Castro. Thus, he nurtured the hope that the book "will take refuge in your camp: in no other place could it be more secure." Together with the copy that he presented to Castro, it seems that Sánchez had sent a set of instructions with the precise intent of the book, "and in order that you would not discard it since you don't know it, I am sending it to you with my instructions." Since his own situation precluded his bringing to fruition the ultimate implications of the book, Sánchez counted on Castro to carry on such a battle. Accordingly, he sent the book, "to greet you in my name, to confirm our friendship, and that it should battle under your flag."

There is reason to believe that the reader for whom Sánchez wrote *Quod nihil scitur* was, like Castro himself, an individual with a Jewish background. In neither of the books that he dedicated to Castro did Sánchez conclude with the obligatory "praise to Virgin Mary."[5] At the end of *Carmen de Cometa,* furthermore, there is a reference to the Christian religions in Europe as *cultum . . . deorum* ("the worship . . . of gods").[6] With a writer as careful as Sánchez, one cannot attribute the plural "gods" (*deorum*) to a mere slip of the pen. Rather, it must be taken as evidence that, like many other *conversos,* he regarded Christianity as polytheistic.

## SÁNCHEZ' CRITIQUE OF AUTHORITY

The principal objectives of Sánchez' *Quod nihil scitur* were, first, to discredit the notion of *authoritas* in the realm of scientific investigation; second, to discredit the use of Aristotelian and scholastic methods or investigation; and, third, to establish the grounds for a scientific method of inquiry. These goals were intimately linked with one another. Once the notion of *authoritas* was dismissed, it would be possible to show the futility of Aristotelian thinking and propose a *modus sciendi* or "scientific methodology" based on experimentation and theory (Sánchez was the first to have coined this expression).

In scholastic thinking, "authority" (*auctoritas, authoritas*) was a fundamental concept of those who believed that truth was conditioned by the opinions and views of "authors" (*auctores, authores*), in people invested with "authority," and that it needed to be processed through a hierarchy of such opinions. "Medieval reverence to *auctores* went so far," writes Curtius, "that every source was held to be good. The historical and critical sense were both lacking."[7] An investigator could not approach the subject at hand directly, but only through the mediation of a hierarchy of authorities, ecclesiastic or secular, such as Aristotle in physics, Galeno in medicine, and Orosius in universal history.

Sánchez' critique of authority had its setting in the special situation of Jews and *conversos* under the oppressive rule of ecclesiastical powers. The medieval church derived its authority to rule from the assumption that ecclesiastical authorities were in possession of "the truth" and therefore had the right to impose it on others. Because the truth depended on *authoritas* and could not be approached directly, ecclesiastical interpretations could not be contested. By challenging the very notion of *authoritas,* Sánchez sought to undermine the foundation of medieval ecclesiastical authority and, with it, the source of the church's oppressive rule. As we will see, Sánchez carefully distinguished between matters of faith, depending on authority, and matters of science, which depend on direct investigation and objective demonstration. Through this distinction, Sánchez relegated *authoritas* to the realm of the subjective, thereby denying ecclesiastical powers the right to claim that their truths were categorical and universally valid.

## RABBINIC HERMENEUTICS AND THE AUTHORITY OF FAITH

Sánchez' recognition of *authoritas* in the realm of faith was consistent with Jewish tradition, specifically his own Iberian tradition as explicated by Maimonides. In effect, Jews recognized the rabbis of the Talmudic period as the supreme *authoritas* of Judaism and Jewish law. The rabbis' authority, however, was not grounded on some metaphysical doctrine, but on the political and judicial institutions of the Jewish people. It was limited to the legal and judicial application of the law and did not extend to the realm of dogma and biblical interpretations. A few remarks about the rabbinic concept of hermeneutics would further elucidate this point. For the rabbis, the object of interpretation was not to "discover" the mind of the author, but, rather, to *generate* new meaning from the text. From this perspective, meaning is not *present* in the text, but effected by the active participation of the reader functioning as an *ecrivain.* This is why Maimonides established the second principle of his *Sefer Ha-Mitsvot* ("The Book of the Scriptural Commandments"): that all doctrines that the rabbinic authorities derived through the interpretation of the scripture (for example, the duty to respect an older brother or a step-parent) cannot be classified as "scriptural" doctrines per se (*de-'oraita*), but rather, they must be regarded as "rabbinic obligations" (*de-rabbanan*).

Intrinsic to rabbinic thinking is the belief that the text of the scripture is polysemic, containing the possibility of countless readings and interpretations.[8] Accordingly, the rabbis regarded a vocalized Scroll of the Torah as liturgically invalid (*pasul*), since they feared that the univalent appearance of a vocalized text would somehow restrict the polysemic character of the Torah.[9] Interpretation, more importantly, can neither displace nor restrict the polysemic character of the scripture. From this it follows that a rabbinic doctrine or legislation based on the hermeneutics of the Torah is not valid because the rabbis have determined the "true" meaning of the text-supplanting all other interpretations, but solely because they, as legislators and teachers of the Jewish people, have the authority to promulgate and instruct. This point is evident in the position maintained by the Geonim (heads of the Talmudic academies in Babylonia) and Sephardic scholars, that rabbinic hermeneutics (*derasha*) is not restrictive and cannot exclude other interpretations of the same text.[10] Accordingly, the Geonim as well as many distinguished Sephardic scholars, such as Maimonides, Meir Abul'afya (ca. 1170–1244), and David ibn Abi Zimra (1479–1573), maintained that although a court cannot abrogate a decree of another court unless it is of a higher rank, if a decree was based on biblical exegesis it may be abrogated by a lower court: *authoritas* is not operative in the interpretation of the scripture, even when resulting in legislation.[11]

Maimonides therefore rejected the application of *authoritas* in post-Talmudic jurisprudence. In accordance with the school of Lucena, Spain, he rejected the notion that the Geonim were invested with special authority in the field of Talmudic law and that their views must be accepted unequivocally.[12] He was careful to distinguish between the law of the Talmud itself, "which is binding on all Israel,"[13] and that of the post-Talmudic era. Since the Talmud comprised the views and opinions "which were agreed upon by all Israel," it represents national consensus and public authority.[14] Its ultimate foundation is political: the nation of Israel (in exile). Therefore, it is binding on all Jewry. On the other hand, post-Talmudic interpreters, including the Geonim, did not represent the nation as a whole; accordingly, they lacked Jewish *public* authority. With the conclusion of the Talmudic era (499 C.E.), the period of a national Jewish court came to an end. All Jewish courts to come henceforth have local jurisdiction alone (*bet din shel yehidim*).[15] It is on the basis of their *expertise* on Talmudic law, not on legal *authority,* that the decisions of the post-Talmudic courts are to be accepted.[16]

Maimonides' distinction contradicts the current notion that, according to Jewish law, later jurisconsults (*acharonim*) must subordinate their views to the earlier jurisconsults (*rishonim*). This notion displays the principle of authority that Maimonides rejected and that, in fact, derives from the well known scholastic distinction between *auctores maiores* and *minores.*[17] For Maimonides, when conflicting opinions arise, one should follow the most reasonable view, whether it comes from an early or from a late scholar.

> Every court of justice in every city which was established after the Talmud, which legislated a prohibition, promulgated a statute, or established a custom for the people of its city or of many cities, its decisions did not disseminate throughout Israel, because of the distances and poor traveling conditions. And because the court of justice of that city was local, whereas the supreme court of seventy-one members had ceased to function many years before the

compilation of the Talmud. Accordingly, one cannot coerce the people of one city to adopt the custom of another city. Nor may one say to a court of justice to legislate a prohibition which was legislated by another court in its own city. Similarly, if one of the Geonim taught the principle of the law to be one way, and another court coming afterward came to the conclusion that this is not the principle of the law written in the Talmud, the opinion of the earliest must not be accepted, but that which seems more reasonable, be it of the earliest or the latest.[18]

Along with the authority of post-Talmudic interpreters, Maimonides also rejected the authority of divine interventions into the realm of judicial analysis and judgment: no one can base a legal decision or interpretation on divine inspiration or prophecy. Since it was axiomatic that the heavens will not interfere in the legal process, anyone claiming authority on divine intervention must be regarded as a false prophet.[19]

## MAIMONIDES AND THE CRITIQUE OF AUTHORITY IN SCIENCE

Sánchez was the first modern thinker to reject authority in the natural sciences. Anticipating Galileo (1564–1642), he flatly rejected authority in the realm of natural phenomena and insisted on the direct examination of things themselves. He mentioned these two points in the "Introduction to the Reader" of *Quod nihil scitur:*

Don't ask me for many authorities (*authoritates*) or reverence for authors (*authores*), since this is of a servile and unlearned spirit, rather than of one who is free and wants to investigate the truth. I shall only follow the reason of Nature.[20]

Addressing Aristotle's authority in particular, Sánchez asked: "Why, if Aristotle had written about something, must I remain silent?" One must be free to examine the things directly, without the intercession of authority. "Had he actually determined in his works all the forces of nature, and comprehended all the complexities of things? No. But in the realm of science, in the tribunal of truth, no one can judge, no one can . . . rule except for the truth itself."[21] Since scholars had refrained from examining natural phenomena directly, what passed as science is nothing else but sheer fantasy and fiction. He described the endeavors of the learned men of his time as follows:

> Each of them had built a science out of his own or other people's imagination, from which they make further inferences, and from those, others, transcending already the boundaries of the things themselves, resulting in a labyrinth of words, with no foundation whatsoever in the truth. Therefore, instead of a direct understanding of the natural things, we have a new thing, the fabric of fiction, which no intelligent mind could ever accept.[22]

"Accordingly," Sánchez wrote, "it is easy to see how stupid are those who search for science in authority (*authoritas*), without examining the things in themselves."[23] The purposes of authority and reason are fundamentally different. "The object of authority is to believe, of reason is to demonstrate. One is for faith; the other is fit for science."[24] Sánchez therefore claimed that the knowledge of nature that is gleaned from books rather than from direct experimentation is to be included among the matters of faith, rather than of science. Indeed, if the truth had to be acquired from books alone, then knowledge of any sort would have been impossible; the volume of knowledge would be so enormous, and the different views and opinions so varied, that no individual could possibly cover it during a single life span. Moreover, "it would generate in me faith, rather than science; from which it follows that the majority of modern writers are more faithful than wise."[25] The only means for genuine knowledge is in the direct examination of nature. Authority cannot be accepted as a source of science. "Therefore, one speaks the truth, not by citing someone else, but by saying what the thing is." Labeling those who invoke Aristotle's authority "unintelligent guides of authors, who don't see or at least pretend not to see," Sánchez argued that Aristotle himself disagreed with Plato, saying that he loved the truth more. "Now, we see ourselves [that] an Authority coming from without has little value."[26] Faith, which is knowledge based on authority, "suffices only for the ignorant."[27] Accordingly, at the end of his book, Sánchez promised to lay the foundations for a scientific methodology (*modus sciendi*) which will not be divorced from nature.

Sánchez' critique of authority in the realms of metaphysics and science had its roots in the Maimonidean tradition. Concerning physical phenomena, Maimonides formulated the principle that "facts do not follow opinions, but true opinions ought to follow the facts."[28] Although Maimonides regarded Aristotelian physics as sound and based his twenty-six propositions for the proof of creation on it, his reason was that he believed that, on the whole, Aristotle's views were demonstratable. However, he never invested Aristotle with authority, as did the scholastics, but argued instead that Aristotelian physics was to be dismissed when it contradicted "perceptible experience" (*amr muṣhahad*). Maimonides thus declared, "I shall not contradict at all what [Aristotle] had actually proven,"[29] while at the same time criticizing claims that Aristotle could prove, in particular, his metaphysical theories.[30] For Maimonides, since Aristotelian metaphysics cannot be verified, it must be regarded a pure fabrication, leading to the dissemination of harmful misconceptions. Carefully distinguishing between Aristotle's metaphysics (and related matters above the lunar orbit) and Aristotelian physics of the sublunar world, Maimonides declared:

> Let me tell you a general principle. Although I am quite aware that many of the [Aristotelian] zealots would attribute this to my lack of understanding or to my being deliberately misleading, I will not refrain on this account from communicating what I perceived and understood despite my limitations. This general principle is that whatever Aristotle had said about all that which exists below the moon's sphere up to the center of the earth is undoubtedly true—and one would not depart from him, unless he has misunderstood him, or has already an opinion which he now wants to defend, or because those [Aristotelian] views lead him to deny a perceptible experience (*amr mushahad*). However, Aristotle's discussions on [subjects] from

the moon's sphere and above, are a kind of conjecture and fancy except for a few items. This is all the more true in his discussions about the order of the [disembodied] intellects and some of those theological opinions which he happens to believe in, containing many absurdities and resulting in distinct harm which is evident among all the nations, and the [cause for the] propagation of injuries. And there is no proof of them.[31]

Maimonides disavowed the notion of *authoritas* in the realm of natural phenomena, even when pertaining to Jewish law.[32] Forcefully, he insisted that, on matters connected with physical phenomena, there should be no difference between the opinion of a prophet and a Gentile. A view pertaining to physical phenomena ought to be incorporated into law or rejected on the basis of objective demonstration alone, regardless of who had issued it. In justifying the introduction of astronomical computations by non-Jewish scientists for the determination of the Jewish calendar, Maimonides wrote:

The proofs for every item are [to be found] in the science of astronomy and geometry about which Greek scholars wrote abundantly, and they [their writings] are now found in the hands of scholars. However, the books [on astronomy] by Jewish scholars from the children of Issachar, at the time of the prophets, have not reached us. Nonetheless, since all these matters are [based on] clear and unambiguous proofs, which no one can doubt, it is unimportant who the author is, whether a prophet or a gentile. Because every item whose reason is exposed, its truth is discerned with unambiguous proofs, we may rely on the person who said it or taught the proof which was exposed and the reason which was discerned.[33]

Some Jewish jurisconsults extended this principle to the abrogation of rabbinic legislation. To illustrate, the rabbis legislated that a premature baby born at the eighth month of gestation has the status of a non-person, since he would surely die. Solomon Semah Duran

(c. 1400–1467) declined to apply this legislation on the ground "that experience contradicts it."[34] This principle was registered by a contemporary of Sánchez, Joseph Caro (1488–1575), the highest Sephardic authority in Jewish law.[35] It was incorporated into the code law of another contemporary, Moses Isserles (ca. 1525–1572)—the highest legal authority of Ashkenazic Jewry.[36]

The Catalonian Jewish philosopher Hasdai Crescas (d. c. 1410) continued the Maimonidean tradition even while criticizing Maimonides' own work. In his book, *Or Adonay,* Crescas offered a systematic critique of Aristotle's physics, presented in the form of a critique of Maimonides' attempt, in his twenty-six propositions, to demonstrate the Jewish doctrine of creation in Aristotelian terms. Rather than the mere details of any of the Aristotelian systems, the ultimate object of Cresca's critique was the scholastic method of reasoning itself: the attempt to achieve rational certainty. Implicit in his critique was the need for a new type of rationality. True to his own skepticism, Crescas refrained from offering some new method of reasoning to replace the one he doubted. As Wolfson noted:

> In a larger sense, we may see in Crescas' critique of Aristotle the fluctuations of the human mind at the point when it began to realize that reason, which had once helped man to understand nature, to free himself from superstition and to raise his desultory observations to some kind of unity and wholeness, had itself in the system of Aristotle gone off into the wilds of speculation and built up an artificial structure entirely divorced from nature. A new way of returning to nature was sought, but none was as yet to be found. Crescas had passed the stage when man condemned reason; he had reached the stage when man began to doubt reason, but he had not yet entered upon the stage when man learned to control reason by facts.[37]

Crescas' reluctance to present his own world view, or to develop a theory of physics, is consistent with the skeptic posture that he intended to promote. In this way, he contributed to a movement that by the sixteenth century would bifurcate into mysticism, on the one hand, and Sánchez' scientific methodology on the other. Both these approaches were predicated upon the realization that human reason alone cannot attain certainty: one would invoke divine illumination, the other scientific experimentation.

## THE CRITIQUE OF AUTHORITY AND RADICAL HERMENEUTICS, FROM SÁNCHEZ TO SPINOZA

Sánchez' critique of authority contributed to the modern European search for a new model of rationality and to the undermining of religious authority. For the ecclesiastical leaders of medieval Christianity, religious authority derived from divine revelation and from authoritative interpretation of scripture. Those who sought to undermine ecclesiastical authority therefore began by questioning the authority of the biblical text and of its traditional interpretation.

Contrary to what many believe today, the decline of the Bible in seventeenth and eighteenth century thought was not a reflection of increased confidence in human reason. To the contrary, the decline of the Bible was the result of the skepticism which brought into question the established methods of both philosophy and biblical hermeneutics. Increased confidence in human reason emerged only as a consequence of the skeptics' critique of biblical authority. Three individuals of *converso* descent contributed significantly to this critique. Biblical criticism and radical hermeneutics—that is, the interpretation of scripture without regard to ecclesiastical tradition and authority—were initiated by Isaac La Peyrère (1596–1676). *Structurally,* his hermeneutics combined the two essential elements of Sánchez' "scientific methodology": *experimentation,* which in the field of biblical history must be replaced by anthropology, and *theory* based on the facts at hand, rather than on authority. Based partially on radical hermeneutics and partially on the data obtained through the discovery of the new worlds and civilizations, he reached the conclusion that there were human beings before Adam. According to La Peyrère, Adam was the first Jew, not the father of all humankind. An important consequence of his thesis was the emergence of the first principles of biblical criticism. In the presentation of his views, La Peyrère developed the thesis that the text of the Bible in its present version is corrupt. He further concluded that it contains inaccurate documents and could not have been written by

Moses. Rather, it was the product of various authors, writing at different epochs:

> La Peyrère next developed what has been a major aspect of biblical criticism over the last three centuries. From various textual examples, he showed that there seemed to be different authors of different portions of Scripture; these things were diversely written, being taken out of several authors.[38]

The most successful attempt to free human reason from the authority of religion was that of Spinoza (1632–1677). In his *Theologico-Political Treatise* (1670), he rejected the claims for divine authority based on the text of the scripture and religious tradition. He accomplished this by further developing the radical hermeneutics and criticism initiated by La Peyrère. In his *Ethics* (1677), published after his death in *Opera posthuma,* he undermined the metaphysical notions used to justify religious ideology and authority. Although Spinoza confined his criticism to the Hebrew scriptures alone ("I do not myself possess a knowledge of Greek sufficiently exact for the task," he writes, and "I prefer to decline the undertaking"[39]), there is little doubt that both he and La Peyrère meant also to include the Christian scriptures. Concerning this fundamental point, Leo Strauss remarked:

> It was infinitely less dangerous to attack Judaism than to attack Christianity, and it was distinctly less dangerous to attack the Old Testament than the New. One has only to read the summary of the argument of the first part of the *Treatise* at the beginning of the thirteenth chapter in order to see that while the explicit argument is chiefly based upon, or directed against, the Old Testament, the conclusions are meant to apply to "the Scripture," i.e., to both Testaments alike.[40]

Distinguishing between the Jewish concept of the law, with its political and judicial institutions, and the Christian concept of religion as a matter of pure faith, Spinoza insisted that unlike the (Mosaic) law, (Christian) religion "stands outside the sphere of law and public authority" (*nullius juris neque authoritatis publicae est*).[41] In developing this argument, Spinoza was following rabbinic tradition, which distinguished between the political and judicial aspects of the law, which depend on authority, and matters pertaining to doctrine and faith, which transcend public authority. This position had been formulated by Bahye ibn Paquda (eleventh century), the revered author of *Duties of the Hearts,* one of the most important works to have been produced in Jewish Spain. Commenting on the passage in which scriptures establish the authority of the Supreme Court of Israel (Deut 17:8–11), he observed that their jurisdiction pertains only to what he designated as "duties of the limbs," that is, external obligations—not on matter of faith, or "duties of the heart":

> The (Torah) did not say that, when you entertain doubts concerning the unity of God, or [the meaning] of God's name and His measures, or one of the doctrines of religion which humankind can arrive at through [common] intelligence and reason, you must subordinate them to the authority of the sages of the Torah, and that you should rely on mere tradition.[42]

Accordingly, Spinoza rejected the concept of authority in the realm of faith. In the footsteps of Maimonides and ibn Paquda, he distinguished between matters subject to public authority (for ibn Paquda, "duties of the limbs") and strictly private matters that concern the individual alone (for ibn Paquda, "duties of the heart"). Negating the scriptural basis for a supreme religious authority, Spinoza observed that Moses and the Jewish priesthood cannot serve as a model for purely religious institutions, such as the Christian churches.

> [N]or should anyone be deceived by the example of the Jewish high-priests and think that the Catholic religion also stands in need of a pontiff; he should bear in mind that the laws of Moses, being also the ordinary laws of the country, necessarily required some public authority (*authoritate quadam publica*) to insure their observance; for, if

everyone were free to interpret the laws of his country as he pleased, no state could stand, but would for that very reason be dissolved at once, and public rights would become private rights.[43]

At the same time, Spinoza insisted that religion (as defined by the Christian faith) stands outside the boundaries of the law and consequently outside the boundaries of *authoritatis publicae* ("public authority"). Touching upon ibn Paquda's distinction between "duties of the limbs" (="outward actions") and "duties of the heart" (="truth and simplicity"), he argues:

> Inasmuch as it consists not so much in outward actions as in simplicity and truth of character, it stands outside the sphere of law and public authority (*authoritatis publicae*).[44]

On the basis of the Hebrew scripture and Jewish tradition, it would follow that *authoritate* only concerns public right, never private rights. Hence, Spinoza's plea for freedom of interpretation and radical hermeneutics:

> The only reason for vesting the supreme authority (*summa authoritas*) in the interpretation of law, and judgment on public affairs in the hands of magistrates, is that it concerns questions of public right. Similarly the supreme authority (*summa authoritas*) in explaining religion, and in passing judgment thereon, is lodged with the individual because it concerns individual rights. So far, then, from the authority (*authoritate*) of the Hebrew high-priests telling in confirmation of the authority (*authoritas*) of the Roman pontiffs to interpret religion, it would rather lend to establish individual freedom of judgment. Thus in this way also, we have shown that our method of interpreting Scripture is the best. For as the highest authority (*maxima authoritas*) of Scriptural interpretation belongs to every man, the rule for such an interpretation should be nothing but the natural light of reason which is common to all—not any

supernatural light nor any external authority (*externa authoritas*).[45]

In this last point, Spinoza is indebted to Joseph Albo (ca. 1350–ca. 1444), one of the most illustrious religious thinkers to emerge from Spanish Jewry in the generation before the expulsion. According to Albo, the religious doctrines and principles of Judaism are not, strictly speaking, subject to authority. Although all Jews are duty-bound to believe in the Torah, they cannot be classified as heretics or unbelievers if their own reasoning leads them to deny a particular principle or interpret it in a radical way:

> Every Israelite is obliged to believe that everything that is found in the Torah is absolutely true, and any one who denies anything that is found in the Torah, knowing that it is the opinion of the Torah, is an unbeliever.... But a person who upholds the law of Moses and believes in its principles, when he undertakes to investigate these matters with his reason and scrutinizes the texts, is misled by his speculation and interprets any given principle otherwise than it is taken to mean at first sight; or denies the principle because he thinks that it does not represent a sound theory which the Torah obliges us to believe; or erroneously denies that a given belief is a fundamental principle, which however he believes as he believes the other dogmas of the Torah which are not fundamental principles; or entertains a certain notion in relation to one of the miracles of the Torah because he thinks that he is not thereby denying any of the doctrines which is obligatory upon us to believe by the authority of Torah—a person of this sort is not an unbeliever. He is classed with the sages and pious men of Israel, though he holds erroneous theories.[46]

Since beliefs express the perceptions and understandings of individuals, individuals cannot be faulted or censored if their minds have led them to radical interpretations or understandings.

We say, therefore, that a person whose speculative ability is not sufficient to enable him to reach the true meaning of scriptural texts, with the result that he believes in the literal meaning and entertains absurd ideas because he thinks they represent the view of the Torah, is not thereby excluded from the community of those who believe in the Torah, Heaven forbid! Nor is it permitted to speak disrespectfully of him and accuse him of perverting the teaching of the Torah and class him among unbelievers and heretics.[47]

The radical hermeneutics of La Peyrère and Spinoza served as the foundation for the revolutionary biblical criticism of Jean Astruc (1684–1766). Unlike his predecessors, however, Astruc carefully avoided examining the theological and philosophical implications of his criticism. In this way, he initiated the kind of biblical criticism which has dominated biblical studies in the last two centuries.

## CONCLUSIONS

In order to protect their personal and religious freedom, *converso* thinkers sought to undermine religious authority and thus the legitimacy of religious and ideological coercion. Their method was to challenge the general claims for rational certainty that supported religious authority. The object of *converso* skepticism was therefore to question the validity of *authoritas,* rather than the validity of knowledge in general (or of one kind of knowledge). The first challenge against *authoritas* came from Sánchez. For reasons of prudence—it would have been suicidal for him to have questioned the authority of religion—he confined his criticism of *authoritas* to the realm of the natural sciences in general and of the Aristotelian and scholastic methodologies in particular. While conceding that *authoritas* is valid in matters of faith, Sánchez limited such matters to the realm of the subjective. Criticism of religious *authoritas* came from Spinoza. By applying the Maimonidean distinction between public and private authority, Spinoza further extended the criticism of *au-*

*thoritas* to include matters of faith. Without touching the Christian scripture, La Peyrère and Astruc questioned the integrity of the Hebrew scripture, thus denying Christianity (and the Christian scripture) its source of legitimacy. Spinoza went further, questioning the very notion of religious authority in Christendom. By applying ibn Paquda's distinction between "duties of the heart" and "duties of the limbs," Spinoza rejected the claim of Christianity authority. By rejecting the political and legal aspects of the Torah, and claiming sole concern for the spiritual salvation of the individual (his corporal welfare being relegated to the political and legal institutions of the state), Christianity has forfeited any claim to *authoritas*. *Authoritas* is inoperative in systems dealing exclusively with "duties of the heart." By placing biblical hermeneutics outside the realm of *authoritas*, in accordance with rabbinic tradition, Spinoza provided a basis for religious freedom and for the elimination of religious persecution: the two major objectives of the *converso* community.

Paradoxically, the rise of secularism that followed the demise of religious *authoritas* allowed for the possibility of genuine religious life and experience: the discovery that religion need not be the effect of external compulsion, but of the purely subjective faith and free choice of the individual.

## NOTES

1. Mexico: Fondo de Cultura Economica, 1966.

2. For some interesting examples, see Richard H. Popkin, "L'Inquisition Espagnole et la Diffusion de la Pensée Juive dans la Renaissance," *Sciences de la Renaissance* 5 (1973), 49–66. See also Richard H. Popkin, "The Sceptical Origins of the Modern Problem of Knowledge," in eds. N.S. Care and R.H. Grimm, *Perception and Personal Identity* (Cleveland: The Press of Case Western Reserve University, 1969), pp. 3–24.

3. The best work on Sánchez is by Arturo Moreira de Sa, *Francisco Sánches*, 2 vols. (Lisbon, 1947). There is a fine study on Sánchez in the Introduction of Joaquim de Carvalho, *Francisco Sánches: Opera Philosophica* (Coimbra, 1955). On his Jewish background, see *Francisco Sánches*, vol. 1, pp. 82–87. On his skeptical

philosophy, see Richard H. Popkin, *The History of Scepticism from Erasmus to Descartes* (Assen: Van Gorcum & Comp., 1960), pp. 38–43; *idem*, "Sánchez, Francisco," *The Encyclopedia of Philosophy,* vol. 7 (New York: Macmillan, 1972), cols. 278–80; *idem,* "Sánches, Francisco," *Encyclopaedia Judaica,* vol. 14, col. 825; C. Rosso, "Sánches," *Enciclopedoa Filosofica* (Firenze: G.C. Sansoni, 1967), vol. 5, cols. 991–992. On his theory of cognition, see my "Francisco Sánchez's Theory of Cognition and Vico's *verum/factum,*" *New Vico Studies,* vol. 5 (1987), 131–46.

4. He was the son of Dr. André de Castro. For some biographical notes, see Diogo Barbosa Machado, *Bibliotheca Lusitana* (Lisbon, 1741), vol. 1, p. 644.

5. All references to Sánchez' works are from ed. Joaquim de Carvalho, *Opera Philosophica* (Coimbra, 1955). Cf. *Opera Philosophica,* pp. 90, 122.

6. *Ibid.,* p. 145.

7. Ernst Robert Curtius, *European Literature and the Latin Middle Ages,* trans. Willard R. Trask (Princeton: Princeton University Press, 1973), p. 52.

8. See José Faur, *Golden Doves with Silver Dots: Semiotics and Textuality in Rabbinic Tradition* (Bloomington: Indiana University Press, 1986), pp. xv, 120.

9. *Ibid.,* pp. 10–12.

10. *Ibid.,* p. 15.

11. See my *Studies in the Mishne Tora* (Heb.) (Jerusalem: Mossad Harav Kook, 1978), pp. 31–32.

12. *Ibid.,* pp. 41–42; cf. pp. 45–46.

13. Introduction to the *Mishne Tora, Sefer ha-Madda',* eds. Katzenelenbogen and Lieberman (Jerusalem: Mossad Harav Kook, 1964), p. 11.126–127.

14. *Ibid.,* 1.129.

15. *Ibid.,* 11.119–120; see *Studies in the Mishne Tora,* pp. 43–45.

16. See *Studies in the Mishne Tora,* p. 41.

17. See *European Literature and the Latin Middle Ages,* pp. 465–67.

18. Introduction, *Sefer ha-Madda',* p. 11.117–125.

19. *Mishne Tora, Yesode ha-Tora* 9:4.

20. *Quod nihil scitur,* in Opera Philosphica, p. 2.

21. *Ibid.*

22. *Ibid.*

23. *Ibid.,* p. 10.

24. *Ibid.,* p. 3.

25. *Ibid.,* p. 50.

26. *Ibid.,* p. 48.

27. *Ibid.,* p. 10.

28. *Guide* I, 71, p. 123 (11.29–30). All references to the *Guide* are from eds. Joel and Munz, *Dalalat al-Ha'irim* (Jerusalem, 1931).

29. *Guide* I, 71, p. 126 (11.5–6).

30. Specifically, Maimonides accuses Aristotle of following in the footsteps of the Sabeans; see *Guide* II, 23, p. 255 (1.4). Cf. *Studies in the Mishne Tora,* pp. 7–8.

31. *Guide* II, 22, p. 223 (11.14–24).

32. This position itself is based on rabbinic tradition; see *Guide* II, 8.

33. *Mishne Tora, Qiddush ha-Hodesh* 17:24. Cf. *Guide* II, 8; III, 14, p. 331 (11.15–22).

34. *Teshubot ha-Rashbash* (Leghorn, 1742), #413, 101d.

35. *Bet Yosef, Eben he-'Ezer* #156 s.v. *katub.*

36. *Haggaha, Shulhan 'Arukh 'Eben ha-'Ezer* 156:4.

37. Harry A. Wolfson, *Crescas' Critique of Aristotle* (Cambridge: Harvard University Press, 1929), p. 127.

38. *Ibid.,* p. 49.

39. *A Theologico-Political Treatise,* trans. R.H.M. Elwes (New York: Dover Publications, 1951), p. 156.

40. *Persecution and the Art of Writing* (Glencoe: The Free Press, 1952), pp. 190–91.

41. *A Theologico-Political Treatise,* p. 118.

42. *Kitab al-Hidaya illa fara' id al-Qulub* (= *Hobot ha-Lababot*), ed. A.S. Yahuda (Leyden: Brill, 1919), p. 16.

43. *A Theologico-Political Treatise,* p. 118.

44. *Ibid.*

45. *Ibid.,* p. 119.

46. *Sefer ha'Iqqarim,* ed. and trans. Isaac Husik (Philadelphia: The Jewish Publication Society, 1946), I, 2, vol. 1, pp. 49–50.

47. *Ibid.,* p. 52.

# Chapter Ten

# JONATHAN EDWARDS:
# PIETY AND ITS FRUITS

## JOHN E. SMITH

Despite the negative image that was attached to his name—due largely to the notorious, atypical sermon, "Sinners in the Hands of an Angry God"—Jonathan Edwards has proved to be the most able religious and philosophical thinker on the American scene until the time of Charles Peirce. Not only did he introduce some basic ideas of Locke and Newton and put the ideas of the Cambridge Platonists to creative use, but he also had original ideas of his own concerning God, regeneration, moral virtue, freedom and the pattern of human history. It is clear that Edwards, while insisting on biblical foundations for theology, was a philosophical theologian in his desire to enlist the resources of experience and rational thought for elucidating "the things of religion" and showing their relevance for human life.

Protestant theologians have been repeatedly forced to face the problem of relating faith and reason, theology and philosophy, because of the lack of any clear consensus about the matter of the sort enjoyed by Catholic theologians. Some decades ago, for example, Tillich was arguing for a correlation between theology and philosophy while Barth was claiming to have a purely biblical theology equally disconnected from all philosophical positions. By contrast, the Catholic tradition continued its two major approaches, that of the Augustinians, on the one hand, and of the Thomists, on the other. The Augustinian tradition pursued the reflective and meditative way, beginning with the self and seeking to find in its depths the divine Presence in the form of the Uncreated Light of *Sapientia*. The watchword of this approach was "faith seeking understanding," in which the boundary between philosophy and theology cannot easily be drawn, so close was the penetration between the two. The emphasis was on understanding and intelligibility, not on proof in the demonstrative sense. Anselm, it is worth noting, belonged to this tradition despite his effort, under the influence of Boethius, to find a single *argument* for the existence of God.[1] His Augustinianism is often overlooked because the meditative background of his famous argument is frequently ignored as something merely rhetorical. For reasons too complex to be gone into, this approach was overshadowed by the synthesis of Aquinas, based on a different principle and method. The world, not the self, became the starting point and Aquinas set out to prove the existence of God from the existence of the world in accordance with a complex principle of causality. Under the aegis of Aristotle, the aim was to achieve demonstration as something both more objective and more secure than the quest for understanding. The most influential among the doctrines of Aquinas was his clear distinction between natural and revealed theology, or between what reason can know of God out of its own resources and what comes from revelation alone. This distinction has persisted and still provides a framework for Catholic theology.

Jonathan Edwards made a new beginning in philosophical theology. It was closest to Augustine's "faith seeking understanding" with its aim of apprehending the meaning of divine things through the likenesses and similitudes we find in our experience refined by the power of thought. This approach is echoed in Edwards' *Images and Shadows of Divine Things* and is illustrated with the greatest clarity in his *Treatise Concerning Religious Affections*.[2] In his attempt to interpret, defend and also criticize the piety manifested in the Great Awakening, Edwards fastened upon the emphasis to be found in the Bible on the "fruits of the Spirit"—love, hope, humility, desire, joy, sorrow, gratitude, compassion and zeal—as a touchstone for detecting and assessing genuine piety. To accomplish his goal he needed a generic concept capable of expressing the meaning of these fruits in a clear and consistent way. His quite original concept of "religious affections" is what enabled him to carry out the analysis. He was well aware that this term as such is not a biblical one, but he maintained that, with the help of experience and reason, we can elucidate the meaning of the biblical fruits as "affections" and thus make them available as "signs" or criteria for critical judgment. We shall return to this analysis shortly, but before doing so some brief indication must be given of the situation in which he worked.

Puritanism, as is well known, placed its main emphasis on the personal and individual dimensions of the relation to God; it was inevitable that immediacy, intuition and feeling, taken in the older sense of direct experience, would be regarded as the channel through which the religious relationship was first established and through which its validity might be appraised. At bottom lay the fundamental problem of *salvation* and how one might have "assurance"—the favorite expression in the tradition—about the condition of one's soul. For it was one thing to be under the sway of some version of the doctrine of election and the belief that there is a real difference between sincere believers and hypocrites, and quite another for an individual to have some way of knowing to which of these two groups he or she might belong. The solution of that problem was *the* paramount concern for all believers or those professing religious faith; this explains the prevalence of the "soul-searching" that we associate with American Protestantism, especially on its Calvinistic side, from its beginnings to roughly the middle of the eighteenth century.[3]

For the individual, the major method of approaching this problem was introspection, inner self-examination and judgments about states of mind. This method was often guided by the belief that the process of conversion followed a fixed *order* so that one progressed from initial faith through stages of legal and evangelical "humiliation" that resulted in a conviction that one was sealed in the Spirit. This practice of introspection did not, of course, always lead to comfort and assurance, but, more often than not, led to despair and hopelessness accompanied by the sense that one was doomed and excluded from the realm of grace. Whatever the outcome, positive or negative, the scene of this self-examination was the recesses of individual consciousness; the drama of salvation was thought to unfold within the individual soul.

Perry Miller has well focused the situation in his discussion of personal writings and diaries recording the spiritual odyssey of the individual in Puritan New England.[4] According to Miller, the Puritan confronted a certain antithesis in writing a biography or autobiography. On the one hand, he or she had to record as much as possible of the daily round, for, as life stands under divine providence, even the seemingly insignificant event may be of the highest importance in God's economy. On the other hand, the story had to have a didactic force; it had to be an example, whether of grace abounding or of spiritual doom, with a final message that brought all the events together and expressed their ultimate significance. David Brainerd's *Journal,* especially as edited by Jonathan Edwards, is a perfect illustration of Miller's view.[5] Brainerd had traced his missionary journeys and the odyssey of his soul in great detail, revealing his hopes and fears, his moments of elation and of depression, his appraisals of his efforts and judgments on his successes and failures in carrying the gospel to all who would listen. Firm in his conviction that Brainerd was to be accounted among the "visible saints," Edwards reworked the narrative, softening, for example, the moments of greatest depression and of exuberant zeal as being too extreme to be worthy of the true saint. At the end, however, a unified picture of Brainerd's entire life and its meaning emerges, and the example is set.

The focus of all such narratives was the hope for the coming of grace. Thus Miller wrote:

> The grace of God, as most men experience it, is elusive; though certainty is written in the tables of divine election, and though the true saint will persevere no matter what sins he falls into, still the sins of the best of men are terribly visible, while the book remains inaccessible to mortals. The creature lives inwardly a life of incessant fluctuation, ecstatically elated this day, depressed into despair the next.[6]

Edwards transformed the entire approach to the problem in a clear and dramatic way. However, his way of doing so has not always been properly understood, because his thought took shape within the turbulent events of the Great Awakening, which he was both defending and criticizing at the same time. The ensuing debate predictably turned into a two-sided affair governed by the dichotomy of the "head" and the "heart," with rationalists defending doctrine and decorum and revivalists upholding the force of experience, even to the point of condoning "enthusiasm" and its excesses. Edwards stood between the two extremes, maintaining a definable alternative that exposed the error and one-sidedness of each position. From the one side, he was aware of the extent to which Puritanism had understood faith as the profession of orthodox *doctrine* as in, for example, the vaunted "five points of Calvinism." He responded to this dry rationalism by insisting on the primacy of love and of what he would call the "sense of the heart," which, as we shall see, is not heat without light. From the other side, he had to contend with the excesses of the new wave of evangelical piety—mere emotionalism, vain imaginings and claims to private revelations—and he set over against those tendencies his signs, or criteria for assessing what he would call the "religious affections." The failure of his contemporaries to understand what he was doing can be traced in large part to the fact that he offered little comfort to either side in the debate. The opponents of "heart religion," like Charles Chauncy, were put out by Edwards' defense of the Awakening as being "on the whole" a genuine work of the Spirit. The advocates of the new piety were greatly troubled by his demand for a critical testing of the spirits in accordance with the biblical picture of the sincere believer.

We may now return to the discussion of Edwards' conception of the religious affections and its bearing on the main problem of overcoming the chasm that had opened up in the interpretation of the Awakening. There are five points to be covered, and I shall indicate them in a general way as a prelude to considering each in more detail: first, the meaning of "affections" and their place in the religious life, along with Edwards' novel idea of signs as a means of assessing genuine piety; second, the emphasis he placed on experience and the involvement of a total self; third, the importance of love and the indwelling of the Spirit to go hand in hand with faith; fourth, his attack on the belief that there is some canonical "order" in the work of regeneration; and, finally, but most importantly, his move away from introspection and interiority in the direction of more visible and public manifestations of the presence of the Spirit.

Edwards understood affections to refer to the "more vigorous and sensible exercises of the inclination and will of the soul."[7] Our capacity for perception and speculation, for discerning and judging, he called the *understanding,* which he regarded as providing the view of a spectator. Our capacity to respond to things, to be in "some way inclined" or to be pleased or displeased, approving or rejecting, he called the *inclination.* With respect to overt actions, inclination is called will, and with respect to the mind, it is called heart. The will and affections, he insisted, are not two faculties of the soul, but are rather distinguished in the liveliness and sensibleness of their exercise. In every act of the will the individual is either inclined or disinclined to what is contemplated, and Edwards identified the two with the affections of love and hatred, respectively. As we shall see, much depends on his regarding affections as *responses* of the person to a meaningful grasp of the *nature* of what he or she is responding to. By contrast, passions are said to be sudden, violent and such as to overpower the mind so that it is "less in command."[8] Passions are not so much responses as reactions to what comes over us.

It is important to bear in mind that a more complete understanding of the nature of the affections, both in themselves and in their role for testing the spirits, is to be gained through Edwards' analysis of the twelve signs, which forms the substance of his *Treatise.* To begin with, the "positive"[9] signs are meant to be manifestations in the life of the individual of the indwelling of the Spirit in accordance with its own essential nature. Edwards distinguished between the Spirit as "acting upon" a person and as "dwelling in" a person; the latter alone is the mark of gracious affections. Edwards never spoke of the signs as something from which we *infer* the presence of the Spirit; instead, he thought of them as indicating or *pointing to* that presence, something that is fully in accord with his belief that the Spirit is an animating presence making itself felt in the experience and conduct of the person.

The first sign tells us that only affections arising from influences *spiritual, supernatural* and *divine* are to be regarded as gracious. Although the full meaning of what it is for an affection to "arise" or "be raised" is not made clear until the fourth sign with its idea of a spiritual understanding, we may anticipate this meaning by recalling what was said previously. Affections are responses of the self made in connection with some understanding of the object to which the self is responding; this understanding is integral to the nature of the affection that arises. In referring to affections coming from supernatural influences, he introduced his basic idea of a new sense, a new inward perception, a sense of the heart, as he sometimes called it, which cannot be created by us and is not compounded of anything entirely natural. Edwards had clearly not read Locke in vain, and he knew how to engage his idea that the simple ideas are beyond any human power to create. The presence of the new sense in the person stands as a possession that *makes a difference* to that person's being at the most fundamental level and that is thus distinguished from any particular perception he or she may have or any particular action performed. Edwards put this in the following way:

> So this new spiritual sense is not a new faculty of understanding, but it is a new foundation laid in the nature of the soul, for a new kind of exercises of the same faculty of understanding. So that new holy disposition of heart that attends this new sense, is not a new faculty of will, but a foundation laid in the nature of the soul, for a new kind of exercises of the same faculty of will.[10]

The change in being involves the self as a whole and cannot be understood as having to do merely with some aspect or feature of that self.

The second sign expresses Edwards' firm belief that the purity of the soul is most manifest in a love for the *excellence* of divine things that is not based on any estimate of the benefit that may follow from it. There are, to be sure, benefits in the offing, but these are not to be allowed to enter in as motives or conditioning factors. What Edwards meant by "excellence" is not a simple matter and embraces religious, moral and aesthetic elements, all of which are combined in God's *gloria.* Love, however, is to be undivided and unmixed and, as an affection raised, it can be pure only if it is based on a sense of that divine excellence. The third sign is closely connected and adds the esthetic dimension expressed in the "beauty of holiness." The love that is pure arises from the appreciation by the heart of the "love-liness" intrinsic to the excellence of God. Here, again, Edwards relied heavily on the basic idea that the appropriate affections arise through the medium of a true sense, perception and appreciation for the object of love as apprehended by the understanding.

The role of understanding is made clear in the fourth sign, where the meaning of a "spiritual understanding" is set forth. Here Edwards struck a definite blow against some of the excess and aberrations of revivalism. No evidence of gracious affections is to be found in the fact that someone is "affected" to a high degree by having a vivid image, by seeing a shining countenance or, even more, by having the sense that the inner meaning of some scripture passage is being communicated to him or her immediately; for all these latter affections do not proceed from that light in the mind that is essential. Edwards wrote:

> Holy affections are not heat without light, but evermore arise from some information of the understanding, some spiritual instruction that the mind receives, some light or actual knowledge.[11]

Without understanding, then, affections are not genuine. This leads us to ask what sort of understanding is involved, especially when we recall that the understanding by itself is "speculative" or "neutral" and "merely notional" without inclination. Edwards answered this question by means of the idea of a "spiritual understanding" that has distinct affinities with the idea of a "spiritual sensation" about which he had read in the works of the Cambridge Platonist, John Smith. Edwards insisted that spiritual understanding *is* understanding, but spiritual understanding has within itself the sense of the heart; it is not merely a matter of *observing* without inclination, but is, rather, *participating* so that the one who understands also has a *taste* of what is being grasped. One may understand what is meant by the term "honey" and still have no sense of what it tastes like. For that, we need experience of a personal sort that each can have only for himself or herself. A new mode of illumination is envisaged; the understanding becomes fused with sensible perception, and the result is a spiritual understanding.

Edwards was, of course, aware that the affections, love, hope, joy, etc. are more complex than the perceptions of the ordinary senses, but the structure of the understanding persists. The "dry" light of understanding is by itself not enough; there must also be the sense of the heart, if the religious affections are to arise. On the other side, however, the understanding is essential if these affections are to be suffused with light and be a proper response to the true nature of God, Christ and the scripture. With these conceptions Edwards could correct the errors of both extreme positions adopted in face of the revival. Trying to exclude the affectional dimension—by going back to a merely notional understanding in the form of doctrine alone—flies in the face of experience and the model of genuine religion as consisting of gracious affections. Trying to safeguard the wild and uncontrolled emotionalism of popular revivalism—by denying all need for rational control in the belief that "having the spirit" sets all book-learning and knowledge at nought—is an even greater error and fails to discern the great difference between emotions devoid of light and genuine affections.

The fifth sign carries the development one stage further. Those who truly apprehend the excellence of the scripture find that there arises a *conviction* of its truth through what is essentially an illumination of understanding. The place of understanding here is crucial, since, as Edwards said, "the conviction of the judgment arises from the illumination of the understanding" in having a right view of the excellence of the word.[12] This view runs counter to the idea that the Spirit simply forces the will to accept what the understanding does not really grasp. Ever circumspect, Edwards called attention to the twofold meaning of conviction; on the one hand, it expresses a certainty that it is "just so," a sort of rational certainty, but, on the other, there is the element of risk involved in a person's being willing to "venture his all" on the truth of scripture. Conviction, consequently, is not a merely theoretical state of mind, but, in Jamesian fashion, commits the person to carry it over into the whole fabric of life where it will eventually manifest itself in a more visible, overt and public way. Without this dynamic element, conviction might remain no more than an inert and even complacent certainty, bringing forth no fruit in individual and social life.

The sixth sign represents Edwards' reinterpretation of the familiar distinction between *legal* and *evangelical* humiliation, the well-known term for self-denial. Legal self-denial is something forced or exacted from the self by the greatness and awesomeness of God, while evangelical humiliation flows from the sense of the heart that gladly "gives all to God" from the outset. The great temptation is spiritual pride, and, paradoxically enough, it is possible only for those who do have a zeal for self-denial. Just on this account, however, there is the danger that one will make claims for his or her spiritual attainments in comparison with others who remain, in one of Edwards' favorite expressions, in "a dull and lifeless frame," and there is the further temptation to suppose that one is better than others or has a just claim upon God. The humility that freely acknowledges the divine *gloria* in love makes no such judgments and claims. When someone thinks first of himself and of his spiritual eminence, "he is certainly mistaken," Edwards says, and the truth is that "he is no eminent saint; but under the great prevailings of a proud and self-righteous spirit."[13] It is important to notice, once again, what we may call the consequential character implied in the application of this sign. If people find that, as a *result* of contemplating spiritual attainments and a sense of self-denial, they are led to set themselves above others or to appear better than they are, that is a sign of false humiliation. In effect, Edwards was saying, look within and see whether what you are *doing* is setting yourself above others, and, if so, know that your affection is not genuine. Evangelical self-denial gives all to God and makes no calculations.

In the seventh sign, Edwards focused on what is really the central point of the entire analysis, the change of nature of the self as a whole in the turning toward God and away from the realm of corruption. Nature, he said, "is an abiding thing," and this means that the new nature must be such as to continue to manifest itself over the course of a lifetime. As we shall see, the connection with the twelfth sign of holy practice is very close. In comparison with the enthusiasm of a moment, a sporadic heightening of emotions and imaginings so much evident in the firewords of the Awakening, the new nature is something enduring and is no triumph of an hour, since God's work has "proportions" and takes the form of a progressive renovation of nature. The old sins and evils are not simply wiped out, but their dominion is broken and a new foundation is laid in the self that is to continue to make itself felt in the future. No mention is made here of any "moment" of conversion—an idea much in evidence at the time. In fact, Edwards repeatedly insisted that, while the Bible says much about the nature of what he called affections, nothing is said about the Spirit's "method of producing them." The point is that the idea of a "moment" is entirely inappropriate in this connection, because what is in question is a new self, an enduring character that cannot be compressed into an instant. That the course of life and time are involved makes it impossible for anyone to catch an intuitive grasp at some point in time of the existence of this new nature. Its being is in being manifested ever and again in the course of an entire life lived in the company of others.

Signs eight and nine may be taken together as pointing to further features of the person who has genuine affections. Meekness and tenderness—Edwards has in mind the beatitudes—are hallmarks of Christian character and define the way in which the person is to relate to the world and to others. Here, as in the final sign, emphasis is being placed on conduct in the world and its moral and social dimensions. These virtues are not enclosed states of mind but are ingredient in the way one behaves, so that, once again, they are not to be apprehended by introspection. That approach, moreover, is further excluded by the fact that meekness and tenderness are not passive feelings but express a tone and a manner of acting in the world and make their presence felt only in what we do.

The aesthetic aspect of the world and human experience was of great concern to Edwards, and the tenth sign—symmetry and proportion—makes that clear. The creation is shot through with order, and this order is to be manifest in human beings. The affections are to stand in proper relations to each other; hope, for example, must always be accompanied by fear, lest an excess of the former lead us to fall into an irreverent frame of mind. Or again, a person may have much love for God and fail to extend this to the neighbor, or, vice versa, a person may have great regard for his neighbor and not think about God at all. Here Edwards was drawing a contrast between a religion of fits and starts so characteristic of many revival experiences and the well-ordered life of the true believers. In one of his finest figures of speech, Edwards likened the hypocrites to meteors that appear at times with a mighty blaze of light and then fall to earth as lifeless matter, while the saints are like the fixed stars whose light shines steady and sure.

The eleventh sign—true affections are such that the higher and purer they are, the more an appetite for God is increased—is directed against complacency and the tendency to believe that "some high experiences that are past" suffice so that nothing more is to be done. True piety, by contrast, lives with the sense of the great gulf between God and humanity and does not rest with any simple assurance. Actually, something even more important is at stake here. Edwards was attacking those who remain content and self-satisfied in virtue of their "high experiences," except that these mean nothing in themselves unless they serve to heighten our desire for God. In short, faith itself is not to be faith in affections, even genuine ones, but faith in God to whom they all point; without pointing beyond themselves to the reality of the Spirit from which they flow, affections become no more than episodes in human experience. The stress on continuing into the *future* and on sustaining and enhancing the sense of the divine excellence means that no experience of the *past* can provide a sufficient ground for the belief that one is to be numbered among the saints.

The last sign in which true piety is identified with "holy practice" was regarded by Edwards as the "principal" sign, "the chief of all the signs of grace." Accordingly he devoted more space to this sign than to any other. The relation of piety to practice is not such a simple matter as might be supposed and involves theological considerations, such as the relation between faith and works. The important point is Edwards' claim that "men's deeds are better and more faithful interpreters of their minds than their words."[14] Through the powerful rhetoric of his sermons, he expressed this claim in a favorite sentence: "it is much easier to get 'em to talk like saints than to act like saints." The move to an emphasis on overt behavior and public performance cannot be mistaken; it takes us beyond all inner states and into the light of day. No better indication of the shift is to be found than in the following declaration: "I proceed to show that Christian practice . . . is . . . much to be preferred to the method of the first convictions, enlightenings and comfort in conversion or any immanent discoveries or exercises of grace whatsoever, that begin and end in contemplation."[15] All affections, to be sure, are to be seen as the fruits of piety, but the final test is to be found in practice and the outward manifestation of the heart that God alone knows and judges. Practice transcends "contemplation" and is the most reliable sign of the new nature wrought by the indwelling of the Spirit. It is no longer true that everything takes place "in the mind" and, therefore, that the proper inspection of that mind is sufficient for detecting the presence of the Spirit. In the end, all the signs are signs of dynamic transformations in the integral self, and these changes are meant to have a permanence far beyond what is contained in any state of mind. In this regard, Edwards signaled a turn away from Locke and static "ideas" in the mind and on toward the pragmatists who were to identify their insights by appropriating the biblical injunction, "By their fruits, ye shall know them."

Edwards' fundamental idea of signs as distinguishing marks along with the particular signs themselves can be interpreted in terms of what James meant by "differences" and "making a difference."[16] All the signs (and quite apart from the differences between them) are meant to focus upon objective modifications and transformations in the life of the individual so that, for example, having the proper perception of the divine excellence makes a difference to the nature of the response. Without that perception there can arise no affection of the sort that Edwards described as a conviction of the truth of the scripture. In establishing this connection of the signs with making a difference, however, it is essential that such differences not be understood merely as a difference in ordinary sensible fact. The differences in question will vary in accordance with the particular affection at hand, and in all cases there will be reference to attitudes, motives, the orientation of the self and the character that reveals itself over an entire course of life. In short, the differences made will be of a complex and subtle kind, and to detect them will require insight and judgment passing far beyond differences in sensible fact. The advance that Edwards made over the past in the description and assessment of true piety resides in his having marked out the signs—what we are to look for—that indicate noticeable changes in the life and experience of the person, changes that, as should now be clear, cannot be understood by taking them to be merely states of mind.

## NOTES

1. On this approach to Anselm and Augustine, see John E. Smith, *The Analogy of Experience* (New York: Harper & Row, 1973); also, "The Two Journeys to the Divine Presence," in *The Universe as Journey,* ed. Gerald H. McCool, S.J. (New York: Fordham University Press, 1988), pp. 131–50.

2. *A Treatise Concerning Religious Affections,* ed. John E. Smith, vol. 2 of *The Works of Jonathan Edwards,* Perry Miller, ed. (New Haven: Yale University Press, 1959). Future references will be to *Affections.*

3. One of the best accounts of the impact of the Great Awakening on the churches and on society at large is to be found in Richard Hofstadter, *America at 1750* (New York: Random House, 1971), ch. VII, VIII.

4. Among Perry Miller's many writings, the following are especially relevant to this essay: "The Great Awakening from 1740–1750," in *Nature's Nation* (Cambridge: The Belknap Press of Harvard University, 1967), pp. 78–89; "Jonathan Edwards and the Great Awakening," "The Rhetoric of Sensation," and "From Edwards to Emerson," in *Errand into the Wilderness* (Cambridge: The Belknap Press of Harvard University, 1956).

5. Jonathan Edwards, *The Life of David Brainerd,* ed. Norman Pettit, vol. 7 of *The Works of Jonathan Edwards,* John E. Smith, ed. (New Haven: Yale University Press, 1985).

6. Perry Miller, *The American Puritans* (New York: 1956), p. 225.

7. *Affections,* p. 96.

8. *Ibid.,* p. 98.

9. "Positive" here must be explained in view of the fact that I am omitting discussion of what Edwards called "negative" signs, or those that are not decisive in determining the genuineness of the affections one way or the other. Among these signs he included

what he regarded as accompaniments or "occasional causes"—heightened sentiments, powerful visions, "great heat with no light" and similar phenomena—manifested in the revivals but inadequate as criteria for judging true religion.

10. *Affections,* p. 206.

11. *Ibid.,* p. 266.

12. *Ibid.,* p. 296.

13. *Ibid.,* p. 329.

14. *Ibid.,* pp. 409–10.

15. *Ibid.,* p. 426.

16. Cf. William James, "Philosophical Conceptions and Practical Results," *The University of California Chronicle* (Berkeley: 1898), repr. in William James, *Collected Essays and Reviews,* ed. Ralph Barton Perry (New York and London: 1920); and William James, *Pragmatism* (New York and London: 1907), repr. (Indianapolis and Cambridge: Hackett, 1981); and John E. Smith, *Purpose and Thought: The Meaning of Pragmatism* (New Haven: Yale University Press, 1978), ch. 1.

# PART FOUR: POSTCRITICAL HOMILIES

To say that knowledge is knowledge-in-use is, for postcritical thinkers, to say that knowledge is displayed in character, which character is itself manifested in a person's participation in the life of a community of interpreters. Part of postcritical scholarship is, therefore, to share with the broader community one's interpretive responses to the scriptural word on which the community founds its life. For these scholars, such a community appears to be a community, at once, of academics and of fellow Christians or Jews. In this section, two Christian scholars offer homilies through which the scriptural word speaks as a lesson in the virtues, at once, of postcritical interpretation and of the renewed religious practice which that interpretation allows.

Theologian Paul van Buren explores the truth of the Pentecost story, whether "it happened" or not, and what it shows about how Israel does—and does not—represent a speech community, or a community of interpreters. He teaches that "to share a language is to share a whole pattern of behavior." Christians share a story rather than a single, natural language, but while sharing a story "is not quite the same thing as sharing a language . . . it too has extensive behavioral consequences." Here, then, is a tale about what Jews and Christians share, and do not share. They share the story of Israel, but Jews speak the language of Israel, while Christians speak the language of Israel's story.

Ethicist Stanley Hauerwas offers a scriptural meditation on the language of Christian virtue. The scriptural doctrine of justification through faith might seem at odds with the language of virtue, with its connotations of achievement and development. But Hauerwas teaches that "character is an achievement that comes only as a gift," and the development of Christian virtue is "ultimately circular . . .

from hope to hope," since "it is love at the beginning generating hope and it is love at the end rejoicing in what is created." Life is an enacted narrative which, through grace, redeems a history of suffering.

Chapter Eleven

# ACTS 2:1-13—THE TRUTH OF AN UNLIKELY TALE

## PAUL M. VAN BUREN

The story told in the opening verses of the second chapter of the Acts of the Apostles is the tale of the church's first Pentecost, of the outpouring of the Holy Spirit, and so, by one reckoning, of the birthday of the church. It has consequently always been dear to the church. It has been dear to the church read more or less literally, in that lovely way in which a precritical age could read texts "literally" without being too literal about it. It read the story for its main point, the outpouring of the Spirit, letting the details fall where they may.

Having passed through the painful fires of Cartesian rationalism and enlightenment criticism, it is difficult for us today to read this text without wondering about those details, and when we do, we begin to find the story improbable at best. We might conclude that the story depends for its appeal to the church on our not paying close attention to the details: one hundred and twenty Galileans all in one room of what we now know as the Old City of Jerusalem, scarcely rich enough to have hired a hall large enough for such an assembly, and all speaking at once? Then well over three thousand Jews join them—where? Hardly in their one room, but where—other than on the temple mount—would there have been an open space sufficient to hold such a crowd?

These Jews have come from all over the ancient world— judging by the places listed, evidently from the wider world of Alexander the Great's conquest, rather than the more limited realm of Roman conquest. Their mother or native tongues appear to be those of their lands of origin, yet they were all Jews enough to have come to Jerusalem for this pilgrim festival of *shavuot*. More importantly for our interest in this story, they all seem to have learned how to use the expression, "the mighty acts of God" (Pss 106:2; 145:4.12). That would mean that they had some acquaintance with the scriptures, as their presence for the pilgrim festival also implies. And that presupposes, further, that they knew enough Hebrew to read the scriptures, there being no known translation into most of the native languages of the members of this gathering.

The story may be based on a total misunderstanding of the phenomenon of "glossolalia" ("speaking in tongues"), which appears to have been a sort of ecstatic babbling characteristic of some of the members of the Christian congregation in Corinth and referred to in chapters 12 to 14 of Paul's first letter to that church (and only there in the New Testament, other than in this story plus two other references in Acts, where it is also a mark of the gift of the Spirit). At this point in his book, the author seems ignorant of the Corinthian phenomenon and tells his tale of tongues as a sign of what really concerned him: the outpouring of the Spirit on every member of the early Christian community as that which empowered and authenticated its message and movement for the whole world.

Having learned from Wittgenstein to keep my eye on language —on words in our actual use of them—if I want to understand "what the words are about," I realize that I will come no closer to the truth of this story by first trying to decide whether its author has ignored or misunderstood the Corinthian phenomenon of "tongues." It just could be the case that what he tells us about the linguistic consequences of the outpouring of the Spirit is of more importance than whether he has understood Paul correctly. The story interests me, in any case, for what it tells us about the role of language in the new movement that was becoming the Christian church, especially as this compares with the role of language among the Jewish people. My concern, then, is not with "*wie es eigentlich gewesen ist,*" but with what the story suggests—and invites us to say—about the church and the Jewish people as linguistic communities. Let us begin with the latter.

I

There were in Jerusalem at that time "Jews, devout men from every nation under heaven." By the end of the story, we are told that about three thousand of them end up being baptized, whereas others were quite unmoved by the apostles, so we are led to think of a rather large crowd. But they are all Jews. Although "from every nation under heaven," the Jews are one nation. They are united, according to this story, by Jerusalem and so by all that Jerusalem means for the Jewish people. It was (and in our day it has become again) their capital city, the city of David, but it was then also the city of the temple, the place where God's name dwells. They are united then by nationhood, by a common story and by a life lived in following out that story (e.g. by obeying the *mitzvah* [commandment] to come to Jerusalem for the festival of *shavuot*). Moreover, as an important aspect of their nationhood, they have a common language, that of the biblical story, Hebrew. Their common language is the one in which the revelation, the word of God, was given to them.

As the Acts story reminds us, however, the common language of the Jewish people was (is?) for many (most?) not a mother tongue. For getting along in the various lands in which they reside, they speak and were brought up speaking the language of that land. Yet when it comes to getting along precisely as Jews, for living Jewishly in their various lands, their language is the one in which they learn how to speak of "the mighty works of God." And so when they make pilgrimages to Jerusalem, it will be with the one language that they have in common with all other Jews.

As we have also learned from Wittgenstein, to have a language in common is to share a whole pattern of behavior. If that language is biblical Hebrew, as in the story under consideration, then that pattern of behavior will include the use of a vocabulary rich with terms of memory and hope, of justice and mercy, of concern for the land and concern for one's people. Above all, it is rich with terms for commandment and obedience. To speak this language is to enter the community of Torah and *mitzvot* (commandments). To speak any language is to share a whole pattern of behavior; to speak this language also entails moving into the framework of the biblical concern for human behavior, for this is a language on its way, at the time of our story, to focusing increasingly on *halakhah* (what to do, how to walk).

To have in common the language of *Torah* and *halakhah* is to find oneself a people with a history remembered, a destiny hoped for, and so a distinct identity in the intersection of the two. It is to be a Jew as a part of the Jewish people or nation. It is to accept or reject, to acknowledge or endure or deny, but in any case to live in relationship to the vocation of the Jewish people as the people of God. It is to live in the light of or under the shadow of the biblical story of "the mighty works of God." The story defines the identity of this people.

Finally, the common language of the Jewish people is the language in which the revelation was given to them. They speak the language of Torah, of God's commandments, of the word of God. It will not be impossible but it will be at least awkward to be an atheist or totally secularized in this language, on the one hand, as it will be just as awkward to be "religious." The distinction of secular/religious comes from other languages and forms of life. In this language, and so in this form of life which is that of the Jewish people, "the word of God" is all of a piece with the words of the streets and fields. The sacred language is no other than the language of everyday. This suggests that for this nation, speaking this language is sharing in a quite particular pattern of life/behavior. Israel is not likely to be or become like any other nation, not if it continues to speak its common language.

## II

The Christian church is not the community of those one hundred and twenty Galileans, or of the one hundred and twenty plus the "about three thousand" added to them on that day of

Pentecost/*shavuot*. We can tell that it is not, because it does not have Hebrew—or any other language, for that matter—as a common language. To put it another way, the church, unlike that gathering of Pentecost, is not Jewish. Within the first century of its life, the church lost its original Jewish identity and found another hinted at in the Pentecost story: that of the church of Jesus Christ, drawn "from every nation under heaven." If Hebrew or more likely Aramaic had been its first and only language, it soon went over to the *lingua franca* of the Hellenistic world about it. Its scripture from a very early point in its life was that of the Greek-speaking diaspora of the Jewish people, the *septuaginta,* but it lost no time producing translations of this as well as of its own Greek writings into Latin and other languages as these seemed needed.

In contrast to the Jewish people, the church had no common language. It had recourse to what we may call diplomatic or functionally common languages, such as Greek and then Latin. It may be that English is on its way to becoming such a functional common language, but it too can and will undoubtedly be superseded by others. The point is that the church, when gathering or otherwise conversing across the borders of natural languages, such as English, German, Spanish, or Swahili, has always found one or another of these natural languages useful for its purposes, but there has never been a sacred language for the church. The church does not seem to need a common language because it lives by the possibility of translation. Given that possibility, then the church in fact lives from a shared story, translatable, translated and told in many natural languages.

I do not wish to attempt a definition of a "natural language." Instead, I wish to point to examples of what I am calling a natural language: Greek, English, French, German, Italian, Russian, Arabic, Chinese. In ancient times, and now again in modern times, Hebrew was and is a natural language. A natural language is any system of speaking and writing whereby a society goes about living its life and doing all the various things it does.

However we are to assess the relationship of the Jewish people to the Hebrew language between the end of the second Jewish commonwealth and the beginning of the third, when it comes to the church it is clear that it has never had nor felt the lack of a common natural language. It always spoke the languages of the various lands in which its members lived. It used the languages of "every nation under heaven." What is decisive and definitive about the church, however, is that its members are united by the fact that they can all say "we hear (the apostles and evangelists) telling in our own tongues the mighty works of God." The church does not share the language in which the revelation was given; what it shares is the translatable story of revelation.

## III

I chose to read the author's question in the middle of his story as more than rhetorical: "How is it that we hear? . . . We hear them telling in our own tongues the mighty works of God." How indeed! The answer in the story is that they were all filled with the Holy Spirit. One could say that the gift of the Spirit of God is an immediate simultaneous translation, or that the Spirit in effect is that translator. The result of the gift of the Spirit is that a community that wills to be and to some extent is being shaped by or conformed to the story of God's revelation becomes a possibility even in the absence of any knowledge of the language in which the story was first told. The tale of Pentecost in Acts, then, points to the heart of the very possibility of the Christian church. It will be in full accord with this tale that when the church later came to write its major creeds, it placed itself in the article that begins, "We believe in the Holy Spirit."

As the story in Acts continues, Peter asserts that what was happening was a realization of that of which the prophet Joel had spoken: God was pouring out his Spirit "in the last days." The event of the Christian church is not simply a continuation of God's dealings with Israel. On the contrary, God was doing a new thing. The identity of the church depends absolutely on both sides of this, and for any understanding of the church, both sides must be recognized: it was truly the work of the one God, Israel's God, the God of Israel's story; and it was also a new work leading to a new and different community. Only when we hold these two together is it possible to understand the peculiar sort of community that is the Christian church. The church is a linguistic community in the special sense that it is a community other than Israel that hears Israel's story by way of the story of Jesus as also its own. In order to understand this, we need to consider each of the steps leading to it: that the church hears the story of Jesus; that through it it hears Israel's story; that it hears this as its own; and that it is in sharing this story that the church is a linguistic community.

1. The church hears the story of Jesus. Historically the church came into being around the story of Jesus, which, as the story about him, included many of the stories about God and the kingdom that Jesus himself had told. That is to say, the church's story about Jesus was a story about the storyteller of Nazareth. In hearing about him, the members of the church, and then also those who listened to them, heard about God and about God's relationship to them and their relationship to God. As it had been before, when the first disciples heard Jesus and his stories, so it was with the later disciples' telling about Jesus: the fundamental effect on the hearers was that they found themselves confronted by the awesome and wonderful love of God. The gospel traditions grew up among people to whom that had happened, and as that tradition in its eventual written forms makes clear, it grew because it happened.

It happened first of all among Jews. All the disciples were Jews, and the whole three thousand of our Pentecost story were also Jews. Originally, then, it was always a case of some Jews hearing a story told by other Jews about the Jew Jesus and his stories about their God. And the result for those who joined themselves to this developing community was that they rediscovered, or discovered in a new way, their own elect identity as the people of their God. Their God became for them, we might say, a matter of *hic et nunc,* not just a matter of tradition or custom or culture, or whatever else the God of Israel had been for those particular persons. "The mighty works of God" became for them a matter of the present, involving themselves, not just a matter of the patriarchs, Moses and the prophets.

And then came the great novelty: it began also to happen among some Gentiles who also heard the disciples' story. Probably it began with so-called "God-fearers," Gentiles already attracted to

Judaism and Israel's story of God. Nevertheless, Gentiles, non-Jews, now began to become hearers of the story of Jesus and for them the result was not a return to their own God, but a discovery for the first time of the reality of the God of Israel as also their God. That was the effect of the story of Jesus on Gentiles. A few chapters after his story of Pentecost, the author of Acts tells the story of Gentiles receiving the Holy Spirit and so becoming fellow-hearers of the story along with the Jewish disciples. The author underscored the consternation of the disciples before this event, but he also pointed out that since the Gentiles too had received the Spirit, there was no denying their part in the community of those who heard the story of Jesus.

From its beginning and on into our own day, then, the church has in fact lived and grown through the telling and retelling of the story of Jesus. Insofar as in this telling of the story has led hearers to find themselves before God, whether for the first time or once again, the Christian church has lived and continues. The story of Jesus both identifies and vivifies the Christian church, and the church has lived through the centuries from what it calls its ministry of word and sacrament, which is nothing other than its telling of the story of Jesus and its celebration of it through the re-enactment of one of its significant moments. Because it is itself grounded in the story of a radically new act of the God of Israel, the church sees itself as part of that new act.

2.   Through the story of Jesus, the church hears Israel's story. To the first disciples and the three thousand Jews in the Pentecost story, it would never have occurred that the story of Jesus could or ought to stand alone. It would have been immediately evident to them that this was a part of Israel's story, even if they regarded it as its climax, for they were all Jews and the story was all about their God, the God of Israel. As the church became increasingly and then overwhelmingly Gentile, the connection between the story of Jesus and Israel's story became more complex. For a Gentile church, the story of Jesus was in fact its introduction to Israel's story, but before long Israel's story came to be seen as only an introductory background for the story that really mattered to it, the story of Jesus. Nevertheless, it remains a fact of the church's life and history that it has always kept Israel's story as a part of its Bible. From time to

time, moreover, it has recalled that Jesus was and remains a Jew and so a member of Israel. Israel has therefore always been at least potentially present to the church whenever Jesus has been present to it. The presence of Israel's scriptures within the church's sacred writings remains a continuing reminder that Jesus will only be misunderstood when he is abstracted from his original context as a Jew within the people Israel. Although the church has not always seemed to be aware of it, the fact remains, that whenever the story of Jesus is told in a way that reflects how it was told by the disciples, the church will be led back into the story of Israel which Jesus is told of as having regarded as his own. Through his story, the church hears Israel's story.

3. The church hears Israel's story as also its own. In its infancy, the church could hear Israel's story as Israel heard and hears it, since it was a sect within Israel. Within a few generations, however, when it had become predominantly Gentile, it could not quite hear it as Israel did. It could hear it as its own, as addressed directly to it, the Gentile church, only by denying that it was a Jewish book addressed to the Jews. And that, in opposition to Marcion, is exactly what it did. Only, in order to hear it as addressed directly to the church, it had to spiritualize much of it, such as the promise to Israel of the land.

This way of reading and hearing Israel's story is a mark of the anti-Judaic church. A church seeking to find an identity for itself that is not inherently anti-Judaic is having to find another way to hear Israel's story. The starting point, of course, is to hear Israel's story as Israel's first and foremost. The direct addressee in Israel's scriptures is Israel and so also its descendants, the Jewish people. When the church reads these scriptures, it reads of a love affair and lovers' quarrel between God and his people Israel, the Jewish people, not the church. If the church is to claim these scriptures as its own in a way that is not inherently anti-Judaic, it can do so only by claiming them as *also* and only indirectly its own.

This is perfectly possible if the church does not forget how it came to be and how it is kept alive. Its origin in and preservation by means of the story of Jesus can remind the church that it has Israel's story indirectly as its own by way of Jesus, whose story it is directly as a Jew. If its story of Jesus is really of Jesus, then it will be of him with his own story, the story of Israel which he shared and shares with his own people.

It is absolutely essential for the church that it claim Israel's scriptures as its own, if only indirectly, that it can and does hear Israel's story and knows itself, however indirectly, to be included in it and addressed by the God of that story. If it did not and could not do so, it would become only a church of an imaginary, non-Jewish Jesus who was not sent by the one God. If it did not and could not know itself addressed by God in Israel's story, it might see Jesus, but it would not thereby see the Father. So its whole claim as to the significance and identity of Jesus would come to nothing. Left to its New Testament alone, divorced from and read without reference to the original Testament, it would be serving some god of its own devising, not the God of Israel, and so not the God whom Jesus called Father. The novelty of God's act in Jesus Christ, and so the novelty of God's calling a Gentile church to his service, would be no novelty were it not the work of the one God, the God of Abraham, Isaac and Jacob, the God of Moses and Sinai, the God of Israel. It would be only the arbitrary or perhaps quite ordinary work of some unknown god. If not anchored in Israel's story, the story of Jesus can become again, as it was for so many centuries of the church's history, the bearer of the virus of anti-Judaism that spawned the disease known as "antisemitism."

4. We come then to the conclusion to which these steps lead: the church is a linguistic community, not in having a natural language, but in the fact that it lives from sharing a story. The story is the story of Jesus in both senses, both the story concerning him, and therefore also the story in which he lived, Israel's story. For this sharing, any and every natural language will serve.

The linguistic character of the Christian church is evident. The church has a gospel to preach. It has developed teaching. Doctrine is a mark of its history and of its life. It has more to it than preaching, teaching and doctrine, but these are surely characteristic of its life. As to its activity, nothing is more characteristic than its liturgy. Liturgy, *liturgia,* means "service," in the sense of service of God. And what does liturgy look like? It is printed in a book and consists of words. The church's life consists of more than language, but its language is woven into everything else it does. Clearly, the church is a linguistic community.

Yet it is a linguistic community without a common, natural language. Students of its life and history need to learn not only several ancient but also several modern natural languages just to get at the primary sources. When large international and cross-cultural gatherings of the church occur, be it at the Vatican or under the auspices of the World Council of Churches, simultaneous translation is essential and normal. As the spread of the church depended on the possibility of translation in the first place, so its present cooperation and unity ordinarily require translation. At ecumenical gatherings, it is common, however, for the church's most familiar words, the Lord's Prayer, to be said together by all present, each in his or her own tongue. That single phenomenon tells us much about the sort of linguistic community that the church is.

The church has translated the primary form of its story, the Bible, into every known written language and has even, on occasion, created a written language for the sake of such a translation where before only a spoken one had existed. Christians have gone throughout the world with their translated story in their hands and also in their mouths, telling the story that first created and continues to create and sustain the church.

The church lives from this shared story. This can be seen from the nearly universal practice of what is usually called Bible study. In all branches of the church, Christians gather together in small groups, from time to time, to read, ponder, meditate on or discuss a small part of the Bible. The practice is more developed and more regular in some traditions than in others, but there is no tradition in which Bible study in some form does not take place. It is evidence of the church's awareness that it is fed by the biblical story.

Further evidence is the universal practice of preaching as an important and central part of the church's regular gathering together, at least on Sundays. In some traditions, the symbol for preaching is the pulpit with an open Bible on its lectern. Preaching means taking up the biblical story and retelling it in the preacher's words. In my own (Anglican) tradition, the sermon is the climax of the first part of normal Sunday eucharistic worship, following upon the readings from the Bible, and it is never optional. The major place accorded to preaching in the church is evidence of the importance of the story from which the church lives.

In Karl Barth's tortured attempt to relate the church and the synagogue as the two forms of the one community of Jesus Christ, the synagogue represents the community as hearing, the church represents it as believing. But, in fact, the church and the Jewish people are two communities of the one God, and therefore both have the task and the possibility to both hear and believe. The church, in any case, is always called to hear the story of God that Jesus presents to it and the story of how the God of Israel, the one Jesus called Father, has also become God for Gentiles and a Gentile church. The church can never be finished hearing this story, for it is called, again and again, anew every day, to trust in this story and in the one of whom it tells. Perhaps even more radically than the Jewish people, the church is called to hear and to trust in the story of its origin, for that is all it has to go on.

To be hearers of the story of Jesus, and therewith hearers of Israel's story, has always been understood to involve being also a doer of the story. That is to say, to hear this story as the church believes it ought to hear it is to find oneself involved in and to some extent shaped by it. It is a story of the past, and yet that past becomes present and the present is drawn into the story, in no small part by living a life of continuing and growing conformation to it. To recall that past has always meant for the church to call the past up into its present retelling and re-enactment, so that it can know that it "was there when they crucified the Lord." Of equal or more importance has been the conviction that the present is part of and a continuation of the story. The story is not over! It lives on in the present life of the church. Thus the actual life of the church is itself a part of, an extension of the story which the church tells. The church lives not only from but also definitely within the story of Jesus in the context of Israel's story. If there were no story, there would be, quite literally, no church. And since the story is quite specific in the life which it portrays and the virtues which it sets before the hearer, for example in 1 Corinthians 13, it not only makes the church to be, but it makes it to be of a certain sort. Because of the story, there is not only the church but a reasonably identifiable Christian life.

The story can do its work, apparently, in any language. The concept of a sacred language or even "the language of revelation," which might make a certain sense for Jews—and also for Muslims, though with Arabic in mind, not Hebrew—makes no sense at all in the church. Christians would always have to understand the phrase "the language of revelation" as meaning some human, natural language, already in use, in which the story of God's revelation came to be told, for the story of Pentecost presents revelation as essentially language-neutral: the Holy Spirit is the revealer who can address human beings in whatever language they speak. Every language is potentially the language of revelation. It could be said, therefore, that, while having no sacred language of its own, the church has the privilege of making every language sacred by putting it to the service of its sacred story.

To share a language, we said, is to share a whole pattern of behavior. To share a story is not quite the same as sharing a language, and yet it too has extensive behavioral consequences. Those who truly hear the story are drawn by it to definite actions and attitudes, for the story of Jesus is largely about human behavior, both good and bad. Since there is a Christian story, there exists the concept of a Christian life. Whether the story is always put into practice is another matter, and Christians have often disagreed over the specifics of how this should be done. What has never been in doubt in the church, however, is that there is a praxis that follows from the story. To be a hearer of this story is to accept the call to be a follower of the one of whom the story tells.

The story of the church's first Pentecost, as we saw, is an unlikely tale. Yet I have tried to show that it contains fundamental truths about the church and its relationship to language and to revelation. It could be said, then, that it is a true story, even if it never happened that way. But that, of course is a judgment made from the position of the church. A quite different judgment is also possible, and the story itself suggests an alternative: those who think that so much should be made out of their translatable story may simply be full of new wine!

## Chapter Twelve

# A MEDITATION ON DEVELOPING HOPEFUL VIRTUES

### STANLEY HAUERWAS

Therefore, since we are justified by faith, we have peace with God through our Lord Jesus Christ. Through him we have obtained access to this grace in which we stand, and we rejoice in our hope of sharing the glory of God. More than that, we rejoice in our sufferings, knowing that suffering produces endurance, and endurance produces character, and character produces hope, and hope does not disappoint us, because God's love has been poured into our hearts through the Holy Spirit which has been given to us (Rom 5:1–5).

What follows is meant to be an extended meditation on this text. I am adopting this strategy because I think this text provides us with some helpful suggestions about the nature, kind and significance of the virtues for the Christian life. At least on the surface the text seems to be about virtue. Suffering is not, of course, a virtue in itself. Endurance, character, and hope, however, seem to name dispositional characteristics that suggest that virtue language is not foreign to the New Testament. Yet it is by no means clear why endurance, character, and hope are given particular status for illuminating the Christian life and/or why Paul seems to think them so closely interrelated. I call this a meditation because I hope to show how close attention to scripture is compatible with and indeed requires critical reflection meant to help us lead better lives.

I think it important to dwell over these issues in order to test the current enthusiasm by many for the rediscovery of the significance of virtue for construing the Christian life. I have obviously been among those attempting to rehabilitate virtue language for Christian ethics.[1] That seems natural enough since not only in the New Testament are there lists that seem to name virtues (Gal 5:22), but the Christian life, for all its variety in the New Testament, suggests that the Christian is characterized by certain enduring dispositional skills that should not be easily lost.

However, things are not quite that easy. I can illustrate this dis-ease by telling you about two encounters. The first was with John Howard Yoder. During a lecture at Duke, Yoder used the phrase "dignity of the person" to suggest the kind of regard Christians should have for all people.[2] I thought I had finally caught Yoder smuggling into his discourse an element foreign to the scripture—an element, moreover, that comes from liberal ideology. Responding to my challenge whether such usage was consistent with his biblical realism, Yoder argued that "dignity of the person" was no less foreign to the gospels than the language of virtue. Moreover, he suggested that the New Testament at least seems to speak more about what we can and cannot do than it does about the virtues we ought to have. Thus in Galatians 5 just before we get the list of what appear to be virtues in verse 22—that is, love, joy, peace, patience, kindness, goodness, faithfulness, gentleness and self-control—we are forbidden in verse 19 to do the works of the flesh—immorality, impurity, licentiousness, idolatry, sorcery, enmity, strife, jealousy, anger, selfishness, dissension, party spirit, envy, drunkenness, carousing, and the like. Given such a list and what it implies about the human condition, maybe we ought to return to rules and law.

The second encounter occurred at a conference on the church and the university at Bethel College in North Newton, Kansas. I had written a paper called "How the Christian University Contributes to the Corruption of the Youth."[3] I had used an argument by Martha Nussbaum that defended Aristophanes' critique of Socrates in *The Clouds* for engaging in dialectics indiscriminately—namely, it does no good to invite some to examine their lives prior to their being trained in virtue. When that is done, the result is only moral cynicism, not virtue. I suggested that is exactly what the university does today since we do not think it possible to expect our students to be virtuous or for the university to enhance or develop the virtues they have. After the paper, I was confronted by a young woman undergraduate who noted that the gospels seemed quite unconcerned with virtue. Rather the issue is one of discipleship. When the virtues are made central, Christians lose that which makes their morality intelligible—namely our lives as Christians are to be determined by our loyalty to a concrete person, not a set of abstract dispositions.

By reflection on this Pauline text, I hope to respond to these challenges. Of course, I cannot pretend to resolve all the disquiet many feel about the language of virtue, but I at least hope I will be able to suggest why the virtues help us express central aspects of the Christian life. Along the way I will also make some suggestions about the troubling issues surrounding how the virtues are individuated as well as interrelated. This will provide the opportunity to explore why some claim the virtues entail a narrative. Discussion of this, moreover, will force me to at least glance at the issue of whether, how, and what kind of an account of human nature is required in the attempt to construe the Christian life in terms of the virtues. This may seem a lot to hang on this text, but like most preachers I am confident that the text is up to the task.

Yet I am going to ask even more of the text. For the text begins with the claim that we have been justified by faith. This emphasis on justification has often been one of the reasons that many in the Christian tradition have thought the language of virtue suspect for displaying the nature of the Christian life. There are several ways this tension has been understood. In particular, justification suggests that our lives are given to us as a gift whereas the virtues seem to imply that the moral life should be construed as an achievement. Moreover, the language of forgiveness that is so crucial for understanding justification seems to strike at the very heart of an ethic of virtue. The whole purpose of the virtuous man or woman is to live in such a manner that he or she will never have to be forgiven for anything. Aristotle even suggests that the virtuous person should avoid receiving favors, as such receptivity makes us vulnerable to fate, thus robbing us of the strength of character necessary to acquire the virtues in the right manner—that is, so they cannot be lost or distorted.[4]

Moreover, the emphasis on justification seems to make any developmental account of the moral life suspect. In contrast, an account of the virtues requires us to provide a sense of how growth in virtue is an intrinsic part of the moral life. From the perspective of justification the virtues cannot help but appear as attempts at self-justification; any attempt to acquire the virtues invites men and women to believe they can achieve rather than be given righteousness. Therefore questions of the nature and status of the virtues for displaying the Christian life must be set in the context of how best to understand moral development.

As usual, Karl Barth in *Church Dogmatics* 2/2 puts the issue in its starkest form—"the relation between God and man is not that of a parallelism and harmony of the divine and human wills, but of an explosive encounter, contradiction and reconciliation, and which it is the part of the divine will to precede and the human to follow, of the former to control and the latter to submit. Neither as a whole nor in detail can our action mean our justification before God."[5] It might be thought that this is a theme peculiar to justification, but following this passage Barth says, "Our sanctification is God's work, not our own. It is very necessary, therefore, that there should be the encounter, the confrontation of our existence with the command of God."[6]

That Barth uses the language of command as primary I think is not accidental given his emphasis on justification. From such a perspective the Christian life appears as a continuing series of responses to particular commands, but there is no continuing effect in those subject to those commands. There is continuity between the commands, but it is the continuity of the commander, not those subject to the commands. For Barth, therefore, the fundamental image for the Christian life is not growth, but repetition. Only God's command is capable of such repetition, for the "repetition and confirmation of all other commands is limited: partly because, so far as content is concerned, they aim only at individual, temporally limited achievements; partly because they aim at attitudes and therefore at usages which once they are established need no new decision. But the necessity as well as the possibility of repetition and confirmation of the command of God is without limit. Even if it aims at definite achievements and attitudes and actions and usages, it always aims beyond them at our decision for Jesus, and just in this substance the decision demanded by God's command is of such a kind that it can and must be repeated and confirmed.[7]

Gilbert Meilaender has observed that this manner of construing the Christian life conceives of our existence primarily in terms of a dialogue. The Christian life has a distinctive nature, but that distinctiveness cannot be characterized by any progression. Rather, the Christian life is a "going back and forth, back and forth. That is to say, the Christian is simply caught within the dialogue between the two voices with which God speaks: the accusing voice of the law and the accepting voice of the gospel. Hearing the law, we flee to the gospel. Life is experienced as a dialogue between these two divine verdicts, and within human history one cannot escape that dialogue or progress beyond it."[8]

This perspective which has dominated Protestant theological ethics assumes that texts like Romans 5:1-5 are supportive of this view of the Christian life—we are justified by faith. It is only the external action of God through Jesus Christ that has given us an access to this grace. Yet the second half of the text is less open to being so construed. We begin in hope made possible by our sharing in the glory of God, but "even more than that" we rejoice in our sufferings, as suffering produces endurance, and endurance produces character, and character produces hope—a movement of hope to hope. But the crucial question is whether this movement is getting us anywhere.

Most accounts of the Christian life have certainly thought such movement entails a sense of growth and development. The Christian life is not seen so much as a dialogue but as a journey through which people are gradually and graciously transformed by the very pilgrimage to which they have been called. "Righteousness here is substantive rather than relational. It consists not in right relation with God but in becoming (throughout the whole of one's character) the sort of person God wills us to be and commits himself to making of us. Picturing the Christian life as such a journey, we can confess our sin without thinking that the standard of which we fell short, in its accusation of us, must lead us to doubt the gracious acceptance by which God empowers us to journey toward his goal for our lives."[9]

The battle lines between these two approaches are so well entrenched that one despairs of finding any way to resolve this dispute. My emphasis on the importance of character and virtue in the moral life has clearly put me on the side of those who think in terms of a journey. Yet I certainly do not think that this "developmental" view of the Christian life "unfolds" what was already there as potential. Growth in virtue either as individuals and/or communities is not an inevitable movement to the higher and better. Our "nature" does not in and of itself provide all that is needed for growth in virtue. The virtues are not the result of the development of a teleology intrinsic to human nature.

I do not wish to deny that the virtues have something to do with our "nature" or that the kind of persons we are should in some way inform how the individual virtues are determined. Yet I think Edmund Pincoffs is wrong to suggest that "a just man is a just man. He needs no imprimatur to show forth what he is. Courage is no more a Catholic than it is a Buddhist virtue; honesty commends itself to Presbyterian and Coptic Christian alike."[10] Just as a Calvinist unbeliever is different from a Catholic unbeliever, the courage of a Christian is not the same as that of a Buddhist. No appeal to human nature is sufficient to ensure such commonality. In this respect I think MacIntyre is right to argue that any account of the virtues requires a teleological understanding of human existence articulated through a community's narrative.[11]

That, of course, is exactly what I want to suggest Paul's appeal to justification by faith is about. It would take us too far afield to discuss recent changes in the interpretation of Paul. Suffice it to say that Paul has finally been rescued from the Lutherans by a recovery of the centrality of apocalyptic eschatology in his theology. As J. Christiaan Beker notes, "Paul's proclamation of Jesus Christ (=the Messiah) is centered in a specific view of God and in a salvation-historical scheme. What does this mean? It expresses the conviction that, in the death and resurrection of Jesus Christ, the Covenant-God of Israel has confirmed and renewed his promises of salvation to Israel and to the nations as first recorded in the Hebrew Bible. These promises pertain to the expectation of the public manifestation of the reign of God, the visible presence of God among his people, the defeat of all his enemies and the vindication of Israel in the gospel. In other words, the death and resurrection of Jesus Christ manifests the inauguration of the righteousness of God."[12] It is only against this background that we can understand why Paul conceives of the Christian life as a movement from hope to hope or why it is that hope is singled out as the virtue that frames the Christian life. For the hope we have been given makes possible the locating of our lives in a new history, a new journey, that was not possible without the life, death, and resurrection of Jesus Christ.

It is a neat, important, and largely unexplored question what the relation may be between this eschatological understanding of the moral life of Christians and the teleological account MacIntyre, following Aristotle, says is needed for an ethic of virtue. While I think there is no necessary incompatibility between the eschatological and the teleological—indeed for theological reasons I would argue a necessary compatibility—it is by no means clear what substantial and material terms best display that relation. I suspect such a discussion—which put abstractly is about the relation of nature (teleological) and history (eschatology)—will involve an account of the nature of happiness and its relation to suffering. When put in those terms the primary difference between Christian thought on these matters and someone like Aristotle is that the former happiness can finally only be understood in terms of the life of a community—eschatologically, the communion of saints. That, of course, will make a great difference for how the virtues are understood.

I do not mean to suggest that my emphasis on the eschatological context for understanding the virtues of Christians makes impossible any comparison of Christian virtues with those of other communities. In fact, I suspect we share enough as humans—we all must die—that provides some basis for comparison if not commonality. Indeed I find Robert Roberts' suggestion that virtues have a grammar—that is, a set of rules embodies a system of relation—that makes comparisons possible very suggestive. Thus gratitude has a structure that involves the reception of a non-obligatory good from another person that has a kind of universality—that is, it is true of gratitude as a virtue wherever we find it.[13] It is unclear to what extent the grammars of the different virtues can be said to be grounded in our nature. However, I have no doubt that Roberts' suggestion allows for some formal parallel to be drawn across various virtue traditions.

Yet as Roberts suggests, appeals to nature are tricky indeed, especially in the Christian context. From the perspective of the gospel the deepest truth about us is not that we share a common nature —even a weak, needy, or fallible nature—but that we are forgiven sinners for whom Christ died. What we have in common is a common predicament that depends on the belief that an historically contingent life has determined the eschatological destiny of the universe. Roberts notes that it seems improbable that such a historical belief could form part of the grammar of any virtue. For "grammar" is a form of an informal sort of logic and logic makes no reference to historical events. Yet Roberts rightly argues that "the doctrine of righteousness through Christ's atoning death for sinners is the hub of the Christian view of the world, the axis upon which everything else turns. And the virtue of forgiveness is especially close to the hub. So in this case, like it or not, a particular historical belief is essential to the grammar of a virtue, and every exposition of Christian forgiveness must give a central place to this belief, just as every instance of distinctively Christian forgiveness involves envisioning the offender in the light of the cross. To put this in the terms of the Christian virtues-system, the historical fact that Christ died for sinners became an essential feature of human nature."[14]

Put in terms of Romans 5, our nature is grounded in hope. That hope is embodied in our most basic needs and wants—to survive, to eat, to love—but such hope leads us to hope finally in God. Thus the movement is from hope to hope as we discover we can hope only because, as Paul says, we discover we stand in grace. More exactly, we do not begin in hope, but we rejoice in our hope as we learn that our hope is possible only as we learn to acknowledge it as a gift.

Yet Paul says we not only rejoice in our hope, but also in our sufferings. For suffering is also something we receive rather than do. Hope and suffering, it seems, are equally matters for rejoicing insofar as they make possible our hope of sharing in God's glory. In order to understand this aright, however, it is crucial that the story of Israel and Jesus that Paul assumes not be forgotten. Otherwise the suffering in which we are told to rejoice might well be but a masochistic delight. Christians are not to suffer as an end in itself, any more than the self is to be sacrificed in and of itself. Rather suffering, as well as self-sacrifice, gains its theological intelligibility only as it is formed after Christ's likeness.

Not all suffering is to be the occasion for rejoicing, but only that which is correlative to the grace in which we stand. We can suffer from illness or tragic loss of a friend but such a suffering is not in itself to be the occasion for rejoicing. That is only possible when such suffering is given a telos through the suffering that comes from the faith that has been made ours through Jesus Christ.[15]

Only that suffering is capable of producing endurance. For what is endurance but steadfast faithfulness to the cause of Jesus Christ? This can easily be misunderstood as endurance can be associated with passive acceptance of evil. But the kind of endurance that Paul calls for us to embrace is that which is capable of turning our fate into destiny—that is, we are given the means to turn our past, which is a history of sin, into love capable of being of service to the neighbor. Endurance in this sense is closely associated with courage since both involve essential stances toward death. Moreover, each gains its intelligibility by the kind of patience required to live in the presence of the hope of the kingdom.

Christians can endure because through Christ they have been given power over death and all forms of victimization that trade on the power of death. The ultimate power of Christ is the victory over death that makes possible the endurance derived from our confidence that though our enemies may kill us they cannot determine the meaning of our death. The power Christians have been given allows us to endure in the face of oppression exactly because we refuse to let our oppressors define us as victims. We endure because no matter what may be done to us we know that those who would determine the meaning of our lives by threatening our deaths have already decisively lost.

Moreover, that is why it is "we" that rejoice in our sufferings that produce endurance, as this is not some individual achievement. The endurance required of Christians is possible only because it is the endurance of a whole people who are committed to remember the saints. For it is from the saints that we learn how to be steadfast in the face of adversity. By remembering them we literally become members of a community and history that gives us the power to prevail.

The saints, of course, make no sense apart from the life and death of Jesus of Nazareth. The memory of the saints, therefore, derives its power from the memory of him who is celebrated in a meal through which we are given the opportunity to share in his destiny. Death on a cross could not blot out Jesus' life as by his resurrection a people are created capable of sustaining the virtues necessary to be a community of memory. Because of that memory we as Christians have the power to make our deaths our own by learning to endure.

Yet endurance, like suffering, is not an end in itself, since it produces character. This is not a means/ends relationship. We do not suffer so that we will endure and we do not endure in order to have character. Rather, the kind of suffering we take up endures, and our endurance has character. For what is character but the naming of that history that we have been given through our endurance? That is why our character is an achievement, but it is an achievement that comes as a gift. (I am indebted to Alasdair MacIntyre for this way of putting the matter.) It comes not by constant effort to realize an ideal, but rather character is our discovery that we can look back on our lives and, by God's forgiveness, claim them as our own. Character, in other words, is that continuity of self that makes possible retrospective acknowledgements that our lives have been made more than we could acknowledge at any one time.

That is why Christian ethics is in such profound tension with accounts of the moral life that assume ethical reflection and behavior is primarily a matter of prospective judgments about this or that kind of decision. Such ethics are built on rationalistic self-deceptions that assume each individual has the power to determine his/her "choices." In contrast Christian ethics, at least the kind I am willing to defend, is not so concerned with decisions and choices, but rather with the kind of person that is prior to all choices.

Of course, it can still be asked if hope, endurance, and character are virtues. Are they habits or dispositions that form us to be what otherwise we have no capacity to be? I am obviously convinced that the language of virtue does help us see better what Paul is about in Romans 5. At the very least it is clear that Paul does not begin with the question: "What ought to be done?" The question of "What ought we to do?" is nonsense if it is asked prior to the question of the kind of character we should have. We can only act in a world we can see, and we can only learn to see by having one kind of character rather than another. As Wittgenstein reminds us, the world of the happy person is not the same as the world of the unhappy. This is not a psychological point, but an ontological claim about the way we are in the world. The character of Christians is only possible if Jesus has in fact risen from the dead.

For Christians the question of being is prior to the question of doing. Virtue is prior to act. Even more strongly put, we cannot even know what an action is until we are able to fit it into an agent's history. This is but to say that there is a strong and inherent relation between the intentional, the social and the historical. Alasdair MacIntyre suggests that we "place the agent's intentions in causal and temporal order with reference to their role in his or her history; and we also place them with reference to their role in the history of the setting or settings to which they belong. In doing this, in determining what causal efficacy the agent's intentions had in one or more directions, and how his short-term intentions succeeded or failed to be constitutive of a long-term intentions, we ourselves write a further part of these histories. Narrative history of a certain kind turns out to be the basic and essential genre for the characterization of human actions."[16]

I think this is essential if we are to understand the relation that Paul has developed between hope, suffering, endurance, and character. For as I have tried to show, the interrelation between these reflects the assumption that in God's action in Jesus Christ we have been made part of an enacted narrative. The kind of hope, the kind of suffering, the kind of endurance, and the kind of character we are to have are but reflections of the story of what God has done in and through Jesus Christ. Hope, endurance, and character are those qualities of self that make possible our participation in that story. The virtues, the unity of self embodied in our character, give us direction by making our past intelligible. We develop by looking back.

That, moreover, is why the movement is ultimately circular— that is, from hope to hope. By being put on the way by hope we discover hope that does not disappoint. Aristotle suggested in the

*Nicomachean Ethics* that the virtues are like a "second nature" because they are not implanted in us by nature nor contrary to nature, but rather "we are by nature equipped with the ability to receive them, and habit brings this ability to completion and fulfillment."[17] In like manner I think Paul is suggesting that through enduring suffering we discover that God has given us a character capable of sustaining a hope that does not disappoint. It is not as if the hope with which we began is deficient, but rather that very hope has put us on a journey that we could hardly anticipate when we began. By nature we cannot help but hope, but our nature is not sufficient to sustain that hope except as we are led by that hope to hope in God.

But why does character produce hope? It does so because as we learn to inhabit the narrative of God's work in Jesus Christ we learn to see all existence as trustworthy. It is not trustworthy in itself but because every part is related to every other part by reflecting the glory of God's creation. So character produces hope by expanding our "nature" as we are taught to ask more and more of God's creation. In the language of the scholastics God's grace rewards itself by increasing in us the ability to enjoy God forever.

The scholastics, of course, called this process "merit." No doubt that was an unfortunate choice of words as it invites the assumption that men and women might be able to place God's grace under necessity. Yet Thomas insists: "Man is justified by faith not as though man, by believing, were to merit justification, but that he believes whilst he is being justified."[18] We are ordained by God to an eternal life, of friendship with God, not by our own strength but by the help of grace.[19] Therefore merit but names the process by which God's grace becomes ours because of God's unwillingness to leave us alone. We can, perhaps, give up the word "merit" but I am convinced we cannot give up what it is meant to signify if we are to be faithful to Paul's insistence that the hope that is produced by our character will not disappoint us.

For what is merit but the love that has been poured out into our hearts by the Holy Spirit? So it is love that is at the beginning generating hope and it is love at the end rejoicing in what it has created. That is why the language of development or growth cannot be avoided in any account of the Christian life as otherwise we deny the power of God's grace. We are destined to enjoy friendship with God, which is the only form of peace worth having as it is activity in its purest form, lacking or needing nothing.

I think it is only against this background that we can appreciate why Aquinas was ultimately driven to the extremely odd category of "infused moral virtues."[20] It is oftentimes overlooked that Aquinas' familiar distinction between natural and theological virtues was qualified by his further contention that with charity all the moral virtues are infused—thus infused fortitude, infused temperance, infused justice and infused prudence. These virtues are different "in species" than the natural virtues as they make it possible for us to act in relation with our life with God. As Robert Sokolowski suggests, "we seem to have not only a contrast between moral and theological virtues but also a contrast between two levels of moral virtues, the natural and the infused. In what sense does one remain a single agent in such differences? And how are the infused moral virtues to be compared with the acquired moral virtues? For example, could a person who is weak in self-control as regards natural virtue be, at the same time, temperate and courageous through his infused virtue? Does he acquire such temperance and courage simply by infusion, without actual performance?"[21] Indeed Aquinas even goes so far, as Sokolowski notes, to say with Augustine that "Where there is no recognition of the truth, virtue is false, even in good habits."[22]

While I have no stake in underwriting the language of "infusion," I think that Aquinas is right to emphasize that the virtues that come from God's love are of a different kind than that of the "so-called" natural virtues. This does not mean that there is no continuity between natural and infused courage, but rather that such continuity cannot be assumed by assertions about there being no disharmony between God's created and redeemed orders. Yet Sokolowski fears that Aquinas' distinction between natural and infused virtues might give the impression that the single human agent is split into two performers with two different contexts of action. He resolves this by suggesting that finally there is no difference between what the good person and the Christian is meant to do in the concrete—i.e. to tell the truth, to be honest, to be temperate and courageous, to defend one's home and country.[23]

But surely this is to solve the problem far too easily, especially when we remember that the life of virtue is also a matter of perception. What Aquinas is rightly struggling with is the fact that the person whose life is lived in love and peace with God simply does not live in the same world as the person who does not. To use the language I have employed, they inhabit different narrative contexts. Yet we know the situation to be still more complex as we know that as long as we are wayfarers, our selves are constituted by those two narratives.

Which, of course, brings me finally to the problem of sin. It is sin, after all, that renders all talk of growth or development problematic. Just to the extent we think we are getting somewhere, that we are making progress, we in fact are only regressing as we attribute to ourselves what only God can do. Because of the undeniable power of sin perhaps it would be better to avoid all talk of development in the Christian life. Such talk is only an invitation to underwrite further our self-deceptive claim that we want to know the truth about ourselves. Moreover, it is the common testimony of the saints that the closer they get to God, the more their sin becomes an overwhelming reality.

Yet that is surely the reason why we cannot let the reality of sin determine our growth in hope. No sin is more damning than to fail to hope in the power of God's love to release us from our sin. Our growth in grace is not a denial of our sinfulness but rather the basis for our knowledge and acknowledgement of our sin. Without God's grace we cannot even know we are sinners. But because God has invited us to be part of his kingdom, the truth of our sin can be known and confessed without that knowledge destroying.

Forgiveness, therefore, is the hallmark of our growth in grace. This forgiveness is not our forgiving which too often simply invites our attempt to dominate others. Rather we must be willing to accept forgiveness. Such acceptance is the means by which our souls are expanded so hope is made possible, and through hope we learn to endure suffering, confident that God has given us character sufficient for such work. In short, God has given us all we need to finally be of one mind to live in God's story so that our virtues might finally be unified—that is why all virtues for Christians cannot help but be hopeful.[24]

## NOTES

1. For example, see my *Character and the Christian Life: A Study in Theological Ethics* (San Antonio: Trinity University Press, 1985) (third printing with new Introduction) and *A Community of Character: Toward a Constructive Christian Social Ethic* (Notre Dame: University of Notre Dame Press, 1981).

2. This was not the first time Yoder had appealed to the notion of dignity in his work. In *The Politics of Jesus* (Grand Rapids: Eerdmans, 1972) Yoder says, "Certainly any renunciation of violence is preferable to its acceptance; but what Jesus renounced is not first of all violence, but rather the compulsiveness of purpose that leads men to violate the dignity of others" (pp. 243–44). Yoder is, of course, free to construe the language of "dignity" in ways that avoid the individualism of liberalism, but I suspect that we are better off avoiding the term entirely.

3. This essay has been published in *Katallagete,* 9, 3 (Summer 1986), pp. 21–28. It appears in my book *Christian Existence Today: Essays on Church, World, and Living In-Between* (Durham: Labyrinth Press, 1988).

4. Aristotle, *Nichomachean Ethics,* translated by Martin Ostwald (Indianapolis: Bobbs-Merrill Co., 1962), 1120a5–20. For an extraordinary account of Aristotle's sense of the vulnerability that is necessarily inherent to the life of virtue, see Martha Nussbaum, *The Fragility of Goodness: Luck and Ethics in Greek Tragedy and Philosophy* (Cambridge: Cambridge University Press, 1986).

5. Karl Barth, *Church Dogmatics,* 2/2 (Edinburgh: T. and T. Clark, 1957), p. 644.

6. *Ibid.,* p. 645.

7. *Ibid.,* p. 612.

8. Gilbert Meilaender, *The Limits of Love: Some Theological Explorations* (University Park: Pennsylvania State University Press, 1987), p. 35. The earlier and more complete version of this essay from which this quote was taken can be found in "The Place of

Ethics in the Theological Task," *Currents in Theology and Mission,* 6 (1979), p. 199.

9. *Ibid.,* pp. 35 and 199 respectively.

10. Edmund Pincoffs, *Quandaries and Virtues: Against Reductionism in Ethics* (Lawrence: University of Kansas Press, 1986), p. 162.

11. Alasdair MacIntyre, *After Virtue* (Notre Dame: University of Notre Dame Press, 1984), pp. 204–25. In *Whose Justice? Which Rationality?* (Notre Dame: University of Notre Dame Press, 1988) MacIntyre argues not only that the virtues are tradition specific but so also are the desires. "We are apt to suppose under the influence of this type of modern view that desires are psychologically basic items, largely, even if not entirely, invariant in their function between cultures. This is a mistake. The role and function of desires in the self-understanding of human beings vary from culture to culture with the way in which their projects and aspirations, expressions of need and claims upon others, are organized and articulated in the public social world" (p. 21). I think MacIntyre is quite right about this and makes doubly problematic any attempt to construe the virtues in terms of the formation of "invariant" desires and/or passions.

12. J. Christiaan Beker, *Paul's Apocalyptic Gospel: The Coming Triumph of God* (Philadelphia: Fortress Press, 1982), p. 30.

13. Robert Roberts, "Virtues and Rules" (unpublished paper), pp. 13–14.

14. Robert Roberts, "Therapies and the Grammar of a Virtue," in *The Grammar of the Heart: New Essays in Moral Philosophy and Theology,* ed. Richard H. Bell (San Francisco: Harper and Row, 1988), pp. 14–15.

15. For more extended reflection on these matters see my "God, Medicine, and the Problems of Evil," *Reformed Journal,* 38, 4 (April 1988), pp. 16–22.

16. Alasdair MacIntyre, *After Virtue,* p. 208.

17. Aristotle, *Nicomachean Ethics,* 1103a23–25.

18. Thomas Aquinas, *The Summa Theologia,* translated by the English Dominican Province (Chicago: Encyclopaedia Britannica, Inc., 1952), I–II, 114, 6 Reply Obj, 1.

19. *Ibid.,* I–II, 114, 2 Reply Obj, 1.

20. *Ibid.,* I–II, 65, 2; 65, 3.

21. Robert Sokolowski, *The God of Faith and Reason* (Notre Dame: University of Notre Dame Press, 1982), p. 78.

22. Aquinas, *S.T.,* 65, 2.

23. Sokolowski, p. 82.

24. For the development of the idea that the Christian moral life involves finding our life as part of God's life see my *The Peaceable Kingdom: A Primer in Christian Ethics* (Notre Dame: University of Notre Dame Press, 1983).

# AFTERWORD: AN EARLY POSTCRITICAL PHILOSOPHY OF SCRIPTURAL INTERPRETATION

It seems fitting that, having emerged out of discussions stimulated by Moshe Greenberg's lectures on methods of biblical interpretation, this volume conclude with what Greenberg considered a primary stimulus of the postcritical method of interpretation: Martin Buber's theory of the biblical *leitwort* (or "leading word"), as presented in his "Toward a New German Translation of the Scriptures." Alan Swensen has translated Buber's essay for this volume; Steven Kepnes has abbreviated the translation and offered an introductory essay.

As explained in Kepnes' introduction, Buber sought a way beyond criticism to reappropriate the Bible's *call* to us. This is, in the terms of this volume, to reappropriate the Bible's performative meaning for its communities of interpreter-practitioners. This reappropriation does not abandon historical-critical study but, instead, re-employs it as a means of achieving more detailed and attentive engagement with the biblical text. As Kepnes notes, Buber's hermeneutic remained romantic, since it idealized the text's simple or unburdened meaning, as if that meaning could be separated from the interpretive contexts of the text's potential readers. In *The Text as Thou: Martin Buber's Dialogical Hermeneutics and Narrative Theology,* however, Kepnes also shows that Buber's idealization countered the critical historian's tendency to displace textual meaning itself in favor of the conceptual or factual objects to which the text purportedly referred. Buber restored scripture's voice as divine word. For strictly critical interpreters, this word may appear to display its meaning only extrinsically, in the objects to which it refers;

for strictly romantic interpreters, the meaning may appear only intrinsically, in the word's inner nature. For postcritical interpreters, however, Buber's legacy is to have taught that the biblical word displays its meaning both without and within, in the dialogue it evokes between word and reader, and between reader and reader.

# Chapter Thirteen

# INTRODUCTORY COMMENTS TO BUBER'S "TOWARD A NEW GERMAN TRANSLATION OF THE SCRIPTURES"

## STEVEN KEPNES

Martin Buber's "Zu einer neuen Verdeutschung der Schrift"[1] is translated and published here in English for the first time. "Toward a New German Translation of the Scriptures" includes a discussion of Buber and Rosenzweig's principles of translating the Pentateuch and the remaining books of the Tanakh, as well as a fine summary of the principles that ruled Buber's larger works of biblical interpretation, such as *The Kingship of God, Moses,* and *The Prophetic Faith.*[2] The central hermeneutical tool here is Buber's famous *Leitwort* or "leading word" principle.[3]

Paul Ricoeur, in "The Symbol Gives Rise to Thought,"[4] coined a phrase that aptly describes the goal of Buber's style of "postcritical" scriptural interpretation: to approach scripture with the attitude of a "second naiveté."[5] Educated by the application of critical theories of history, text, sign, and symbol, postcritical exegetes return to scripture a second time with a desire to get "beyond the desert of criticism" and "be called again."[6] In his "Toward a New German Translation of the Scriptures," Buber points out that the traditional designation for the Hebrew Bible, *miqra,* means "calling out" or "exclaiming,"[7] and the essay shows that all of Buber's efforts at translating and interpreting the Hebrew Bible are focused on getting readers to the point where they can "meet,"[8] hear and respond to the call of scripture.

> He . . . can open the book and let himself be touched by its rays, wherever they may touch him. He can, without antici-pation and without reservation, surrender himself and al-low himself to be tested; he can absorb, absorb with all his powers, and await . . . to see whether or not a new fresh-ness springs up in him toward this or that in the book.[9]

Buber states early in his essay that, for most contemporary per-sons, this calling out, which is the Hebrew scriptures, has been muf-fled and muted and that what they meet when they pick up the Bible is more often the silent letter than the challenging and revealing voice. There are several factors that have led to the silencing of the voice of scripture. Ricoeur points to the arid "desert of criticism" that at once elevates the level of exegesis and destroys any immedi-acy and intimacy with the text. Modernity's critical attitude of suspi-cion, objectification, dissection and analysis—the result of what Buber calls the "progressive augmentation of the world of *It*"[10]— seals the reader off from a direct encounter with scripture. For the "second naiveté" to occur, this critical hermeneutics of I-It must be complemented with an I-Thou hermeneutics that opens readers to the speech of the biblical text.

The ground for such an I-Thou biblical hermeneutic can be found in Buber's *I and Thou.* Here Buber insists that the I-Thou attitude must penetrate our relations not only with fellow humans, animals and the divine, but also with works of literature and art, what he calls "*geistige Wesenheiten,*" "spiritual beings"[11] or "forms of the spirit."[12] It appears to me that there is no better example of a *geistige Wesenheit* than scripture.[13] When the Bible becomes the paradigmatic form of spirit we can begin to understand Buber's curious use of the designation "*Wesenheit.*" To the extent that the Bible becomes a "Thou," it is capable of addressing us and appears as a *Wesen,* a being, addressing its reader. As a Thou, the Bible can be seen as a saving "power"[14] that "thinks"[15] and "wants"[16] certain things from its readers. What it "wants" first and foremost is that the reader become active. In clarifying the I-Thou relationship with *geistige Wesenheiten,* Buber states: "The Thou meets me. But I step into a direct relationship with it. Hence the relationship means being chosen and choosing, suffering and action in one."[17]

An I-Thou relationship with a form of spirit engages us in a "dialogue." Interpreting the Bible as a form of spirit requires us to face the text as we face another being. We open our senses to it; we allow it to move us, to confront us, to speak to us. We try to perceive its special message and disclosure of reality. And we also respond to it. We present our reactions and we look to see if the work confirms it.

Approaching the biblical text as "Thou" required Buber to see it as a gestalt, a "living unity,"[18] rather than as a series of separate and unrelated literary strands or historical documents. This approach also heightened his appreciation for the particularities of Hebrew language and biblical rhetoric. While Buber argued that critical methods of biblical interpretation and the objective attitude of I-It can work against an I-Thou relationship with the text, "Toward a New German Translation of the Scriptures" shows that critical methods of biblical interpretation—historical criticism, philology, analysis of biblical Hebrew syntax, rhythm and rhetoric—can also deepen the reader's appreciation of the biblical text as a living unity. He argued that it is not criticism per se that prohibits readers from an I-Thou encounter with the Bible, but rather how criticism is used. This follows his view that the I-It relationship is not necessarily antithetical to, but can be the prefatory "chrysalis"[19] for, an I-Thou relationship.[20]

Buber argued that poor translation rather than criticism most threatens an I-Thou relationship with the scripture. Poor translations have "transformed the scriptures into a palimpsest."[21] "The original script, the sense and word of that first time, are covered over with a popular abstractness of partly theological, partly literary origins."[22] Poor translations are more the result of inadequate or poorly applied criticism than criticism itself. Indeed, it is translators "without knowledge"[23] who commit the biggest sin of Bible translation by sacrificing the unique characteristics of biblical Hebrew for the end of a more readable, comprehensible, and aesthetically pleasing translation. Buber insists that the Hebrew Bible that was written in a semitic language and in a culture far removed from occidental language and modern culture must appear as unfamiliar and differ-ent. The translator's first obligation is faithfulness to diction and style of biblical Hebrew. For Buber's translation this meant that the German language must be molded in the image of Hebrew and not vice versa. Here, for example, Buber insisted that the German trans-lation must adopt the biblical Hebrew style of the *Leitwort* and use the same German word or word stem for every Hebrew word or word stem no matter how many times it is repeated in a biblical prose unit. This rhetorical style is certain to make the Bible seem unfamiliar and "other," but precisely when the Bible is presented as unfamiliar or even as alien, readers can have fresh transformative encounters with the text.

What gave Buber the confidence that the text as "other" would draw and not repel the modern reader was his belief that in and through the otherness of the Hebrew Bible was the imprint of the eternal other, the eternal Thou. In "The Dialogue Between Heaven and Earth,"[24] Buber states that the biblical writers managed to do what no other writers have done: to fill their text with "the dialogue between heaven and earth" and show "how again and again God addresses man and is addressed by him."[25] Indeed, in the "recorded spokenness"[26] of the Hebrew scripture is the speech of God. When one follows the *Leitwort,* one is led to a divine "message"[27] that is an instruction for life. This instruction has the power to "reach out and take hold and recast" modern readers if only they open themselves as they open the newly translated book.

> He must open himself new to the book which has become new, keep back nothing of himself, allow everything to happen that may happen between it and him. He does not know which saying, which image will reach out and take hold of him and recast him; from whence the spirit will rush and enter into him, to embody itself anew in his life; but he is open. He believes nothing in advance, he disbe-lieves nothing in advance. He reads aloud what is there, he hears the word which he speaks, and it comes to him; noth-ing is prejudged, the current of time flows, and this human being's modernity itself becomes a receptive vessel.[28]

In this quotation, we have a beautiful portrait of the attitude of second naiveté which Buber hopes his modern readers of the scripture will employ. Clearly there are differences here between the modern postcritical biblical hermeneutics of Buber and the *post*modern, postcritical hermeneutics of Lindbeck and Fraade portrayed elsewhere in this volume of essays. Although Buber was sensitive to the language horizon of the Bible, it was not until very late in his life[29] that he came to recognize the mediating role of the language horizon of the interpreter. Buber held to the romantic belief in the existence of "one language of the spirit."[30] He thought that one could shed the prejudices and preconceptions that one's linguistic system provides and get to what Goethe called "that simple common language."[31] In "Toward a New German Translation of the Scriptures," Buber fails to appreciate not only the difficulty of shedding one's given linguistic structures and traditions, but also the crucial productive role such linguistic structures and traditions play in all hermeneutical acts of understanding.[32]

Nonetheless, Buber's attempt to heighten the linguistic otherness of the scriptures shows that he was quite aware that there is dissonance between the biblical and modern western language worlds and that this dissonance can be hermeneutically productive. To frame his biblical hermeneutics in postmodern terms, we would only need to take our lead from the opening paragraph of *Ich und Du* and say that postcritical biblical hermeneutics arises out of a "dialogue" between the reader and the text that takes place in the intersection between the linguistic horizon of the biblical text and the linguistic horizon of the reader.[33] The hermeneutical tools that the interpreter employs are "twofold": on the one hand, there is the critical discourse of the "*Grundwort*" I-It and, on the other, the restorative discourse of the "*Grundwort*" I-Thou.

## NOTES

1. "Toward a New German Translation of the Scriptures" (hereafter, NGT) is a condensation and summary of a number of Buber's essays on biblical translation and interpretation that can be found in Martin Buber and Franz Rosenzweig, *Die Schrift und ihre Ver-*

*deutschung* (Berlin: Schocken, 1936) and in Martin Buber, *Darkho shel Miqra* (Jerusalem: Mosad Bialik, 1964). The essay first appeared as Beilage to Martin Buber and Franz Rosenzweig, *Die Fünf Bücher der Weisung* (Köln: Jakob Hegner, 1954) and can be found in the current Lambert Schneider German edition (Heidelberg, 1981). The latter version of the supplement is translated by Alan J. Swensen by permission of the Balkin Agency and the Buber Estate. Due to space restrictions I have edited out about a third of the essay.

2. Martin Buber, *The Kingship of God.,* trans. R. Scheimann (New York: Harper and Row, 1967 [German, 1932]); *Moses: The Revelation and the Covenant* (New York: Harper and Row, 1958 [Hebrew, 1945]); *The Prophetic Faith,* trans. C. Witten-Davies (New York: Harper and Row, 1960 [orig. 1950; Hebrew, 1942]).

3. NGT, 14ff.

4. Paul Ricoeur, "The Symbol Gives Rise to Thought" in *The Symbolism of Evil* (Boston: Beacon, 1978).

5. *Ibid.,* 352.

6. *Ibid.,* 349.

7. NGT, 7.

8. NGT, 7.

9. NGT, 2–3.

10. Martin Buber, *I and Thou,* trans. R.G. Smith (New York: Scribner's Sons, 1958); orig. *Ich und Du* (Leipzig: Insel Verlag, 1923).

11. *Ibid,* 6.

12. Robert Wood, *Martin Buber's Ontology* (Evanston: Northwestern University Press, 1969).

13. Steven Kepnes, *The Text as Thou: Martin Buber's Dialogical Hermeneutics and Narrative Theology* (Bloomington: Indiana University Press, 1992), ch. 3.

14. NGT, 2.

15. NGT, 27.

16. NGT, 27.

17. Martin Buber, *I and Thou,* 11.

18. NGT, 6.

19. Martin Buber, *I and Thou,* 17.

20. Paul Ricoeur, "Explanation and Understanding," in *The Philosophy of Paul Ricoeur* (New York: Beacon, 1978).

21. NGT, 3.

22. NGT, 3.

23. NGT, 4.

24. Martin Buber, "The Dialogue Between Heaven and Earth," in *On Judaism,* ed. N. Glatzer, trans. E. Jospe (New York: Schocken, 1972 [1951]).

25. *Ibid.,* 214.

26. NGT, 11.

27. NGT, 11.

28. NGT, 3.

29. Cf. Martin Buber, "The Word That Is Spoken," in *The Knowledge of Man,* ed. M. Friedman, trans. M. Friedman and R.G. Smith (New York: Harper and Row, 1965 ["Das Wort, das gesprochen wird," 1960]); and Kepnes, *The Text as Thou,* ch. 4.

30. NGT, 17.

31. NGT, 17.

32. Hans-Georg Gadamer, *Truth and Method* (New York: Crossroad, 1982 [1960]), 258f.

33. *Ibid.,* 273f.

# TOWARD A NEW GERMAN TRANSLATION OF THE SCRIPTURES

Supplement to the Buber-Rosenzweig Translation of
the Five Books of Instruction
by
MARTIN BUBER
translated by
ALAN J. SWENSEN
edited by
STEVEN KEPNES

1

Two things distinguish the scriptures, the so-called Old Testament, from the great books of the world religions.[1] The first is that event and word are definitely located among the people, in history, in the world. What transpires does not transpire in a separate space between God and the individual; through the latter, the word passes to the people, who are to hear and translate it into reality. . . . The second thing is that the law which speaks here is one addressed to the natural life of humans. Meat-eating and animal sacrifice are connected to each other, marital purity is consecrated monthly in the sanctuary; the human being of drives and passions is accepted as he is, and sanctified, that he not become enslaved. . . . The living spirit wants to give spirit and life; wants spirit and life to find each other, spirit to form itself into life, life to refine itself through spirit. It wants the creation to complete itself from within itself. The "Old Testament" is intended as a witness of this will and of the service due to this spirit devoted to life. If one understands it as "religious scripture" belonging to some part of the detached spirit, then it fails, and one must disassociate oneself from it. If one understands it as the imprint of a reality that encompasses life, then one comprehends it and it encompasses one. The specifically modern man is hardly capable of this any more. If he "takes interest" in the scripture at all, then it is, precisely, a "religious" interest—more commonly not even that, but rather a "religious-historical" or a "cultural-historical" or an "aesthetic" interest, and so forth—in any case an interest of the detached spirit which is divided into autonomous "realms." He does not face the biblical word in order to heed it, as did earlier generations; he no longer confronts his life with the word. He files the word away in one of the many unholy chests and prevents it from disturbing him. So he cripples the power that among all existing things is most likely to be able to save him. The thoughtful may well ask me: "And if this human being—or rather, if *we* could succeed, as entire beings, in approaching the entirety of the book of which you speak, would not that which is most indispensable for an authentic reception still be missing? Would we then be able to *believe* the book? Would we then be able to believe *it?* Can we do any more than believe that people once believed, as it reports and proclaims?"

For "modern man" the surety of faith is not accessible and it cannot be made accessible to him. If he is serious about the matter, he knows this and permits himself no illusions. But openness to belief is not denied him. He too—precisely if he takes the matter truly seriously—can open the book and let himself be touched by its rays, wherever they may touch him. He can, without anticipation and without reservation, surrender himself and allow himself to be tested; he can absorb, absorb with all his powers, and await whatever may happen to him; wait, to see whether or not a new freshness springs up in him toward this or that in the book. For this to occur he must of course take up the scriptures as if he did not yet know them; as if he had not had them placed before him in school, and since then placed before him in the light of "religious" and "scientific" certainties; as if he had not throughout his life encountered all sorts of spurious concepts and propositions, citing them as authority. He must open himself new to the book which has become new, keep back nothing of himself, allow everything to happen that may happen between it and him. He does not know which saying, which image will reach out and take hold of him and recast him; from whence the spirit will rush and enter into him, to embody itself anew in his life; but he is open. He believes nothing in advance, he disbelieves nothing in advance. He reads aloud what is there, he hears the word which he speaks, and it comes to him; nothing is prejudged, the current of time flows, and this human being's modernity itself becomes a receptive vessel.

## 2

The special duty of translating the scriptures yet again, a duty which awoke to us in the present and led to our undertaking, arose out of the discovery of the fact that time has again and again transformed the scriptures into a palimpsest. The original script, the sense and word of that first time, is covered over with a popular abstractness of partly theological, partly literary origins, and what the modern man usually reads when he opens up "The Book" is so unlike the listening speaking that has recorded itself here that we would have every reason to prefer a shoulder-shrugging rejection that "can't make anything of the stuff" to such a pseudo-reception. This applies not only to the reading of translations, but to the reading of the original as well: the Hebrew sounds themselves have lost their immediacy for a reader who is no longer a listener; they are permeated with the voiceless eloquence of theology and literature and are forced by the same to express a compromise of the spiritualities of two millennia instead of the spirit that gained a voice in them. The Hebrew Bible itself is read as a translation, as a bad translation, as a translation into worn-out conceptual language, a translation into that which is supposedly well-known but in truth is simply commonly used. A mixture of respect without knowledge and familiarity without intuition has taken the place of reverent intimacy with its sense and its sensuality. It would be hopeless in the face of this fact to expect to achieve anything through a new translation if the scriptures had already been translated in the strictest manner and then disseminated, for then it would of course be the textual truth itself that had become frozen and not simply its paraphrase. Then the vividness, the liveliness, the physicality of biblical speech would already have entered into the occidental consciousness and would only have fallen prey now to a trivializing, from which perhaps the new light cast by new religious events—but not a retranslation into one of the occidental languages—would eventually rescue them. But this is not so. Even the most significant translations of the scriptures that have been preserved—the Greek of the Septuagint, the Latin of Jerome, the German of Martin Luther—are not essentially intent on preserving the original character of the book in diction, syntax, and rhythmical structure. Born by their intention of transmitting a reliable founding document to an actual community —the Jewish diaspora of the Hellenistic era, the early Christian community, the faithful of the reformation—these translators draw the "content" of the text over into the other language, not categorically sacrificing the unique qualities of the elements, the structure, the dynamic, but nonetheless giving them up without struggle when the recalcitrant "form" appears to be hindering the transmission of the content. As if an authentic message, an authentic saying, an authentic hymn contained a What that could without harm be separated from its How, as if the spirit of the speech were to be sought elsewhere than in the bodily form of its language and could be passed on to other times and places by some means other than through a reproduction that is both faithful and impartial; as if to make it commonly understandable at the price of the original physicality were not or would not inevitably mean to make it misunderstandable! Certainly the great translators had the enthused insight that the word of God was for all times and places, but they failed to see that the weight of the "from whence," of the There and Then in all its national, personal, and corporeal specificity would not be reduced through such an insight but rather heightened. Realized revelation is always human body and human voice, and that always means: *this* body and *this* voice in the mystery of their uniqueness. The prophet's proclamation involves not only his symbols and his parables, but also the undercurrent of biblical Hebrew sensuality even in the most spiritual of concepts, the taut stringing of the biblical Hebrew sentence architecture, the biblical Hebrew practice of relating adjacent or even widely separated words by means of related roots or similar sound, the powerful course of biblical Hebrew rhythm that goes beyond any meter. To recognize this means admittedly to assign the translator a task that is in principle unrealizable, for the particular is precisely the particular and cannot be "represented." The sensualities of languages are different, their ideas and their manners of presenting them, their innervations and their movements, their passions and their music. *Fundamentally,* then, message cannot be translated either, in its fateful welding of sense and sound; it can only be translated practically: approximating, coming as close as one is allowed in each case by the limits of the language into which one is translating. Still the translator must again and again press forward to these limits, accepting instruction only at these limits themselves, only from the mouth of the highest guardian, as to what is granted him and what not. In principle not even the prerequisite can be fulfilled—the uncovering of the original writing —for what the primary meaning of a biblical word was cannot by nature be known, but only deduced; and often even this only by conjecture. Not seldom we must be contented with suppositions as to what the "redactor" meant—that is, the unifying consciousness that built the halls of the Bible out of compilations and fragments that had been handed down.[2] But even this may suffice for our task of approximation, for not in the "sources," but rather here is where in truth *Bible* is—that namely which joins up itself to the testimonies and documents, which binds them together into books and into the book: a faith in reception and transmission that unites the ages, the synopsis [*Zusammensehen*] of all changes in the stillness of the word.

The relationship of our translation to the text is determined by this knowledge of this living unity. Analytical science has the right, wherever it deems proper, to replace symbols that are written with others that it finds more appropriate; it is our right, however, to linger in the givenness of the "solid letter," as long as it in any way allows us to. Analytical science may break a narrative, a song, a sentence into actually or supposedly independent components; we, however, may look to and replicate the work that has been forged out of these separate entities. Replication is not to be understood as the sort of undertaking that goes against the spirit—the repetition of a preexisting form in material of another kind—but rather as the striving to create an equivalent or equivalents in the differently-structured language into which one is translating. German phonetic form can never reproduce Hebrew phonetic form, but, growing out of an analogous impetus and exercising an analogous effect, it can correspond to it in a manner possible in German—it can Germanize [*verdeutschen*] it.

In order to do justice to such a demand, the translator must receive from the Hebrew letter the actual phonetic form; he must experience the writtenness of the script for the most part as the recording of its spokenness; that spokenness—as the actual *reality* of the Bible—which awakes anew wherever an ear hears the word biblically and a mouth speaks it biblically. Not only prophecy, psalm, saying are originally born of the tongue and not of the feather, but also report and law. For undisrupted early times, sacred text is usually orally transmitted text, often orally transmitted even when a highly developed profane literature exists next to it. Such sacred text is only written down when its unadulterated preservation has become uncertain, despite its rhythm, which impresses it upon the memory, and despite all strict regulations concerning memorization—or when special purposes demand it. That which came into being through speaking can only come to life again each new time in speaking, indeed, only through it be purely per- and re-ceived. In the Jewish tradition the scriptures are meant to be recited. The so-called accent system, which accompanies the text word for word, aids us in going back legitimately to its spokenness; already the Hebrew term for "reading" means: exclaiming. The traditional name for the Bible is "the reading" [*haMiqra*][3]—in other words actually: the exclaiming; and God does not say to Joshua, the book of the Torah must not leave his sight, but rather it must not go "out of his mouth," he should (this is the actual meaning of what follows) "murmur" therein, that is, reproduce the intonation with quiet lips.

It is to this type of recorded spokenness that the German phonetic form should correspond, and it is of course not meant for silent reading but rather for that real recitation which draws out the full value of the sound. Our German translation of the scriptures is intended to be "exclaimed." Only then will the unfamiliarity of its effect not degenerate into alienation.

This unfamiliarity is necessary in and of itself; it is precisely what is needed if a translation is to help bring about a meeting between the scriptures and modern mankind, after all our false certainty that we know everything about the Bible, after all our efforts to bring it down to our level. It would be a false, superfluous, questionable, late-romantic unfamiliarity if it were to grow out of aesthetic or literary reflections; if, for example, the diction were to be determined entirely or even only partially by a particular taste—no matter whether an archaizing or an arbitrarily neologizing taste— and not by the demands of the text, by its commanding thus-ness, by its characteristic strengths and intimacies. In order to create the occidental, German correspondence, one must often reach beyond the current vocabulary to words that have fallen out of usage or even disappeared—as long as these words have been reliably handed down and yet have no real synonym, and a reintroduction is thus legitimate and desirable. The translator must also not shy away from neologisms from time to time, where he is unable to find a perfect equivalent in the German vocabulary for a biblical institution or a biblical idea. It will then depend on the seriousness of his language-conscience, on the sureness of his language-tact, on his stance in relation to the rules of the language into which he is translating—a stance that must be bold and yet obedient—as to whether the new word—even if only as a designation for a thing in that biblical world —is acknowledged and naturalized by following generations. The reader who is impartially seeking the way to the Bible will, of course, again and again seek to penetrate from those words of the new translation that deviate from the words he is familiar with, to the realities that voice themselves therein. He will consider whether the familiar transmission satisfies this reality in its peculiarity; he will measure the distance between the two, and then test how well the new choice of words holds up in comparison. And so, as he reads, the biblical world will dawn before him, realm by realm, as will its otherness in contrast to much he has grown used to, but then also the importance of incorporating this otherness into the structure of our own lives. Admittedly this world will often appear linguistically sharper, more emphatic than it did to those who lived in it, since, standing in contrast to that with which we are familiar, the concept in the German translation will convey its sensual root meaning more emphatically than in the original, where the sensual, imagistic elements simply resonated along with the word in its conceptual usage. But it is precisely from this that, for the serious reader, the task of familiarization, of immersion arises, a task that cannot help but be fruitful. It is the same task which, in another form, the reader of the original undertakes when he sets out to liberate the living There and Then, and thereby the physicality of the biblical spirit, from the lexical familiarity that rapidly clouds the reading of the learner of Hebrew in our times, regardless of whether it is out of a dictionary or in the colloquial talk of the conversational method that he learned what the words supposedly mean.

3

The Hebrew Bible is essentially shaped and formulated by the language of the message.

"Prophecy" is only the clearest, the naked appearance of the message, as it were. What is to be made known here is made known openly. But there is hardly any part, hardly any stylistic form in the scriptures that is not directly or indirectly bound to the message and sustained by it. We read the early genealogies, and the lists of names, which appear to be without purpose, turn out—in selection and arrangement—to be representatives of the message. We read narratives that seem to us to be purely profane history—as for example that of Abimelech, the son of Gideon—until we notice that a counter-image has been drawn here to a major concern of the message, to the "naive theocracy" in the cited example.[4] We read legal and ritual regulations of the most sober, factual, casuistic precision and suddenly out of it a concealed pathos communicates itself to us. We read psalms that seem to say nothing else to us but the tortured human's heaven-ward cries for help; but we only need to listen properly in order to recognize that it is not just any human who speaks, but rather one who lives under the revelation and even in crying out testifies to it. We read wisdom that is considered skeptical, and from within its midst great sayings of the message strike us like lightning. Whatever the case may have been with a given piece of the Bible before it was incorporated into the Bible: in every limb of its body, the Bible is message.

If this is the case, then the message must have modified the biblical language in many of the places where this message expresses itself indirectly, just as it formed its own unique language in the speech of the messenger. For it would mean a thorough mistaking of the nature of the Bible, if one were to assume that the Bible has tacked on the message in each case, as a "moral" is attached to bad parables. Indeed nowhere else can one refine a "content" from the biblical bronze castings, but rather each exists in its uniform, insoluble shape—more insoluble even than that of the true poem. Nowhere here can one reach back to an original What that has been given this How but could also tolerate another. Everything in the scriptures is authentic spokenness, in the face of which "content" and "form" appear to be the results of a pseudo-analysis; thus the message cannot shrivel up to annotation or commentary, even when it expresses itself indirectly. It penetrates into the shaping, it participates in determining the shape, it transforms it, enters into the shape, but without even the slightest disfiguring, blurring, didactic effect. The narrative retains its epic unity undimmed, the regulation its strict objectivity, but the modifying activity of the message is carried out within these formations.

It can be none other than precisely a formal principle whereby this modifying activity is carried out. This formal principle is rhythm, rhythm both in a broad and in a particular sense.

By rhythm one is to understand here not any structured movement in general, but rather the phonetic joining of a constant with a multiplicity, appearing within an ordering rich in meaning. The constant can either be purely structural—recurrence of the intonation, the intensity of movement, the measures—or phonetic—recurrence of sounds, clusters of sounds, words, clusters of words. The formal principle of the message is accordingly dual. In fact, the phonetic rhythmics—"paronomasia" and its relatives—is taken into its services as is, whereas the structural rhythmics becomes the message's means of expression through *alterations* that come into play in the given moment.

## 4

The text that has been translated into German here is the Masoretic one, the one handed down [*haMasorah*]. To comprehend it is the unavoidable task of the translator. He has been entrusted with a fixed entity, in the face of which even the most tempting conjecture must appear arbitrary. . . .

The effort to preserve the Masoretic text proceeds from the view that it is not possible to reach back behind what is there, without replacing the reality with various and mutually contradictory possibilities. We must attempt to understand what the one who was responsible for the form of the text, the "redactor," meant by this form. We must seek to follow the latest consciousness, since it is only seemingly possible to penetrate to an earlier one. The diction of this translation is connected to this very same view, since it is a translation that has as its goal to translate the Bible, and not biblical national literature, into German. It is concerned with comprehending a whole that has, after all, become an authentic unity, regardless of how many and diverse the pieces are out of which it grew.

The Bible is meant to be read as one book, so that no one of its parts remains self-contained, but rather each is held open toward all; it is meant to become present to the reader as one book with such intensity that, while reading or reciting a weighty passage, he will recall the passages that can be related to it, in particular those to which it is linguistically identical, approximate, or related. And all of these passages will illuminate and clarify each other for him, join themselves together for him to a unity of meaning, not to one expressly taught but rather to the theologumenon which is immanent in the word and surfaces out of its connections and correspondences. These connections are not made after the fact by interpretation, but rather the canon came into being precisely under the workings of this principle, and one may rightfully assume that it was influential in the selection of that which was incorporated, in the choice between different versions. But it is unmistakably at work already in the composition of the individual parts: the repetition of words or word clusters that have identical or similar sound, or identical or similar roots, occurs within one section, within one book, within one group of books with a force that is quiet, but that overpowers the reader who is prepared to hear. If, starting with this insight, one considers the linguistic connections between, for example, the prophets and the Pentateuch, between the psalms and the Pentateuch, between the psalms and the prophets, one will recognize again and again the powerful synoptic nature of the Bible.

Biblical root-words do not reveal their breadth and depth of meaning from a single passage; the passages complement, support each other. Declaration flows constantly between these root-words, and the reader who has developed an organic Bible-memory will not read the individual context for itself in any given case, but rather as a context embraced by a wealth of contexts. The latent theology of the text appears directly wherever the content of the individual root words from different sentences, different text forms, different levels of expression, turns out, in this manner, to be the same. No doubt it is not the word, but rather the sentence that is the natural unit of living speech, and the word, by contrast, the product of an analysis; but the biblical sentence is meant to be grasped biblically, that is, in the atmosphere that is created by the recurrence of the same root words.

To make this inner band visible is a service into which the translator is also placed. He knows the power of laziness, of familiarity, of superficial reading, in Hebrew and in German; he knows that those who have been reading the Bible since childhood succumb to this power particularly easily; he must do his part to stop this power. This involves choosing—whenever it is necessary and feasible—the succinct, easily remembered word that will be recognized immediately wherever it recurs, and in so doing not shying away from an unaccustomed word, if the language willingly offers it up from a forgotten chamber. It involves endeavoring to render a Hebrew word stem by means of a single German one—when it is necessary and when it is feasible; not one by means of many, not many by means of one. Whenever it is necessary: for in the case of words that have little or no spiritual emphasis, one may loosen or rescind the principle, to the extent that it is not essential to practice the office of all translators here as well, not to confuse the "synonyms," but rather to leave them in their differentiated meanings.[5] And whenever it is feasible: for often the particular qualifying circumstances of a passage will create an obligation to treat it as an exception. Every translator is of course placed under dual laws that from time to time appear to conflict with each other: the law of the one and of the other language. For the translator of the scriptures there is another duality: the one law that speaks from the particular right of the individual passage, and the other that speaks from the biblical totality. But as the former two are reconciled or, more precisely, allied by the fact that there are only penultimate languages and in the end—inaudible and yet not to be ignored—the one language of the spirit, "that simple, common language" (Goethe), so the conflict between the right of the sentence and the right of the book is overcome again and again by the fact that both derive their meaning from the same dialogue-encounter. In the former case the dialogue-encounter is directed to the human person and to the moment, and in the latter to the people and to the world-time; the people, among whom the independent person is placed, and the world-time, into which the independent moment is placed.

5

By *Leitwort* one is to understand a word or word-stem that is meaningfully repeated within a text, a series of passages, a constellation of passages. To those who follow these repetitions, a meaning of the text is opened up or clarified, or perhaps simply more vividly revealed. As stated, it need not be the same word but rather only the same root that recurs in this manner. Often the differences in the individual cases even enhance the dynamic overall effect. I call it dynamic, because a movement, as it were, takes place between the constellations of sound that are thus related to each other: anyone for whom the entirety is present will feel the waves breaking back and forth. The measured repetition, corresponding to the inner rhythm of the text, or rather springing forth from it, is certainly the strongest of all means of proclaiming a figure of meaning [*Sinncharakter*] without directly presenting it. And whether it is a case of actual "paronomasia," which appears within an individual syntactic context, or a more generally defined case, which includes alliteration and assonance, or of paronomasia *over a distance*—in other words paranomasia that is at work not in juxtaposition but rather across a larger textual space—in any case paranomasia is always able to achieve a particular expressive value which cannot be replaced by anything else. This is so even independently of the aesthetic value—which we find in exemplary manifestation in the alliteration of the *Older Edda.* This special expressive value lies in the fact that the meaning to be expressed does not appear in a didactic codicil and thus does not burst or distort the pure shape. This presupposes therefore that such a shape, a unified art form, already exists; at the same time, however, it presupposes that a meaning and a message are to be communicated that transcend this art form and that cannot therefore record themselves in this art form without the use of special means—as is possible with a poem and its meaning. Rather, because of their very essence, they must clear their own expressive path. Nowhere is this precondition so present as where the strictly unified epic form and a "religious" message pervaded by the descending spirit meet together.

Certainly there is no place where this has occurred with such unique force as in the narrative of the Pentateuch. The strictness of the form stems here from the profound intent to report and only to report, and for this reason the message is not allowed to impose upon it. There is no room here for an instructive presentation of the religious content that transcends the pure report; the narrative has by its nature no seams. The message cannot enter in here other than by recognizing the epic law and placing itself under the protection of that law. The message accomplishes this by giving the narrative a meaningful rhythm, namely by means of *Leitworte,* without touching the structure of the narrative. For those who listen properly now, the higher meaning will rush over them out of the accord. Between one passage and another, in other words between one stage of the story and another, a connection has been established that expresses the very essence of the narrated event more directly than a tacked-on saying could. Nowhere does the epic language well over, nowhere does it rhetoricize, but nowhere does it lyricize either; the *Leitwort*-rhythm[6] is an authentic epic rhythm here, the rightful artistic signum of a mystery that also comprehends and transcends the world of the form.

6

For phonetic rhythmics (recurrence of the same within a multiplicity) I will give a few examples from the first of the five books of instruction, the so-called Pentateuch; for structural rhythmics (transformation of the rhythmic structure within a textual unit), a few from the second and fourth books.

In the narrative of the building of the tower (Genesis 11:1–9), seven *Leitworte* [*qol haaretz, safah, habah, banah, ir, sham, patz*] illustrate the correspondence between the action of the humans and the opposite action of God, a correspondence that is to be expressed only in this manner, not *expressis verbis.* "All the earth," reads the beginning, meaning the as yet still united people of the earth; "all the earth" in the same sense stands at the end of the first part, before the opposite action begins; and "all the earth," repeated three times, recurs again finally to designate the surface of the earth, over which the people in their tribes have now been scattered. Similarly we hear the word "tongue" (actually "lip" [*safah*]) in the beginning, where the unified language of the human race is mentioned; then again in the speech of God; and once again in the final account—all passages that deal with the act of God that "mixes" ("confuses"—the word occurs here twice, as verb and as noun) this language. "Come!" the agitators call to each other twice, and "Come!" says the descending God to himself. In addition, likewise in corresponding action and opposite action, there is the act of "building" and the "city," the "name" and the "scattering." The undertaking of the humans has as its cause the fear of being scattered—a fate that supposedly threatens them—and as its consequence the real scattering.

The prophets made no secret of the fact that, despite Jacob's chosen status, they understood his behavior toward his brother to be a sin (Jer 9:8, no doubt also Hos 12:4). The narrator—who after all had to recount the choosing of Jacob as the one through whom the covenant would continue—could not say this in any other way than by means of repetition, that is, in an even more reserved form of suggestion than for the choosing. "Deceit" [*mirmah*] (Gen 27:35) is the sin, and the suffering of "Deceit" (29:25) belongs to the atonement. The sin concerns the "first-birth" [*bkhorah*] [*Erstgeburt*] (25:31, 33, 34 as well as 27:19, 36), and the most sensitive punishment is that Jacob receives the "firstborn" (29:26, actually "first-birth") instead of the woman he loves. In the narrative of the completion of the atonement, however, one finds, as one did there (27:4, 10, 12, 19, 23, 25, 27 twice, 29, 30, 31, 33 twice, 34, 35, 36 twice, 38 twice, 41 twice, altogether 21 times), the word "to bless, blessing" [*barakh, barakhah*] at the center: in the story of the wrestling, after which Jacob is blessed by the "man" [*ish*] (32:27, 30), and in that of the reconciliation of the brother, where Jacob's conciliatory gift is designated by the word "blessing," a word otherwise not commonly used for such a thing. The intended connection between the reconciliation of the divine and that of the human sphere also appears in this narrative—a further example of paronomasia as a means of expression—in the manner in which the word "face" [*panim*] is repeated here time and again, alternately in the one and in the other realm, until finally Jacob says to Esau: "I have now indeed looked upon your face as one looks upon God's face."

The structural form of rhythmics, the meaningful transformation of the rhythm, is most clearly recognizable in some of the divine speeches. As already Jerome had discovered, the "scriptures" are divided into breath-units, lines of meaning, "cola," in accordance with their original character as spokenness, and we have translated it this way for the first time. In doing so, however, we had to take into consideration the diversity of genre forms which persists within the prose of the Bible. Even the speeches that contain commandments and regulations are divided in this manner. But once in a while the rhythm transforms itself in midstream, namely where a regulation closes with an instruction that points to what is essential or even merges into a divine interpretation of that which is prescribed. Thus the description of the high-priestly breastpiece of judgment, which conceals the mysterious *Urim* and *Thummim*—"the clarifying and the arbitrating ones"—this description, which enumerates the materials and precious stones and indicates the manner of construction and arrangement with sacred-sober precision (Ex 28:13–28), is followed by a final instruction that differs in lexical stance, in syntax, and in rhythm, and is interwoven with repetitions that are rich in meaning, without disrupting the context and the compositional unity. Thus the regulation for the daily *Darhöhung* [*olah*] [=the raising-up-toward] (more precisely "the one that climbs up," that is the real meaning of the word "burnt offering," as it is called), a regulation precisely factual in both word and sound (Ex 29:38–41), merges into a saying of the higher message (verses 42–46), a pure creation of sacral proclamation. And again from within a regulation concerning sacrifices (Num 15:1–16) a statute grows that reaches far beyond it, different in tone and structure, whose meaningfulness is underscored by the otherwise unknown call, "Assembly!" This statute proclaims the equal rights of the stranger living in Israel, of the "guest-dweller," and apparently not for a single ritual, but rather for the entire communal life: "let there be a single instruction and a single law for you and for the guest-dweller who is a guest among you."

7

Several concepts from the sacral and related spheres will serve as examples to elucidate the choice of words dictated by our task of translation.

One usually finds the concepts related to sacrifice translated by the general terms "sacrifice or offering, to sacrifice or offer," to which then the subdivisions "burnt offering" and "food offering" are added. Thus, a particular, cultic-theological set of circumstances has given way to the generality of religious history. In truth, almost all Hebrew concepts related to sacrifice go back to the relationship of the offerer to his God and to a process between them both, or at least to the initiation of this process. This is why the comprehensive designation *qorban* is derived from a verb that means to approach, draw near. The meaning of the offering, then, is to bring oneself near to

God through it; therefore in German: *Nahung, Darnahung, nahen, darnahen* [=the nearing, the nearing-toward, to near, to near toward]. The so-called "burnt offering," *olah,* means "the one that climbs up" high, to the heavens, in its entirety; thus *Höhung, Darhöhung, höhen, darhöhen* [=the raising, the raising-up-toward, to raise up, to raise up toward]. The so-called "food offering," *minchah,* may simply mean "gift," but the verb *nachah* (to escort) resonates with it and was easily associated with it, hence *Hinleite* [=that which is guided hither]. The word *zebach,* on the other hand, means "slaughtering, slaughter-donation." One slaughters an animal, offers a part of it and eats the rest together: community is brought about with God and at the same time among humans, and each communal meal includes an offering. The fact that the word "thanks" and a word strongly resonating of "peace" are associated with *zebach* belongs in the same context. The Hebrew word for "altar" stems from the same root as *zebach,* because it was precisely at the *mizbeach* that the slaughter occurred and biblically speaking the slaughtering of the "slaughter-meal" at the "slaughter-place" is precisely the primary matter. The odor of the offering smoke is called *reach nichoach,* a refrain-like, recurring assonance, whose second part—a word used only in the sacrificial service—has the same root as "rest" [*Ruhe*]. But even "calming" [*Beruhigung*] would not capture the objectified concept; our "*Ruch des Geruhens*" [odor of profound rest] comes closest in meaning and form. The noun *qodesh,* usually rendered as "sacred or holy, that which is sacred (holy)," is a dynamic concept that designates first of all a process, that of sanctification, of hallowing, of being hallowed; and only later the sacred object [*Heiligtum*]. Therefore, not "*heilige Menschen*" [=holy people] but rather "*Menschen der Heiligung*" [=people of hallowing] and not "*heilige Gaben*" [=holy gifts], but rather "*Darheiligungen*" [=things hallowed through giving]. The priestly shares of these are "*Abheiligungen*" [=things taken from hallowing], the objects that make everything that touches them into things sacrally singled out, "*verheiligen*" [=thoroughly sanctify] them. And the innermost of the sanctuary is not called "the Holy of Holies," but rather—the place from which the sanctuary receives its sanctity— "*das Heiligende* (actually: *die Heiligung*) *der Heiligtume*" [=that which sanctifies (actually: the sanctification) of the sanctuary].

The opposite of this is *chol:* not the "unholy" or "non-holy," but rather that which is "abandoned" to common use, since it is not subjected to cultic singling out. Thus, the beginning of one's own use of the vineyard that was dutifully consecrated during the first four years after it was planted (Lev 19:23) is called a *Preisgabe* [=abandoning] or rather *Preisnahme* [=taking as booty] (Deut 20:6; 28:30). The opposite of "pure" is not "impure," no simple absence of purity, but rather "*maklig*" [=blemished], the *Makel* [=blemish] understood as a miasmatically working power. . . .

8

The difficulty of an adequate translation is heightened to the point of paradox in the case of the translation of the designation for God, namely the tetragrammaton, the name YHVH (the vocalization is uncertain; that of the Masoretic text is a convention, the forbidden pronunciation of the name was certainly not supposed to be made easier thereby).[7] We assume that it was, originally, in the primal form Yah, pure exclamation, primal sound.[8] It was later expanded by one syllable to Yahu, an exclamation composed of a pronoun and an interjection, just like the similar sounding cry of the dervish. Both forms have been preserved as components of proper names, the first form also independently.

In the conversation at the burning bush (Ex 3:14) the name is verbalized by adding another letter.[9] God responds to Moses' question as to his name, or rather as to its meaning, by saying—transposing the verb from the third into the first person—*ehyeh,*[10] "Ich werde dasein" [=I will exist, I will be-there], and adding, *asher ehyeh,* "als der ich dasein werde" [=as who I will exist, be-there]. That the *Ehyeh* is to be understood as the disclosed name emerges from the sentence immediately following, "Thus shall you speak to the sons of Israel: *Ehyeh* sends me to you." It has been the tendency from the beginning to translate *ehyeh asher ehyeh* as "*Ich bin der ich bin*" [=I am that I am], and what was understood by this was (if one does not wish to have God indicate his rejection of any answer by means of this expression, which in this usage is not uncommon among humans, though rather trivial) a statement by God about his eternity or even about his being-from-within-himself. This interpretation is already precluded, however, by the fact that a use of this verb in the sense of his existence is otherwise foreign to the Bible. It means (aside from its use as a copulative verb or in the sense of "there is" and so forth) *werden, geschehen, gegenwärtig werden, gegenwärtig sein, da sein* [=to become, to occur, to become present, to be present, to be *there*]. In order to protect the meaning of this central passage from any misunderstanding, the last narrator or editor—applying in a grand manner the biblical technique of repetition, referred to above—has God speak to Moses, in the section almost immediately before our passage, with the same *ehyeh:* "I will be-there with you" (3:12), and has *ehyeh* recur twice soon thereafter in the same unambiguous sense (4:12, 15). These connections have been pointed out repeatedly in the Jewish tradition, by Jehuda ha-Levi among others. "What sense," says Rosenzweig, "would a lecture on God's necessary existence have for the desperately unhappy? Just as the hesitant leader himself, they need a reassurance of the *"Bei-ihnen-Sein"* [=the being-with-them] of God, and they need it—in contrast to the leader, who of course hears it from God's own mouth—in the form of an illumination of the ancient, obscure name that confirms the divine origin of the reassurance." Moses reasons that the people, in their need, would want to know how they could conjure up this God with the secret of his name, as the Egyptians believed one could. God answers that they had absolutely no need of conjuring him up, for he would of course be there with Moses, would be with them. But, he adds, there is no way they could conjure him up, for he does not become present for humans in the form that they wish, but ever and always in the form that he himself intends for the specific life-situation of his people: *"als der ich da-sein werde"* [=as which I will be there] or *"wie ich (eben) dasein werde"* [=(simply) as I will be there].

Accordingly, we could not adopt any of the previous ways of translating the tetragrammaton. The circumlocution "the Lord," with which the Septuagint, the Vulgate, and Luther make do—following the Jewish custom of saying the word *'adonai,* my lords, later my lordship, in place of the unspeakable name—was just as unacceptable as the misinterpretation of Calvin and Mendelssohn, "the Eternal." The common transcription in the scholarly translation was not permissible for us either—aside from the questionable nature of its vocalization—because by doing so in the middle of the scriptures the divine name that speaks its own message is equated with the mute proper name of the gods. But we also could not write "*der Daseiende*" [=the one who exists, is there] or "*der Gegenwärtige*" [=the one who is present], because this would be tantamount to replacing the name whose meaning flashes forth, with a fixed concept that can only grasp the "always" of the disclosed meaning and not the "ever anew." It was a question of finding a rendering that would engender in the hearing reader a feeling related to that certainty that flows from the name, in other words, a rendering that does not express the "being-with-them" or "being-with-us" of God conceptually, but rather bestows it in the present. The insight into the pronominal character or content of the original form of the name indicated the direction we should take. Therefore *ICH* [=I] and *MEIN* [=MY] are used where God speaks, *DU* [=THOU] and *DEIN* [=THY], where he is addressed, *ER* [=HE] and *SEIN* [=HIS] where he is spoken of. Where the name occurs in divine speech and the passage is also supposed to function by itself, according to its apparent intent, without reference to the speaker as such— for example as an objectively existing regulation—the third person has been retained. In individual passages of the scriptures—outside of the Pentateuch—where the name manifests itself in its full unfolding, "*ER IST DA*" [=HE IS THERE] had to be ventured, since precisely the presentness of God is to be proclaimed.

The rendering of the shortest form of the name, YAH, posed a particular difficulty. We have determined to use a paler "*Er*" [=He] and "*Du*" [=Thou] for this, but, in order to preserve the original exclamatory character of this form of the name—occurring throughout in hymnic and related texts—we have placed an "Oh" before it everywhere it is feasible; thus also in the compound Hallelu-Yah: "*Preiset oh Ihn!*" [=Praise oh Him!]. . . .

11

The fact that we had to use the biblical proper names themselves, in accordance with our conception of fidelity, instead of the familiar Graecizations and Latinizations, need not be explained. The time has passed in which one said Zoroaster for Zarathustra, and the time will yet pass in which one says Ezechiel or Hesekiel for Yecheskel. But here too there is a limit: one may not make generally known geographical names unrecognizable, for example by writing Mitzrayim instead of Egypt; namely, because the earth is still there and the human beings have died. Inconsistency belongs to the essence and fate of this work—done for the first time—the goals and limits of which have been set, not by an abstract principle, but rather by the reality of a book and of two very different peoples and languages—but precisely by the full reality.

## 12

The history of this German translation of the scriptures, the so-called Old Testament—the first section of which is being republished here—began in the spring of 1925. . . . Rosenzweig's opinion at that time was that Luther's great work still had to be the foundation for any attempt in the German language; in other words, that a new translation could not be undertaken, but rather only a Luther-revision—admittedly an uncomparably comprehensive and more penetrant one than anything that has thus far been designated as such. . . . Naturally we started with the attempt to revise Luther. We worked on one verse after another and changed whatever seemed in need of alteration, based on our knowledge and language-consciousness of the Hebrew language. After one day's work we stood before a heap of rubble. It had become clear that one would get nowhere in this manner. It had become clear that Luther's "Old Testament" remained for all time a glorious construction, but was already today no longer a translation of the scriptures.

Now I undertook to draft a German translation of the first chapter of Genesis according to my conception. When Rosenzweig had read the manuscript he wrote me: "The patina is gone, in exchange it shines like new, and that is also worth something." This sentence introduced exhaustive comments that had already been preceded by a series of others—taken together, already a masterpiece of helpful criticism. Thus the joint work had begun.

The form of the interaction remained the same to the end. I translated, and then sent the pages of this first version (the so-called quarto-manuscript), usually in chapters, to Rosenzweig. He answered with his comments: complaints, advice, suggestions for changes. Of the changes, I immediately made use of whatever directly made sense to me; concerning the rest, we corresponded. Whatever remained in dispute was talked through during my Wednesday visits (every Wednesday I traveled from my residence, Heppenheim an der Bergstrasse, to Frankfurt am Main, where I lectured at the university, and spent the rest of the day at Rosenzweig's). When we finished with the first version of a book, I proceeded to the second, the clear copy which was intended for the printer (the so-called folio-manuscript), and the process repeated itself: again there were an enormous number of comments. It repeated itself during the first, during the second proofreading. After the latter, the book was read aloud to us together, and together we compared it with the original text. Still there were always discussions that lasted for days. After the third proofreading, the imprimatur was given. . . .

### 13

Franz Rosenzweig died on December 10, 1929. The last sentence he began to "dictate" on the day before his death—the end of which he postponed until the next day—concerned the interpretation of chapter 53 of Isaiah, on which we were working at the time, the section concerning the servant of God.

Since that time I have worked alone on the translation. Up until Rosenzweig's death the first nine volumes (up to and including "Kings") had appeared; thereafter six more volumes appeared (up to and including the book of "Gleichworte," the so-called Proverbs of Solomon). In the fall of 1938, Schocken Publishing House, into whose hands the work had passed in 1932, was officially dissolved and it was not possible to publish the remaining volumes.[11]

## NOTES

1. *Translator's note:* Since this essay deals with Buber's efforts to produce a German equivalent of the Hebrew scriptures, some of the examples had to be left in German in order to make the discussion intelligible. This is particularly true for sections seven and eight of Buber's essay. Where it was necessary to preserve the German original, I have supplied an English translation, enclosed in brackets. Any material enclosed in parentheses is Buber's, any material in brackets is that of the translator or editor of this essay.

The English translations attempt to convey not only the meaning of the German, but also some of the principles of Buber's translation. They are therefore very literal in most cases, and often rather awkward, since they are meant to show not only the meaning of Buber's German, but also the relatedness to other words based on the same root, and the original concreteness of abstract words or expressions. In contrast to modern German, which still consists primarily of words of Germanic origin, modern English is based to a large extent on foreign roots. The "sensual" meanings Buber tries to render in his translation are thus difficult to reproduce in English, since the roots available are often Latin ones, and their original, sensual meaning is not immediately intelligible to the average speaker of English. (A.S.)

2. In a profound jest Franz Rosenzweig liked to complete the abbreviation R not as "redactor" but rather as Rabbenu, "our teacher."

3. *Editor's note:* In this and several subsequent instances, I have supplied the Hebrew in brackets as an aid to the reader. (S.K.)

4. Cf. chapter 2 of my book *Kingship of God.*

5. This postulate is ignored even today by translators of the Old Testament. Even a psalm-translator as important as Gunkel, for example, renders four different word stems by means of the one "Spott," and five by means of the one "Schrei."

6. A different kind of *Leitwort*-style is at work in many of the psalms, where in the individual psalm two or more repeating *Leitworte* point to that which is essential in the given case. It is not uncommon that in a psalm the *Leitwort* of the immediately preceding one recurs once, so that in effect a bridge is created from the one to the other.

7. Cf. Rosenzweig's essay "Der Ewige" (*Kleinere Schriften,* 182ff) as well as my books *Kingship of God,* 82ff and *Moses,* 60ff.

8. "Word in the original condition of encounter, even before recollection; pure vocative before any possibility of other cases" (Rosenzweig).

9. Mowinckel, however, assumes (in a letter to Rudolf Otto) *Yahuva* as the original form, a compound of the interjection *ya* and a pronominal form *huva.* In this case the number of letters would have remained unchanged, and the tetragrammaton would have to be seen rather as an abbreviation of the original exclamatory name.

10. *Havah* is the older, *hayah* the younger form of the verb.

11. *Editor's note:* The publication was resumed with the Hegner editions beginning in 1954 and the new Lambert Schneider editions beginning in 1975.

# CONTRIBUTING AUTHORS

**Hans Frei** taught in the Religious Studies Department of Yale University from 1957 until his death in 1988. An expert in biblical hermeneutics and modern Christian theology, he was the author of two highly influential books, *The Eclipse of Biblical Narrative* (Yale, 1974) and *The Identity of Jesus Christ* (Fortress, 1975).

**Kathryn Tanner** is the author of *The Politics of God: Christian Theologies and Social Justice* (Fortress, 1992) and *God and Creation in Christian Theology: Tyranny or Empowerment?* (Blackwell, 1988). She is Associate Professor of Religious Studies at Yale University.

**George Lindbeck,** Pitkin Professor of Historical Theology at the Divinity School and the Department of Religious Studies, has taught at Yale since 1951. The child of Lutheran missionary parents, he was born and received his early education in China, his B.A. from Gustavus Adolphus College, and his Ph.D. from Yale. In addition to academic responsibilities, he has been active in ecumenical work. His two best known books are *The Future of Catholic Theology* (1971) and *The Nature of Doctrine* (1984).

**David Weiss Halivni** taught at the Jewish Theological Seminary from 1967 to 1986. He has been a professor of Religion at Columbia University since 1986. He is a member of the Institute of Advanced Studies at the Hebrew University of Jersulem and is author of ten books and over fifty articles.

**Steven D. Fraade** is the Mark Taper Professor of the History of Judaism at Yale University. He received the A.B. degree from Brown University in 1970 and a Ph.D. from the University of Pennsylvania in 1980. He is the author of several books and many articles and reviews, including *Enosh and His Generation: Pre-Israelite*

*Hero and History in Post-Biblical Interpretation* (Scholars Press, 1984) and *From Tradition to Commentary: Torah and Its Interpretation in the Midrash Sifre to Deuteronomy* (NY: SUNY Press, 1991). The latter, from which the contribution to this volume is adapted, was the winner of the 1992 National Jewish Book Award for Scholarship.

**Michael Fishbane** is Nathan Cummings Professor of Jewish Studies, University of Chicago. He is also author of *Biblical Interpretation in Ancient Israel, Judaism: Revelation and Traditions,* and many other books and articles.

**Moshe Greenberg** received his Ph.D. from the University of Pennsylvania. He was Professor of Hebrew and Semitic Languages and Literature at the University of Pennsylvania for sixteen years. Currently, he is Professor of Biblical Studies at the Hebrew University of Jerusalem. He is the author of numerous essays and books, including *An Introduction to Biblical Hebrew, Biblical Prose Prayer* and translations and commentaries on *Ezekiel, Deuteronomy,* and *Exodus.*

**David Burrell** is Theodore Hesburgh Professor of Philosophy and Theology at the University of Notre Dame. He received his B.A. from Notre Dame, and his S.T.L. from Gregorian University in Rome. He received his Ph.D. from Yale University. He has published numerous articles and several books on analogy, medieval philosophical theology, and most recently on comparative topics in Jewish, Christian, and Muslim thoughts.

**José Faur** is a rabbinic scholar who has published extensively in the field of hermeneutics, linguistics, and Jewish jurisprudence. His two recent volumes are: *In the Shadow of History: Jews and Conversos at the Dawn of Modernity* (NY: SUNY Press, 1992) and *Golden Doves with Silver Dots: Semiotics and Textuality in Rabbinic Tradition* (Indiana University Press, 1986).

**John E. Smith** is Clark Professor Emeritus of Philosophy at Yale. He is a former president of the American Philosophical Association,

Eastern Division, and of the Metaphysical Society of America. He is the recipient of an Honorary LL.D. degree from the University of Notre Dame. His books include *Reason and God; The Spirit of American Philosophy; Experience and God; Purpose and Thought;* and *America's Philosophical Vision.*

**Paul M. van Buren** is Honorarprofessor für Systematische Theologie at the University of Heidelberg and Co-Director of the Center for Ethics and Religious Pluralism of the Shalom Hartman Institute in Jerusalem, and Emeritus Professor of Temple University, where he taught for twenty-two years. He is a member and past-president of the American Theological society, the World Council of Churches' Consultation on the Church and the Jewish People, and the (Episcopal) Presiding Bishop's Committee on Christian-Jewish Relations. He has written eight books and a number of articles.

**Stanley Martin Hauerwas,** Professor of Theological Ethics at the Divinity School, Duke University, is a theologian whose task has been to display how Christian convictions shape lives. He is a graduate of Yale Divinity School and Yale University Graduate School. He is a member of the Society for Christian Ethics, the American Academy of Religion, and the American Theological Society. He is the author of numerous books and articles on the topic of Christian ethics.

**Steven Kepnes** teaches Jewish Studies at Colgate University. He is the author of *The Text as Thou: Martin Buber's Dialogical Hermeneutics and Narrative Theology* (Indiana University Press, 1992), and the editor, with David Tracy, of *The Challenge of Psychology to Faith* (Seabury, 1982). Currently he is editing *Post-Modern Jewish Hermeneutics* (New York University Press, 1994).

**Alan J. Swensen** received a B.A. from Brigham Young University, and an M.A. and a Ph.D. from Princeton University. Currently, he is Assistant Professor of German at Colgate University.

# INDEX OF PRIMARY SOURCES

## RABBINIC SOURCES

## TANNAITIC MIDRASHIM

# INDEX OF ADDITIONAL NAMES AND WORKS CITED

159, 161, 170*n*28, 172, 178,
179, 187–188, 212–214, 301,
352
Mowinckel, Sigmund: 357*n*9
Mudge, Lewis S.: 81*n*6
Muggeridge, Malcolm: 47*n*28

Nadab: 159, 170*n*28
Nahmanides (R. Moshe ben
Nahman): 137*n*29
Nahum: 145
Nehemiah: 111, 112
Neusner, Jacob: 44*n*1
Newton, Isaac: 277
Niebuhr, Reinhold: 99
Nietzsche, Friedrich Wilhelm: 67
Nissim ben Reuben Gerondi (Ran):
135*n*15
Norris, Christopher: 81*n*13, 101*n*8
Novak, David: 44*n*1
Nussbaum, Martha: 253*n*18, 309,
322*n*4

Ochs, Peter: 45–46*n*16
Orlinsky, H.: 188*n*3
Orosius, Paulus: 260
Otto, Rudolf: 357*n*9

Paul: 296, 308, 313–314, 315, 317,
318, 319
Peirce, Charles: 3, 12, 13, 18–20,
22, 38, 43, 46*n*22, 50–51*n*85,
193, 196, 277
Perry, Ralph Barton: 291*n*16
Peter: 300
Pettit, Norman: 290*n*5
Petuchowski, Jacob: 44*n*1
Pincoffs, Edmund: 313, 323*n*10
Placher, William C.: 43*n*1
Plato: 97, 149, 264
Plutarch: 187
Pockock, J. G. A.: 171*n*37

Polanyi, Michael: 44*n*1
Popkin, Richard H.: 274*n*2, 275*n*3
Preus, James: 57, 80*n*1
Przywara, E.: 253*n*13
Pseudo-Philo: 167*n*5, 180

Rabbah b. Nachmani: 139*n*50
Rabinow, P.: 47*n*39, 81*n*12
Rad, Gerhard von: 97, 103*n*24
Rahab: 208
Ran: *see* Nissim ben Reuben
Gerondi, R
Raposa, Michael: 46*n*22
Rashba: *see* Solomon ben
Abraham Adret
Rashbam: *see* Samuel ben Meir
Rashi (R. Solomon ben Isaac):
134*n*13, 135*n*15, 136*n*27, 181,
189
Rava: 130
Rava bar Zimuna: 122
Rawidowicz, Simon: 225*n*5
Ricoeur, Paul: 14, 44*n*1, 60, 62, 63,
64, 65, 80*nn*4–6, 81*n*12,
102*n*8, 170*n*35, 327, 328
Roberts, Robert: 314–315, 323*n*13,
*n*14
Rorty, Richard: 103*n*23
Rosenak, Michael: 44*n*1
Rosenzweig, A.: 189*n*7
Rosenzweig, Franz: 37, 50*n*84,
331–332*n*1, 352, 354–355,
356*n*2, 357*n*7
Rossi, Azariah: 135*n*19
Rosso, C.: 275*n*3
Rosso, L.: 190*n*23
Ryle, Gilbert: 21, 76, 88

Saadya ben Joseph: 108, 133*n*3
Samuel ben Meir: 29, 31, 48*n*59,
127

# INDEX OF TOPICS

# THEOLOGICAL INQUIRIES:

Serious studies on contemporary questions of Scripture, Systematics and Moral Theology. Also in the series:

J. Louis Martyn, *The Gospel of John in Christian History: Essays for Interpreters*

Frans Jozef van Beeck, S.J., *Christ Proclaimed: Christology as Rhetoric*

John P. Meier, *The Vision of Matthew: Christ, Church and Morality in the First Gospel*

Pheme Perkins, *The Gnostic Dialogue: The Early Church and the Crisis of Gnosticism*

Michael L. Cook, S.J., *The Jesus of Faith: A Study in Christology*

Joseph F. Wimmer, *Fasting in the New Testament: A Study in Biblical Theology*

William R. Farmer and Denis M. Farkasfalvy, O.Cist., *The Formation of the New Testament Canon: An Ecumenical Approach*

Rosemary Rader, *Breaking Boundaries: Male/Female Friendship in Early Christian Communities*

Richard J. Clifford, *Fair Spoken and Persuading: An Interpretation of Second Isaiah*

Robert J. Karris, *Luke: Artist and Theologian: Luke's Passion Account as Literature*

Jerome Neyrey, S.J., *The Passion According to Luke: A Redaction Study of Luke's Soteriology*

Frank J. Matera, *Passion Narratives and Gospel Theologies: Interpreting the Synoptics through Their Passion Stories*

James P. Hanigan, *Homosexuality: The Test Case for Christian Sexual Ethics*

Robert A. Krieg, *Story-Shaped Christology: The Role of Narratives in Identifying Jesus Christ*

Brad H. Young, *Jesus and His Jewish Parables: Rediscovering the Roots of Jesus' Teaching*

Dimitri Z. Zaharopoulous, *Theodore of Mopsuestia on the Bible: A Study of His Old Testament Exegesis*

William R. Farmer and Roch Kereszty, *Peter and Paul in the Church of Rome: The Ecumenical Potential of a Forgotten Perspective*
Urban C. vonWahlde, *The Johannine Commandments: 1 John and the Struggle for the Johannine Tradition*